THE FALL OF
KRUGER'S
REPUBLIC

Oxford University Press, Amen House, London E.C.4

GLASGOW   NEW YORK   TORONTO   MELBOURNE   WELLINGTON
BOMBAY   CALCUTTA   MADRAS   KARACHI   KUALA LUMPUR
CAPE TOWN   IBADAN   NAIROBI   ACCRA

THE FALL OF KRUGER'S REPUBLIC

BY

J. S. MARAIS

PROFESSOR OF HISTORY IN THE
UNIVERSITY OF THE WITWATERSRAND

OXFORD
AT THE CLARENDON PRESS
1961

61 - 3848

© *Oxford University Press 1961*

PRINTED IN GREAT BRITAIN

TO MY WIFE

PREFACE

THIS book tries to explain how the discovery of gold on the Witwatersrand led to war between Britain and the Boer republics. The opening in 1949 of the British archives to the end of the nineteenth century—the republican archives were open long before—and the access to Joseph Chamberlain's papers kindly given to me by the trustees (through the good offices of Miss Ethel Drus) have made possible another attempt to reach some definitive conclusions with regard to the coming of war. These conclusions emerge clearly (I hope) from the fresh synthesis which it has been my aim to make with the help both of this new material and of the publications of recent years.

The chapter entitled 'Joseph Chamberlain and the Raid' and part of 'The Aftermath' had been written when Dr. Jean van der Poel began sending me her typescript, which was later published with the title of *The Jameson Raid*. I read Dr. R. H. Wilde's work *Joseph Chamberlain and the South African Republic, 1895–1899* when I had already completed the relevant chapters of my book. Where I altered my manuscript after reading these two works, I have indicated my indebtedness to them.

I have thought it necessary to criticize professor Eric A. Walker's work, particularly his chapter entitled 'The Struggle for Supremacy, 1896–1902', in *The Cambridge History of the British Empire*, volume VIII. Such criticism does not imply any lack of appreciation of his achievements as a writer of South African history. He has placed all succeeding South African historians in his debt.

There are a number of other obligations I should like to acknowledge. The commonwealth relations office made available to me, in the office of the high commissioner of the United Kingdom in Pretoria, certain papers printed for the use of the colonial office. Sir Keith Hancock obtained access for me to General Smuts's private papers, and he as well as professor Kenneth Robinson, the director of the Institute of Commonwealth Studies, read my work in typescript. Mr. Rodney Davenport of the University of Cape Town asked to be allowed to read the typescript and gave me a number of extracts from the Hofmeyr papers in the South African public library in Cape Town. I thank these scholars for their valuable comments on the manuscript.

Several financial grants have facilitated the writing of this book and its preparation for the press. A grant by the National Council for Social Research helped to finance a visit overseas in 1951; and a longer visit was made possible in 1958 by the award of a British Commonwealth Fellowship. Finally, the research committee of the University of the Witwatersrand made a grant to meet the costs of typing. I hereby express my gratitude to the donors.

J. S. MARAIS

Johannesburg
March, 1960

CONTENTS

I. GOLD AND GOVERNMENT IN THE TRANSVAAL   1

The discovery of gold and the founding of Johannesburg. Its population in 1896. Did the Uitlanders in the South African Republic outnumber the Boers during the nineties? The mines and their owners. The backwardness of the republic. The effect of the gold discoveries on the Boer farmers. Rural retrogression (1–5). Paul Kruger, the president of the republic: Early years. Election as president in 1883, after the retrocession of the republic by Britain. Personality and religious beliefs. The influence of religion on his statecraft. Oratorical manner. Attitude to Boer opponents and political parties. The 'opposition' in the executive council and the volksraad. Kruger's way with volksraad committees. The last years (5–14). The state secretary, Dr. W. J. Leyds: An able and incorruptible official, and the fountain-head of Hollander influence in the republic. His enemies (A) among English-speaking settlers and officials in South Africa, (B) among Cape Afrikaner immigrants into the republic, (C) among the Boers. Attitude to Boer politicians. Influence on the foreign policy of the republic (14–18). The alleged inefficiency and corruption of the government. Proposal to appoint a 'state financier' (18–22).

II. THE CONCESSIONAIRES   23

Kruger's concessions policy. Industrial and municipal concessions. The waterworks company of Johannesburg (23–25). The most criticized concessions, those relating to liquor, dynamite, and railways. The liquor concession. Liquor legislation. Drunkenness among Native mine-workers on the Witwatersrand (25–27). The dynamite concession: E. A. Lippert, the original concessionaire, cedes the concession to a French company, but after protests from the British and German governments Nobels acquire a controlling interest in it. The republican government's contract with the new company transgresses the stipulations laid down by the volksraad to regulate the monopoly. Enormous profits of Nobels and the new company. The reasons why the monopoly survived the attacks made on it in many quarters: (A) Bribery by the company. (B) Kruger's belief that the monopoly was 'the corner-stone of the independence of the republic'. Explanation of Kruger's statement. (C) The government's fear of exposure if it abolished the monopoly (27–33). The most important of the concessions was the one which granted the right to build trunk railway lines in the republic. Formation of the Netherlands railway company. The so-called Rand tram. The company's principal line was that connecting Delagoa Bay with the Rand. This line entered the republic in 1889, but the company could not complete it until October 1894, when the line from the Cape to Johannesburg had already been in operation for two years. By the end of 1895 a third line to the Rand—a line from Natal—had been completed. The South African Republic and Natal became commercial allies against the Cape and the Orange Free State and a tariff war began. Its outcome. The high-tariff policy of the Netherlands railway company (33–41). The Selati railway concession: This concession had, like that of the Netherlands company, political as well as economic objectives. Methods employed by the Oppenheim brothers to obtain the concession. Fraudulent bookkeeping of the Selati railway company. Stoppage of the railway and lawsuits in the courts of three countries. Other railways built in the time of the republic (41–45).

III. THE PRELUDE TO THE JAMESON RAID   46

By 1894 Kruger and Leyds had succeeded in enlisting the support of Germany, particularly in order to counteract the pressure of C. J. Rhodes and the

British government on Delagoa Bay and its railway. British statesmen resented Germany's interest in the republic. The real aim of German policy (46–49). Kruger's desire for a port of his own. His way to the sea is barred, however, by the London convention. He tries to make a deal with Britain which would give him access to the sea, but refuses to accept the British terms. He is allowed to acquire Swaziland, but Britain annexes the territory between Swaziland and the sea (49–52). The republic's main problems were internal ones—how to achieve efficient administration and on what terms the Uitlanders were to be given a share in the government. In 1890 the Uitlanders were rendered politically impotent, but a second volksraad was established to further their interests. The local government of Johannesburg. The education of Uitlander children. In 1891 the Hollander Nicolaas Mansvelt became superintendent of education. His policy antagonizes not only the British Uitlanders but also the Cape Afrikaner immigrants and many of the Boers (52–56). Political associations among the Uitlanders. Formation of the Uitlander national union (1892). Its leadership and activities. Its petitions are rejected. Decline of Kruger's prestige and *rapprochement* between prominent supporters of Joubert, Kruger's rival, and the national union. Kruger appoints Esselen, a leading 'progressive', as state attorney. Reason for and effect of Esselen's resignation of the post. Increase in 'progressive' influence in the volksraad in 1895. The temper of the British Uitlanders (56–60). Attitude to the republic of Lord Ripon, the Liberal colonial secretary (1892–5). The commandeering 'crisis'. Loch, the high commissioner, proposes British military intervention in support of an Uitlander rising, but Ripon turns down his proposal. Some of the mining magnates on the Rand decide to lead the insurrection, and they obtain a promise of support from Rhodes (60–63).

IV. JOSEPH CHAMBERLAIN AND THE RAID   64

Joseph Chamberlain: His early career as a Radical reformer. Founder-in-chief of the National Liberal Federation. President of the board of trade in Gladstone's government of 1880–5. In 1886 he splits the Liberal party on the question of Irish home rule and allies himself with the Conservatives. Chamberlain as an imperialist and an advocate of imperial federation. His interest in South African affairs. In June 1895 he becomes colonial secretary in Salisbury's Unionist government (64–70). The Jameson raid. A Cape committee of inquiry exposes Rhodes's part in the raid. The principal task of the Commons committee of inquiry should have been to discover the part played by the colonial office and its representatives. The reasons why this committee has rightly been called the 'Committee of No Enquiry' (70–76). The complicity of the high commissioner (76–78). The complicity of the colonial office. Interviews of Rhodes's agents with Chamberlain. The 'missing telegrams'. Fairfield's letter to Chamberlain (79–87). Under what flag should the 'revolution' take place? The eve of the raid. Chamberlain advises against postponement. Collapse in Johannesburg. The reason why Chamberlain repudiated the raid (87–93). Recapitulation and verdict (94–95).

V. THE AFTERMATH   96

The effect of the raid in South Africa (96–97). Kruger invites Sir H. Robinson, the high commissioner, to come to Pretoria. The attitude of Germany to the raid. The Kruger telegram. The German government withdraws from the position it had taken up at the side of the republic (97–100). The situation in Johannesburg: C. Leonard's manifesto. The insurrectionary leaders. Open talk of 'revolution'. Concessions by the government. When it became known that Jameson had entered the republic, Johannesburg assumed the air of a town in revolt. The reform committee and the government. On Jameson's surrender the Johannesburg leaders decided that the game was up. They now pinned all their hopes on the high commissioner (100–4). Disagreement between Robinson and Chamberlain. Robinson advises Johannesburg to surrender unconditionally. Kruger versus his burghers (104–8). Chamberlain invites Kruger to visit London. The publication of the dispatch on Uitlander grievances. The reasons why Kruger refused Chamberlain's invitation (108–14). Strained relations between Britain and the republic. Robinson refuses to ask for reinforcements and sends Chamberlain a stiff warning. The latter retreats from the policy of interference in the internal affairs of the republic. Should Rhodes take his place in the dock by the side of Jameson? (114–21). Renewed tension during the latter half of 1896 owing to alleged republican infringements of the London convention: Extradition treaties of the republic. The republic's expulsion, immigration, and press laws. Suppression of the *Critic* and the *Star* (121–32). Other volksraad legislation: state schools on the gold-fields, mainly for Uitlander children; extension of the franchise; a *stadsraad* for Johannesburg (132–5).

VI. THE CRISIS OF APRIL 1897   136

A depression hits the republic. Chamberlain's attitude by the beginning of 1897. Chief justice Kotze and the constitutional crisis in the republic. Sir H. de Villiers to the rescue. The colonial office, *The Times*, and de Villiers. New treaty of alliance between the two Boer republics (136–48). Chamberlain sends two dispatches to Kruger, the one dealing with the republic's breaches of the London convention, the other demanding the repeal of the immigration law. 'A considerable force of ships' is sent to Delagoa Bay (148–51). Republican and British action with regard to Delagoa Bay in 1896–7. Germany shows little interest (151–6). The strengthening of the British garrison in South Africa. The republican armaments. The reasons for the British reinforcements: (A) To strengthen British diplomacy. (B) to strengthen the loyalty of 'all the English in South Africa' (156–61). The formation of the South African league. Its action (A) in Natal. (B) In the South African Republic. Comparison between the league and the defunct national union. The British agent and the league. (C) In the Cape Colony. The league, the Afrikaner bond, and the progressive party. The position of Rhodes. Sir A. Milner and the Sprigg ministry. W. P. Schreiner succeeds Hofmeyr as the parliamentary leader of the bond (161–70). The South African association in Britain (170).

VII. SIR ALFRED MILNER   171

Milner's antecedents. His political outlook and character (171–4). His initial 'policy of patience' and relations with certain Cape statesmen (174–7). The publication of the report of the committee of inquiry into the raid. Chamberlain defends Rhodes in the house of commons. The effect of this in South Africa. G. V. Fiddes succeeds Bower as high commissioner's or imperial secretary (177–9). The attitude of the high commissioner and the colonial office to the treatment of non-Whites in the republic: (A) The Cape Coloured. (B) The Asiatics. (C) The Natives or Bantu. Chamberlain had come close to intervention on behalf of the Natives shortly before the raid (179–85). The president of the Orange Free State proposes a conference of the South African states and colonies to discuss the control of immigration. His proposal is still-born because he wishes to exclude the 'imperial factor' (185–6). Kruger's government appoints an 'industrial commission'. Views of experts on the depression in the mining industry. *Rapprochement* between the chamber and the association of mines. The commission's report. The volksraad appoints a committee to consider the report. Milner refuses to present a dispatch from Chamberlain objecting to the dynamite monopoly. Milner, Schalk Burger, and chief justice Kotze. The report of the volksraad committee. The amalgamation of the chamber and the association of mines. Chamberlain upholds Milner's decision not to present the dynamite dispatch (186–95). The assertion of British suzerainty over the republic. Arbitration and suzerainty. Suzerainty and the assertion of Britain's position 'before all the world'. The validity of the suzerainty claim. Suzerainty and paramountcy. Milner's standpoint (195–200).

The presidential election in the republic: The candidates and their platform. The attitude of the mining magnates and the South African league. The influence of the suzerainty claim. Kruger overwhelmingly re-elected (200–2).

VIII. 'THE GREAT DAY OF RECKONING'   203

Kruger dismisses chief justice Kotze. Milner advocates the use of force, and assembles his civilian 'army'. His Graaff-Reinet speech. Chamberlain puts a curb on Milner. The British agent curbs the South African league. A period of irksome waiting for the high commissioner (203–10). Further arming of the republic. Attitude thereto of the British authorities (210–12). Leyds appointed the republic's diplomatic representative in Europe. The British ministers abroad refuse to recognize his status. Milner vetoes the appointment of a republican consul-general in Cape Town. The Anglo-German agreements of August 1898 with regard to the Portuguese colonies. Significance of these agreements for the republic. The Eiffe or Katembe concession at Delagoa Bay (212–17). F. W. Reitz succeeds Leyds as state secretary and J. C. Smuts is appointed state attorney. Their attitude. Milner's policy remains unaltered (217–19). The departure of Leyds means a weakening of Hollander influence in the republic. Effect of this in the field of education (219–21). Trouble in Swaziland. Chamberlain restrains Milner. An amicable settlement between the high commissioner and the republic (221–3). The defeat of Sprigg's ministry in the Cape house of assembly. Sprigg appeals to the constituencies. Rhodes as leader of the progressive party. Schreiner leads the South African party, consisting mainly of supporters of the Afrikaner bond. Schreiner wins the election. The personnel of his ministry (223–8). The republican government levies a tax on mining profits. Kruger tries to raise a state loan. Views of his advisers, the volksraad, the financiers, and the colonial office. The president obtains his loan (228–30).

IX. THE BEGINNING OF THE END   231

Milner on leave in England. The officials who dealt with the situation in South Africa during his absence: J. E. Evans, the vice-consul in Johannesburg; Edmund Fraser, the acting British agent in Pretoria; and lieutenant-general Sir W. Butler, the acting high commissioner. The South African league in the republic prepares for action (231–4). The 'Zarps' or republican police. The league takes action over alleged outrages perpetrated by the police on Coloured people. Milner's reaction (234–7). The shooting of an Uitlander, Edgar, by a policeman. The league calls an open-air meeting and asks Evans to transmit a petition to the Queen. Butler advises Fraser to reject the petition. Arrest of two officers of the league in Johannesburg. All three 'provinces' of the league up in arms. Attitude of Schreiner's ministry. A meeting of the league in Johannesburg is broken up by a hostile crowd. The sequel (237–41). The views of Milner and the colonial office on the Edgar incident. Milner on the results of his visit to England (241–3). The republican government proposes an extension of the dynamite monopoly. Milner (in London) recommends that the acting British agent should ask the chamber of mines to protest. Chamberlain agrees. Significance of this move. Action of the chamber of mines. Chamberlain's protest against the monopoly rejected by the government of the republic. The volksraad resolves to continue the monopoly. Were some of the members bribed? (243–7). The Boer government opens negotiations with the leaders of the mining industry. The course of the negotiations and the reason why they came to a premature stop. The end of the depression in the republic and the volksraad elections of February 1899 (247–56). The second petition to the Queen sponsored by the South African league. A counter-petition of Uitlanders (257–8). Coloured persons and Indians in the republic (December 1898–October 1899). Conferences, actual and proposed, of delegates from the South African states (258–62).

X. THE BLOEMFONTEIN CONFERENCE 263

Milner gets 'things forrarder' in South Africa, and sends a series of dispatches to the colonial office advocating intervention within the republic. His 'helot' telegram. Chamberlain's dispatch indicting the republic is endorsed by the cabinet in spite of Balfour's misgivings (263–70). Cape statesmen take a hand. De Villiers at Pretoria. Interviews between Schreiner and Milner. Milner's tactics. Ideas about a conference of Schreiner and his friends on the one hand and of Milner and Chamberlain on the other. Schreiner's view prevails (270–4). Alleged conspiracy by ex-officers of the British army (and others) in the republic. Reitz's claim that the republic was 'a sovereign international State' (274–6). Milner publishes an interim reply to the signatories of the second petition. 'Frightening' Hofmeyr. Schreiner wishes in vain to be present at the conference. The decision to have an essentially public conference (276–80). The Bloemfontein conference: Milner unwilling to discuss any question except the enfranchisement of the Uitlanders. Milner's and Kruger's franchise proposals. Chamberlain advises Milner—too late—not to 'break off hastily' (280–4).

XI. BRITISH SUPREMACY 285

Milner asks for troops to ensure a republican 'climb down', but deprecates an immediate ultimatum. The publication of the British grievances blue book and the effect thereof in South Africa. The cabinet averse to the dispatch of troops. Milner versus Butler (285–90). Cape and Free State statesmen bring pressure to bear on the Transvaal government to grant a franchise acceptable to Milner. Chamberlain speaks out at Birmingham. Repercussions of the speech in South Africa (290–3). During the six weeks following the Bloemfontein conference the attitude of the Natal ministry causes Milner some anxiety. But by about the middle of July the ministry has been brought to heel (293–5). Hofmeyr visits Pretoria and obtains a seven years' retrospective franchise 'with a simplification of procedure'. Milner's despondency (295–9). The volksraad passes the new franchise law on July 19. The reasons for the complicated look assumed by the law (299–302). The British government commits itself to formal intervention on the franchise question. It proposes a joint inquiry into the franchise law to be followed by another conference between Milner and Kruger. Chamberlain speaks in the house of commons. The republican government considers acceptance of the joint inquiry to be 'equivalent to a destruction of our independence'. Views of that government, Milner, and Chamberlain on the manner in which the president and the com-mandant-general should be elected in future (302–7). The question of arbitration about disputed points in the London convention. Chamberlain accepts the principle of arbitration. Ideas of Milner and Chamberlain about a suitable arbitration tribunal (307–8). In order to avoid the joint inquiry, the republican government offers to accept Milner's Bloemfontein proposals regarding the franchise and Uitlander representation in the volksraad. But it attaches three conditions to its offer. Two of these are rejected by the British government. This virtually ended the negotiations, though the protagonists continued sending each other notes for some weeks after (308–14).

Addendum: Note on *The Cambridge History of the British Empire*, viii. 595–7 (314–16).

XII. THE ULTIMATUMS 317

Views of Smuts, Salisbury, Chamberlain, and Milner. The cabinet decides to send a force of 10,000 men to take up positions near the republican frontier and foreshadows the dispatch of an army corps (8 September). The republican and British governments begin preparing their ultimatums. Delay in the presentation of the British ultimatum. The Boers declare war (317–22).

XIII. CONCLUSION   323

Was war between Britain and the Boer republics 'inevitable'? Historical
determinism and omniscience. The role of the mining magnates (323–5).
The security of the naval base at Simonstown. The 'necessity' of South
African federation. The duality of political power (or will) in South Africa.
The assertion of British paramountcy (325–7). The growth of the gold-
mining industry poses the duality problem in an acute form. An independent
United States of South Africa? The importance of Milner. 'The Afrikander
Nation idea' (327–31). A question of self-respect (331–2).

NOTES ON SOURCES   333

INDEX   339

CHAPTER I

GOLD AND GOVERNMENT IN THE TRANSVAAL[1]

I

THE historian of the fall of the South African Republic must take as his starting-point the great gold discoveries of the 1880's in that state. They took place first at Barberton and then along the Witwatersrand—a line of bleak ridges, cool and salubrious, constituting almost the highest portion of the South African highveld. The apparently inexhaustible Witwatersrand soon eclipsed Barberton, and people came in their thousands to swell the population of Johannesburg, its metropolis, and the smaller towns that grew up along the line of the ridges and beyond them as the mines extended eastwards. In July 1896, ten years after the foundation of Johannesburg, its sanitary board took a census of the inhabitants living within a three-mile radius of the centre of the town—the only proper census taken in the Transvaal during republican times.[2] It gave a White population of 50,907, of whom 6,205 were Transvaalers and the rest aliens. Of the latter the great bulk came from the neighbouring South African states and the United Kingdom, the United Kingdom contributing 16,265, the Cape Colony 15,162, and Natal 1,242. The remainder of the Uitlander population consisted of 3,335 Russian Jews,[3] 2,262 Germans, 992 Australasians, 819 Netherlanders, 754 Americans, 402 Frenchmen, and some others. The rest of the population comprised 42,533 Natives (Bantu), 4,807 Asiatics (mainly Indians), 952 Cape Malays, and 2,879 persons of mixed race (mainly Cape Coloured).

In the absence of reliable data it was impossible to state the number of Boers (including Boer immigrants from the Orange Free State)

[1] Topics dealt with in this and subsequent chapters are also discussed in J. P. Fitzpatrick's book *The Transvaal from Within*. Fitzpatrick had been a resident in Johannesburg since 1892, but his book is inaccurate and written in a partisan spirit.

[2] President Kruger gave a biblical reason for his objection to 'numbering the people'. He probably had reasons of state too. See Kotze, ii. 126 and below, p. 8.

[3] In June, 1899 the chief rabbi put the number of Russian Jews in Johannesburg at some 7,000. African (South), 600, p. 204.

and White Uitlanders in the South African Republic as a whole during the years 1886–99. One man's guess was therefore as good (or almost as good) as another's. Such checks as we can apply today indicate that the ratio of Uitlanders to Boers was often wildly exaggerated. In the nineties estimates of 10:1 were given, and estimates of 4:1 or 3:1 were frequent. Two reasons may be suggested for these exaggerations. First, the striking inrush of immigrants into a sparsely populated state; second, the political agitation of the nineties, which overstated the numbers of the Uitlanders in order to demonstrate more effectively the unreasonableness of denying them any voice in the government. The tendency to overstatement is found even in responsible quarters. To give a few examples: 'The Transvaal and President Kruger will have to consider whether a system should continue which refuses nine-tenths of the population under it the franchise' (C. J. Rhodes,[1] 1894); 'I conceive that I am well within the mark in estimating the white population along the Rand at something like 110,000' (Joseph Chamberlain,[2] 4 February 1896); 'the immigrant population . . . is generally believed to far outnumber the burghers' (Joseph Chamberlain, 10 May 1899); 'the unenfranchised population . . . are a great majority of the white inhabitants of the state' (Sir Alfred Milner,[3] 4 May 1899). Kruger agreed that the Uitlanders outnumbered the Boers. But *his* object was to show the unreasonableness of the demand for the franchise: 'Our enfranchised burghers are probably about 30,000, and the newcomers may be from 60,000 to 70,000,[4] and if we give them the franchise tomorrow we may as well give up the Republic' (Bloemfontein conference, 31 May 1899).

The first census of the Transvaal as a whole was taken in April 1904. The returns showed that 49·32 per cent. of the European population belonged to the Dutch Reformed Churches. This figure included, however, not only Boers from the Orange Free State, but also Afrikaner immigrants from the Cape Colony and Natal. Before the Anglo-Boer war the latter had been included among the Uitlanders. On the other hand, the Boer population of the two republics had suffered serious losses during the war: some 5,000 men killed or dead of wounds and disease, some 4,000 women and 16,000 children

---

[1] Prime minister of the Cape Colony, 1890–6. Rhodes was referring to the White population.
[2] Secretary of state for the colonies, 1895–1903.
[3] British high commissioner in South Africa, 1897–1905.
[4] The figures given by Kruger refer to adult males. C. 9404, pp. 19, 25.

dead in the concentration camps.[1] At the end of the war a further loss
was sustained when two districts and part of a third were detached
from the Transvaal and annexed to Natal. As regards the Uitlanders,
large numbers of them had left the Transvaal on the eve of the outbreak of war. But many had returned even before the peace treaty
was signed and during the succeeding months most of the rest followed suit. In addition, 31,025 new immigrants arrived during the
year ending 30 November 1903.[2] I conclude, first, that in January
1899 there were more Boers in the Transvaal than in April 1904 and
fewer Uitlanders (counting the Afrikaner immigrants from the Cape
and Natal among the Uitlanders in both years); second, that in
January 1899 (a) there were probably more Boers (men, women, and
children) than Uitlanders; (b) there may have been more Uitlander
than Boer male adults owing to the fact that adult males formed
a relatively large proportion of the Uitlander population.

From the Uitlanders we come to the mines, which had been the
cause of the immigration. The winning of gold on the Rand required
the application of large amounts of capital. This explains why the
lion's share of the industry soon fell into the hands of a small number
of companies controlled by big capitalists who had in most cases
made their mark on the diamond fields of Kimberley. The republican
mining law (the so-called gold law), amended from time to time in
consultation with the capitalists, favoured large-scale operations and
enabled the industry to be established on a secure basis. One of the
magnates declared in 1898 that the gold law placed 'in our hands
as our own probably a higher percentage of the . . . extracted mineral
than is done by the mining laws of any other country'.[3] Favoured
by the gold law, the nature and situation of the gold-bearing ore, and
the availability of large supplies of cheap native labour, the gold-
mining industry of the Rand rapidly developed into one of the great
capitalist enterprises of the late nineteenth century. When the
Anglo-Boer war broke out the republic had become the principal
gold-producing country of the world.

By the mid-nineties the following were among the important
capitalists in control of the mines on the Rand: Julius Wernher and
Alfred Beit (of the firm Wernher, Beit, and company—by far the
most important of the Rand firms), Cecil John Rhodes (Consolidated

---

[1] Walker (b), 499.
[2] Ibid. 505. Headlam, ii. 524.
[3] Speech by George Albu in Nov. 1898. African (South), 543, pp. 648–50.

Goldfields), J. B. Robinson, Barney Barnato, George Farrar, S. Neumann, Adolf Goerz, George Albu, Samuel Marks, and Abe Bailey. In order to promote the interests of the industry as a whole, some of the leading capitalists had come together as early as 1889 to establish the chamber of mines, which by 1895 included among its members all the mining firms of any importance. The government refused to accede to the chamber's repeated requests for incorporation; but it did in practice recognize the chamber as the accredited spokesman of the industry.

The immigrants brought in by the new industry came to the part of South Africa where they were least assimilable to the existing population: for the South African Republic was the most backward state in the land. Its White inhabitants—the Boers—were mainly cattle graziers owning large ranches, as their ancestors had done before them for generations. They had grown up in the traditions of the frontier, and every man had from boyhood learnt to ride and to handle a gun. Until the opening up of the gold-fields on the Rand they had lived farther from civilizing influences than the rest of South Africa. The new immigrants were largely urban in their outlook and habits. In addition they were mainly British: and fighting *Rooinekke* was becoming almost as much a part of the Boer tradition up north as fighting 'Kafirs'. A fermentation was bound to follow the pouring of so much new wine into the old republican bottles. The situation was in fact unprecedented, and a challenge to statesmanship.

Only a small proportion of the wealth produced on the Rand found its way into the pockets of the Boers. Though some farmers did benefit from the enormously increased demand for pastoral and agricultural produce, much of this demand was actually supplied from outside the republic, especially after the railways from the south and east reached the Rand in the nineties. The market gardening and dairy farming which developed rapidly in the vicinity of Johannesburg was mostly in the hands of foreigners. In the early days of the Rand, Boer carriers of goods by ox-wagon and Boer breeders of trek oxen had done well. But when the railways arrived on the scene, the palmy days of transport-riding were over. At the same time the republic, sparsely peopled as it was, was experiencing a shortage of land. The old extensive farming needed large supplies of land, preferably land acquired without payment. By 1890 the supply of free land had come practically to an end. To the west, east,[1] and north of the republic the

---

[1] Except for Swaziland and a strip of territory between it and the sea.

land had come under British control. Inside the country foreigners were buying up large areas.[1] In 1893 about 1,000 Boers (men, women, and children) emigrated to German South-West Africa and Angola.[2] In order to find land for their children many Boers subdivided their farms.[3] This often led to impoverishment. Another phenomenon which was becoming increasingly manifest in the nineties was landlessness. The great majority of the 6,205 Transvaalers enumerated in Johannesburg in 1896 were landless and impoverished Boers. The later nineties were a particularly unhappy period for the farming population. Locusts, drought, and above all rinderpest, visited the land together. The Boer government was faced with something like a crisis. A great effort of rehabilitation was required, but the government merely tinkered with the problem of rural backwardness and retrogression.[4] No doubt it was engrossed in 'high politics'; but the crisis had clearly caught it unprepared.

II

There is some justification for the statement that the government was in fact Paul Kruger, the president of the state since 1883. A born leader of men, Kruger had grown up with the state. As a boy of ten he accompanied his parents on their trek out of the Cape Colony in 1835. At the age of seventeen he was a field-cornet. As commandant he played a leading part in the formation of a united republic beyond the Vaal.[5] During the troubled years (1860–4) that followed the adoption of the *grondwet* or constitution he showed himself to be a man of law and order; a conciliator also and a man of peace, but not peace at any price. It was he who struck hard in 1864 so as to bring the civil disturbances to a close.[6] At the end of the troubles he was elected commandant-general of the republic with a seat in the executive council. When president T. F. Burgers (1872–7) lost the confidence of the majority of the burghers, Kruger stood forth as his rival. But at this point the British government annexed the republic. The annexation became Kruger's great opportunity—the tide in his

---

[1] Early in 1899 a certain F. Young wrote to the colonial office in the name of a committee representing companies owning over 8 million acres in the republic. African (South), 571, p. 225.

[2] C. 7633, p. 4.

[3] Tables of subdivided farms given in P. Naude, 492.

[4] See below, p. 193.

[5] *Kruger's Amptelike Briewe*, 18–32.

[6] McGill, ch. xvi; *Kruger's Amptelike Briewe*, 88.

affairs which he took 'at the flood'. He handled the situation skilfully and with great patience. He went twice to London to negotiate, and only after it had become clear that the British government—or rather two successive British governments—were determined to maintain the annexation did he take up arms with the burghers united behind him.[1] After the retrocession he was the obvious choice for the presidency. As the years passed, public criticism of his administration became louder and his popularity waned. There was nothing unusual about that. What was unusual was his election for four successive terms, though on one occasion (in 1893) it was touch and go.

For a political leader to maintain his ascendancy so long was no mean feat. It becomes more remarkable if the character of the Transvaal Boers be borne in mind. Rugged individualists owing to the isolation in which they had grown up, prone to violent political partisanship,[2] unschooled, and suspicious of the innovations deemed necessary by the president, they required skilful handling.

What manner of man was the president? With the passage of time his stature grows steadily, so that the claim that he was the greatest Afrikaner of them all does not today appear preposterous. The impressiveness of the personality is no longer in doubt: the dauntless courage, iron will, and keen intelligence. But while Kruger stood out among his fellow Boers in character and ability, they recognized him as one of themselves. Therein lay his strength as compared with his predecessor Burgers. Foreigners inside and outside the republic also recognized in him the Boer type. But those of them who could not see below the surface failed to recognize that Kruger, typical Boer though he appeared to be, was no ordinary specimen of the type.

Yet it is true that Kruger suffered to the end from the disadvantages of his upbringing and lack of schooling. Though he learnt much from his association with men of the world, his knowledge of the world and of men remained defective. He never managed to rid himself of his suspiciousness of the foreigner. In spite of this, and of his native shrewdness, he was always liable to be imposed upon by plausible self-seekers and rogues.[3]

In his later years, those who met him for the first time found him somewhat repulsive in his bulk, his features, and his mannerisms.

[1] Kotze, i. 496, 589–90, 671; Jorissen, 60–68; *Gedenkschriften*, 85–92.
[2] Kruger's word was *partyschappen*.
[3] Van Winter, ii. 117–20; *Hertzog-Annale*, July 1953, pp. 172–3; Engelenburg, 10; Kotze, i. 492; van Oordt, 803–4.

He was always dressed in black, like the members of the volksraad when it was in session, and on official occasions, even when addressing the volksraad, he wore a great green sash with or without the orders given him by foreign potentates. He drove to his office daily in a state carriage accompanied by mounted men in uniform. These official trappings appear to have been devised by Dr. Leyds, the state secretary.[1] A more substantial attribute of the presidency was the magnificent salary of £8,000 (reduced in 1893 to £7,000) which Kruger allowed, or induced, the volksraad to vote him in 1889.[2] Since he lived and entertained simply, his savings must have been considerable. He could make good use of them, for he had a very large family. He cashed his treasury draft every month, and invested what he saved in land. This wealth during the last decade of his rule contrasted sharply with the poverty of his younger days when he had been a struggling farmer oppressed by the burden of his debts.[3]

Kruger was, like his people, a devout believer, with a childlike faith in the literal truth of the Bible, much of which he knew by heart. He was also something of a theologian, always ready, not only to argue theological points, but also to preach from 'Dopper' pulpits. Many years before he became president he had helped to found this sect of the 'Doppers', the most fundamentalist of the three Dutch Reformed Churches in South Africa.[4] It was this intense religiousness, which reminded his contemporaries of a sixteenth-century zealot,[5] that was responsible, as much as anything, for his being so often described as 'an anachronism'.

What influence had Kruger's religious beliefs and attitudes upon his statecraft? He recognized fairly early in his career that it was necessary to employ as high officials men whose religious beliefs differed widely from his own provided that they professed some form of Protestantism.[6] But that did not imply any change in his own fundamentalist standpoint. The Bible remained his book of books—the New Testament as well as the Old. He used to quote freely from

---

[1] See, for example, Reitz, 19; *Hertzog-Annale*, July 1953, pp. 56, 104, 110–12, 169–70; ibid., Dec. 1955, pp. 137–8; Juta, 251–2; van Oordt, 565–6, 802.

[2] Leyds, *Eerste Jaren*, no. 92, 2 July 1889; du Plessis, 158. By 1897 the president's salary was still £7,000, the chief justice's £2,750, the commandant-general's £2,500, the state secretary's £2,300, while a member of the volksraad received £3 for each day's sitting. African (South), 536, pp. 404–5, 442; 543, p. 225; 568, p. 20.

[3] Kotze, ii. 31; Engelenburg, 6, 13–15, 17; van Oordt, 809.

[4] Engelbrecht, 147–8; Engelenburg, 14, 18–21; Kotze, ii. 126–7; *Gedenkschriften*, 45–46; van Oordt, 809; Reitz, 19.

[5] Jorissen, 16–17.

[6] Ibid. 16; Kotze, ii. 80–81; Engelenburg, 20.

both. But his experience, outlook, and situation made him a man of the Old Testament more than the New. He loved the Psalms. And was there not a clear resemblance between the story of the Israelites escaping from Egypt to occupy the promised land and the exploits of his own people? His people too, he declared, were God's people, a Chosen People, a People of the Covenant.[1] Calvin would certainly have rebuked his erring disciple for thus presumptuously unravelling God's inscrutable mysteries. And this disciple himself, as a practical statesman, did not venture to presume too far on God's support of His Boer people.

It is difficult in fact to explain the president's significant policies in other than secular terms—as the response of an ingenious and experienced improvisator to the changing situations that confronted him. In other words, Kruger's republic was far from being a theocracy. This does not mean that he had no use for the Bible in public life. He found it very useful as an instrument of statecraft in the sense that he constantly sought to justify his policies by biblical quotation or illustration.[2] A deft—or even not so deft—appeal to the Bible was bound to impress both the volksraad and the man on the ranch.

Kruger's public addresses tended frequently to take the form of homilies, delivered in a somewhat incoherent mixture of Afrikaans and biblical Dutch. He spoke in a gruff, powerful voice, jerkily and at great speed, illustrating his points not only by biblical references, but also by allusions to animal life on the veld.[3] Thus on one occasion, when Uitlanders were attacking his government during a depression in the share market, he told the story of his pet monkey which bit him in the leg after it had burnt its tail at his camp fire. Some years later, referring to the contemplated rising in Johannesburg which Dr. Jameson's troopers were to support, he told an impatient member of his audience: 'Until the tortoise sticks his head out, I cannot cut it off.' The president's oratorical manner is well exemplified in the lengthy fourth 'Inaugural' (May 1898). In this oration, which took two hours to deliver, he covered a number of political issues,[4] and then proceeded to address homilies to the

---

[1] *Kruger aan die Woord*, 100–1 and *passim*; Smit, 1.

[2] Kotze, ii. 126.

[3] Engelenburg, 10; *Hertzog-Annale*, July 1953, p. 111; ibid., Dec. 1955, pp. 138–40; *Kruger aan die Woord, passim*. The edited speeches published in the volksraad *Notulen* and elsewhere give an entirely wrong impression of Kruger's manner of speaking.

[4] A member of his audience noted that he pronounced difficult words like *diplomatieke* with a pained expression on his face.

ministers of religion, the teachers, and the assembled burghers. The most striking part of the speech was that in which he dealt with his dismissal of the chief justice, J. G. Kotze, for claiming the so-called 'testing right'.[1]

The Supreme Power, the Sovereign, God alone [he said] could condemn the law, not a subordinate. The devil invented the testing right in the garden of Eden and tested the Word of God which said: 'Of the tree of the knowledge of good and evil, thou shalt not eat of it: for in the day that thou eatest thereof thou shalt surely die.' But the devil comes and tests that word, and says: 'Ye shall not surely die: For God doth know that in the day ye eat thereof, then your eyes shall be opened, and ye shall be as gods, knowing good and evil.' . . . A judge can only live, if he sticks to the law, like a fish to water. But the Chief Justice did jump out of the pail of water, so wanton was he. And I tried to catch him, but he was too slippery, and I could not throw the little fish back into the water. Then I called my old friend, the Chief Justice of the Cape, and he helped me and together we took the little fish and threw him back into the water. And then he becomes wanton once more and jumps so far out of the water that I cannot get him back again. And of course he has now perished. (*En natuurlyk het hy nou gevrek.*)[2]

Cultivated persons were inclined to underrate the ability of a man often uncouth in speech and manner. But if it seemed important to Kruger to state a case cogently he could be impressive. When he had to expound a difficult and controversial question in the volksraad, he prepared himself by playing the part of devil's advocate with so much acumen and persistence that his counsellors concluded that he intended to reject their advice; whereas he had actually been trying to get a grip of the subject and to obtain answers to the objections he expected the opposition to make.[3] But though he could assume an attitude of sweet reasonableness, he was a man of passionate temper, which he could not always control. He was liable to outbursts of rage when thwarted on important issues. On such occasions he would stump angrily from volksraad chamber or committee room, or give vent to his feelings in a tone and demeanour more eloquent than his words.[4] It was impossible, however, always to be certain that the president's rages were genuine. For he knew well how to act a part.[5]

[1] See below, pp. 143 and 203.
[2] *Gedenkschriften*, 222–42; *Hertzog-Annale*, Dec. 1955, pp. 138–40.
[3] Kotze, ii. 30; van Winter, i. 36–37.
[4] Leyds, *Eerste Jaren*, no. 92 (18 June and 1 Aug. 1889); *Hertzog-Annale*, July 1953, pp. 172–3; van Oordt, 513, 563–4, 814; Smit, 145–8; van Winter, i. 254.
[5] Kotze, ii. 16–17; *Hertzog-Annale*, July 1953, pp. 104, 117.

There is a substratum of truth in the following account, though it was written by an enemy.[1] The writer had it from commandant-general P. J. Joubert, the leader of the Boer opposition, who purported to quote a conversation 'long ago' with general N. Smit, the hero of Majuba. Said Smit to Joubert:

> Old friend it is like this: I *do* stand up against him [Kruger], I know he is wrong and I tell him so; but first he argues with me, and if that is no good he gets into a rage and jumps round the room roaring at me like a wild beast . . .; and if I do not give in then he fetches out the Bible and . . . he even quotes that to help him out. And if all that fails he takes my hand and cries like a child and begs and prays me to give in. Say, old friend, who can resist a man like that?

The writer continues:

> I cannot tell you a quarter of what Joubert said to us. . . . He . . . illustrated Kruger's mannerisms, even to the buffalo rushes about the room and the old man's bellowings. Evidently the Executive's meetings are no curate's tea fights.[2]

Kruger subscribed wholeheartedly to the republican motto *eendracht maakt macht* (unity is strength). He interpreted it to mean that political differences among the burghers should not be allowed to imperil the vital interests—above all the independence—of the state. He knew from his own experience the price that the republic had had to pay for *partyschappen*. He accordingly set his face against the formation of organized political parties, and in 1894 the volksraad legislated to forbid the setting up of election committees.[3] In fact it is true to say that party politics, in the sense in which the expression is understood in Britain and the commonwealth, remained alien to the political life of the republic until the end. Kruger's supporters in the volksraad were often known as 'conservatives', his opponents as 'progressives'. But the label 'conservative' or 'progressive' as applied to a particular member, while it might indicate in a general way his allegiance to Kruger or Joubert, gave no indication as to how he would vote on particular measures. Until the last year of the republic the 'Krugerites' were said to be in a majority in the volksraad. Yet this body often voted down measures advocated by Kruger. As for the executive, it was in no way a Kruger cabinet. Throughout Kruger's presidency his principal opponent, Joubert,

---

[1] For another account, written by a friend, see below, p. 13.
[2] Letter from Johannesburg (to Wernher, Beit, and co.), 15 Nov. 1897. African (South), 532, pp. 139–41.   [3] Law 3 of 1894; Smit, 95.

sat with him on the executive council.[1] Other members of the 'opposition' sat there too, elected to their seats by the volksraad.[2] There can be little doubt that this arrangement met with the president's approval, since it suited his genius for conciliating his opponents. Indeed, Kruger's government was largely government by compromise with the leaders of the opposition.

Commandant-general Piet Joubert was no match for Kruger in ability or strength of character,[3] so that it was fortunate for the republic that he never attained the presidency. Without Kruger's consent and co-operation he could have achieved little,[4] and it was fitting that the stronger man should continue to carry the burden in the testing time that followed the discovery of gold. If there was one man who could achieve the transition from the old dispensation to the new in an orderly and peaceful manner by reconciling both volksraad and burghers to the transformations deemed necessary by far-seeing friends of the republic, that man was Kruger. And the record shows that he was willing to try, though vigorous prods had sometimes to be applied.

The volksraad or legislature of the republic consisted during the nineties of from 24 to 28 representatives elected by one- or two-member constituencies. They were almost all ranch- or farm-owning Boers. Half of them retired every two years but might be re-elected. It was their duty to help the president to keep the government in touch with the burghers. Kruger declared time and again that the *volkstem* or *volkswil* was sovereign. It was *die koningstem* (the royal voice). But he added that the *volkswil* should be an informed will. The people had the right to express their will at public meetings or by means of signed memorials. For such expressions of the popular will Kruger professed great respect. A special committee of the volksraad was set up to report on the large number of memorials that kept pouring in, e.g. on legislative projects, and Kruger frequently expressed the view that the volksraad was morally bound to carry out the wish of the majority of memorialists.[5] The difficulty of applying

[1] He sat by virtue of his office as commandant-general, to which post he was re-elected by the burghers several times with the approval of Kruger.

[2] Besides the president and the commandant-general, there sat on the executive council the state secretary and two other burghers, all elected by the volksraad. Other members were the superintendent of Native affairs and the keeper of minutes.

[3] Kotze, ii. 32; Fitzpatrick, 88; Reitz, 19–20.

[4] African (South), 543, pp. 121–2.

[5] *Notulen*, Eerste Volksraad, *passim*. See also Kruger's statement to Milner in C. 9404, pp. 25–26.

such a theory of government is obvious, and Kruger's own practice was not consistent.[1] Yet it would be incorrect to say that he applied the theory only when it suited his book. He does not seem to have intended the theory as a rule to be obeyed in every particular case. He intended it rather as a warning to the volksraad that though they were sovereign in the legal sense, they ought to consider themselves the servants, not the masters, of the people, and that they should be careful to carry the people with them.[2]

Like the burghers the volksraad, consisting as it did of uneducated, self-opinionated, and suspicious men, required skilful handling. Kruger knew all of them personally, and would sometimes invite honourable members to his house to talk over matters of state.[3] In the volksraad he was constantly on his feet, explaining government proposals, defending government policy, and replying to members. He refused to admit that the rule prohibiting members to speak more than twice on the same topic, applied also to him, going so far as to say that he would speak as often as he considered it necessary, and that no one would stop him. There were protests that the president spent too much time in the raad and influenced members by his mere presence and his gestures even if he did not speak. During the last years of his rule executive councillors and heads of government departments took more part in the debates and the president's share became correspondingly less. But up to the end he would intervene when it suited him, even if (as happened on at least one occasion) the 'opposition' objected that he was infringing the order-paper.[4]

I have said that the volksraad frequently opposed Kruger's will. With volksraad committees he had a less difficult task. Notwithstanding the fact that a new government building had been completed early in 1890, more in keeping with the growing income, needs, and dignity of the state, the president continued the practice of summoning important committees to meet at his house, where it was easier for him to influence the members. Such a committee was the one appointed in August 1897 to consider the report of the famous industrial commission.[5] Another was the committee which in June 1890 had to consider certain proposals to alter the concession granted to a

---

[1] See, for example, African (South), 571, pp. 35–36.
[2] For a discussion of Kruger's view of the *volkstem* see Smit, 112–22.
[3] Jorissen, 132; Kotze, ii. 28; van Winter, i. 254; Leyds, *Eerste Jaren*, no. 92, 26 June 1889.
[4] Smit, 143–4, 166; *Hertzog-Annale*, July 1953, pp. 110–11.
[5] See below, pp. 190, 192; *Hertzog-Annale*, July 1953, p. 104.

Netherlands–German company[1] for the purpose of railway construction in the republic. We have a vivid account of its proceedings from the pen of Middelberg, one of the company's directors. He had agreed with the government earlier on the modifications of the concession which should be recommended to the volksraad. At Kruger's house, says Middelberg,

two committees sat in a large room at two tables, on which there burned two candles. In the secret little room next door sat a third committee. From one table to the other wandered 'old president', the members of the executive council, 'Oom Nicolaas' [Smit] among them (Piet Joubert has been sent away),[2] many volksraad members who have nothing better to do, and Verwey and myself.[3] The two tables continually disturbed each other. . . . The previous evening Kruger had had the railway committee alone and let them have some glimpses of his policy. It had been decided in principle that we should be allowed to build the line to the Vaal, if we proved to be reasonable. With great *naïveté* the minute containing this was read in our presence. Coetzee[4] sat with a letter from Piet Joubert in front of him and began the attack. He said he had agreed that we should build the line, but we ought to have no exclusive right, no I-know-not-what, and he recommended that a new concession be drawn up making provision for the acceptance of the best offer. Then Kruger got wild: 'Honourable member, you just listen to me', and before he had done with him the poor fellow had turned quite pale. Relevant or irrelevant, right or wrong, the sparks flew. Coetzee was for the moment reduced to submission.

Such scenes kept on recurring until the end of the committee's sittings.[5]

During the last years of his rule Kruger was visibly aging. Both sight and hearing were affected. His manner became more abrupt and dictatorial. Middelberg sometimes found him looking worn out and ill. At such times it seemed that his mental powers were failing, that he was losing grip. But whenever a challenge had to be faced, the spirit of former days revived. Then he became alert, animated, even cheerful. The old war-horse seemed to be at his best when he scented battle or had just come through it. So it was at the time of the Jameson

---

[1] Usually referred to in English as the Netherlands railway company.
[2] According to Middelberg it was considered that the desired changes in the concession could be made only if Joubert was sent away on an official mission.
[3] Verwey was the company's chief engineer.
[4] O. Coetzee, a member of the committee.
[5] Middelberg's account is quoted in van Winter, i. 253–4. Another railway committee had smoked tobacco and drunk coffee at Kruger's house in 1886, and had been duly 'talked over' by him in the interests of the Netherlands railway concessionaires. Ibid. 128.

raid; in the summer of 1897–8, when he faced his last presidential election; and during the prolonged crisis of 1899.[1]

III

Kruger's principal adviser was the Hollander Dr. W. J. Leyds. He had been appointed state attorney of the republic in 1884, at the age of twenty-five, immediately after the completion of his legal studies at the university of Amsterdam. He soon gained the confidence of the president, and in 1888 the volksraad elected him to the post of state secretary, the principal political office after the presidency. The president and the state secretary constituted the inner circle of the government, being empowered to act within certain limits as the executive authority of the state. They appointed the heads of the government departments, who were responsible to them. They also appointed the judges of the high court.[2]

Leyds's decision to throw in his lot with the Boer government was an important event in the history of the republic. He turned out to be an able, incorruptible, and most industrious official. He recognized from the beginning that his first task would have to be to bring order into the administration. It was he who was mainly responsible for providing the state with that articulated system of government departments in Pretoria to whose efficiency the British diplomatic representative testified in 1897.[3]

Leyds soon came to be regarded as the fountain-head of Hollander influence in the republic. Long before his arrival Hollanders had been active there in many trades and professions including those of *predikant*, schoolmaster, and public servant. But it was during his time that the influence of his compatriots reached its high-water mark. He left the Netherlands at a time when popular interest in South Africa had been revived by the recent martial exploits of Kruger's Boers, who were regarded as being of Netherlands stock. This interest was further stimulated by the gold discoveries in the Transvaal. It seemed clear to a number of prominent Netherlanders, especially those who were instrumental in founding the *Nederlandsch Zuid-Afrikaansche Vereeniging* in 1881, that their countrymen could

---

[1] *Hertzog-Annale*, July 1953, pp. 35, 48, 108–17, 140, 152, 162, 169–79; Kotze, ii. 233–7, 240–1; Greene to Milner, 2 Mar. 1899 in Milner to Chamberlain, 7 Mar. 1899 (C.O. 417/259).

[2] Van Hoek, 13; du Plessis, 177, 227–8.

[3] Leyds, *Eerste Jaren*, no. 6; van Hoek, 17; du Plessis, 168 n. 71; Greene to Milner, 5 July 1897 in Milner to Chamberlain, 12 July 1897 (C.O. 417/220).

play an important part in the cultural, economic, and political development not only of the Transvaal, but of the whole of South Africa.[1]

With regard to the Transvaal, these hopes were centred in Leyds. While he retained Kruger's confidence, Netherlands influence in the operation of the railways, in education, and in the public service might be considered to be secure. And from Kruger's point of view the fact that the Netherlands state had no political ambitions in South Africa was a point in favour of accepting assistance from the Hollanders.[2]

Leyds made many enemies in South Africa, both inside and outside the South African Republic. Lord Selborne, under-secretary of state for the colonies, wrote in 1897: 'All British South Africa . . . are united in believing him to be *the* enemy. . . .'[3] The dislike of the English-speaking officials and settlers was shared by others, though not necessarily for the same reasons. Within the republic, for example, there was both an immigrant Afrikaner[4] and a Boer opposition to him. The Afrikaner immigrants, as well as a large group among the Boers, resented the appointment of so many Hollanders as public servants and teachers. Yet there seem to have been during Leyds's term of office more Cape Afrikaners[5] than Hollanders in the public service, notwithstanding the defective Dutch (Hollands) of many of the former, who had indeed been taught it as a foreign language, but whose schooling had been in English. But though the Hollander officials were in a minority, they occupied a number of key positions.[6] Leyds certainly (and in his more flexible way Kruger too, at any rate until the Jameson raid) distrusted the men from the Cape. His wife, who in political matters spoke with his voice, resented the fact that the Afrikaner immigrants in Pretoria habitually spoke English. (She noted that they were rather ashamed of Afrikaans—an attitude she and her husband shared with them.) Within two years of their arrival in the republic she was convinced that there would have to be a 'show-down' between the *Kapenaars*[7] 'with their English influence' and the Hollanders. A little later Leyds himself unburdened his soul

---

[1] Van Winter, i, ch. ii.   [2] Ibid. 60, 82.
[3] Headlam, i. 68.   [4] Mainly from the Cape Colony.
[5] Including some in Leyds's own department.
[6] Van Winter, ii. 74–75; Botha, 358–61; Hofmeyr, 439; Leyds, *Eerste Jaren*, no. 92, 6 June 1889. Germans were prominent in the department of mines, which was re-organized by the German J. Klimke, the state mining engineer, during the 1890's. Backeberg, 180–2.
[7] Cape Afrikaners.

in a letter to a relative. He began by stressing the importance for republican independence of making Dutch the language of the country in a real instead of merely formal sense, and then proceeded to give his views on the *Kapenaars*.

I look upon them in general [he wrote] as enemies (though disguised enemies) of our independence. . . . They . . . *want* English supremacy and call themselves 'faithful subjects of Her Majesty'. . . . The *Kapenaars* and our young Boers hate the Hollanders, hate them more than the English. . . . They, the *Kapenaars*, consider that they have a right to this country, look on this country as their prey. . . . According to them it is the Hollanders who are the intruders. But the opposite would be nearer the truth. . . .[1]

It is not surprising that throughout Leyds's tenure of office Afrikaners from the Cape and Transvaalers educated in the Cape should have been in the van of the opposition against him. During his first years in the republic his principal opponent was the Rev. S. J. du Toit,[2] the founder-in-chief during the seventies of a movement to make Afrikaans a literary language as well as of a pro-republican political organization known as the Afrikaner bond. He left the Cape in 1882 to become superintendent of education in the republic and was Kruger's right-hand man until he was ousted by Leyds. After his eclipse, other *Kapenaars* or Cape-educated men like chief justice J. G. Kotze,[3] Ewald Esselen, and Eugène Marais, the editor of the newspaper *Land en Volk*, continued to play a prominent part in the opposition to Leyds.

The Hollander officials (including railway officials)[4] were on the whole unpopular also among the Boers, to whom as a rule they remained foreigners with whom it was more difficult to get on than with English-speaking persons, especially colonials from the Cape and Natal. Furthermore, the Boers (as well as their *predikants*, most of whom had been trained at Stellenbosch in the Cape) regarded the Hollanders as theologically suspect. In the execution of their official functions their efficiency probably roused at least as much resentment as their shortcomings, since the Boers were not accustomed to

---

[1] Leyds, *Eerste Jaren*, nos. 14, 18, 27, 38.

[2] Leyds, in a diary he kept for his wife in 1889, called him 'that accursed hypocrite'. To Mrs. Leyds he was 'that Judas'. Ibid., no. 92, 2 June 1889; no. 93, 8 Oct. 1889.

[3] One of the noteworthy features of Kotze's *Memoirs and Reminiscences* is that they never mention the name of Leyds.

[4] This does not apply to the director of the railways, Middelberg, who liked the Boers and got on well with them. On the other hand, his predecessor Cluysenaer, who spent some months in Pretoria in 1888, said about the Transvaal: 'It is over there such a peculiar (raar) country, inhabited by peculiar people.' Leyds, *Eerste Jaren*, no. 93, 13 Oct. 1889.

methodical and impersonal administration. Even among those who supported Kruger's policy of relying on Hollander assistance there were many who regarded that assistance as a temporary though necessary evil.[1]

To the Boers, as to everyone else, Leyds was the personification of Hollander influence. What was his attitude to them? While he gave himself unstintingly to the service of the Boer state, there was not much love lost between him and the people. He and his family never struck root in the republic. It is doubtful whether either he or his wife made a single Boer or Afrikaner friend.[2] This was understandable enough, since the Leydses were highly cultured and somewhat intolerant folk who much preferred their own kind to all others. Even with Kruger their relations seem to have remained on the official plane. Mrs. Leyds has a story about the president coming to their house at 4 o'clock one morning in 1886, in order to consult her husband on some urgent matter: 'I lay . . . in bed lamenting for my table-cloth and chairs, since you know that not only wise words issue from Oom Paul's mouth but also the necessary spittle. And indeed I found the expected surprise. . . .'[3] This was hardly a social call. A few years later, when Leyds *did* expect a friendly visit from Kruger during an illness, it was not forthcoming. (Mrs. Leyds's comment was: 'Cordiality you must not expect from those people.'[4]) But though he might on occasion be critical of the president's behaviour and policies,[5] Leyds nevertheless had a great deal of respect for him. Of the other Boer politicians he was inclined to be contemptuous. During their early years in the republic he and his wife reacted strongly against the political Boers in Pretoria, executive councillors, as well as members of the volksraad. They referred to them as 'those gentry'—*die luitjes*—(Leyds) 'who have learned nothing, including no virtue' (Mrs. Leyds).[6] In a moment of exasperation Leyds confessed: 'O, de boel kan my zoo de keel uithangen' (Oh, the whole caboodle can disgust me so). On another occasion he remarked to his wife about the members of the executive council: 'You know yourself how little the folk are to be trusted.' The debates of the volksraad he referred to as 'chatter' (*praatjes*).[7] As Leyds grew

---

[1] Van Winter, ii, ch. xviii; *Hertzog-Annale*, July 1953, p. 120.
[2] *Hertzog-Annale*, July 1953, pp. 120, 142.
[3] Leyds, *Eerste Jaren*, no. 28.
[4] Ibid., no. 92, 10 Sept. 1889; no. 93, 13 Oct. 1889.
[5] Ibid., no. 29, 92 (18 June and 19 Sept. 1889); van Winter, ii. 117–18, 120.
[6] Leyds, *Eerste Jaren*, nos. 28, 45, 92 (18 July 1889).
[7] Ibid., no. 92 (2, 3, 18, 26 June and 18 July 1889).

older he learnt to keep a close watch on his tongue and pen.[1] But it would appear that his opinion of the Boer politicians remained unaltered to the end. The British agent in the republic wrote in 1897 that most of the members of the volksraad disliked Leyds 'exceedingly', and resented 'his ill-concealed contempt for their somewhat limited civilization'.[2]

A word must be said in conclusion about Leyds's influence on the foreign policy of the republic. Though Kruger sought advice in many quarters, there can be no doubt that in foreign as in home affairs he relied most upon Leyds. A few years before his death the latter described his task in the republic as having been 'the development of the nation and the defence of its independence'.[3] During his term of office first as a state attorney and then as state secretary, the republic concluded a number of treaties of commerce and friendship and of extradition with European states. It also appointed a diplomatic representative accredited to several of these states and developed a fairly extensive consular service. Leyds believed that the republic would by these means (as well as others which he proposed to use) make herself known and enhance her status among the nations of the world.[4] After the Anglo-Boer war president Steyn of the Orange Free State declared that 'the Transvaal, in order clearly to demonstrate her rights, pushed herself too much into the foreground on the continent of Europe, whereby the suspicion of the British government was exacerbated'.[5] Akin to this is the statement made or implied by several writers, that in his approach to foreign affairs Leyds was legalistic and rigid, and failed to take sufficient account of the realities of power politics. How much substance there is in these statements will become apparent in due course.

IV

When Greene, the British agent, testified to the efficiency of the government departments in Pretoria,[6] he made it clear that he was referring to his personal experience only. Both he and his predecessor,

---

[1] *Hertzog-Annale*, July 1953, p. 52.
[2] African (South), 532, p. 128. In Mar. 1898 the agent sent the colonial office the following newspaper account of an incident in the volksraad: MR. J. DE BEER: On a point of order, Mr. Chairman, the state secretary must be dressed in black. (*Laughter*) DR. LEYDS (*surprised*): Pardon, Mr. Chairman, I will withdraw. . . . Dr. Leyds here [re]entered the Raad dressed according to the Rules of Order. Ibid. 543, p. 295.
[3] Leyds, *Eerste Jaren*, introduction, p. vii.   [4] Nilant, chs. i–iii.
[5] Van der Merwe, i. 117.   [6] See above, p. 14.

Sir Jacobus de Wet, were in fact extremely critical of Boer methods of government.[1] Until the time of the gold discoveries the republic had been run in a manner corresponding to the capabilities and needs of a predominantly pastoral community. With the increase in the revenue after the opening up of the Witwatersrand it became possible to increase the administrative, judicial, and technical personnel of the state as well as to improve its quality. But the improvements effected continued to fall short of the standard to which the rapidly growing Uitlander population, and in particular the managerial and technical staff of the mines, felt themselves to be entitled.

The charge of inefficiency was brought mainly against the Boer members of the public service. Owing to the primitive educational facilities in the republic before the discovery of gold the burghers, except for the small number trained outside the state, were inadequately educated to become civil servants. Yet the Boer government felt obliged to find employment in its service for 'the sons of the soil', usually, it is true, in the Boer districts of the republic, but sometimes also on the Witwatersrand and in high offices in Pretoria. One way of raising the standard of the civil service would have been to insist on a minimum qualification, and in 1898 the government's inspector of offices did in fact propose the institution of a public service examination. But the volksraad rejected the proposal by a large majority.[2] In the absence of any prescribed test for admission to the service, nepotism became easier. One of the most persistent charges brought against the president and the executive council was the appointment of relatives and political supporters to offices for which they were not qualified.[3] It seems clear, in short, that something like a 'spoils system' existed in the republic, albeit in a mild form.

It is clear also that political and administrative office-holding could be made to yield dividends. After the gold discoveries the Boer authorities faced problems and temptations with which their experience had not equipped them to deal. The newly arrived Uitlanders had the money, while political power remained in the hands of the Boers. How far was the political power corrupted by the money power? It is in the nature of the case difficult to give a precise answer

---

[1] For de Wet's views see his dispatch to Ripon dated 15 Oct. 1894 in African (South), 532, pp. 1–8. Greene's reports are in the African (South) volumes relating to the Transvaal (1897–9).
[2] African (South), 543, p. 432; *Notulen*, Eerste Volksraad, 1898, arts. 202–3.
[3] Hobson, 34–35, 76; African (South), 543, pp. 17, 353, 479; 532, pp. 1–8; Greene's and Fraser's reports in the African (South) series, *passim*.

to such a question. It was alleged that there existed a 'third raad'[1] in Pretoria consisting of hangers-on of the government, who were believed to be able to obtain favours for those willing to pay. Even friends of the republic were convinced that payments were often made to government officials, in some cases to perform more expeditiously, in other cases to neglect, their official duties.[2] The allegations made lack precision. But it will become apparent later, when we come to the republic's record with regard to the so-called concessions, that we are not entirely without detailed information on the question posed. Meanwhile, two examples of governmental corruption may be mentioned at once. The first relates to the *bewaarplaatsen*, which were areas granted to the mining companies for the purpose of water storage and the deposit of the residues of crushed ore. The companies contended that they should have the prior claim to mine underneath their *bewaarplaatsen*, but the government, including the president, resisted this contention. In January 1894 Lionel Phillips, the president of the chamber of mines and a member of the Wernher–Beit firm, wrote to Beit: 'The Bewaarplaatsen question will I think be settled in our favour, but at a cost of about £25,000 and then only because Christian Joubert has stuck to us like a leech.'[3] It is not clear how this money was spent. What is clear, however, is that the government succeeded in getting the question shelved, notwithstanding a volksraad decree in favour of the chamber's case. The other example of corruption is in connexion with the patents law of the republic. In general the government was prepared to co-operate with the chamber of mines in the scrutiny of applications for patents which might be harmful to the industry. But in one notable case the government and the chamber disagreed. The patent in question was the valuable Macarthur–Forrest cyanide patent for winning gold from previously resistant ores. The chamber contested the validity of the patent which a company was exploiting at the expense of the mines. For his part Kruger favoured the creation of a state cyanide monopoly with the company as government agent. In June 1894 Phillips wrote to Beit: 'The cyanide monopoly . . . suddenly comes up again and is in a rather dangerous state. Fortunately

---

[1] The constitution provided for two volksraads. See below, p. 53.
[2] See, for example, Hobson, 76–83; African (South), 532, pp. 24–26. Beelaerts van Blokland, the republic's diplomatic representative in Europe, remarked in 1891 on 'the corruption of a number of men in the government (allerlei bewindslieden) in a number of forms'. Nilant, 320.
[3] Quoted by Etheredge, 85. Joubert was the minister of mines.

Dr. Leyds and Esselen[1] are dead against it and we may baulk it this year. . . . Next year however it will come up again[2] even if we succeed in postponing it. The other side is spending lots of money in bribes and we shall probably have to spend more next year than this to oppose it.'[3] Once again we do not know who the recipients of Phillips's bounties were. But he and his friends did succeed in baulking the monopoly.

The lax management of the republic's finances[4] made it more difficult to check corrupt practices and wasteful spending. One of the duties of the inspectorate of offices established in 1896 was to bring irregular practices to light. In 1897 this 'department of inspection' issued its first report which revealed defalcations by officials amounting to £18,590 during the years 1884–96. In its report for 1898 a number of further misappropriations, mostly of a petty nature, were exposed. The British agent writing to his government in 1897 expressed displeasure that none of the offenders had been punished. Some prosecutions did, however, take place in the following year, and in any case it seems clear that the government was seriously tackling one type of misconduct among its officials.[5] Another type of malpractice,[6] for which the blame rests squarely on the shoulders of the executive council itself, including the president, was tackled by the volksraad. In 1898 its estimates committee condemned the practice of irregular disbursements from the treasury. In the ensuing debate it was disclosed that almost £2,400,000 which had been 'advanced' to officials since 1883 had not been accounted for. A motion was thereupon carried that the government should obtain statements showing how the moneys advanced had been spent.[7] It appears that it had become customary for the government

---

[1] The state attorney.

[2] That is to say, it will come before the volksraad again.

[3] Quoted by Etheredge, 92.

[4] Middelberg wrote in Feb. 1898: 'The volksraad has assembled again in order to talk about the budget, to which the government, owing to the circumstances, has never yet kept.' *Hertzog-Annale*, July 1953, p. 129.

[5] African (South), 543, pp. 20–21, 494–8; green book no. 14 of 1898.

[6] Both types of malpractice mentioned in this paragraph were referred to by Joseph Chamberlain in his indictment of the republic dated 10 May 1899. C. 9345, p. 227. The republic's reply is in Cd. 43, p. 76.

[7] *Notulen*, Eerste Volksraad, buitengewone zitting, 1898, arts. 312–13; African (South), 543, p. 263. The whole of the £2,400,000 had not actually been spent: about £500,000 had been deposited with the bankers of the republic in the Netherlands. In his reply to Chamberlain on the subject of the missing £2,400,000 the state secretary of the republic declared that 'large items also frequently appear on that Advances Account, although these were accounted for within a few pounds'. He did not specify what 'items' he had in mind.

to transmit to the treasurer order-forms signed by the president calling for payments from the treasury, and that the latter had not considered it to be its business to inquire whether the sums asked for had been sanctioned by the volksraad. Nor had it taken steps to obtain vouchers for the money spent. It sometimes happened that trust moneys in the keeping of the state were paid out as advances. The evidence does not permit us to bring the charge that the state was actually defrauded in these transactions, but at the same time it must be repeated that the laxity of financial control did facilitate dishonest practices.[1]

Notwithstanding their backslidings, perhaps because of them, the president and executive council recognized the advantage of appointing a man of stature as watchdog over the republic's finances. They made several attempts, from 1884 onwards, to get the post of 'state financier' sanctioned, but encountered opposition from the volksraad. Kruger himself expressed some anxiety lest the new broom might prematurely try to sweep too clean. In 1899 the post was at length agreed to by the volksraad and accepted by Middelberg of the Netherlands railway company, who had on several occasions made uncomplimentary references to the republic's financial management. But before he could assume duty the war had broken out.[2]

---

[1] African (South), 543, pp. 263, 344–5; 568, pp. 24–26; 571, pp. 49–50, 144–5; Hobson, 84–85; *Hertzog-Annale*, July 1953, pp. 102, 129.
[2] Van Winter, ii. 318–20; Nilant, ch. vii; *Hertzog-Annale*, July 1953, pp. 102, 172–3.

CHAPTER II

THE CONCESSIONAIRES

I

THE concessions policy was introduced by Kruger shortly after the retrocession of the republic in 1881. The concessions were actually monopolies, and their purpose was said to be the promotion of industrial development in the Transvaal. Influential burghers and foreigners obtained these grants from the government without much difficulty, but they were insecure until the sanction of the volksraad had been obtained. The original concessionaires were usually mere speculators hoping to sell their rights to others. After the gold discoveries those Uitlander interests which had no share in the concessions condemned the policy as a potential menace to the economic development of the country, since the monopolistic industries would require protective tariffs in order to survive. In 1895 the volksraad appointed a committee to report on the industrial concessions. The committee found that all the concessions granted since 1881 had lapsed with the exception of those for the manufacture of dynamite, liquor,[1] iron, leather, bricks, and paper. Of these the iron and paper concessions appear to have been inoperative and to have remained so until the outbreak of the war. The committee was opposed to the grant of exclusive rights of manufacture and recommended a scheme under which approved applicants would be allowed to set up factories which would receive tariff protection under certain conditions. This scheme was approved by the volksraad in 1896. Under it the government made several contracts, which had issued in the establishment of factories for the manufacture of matches and soap by the time the war started.[2]

Besides the industrial concessions there were others conferring rights of a municipal character. Except at Potchefstroom, the first capital of the state, there were no municipal councils in the republic,[3]

---

[1] For the dynamite and liquor concessions see below, pp. 25–33.

[2] Kotze, ii. 24–25; van Winter, ii. 33–42; African (South), 543, p. 617; Cd. 623, pp. 10–13, 99–105; Cd. 624, pp. 28–29, 101–2; Cd. 625, pp. 244–9; *Notulen*, Eerste Volksraad, 1896, arts. 1866–71.

[3] Johannesburg had a so-called sanitary board, which was converted into a municipal council in 1897. See below, pp. 54 and 135.

and the central government was unwilling itself to provide such amenities and necessities as marketing facilities, tramways, water, gas, and electricity in Johannesburg, Pretoria, and other towns. It therefore looked to private enterprise to supply these services and granted concessions to individuals or companies that were willing to provide the necessary capital. In its contracts with these *entrepreneurs*, who were usually Uitlanders and sometimes British subjects, the government took steps to safeguard the interests of the public as well as to increase the revenue of the state. Maximum charges were laid down, regulations governing the management of the undertaking were imposed, and the *entrepreneurs* undertook to make certain payments to the treasury. While most of these enterprises appear to have been conducted with due regard to the public interest, the government did in certain cases fail to guard against over-capitalization and the making of high profits at the expense of the public. Furthermore, it occasionally imposed regulations that were not in the public interest. In the case, for example, of the Johannesburg and Pretoria tramways, which were operated by horse-power, it was compelled by the volksraad to set its face against electrification in the interest of the fodder-growers.[1]

One of the 'municipal' concessions conferred the right of supplying Johannesburg with water. This concession was granted in 1887 to James Sivewright, a Cape politician and company promoter, who formed the Johannesburg waterworks company and received a large sum of money from the company for the water source which he had previously acquired. Other water sources were subsequently acquired, also at great expense. Small wonder that the company charged the public 10s. per 1,000 gallons for its water. In due course the firm of Barney Barnato acquired an important interest in the company. The inhabitants complained that the water supplied to them was insufficient in quantity and poor in quality. In 1893 the sanitary board of Johannesburg, the majority of whose members were elected by the inhabitants of the town, formulated a plan for the acquisition of an abundant source of water known as Wonderfontein. The scheme was, however, obstructed by the waterworks company and certain property holders. In the following year, at the request of the board, the government appointed a commission to inquire into the town's water supply. The commission recommended that the

---

[1] Cd. 623, pp. 109–36; Cd. 624, p. 60; van Winter ii. 40; *Notulen*, Eerste Volksraad, 1898, art. 1055.

Wonderfontein source should be opened up and worked by the board. But the waterworks company organized opposition to this plan so effectively that the board dropped it. The government thereupon entered into an agreement with one G. H. Goch to exploit the new source, but the war supervened before this could be accomplished. Meanwhile, the company had itself acquired a new water supply which enabled it to improve the quality and increase the quantity of its water. But its charges remained as high as before.[1]

II

The most criticized concessions were those relating to liquor, dynamite, and railways. The liquor concession was attacked not so much on account of the monopoly it conferred as because of the debauching of Native mine-workers to which it contributed. In 1881 the government granted to one A. H. Nellmapius the sole right to manufacture spirituous liquors in the republic in return for an annual payment of £1,000. Shortly afterwards Nellmapius ceded his concession to a partnership consisting of himself, Samuel Marks, Isaac Lewis, and Barnet Lewis, and in 1892 the partnership sold the monopoly for about £120,000 to a company, of which Marks became one of the directors.[2] During the years 1893–6 the company supplied over 300,000 gallons of spirits per annum to retailers, mainly for sale to Natives on the Witwatersrand. It was able to undercut Cape brandy, which was taxed at the rate of 6s. per gallon. But it found itself at a disadvantage with regard to spirits imported from Portuguese East Africa, which in accordance with a treaty between Portugal and the republic, entered the Transvaal duty-free. After the completion of the railway between Lourenço Marques and Johannesburg the company experienced such severe competition from the Mozambique distilleries that it was unable to pay a dividend during the years 1897–9. It had paid, however, 12 per cent. in 1896 and 20 per cent. in 1895.[3]

No proof has been offered that the liquor company was implicated in the illicit sale of spirits to Natives on the Rand. The chairman of the company denied that it had any connexion with the retailers of liquor beyond giving them short-term credit. But he

---

[1] Cd. 623, pp. 124–30; Cd. 624, pp. 83, 236–9; Webb, 28.
[2] Cd. 624, pp. 72–73; Cd. 625, pp. 231–4; Kotze, ii. 25.
[3] Cd. 624, pp. 73–75.

admitted that it made 'certain representations' to the government when the sale of liquor to Natives was restricted.[1] The volksraad did in fact legislate to curb drunkenness among the Native mine-workers. Between 1892 and 1895 it enacted several amendments to the liquor law making it more stringent, and in 1896 prohibited altogether the sale of liquor to Natives on the Rand. In order to make this prohibition more effective, the number of retailers licensed to sell liquor on the Rand was to be gradually reduced. But in 1898 the president himself presented a missive from the executive council asking the volksraad to agree to a re-issue of the licences which had been cancelled in accordance with the law, so as to enable the dealers to dispose of their stocks. The volksraad, however, rejected the request by a large majority. The liquor interests continued making representations to the government, which on the eve of the war persuaded the volksraad to appoint a committee to suggest further changes in the liquor law, this time with the object of legalizing the sale of liquor to Natives. The committee duly recommended that retailers on the Rand should be authorized to supply 2 drams (*soopjes*) to Natives per day, and a bill in this sense was introduced in the volksraad. But at this stage a protest arrived from president Steyn of the Orange Free State, Kruger's staunch ally, and the bill was dropped.[2]

So much for legislation. It proved easier, in the republic as elsewhere, to enact restrictive liquor legislation than to enforce it. Milner made some illuminating comments on this subject when he took over the government of the Transvaal from Kruger. He began by remarking that he had made still harsher the already severe liquor law of the republic. In particular, illicit liquor dealers would in future be sent to gaol without the option of a fine. 'Experience has conclusively proved', he wrote, 'that the illicit liquor dealers laughed at even a heavy fine. They were generally agents of wealthy principals, who could not themselves be got at, and who . . . could easily afford to pay the fines inflicted upon those who worked for them.' The law must therefore be sterner. But this was not enough. 'It is only sound and honest administration that can make the best laws of any use. . . . The real fight has got to come, and it will be a great fight. . . . The . . . difficulty of course is, that in the control of the liquor traffic the government has to employ hundreds of agents, and the profit to be

---

[1] Cd. 624, pp. 73–74.

[2] Etheredge, 80–82; Cd. 624, p. 73; African (South), 543, pp. 65–67, 298–9, 361–2; 600, pp. 429–30, 643–6; *Notulen*, Eerste Volksraad, 1898, buitengewone zitting, arts. 348–9, and 1899, art. 1251; van der Merwe, i. 247–8.

derived from making Natives drunk is so enormous that every one of these agents will be exposed to bribes, and very big bribes.'[1]

The oft-repeated charge[2] that the republican police did nothing to enforce the liquor law may be discounted. But in spite of prosecutions and the imposition of the maximum fine allowed by the law the evil of illicit liquor-selling continued unabated until nearly the end of the Boer régime. The Boer authorities admitted the seriousness of the evil.[3] There was a widespread belief shared by Milner that the failure of the police to cope with it was due to bribery on the part of the liquor dealers.[4] On the other hand, the president of the chamber of mines in January 1899 attributed the drunkenness among Native mine-workers mainly to the fact that there were too few police in certain 'outlying districts' on the Rand.[5]

It was generally agreed that Native drunkenness on the Rand appeared to be increasing during the last decade of the republic.[6] But there the agreement ended. Estimates as to the average number of mine Natives incapacitated by the 'vile' and 'poisonous' liquor supplied by the dealers varied widely. In 1897 the chamber of mines put it at 25 to 30 per cent. of the Native labour force. George Albu thought it was 'probably 20 per cent.' Milner was told by a leading mining magnate that 'he always reckoned upon at least 15 per cent.', while the estimate of the acting British agent in Pretoria was 'perhaps a permanent 12 per cent.'[7] But even if we must give up the attempt at exact measurement, the evidence is clear that the evil was one of considerable magnitude.

III

In 1881 the government granted a monopoly for the manufacture of gunpowder in the republic to A. H. Nellmapius, who has been mentioned already in connexion with the liquor concession. A gunpowder factory was duly established, but the enterprise did not pay. After the discovery of gold it became necessary to procure another explosive—dynamite—for the blasting operations in the mines,

[1] Headlam, ii. 308–10.
[2] See, for example, the *Star*, 15 Oct. 1897; African (South), 543, pp. 65–66, 361.
[3] Etheredge, 82–83; Scholtz, ii. 208.
[4] Hobson, 80–81; African (South), 543, pp. 65–66, 361; C. 9345, p. 43.
[5] C. 9345, p. 180.
[6] Etheredge, 83; Scholtz. ii. 208; African (South), 543, pp. 65–66; C. 9345, pp. 31, 43.
[7] Etheredge, 81–82; African (South), 543, pp. 648–50; C. 9345, pp. 31, 50; Headlam, ii. 309; Fitzpatrick, 96–97.

which soon became the best market for dynamite in the world. At first the mine-owners were allowed by the government to import their requirements under a permit system, but in 1887 E. A. Lippert obtained from the government, which had in the meantime acquired the gunpowder factory, the exclusive right to manufacture dynamite and sell it in the republic. He was to pay the government a small royalty on each 50-lb. case of dynamite sold and take over the gunpowder factory at an annual rental. Lippert was an enterprising German-Jewish financier who was to have a finger in many South African pies, from land speculation in Rhodesia to cement making, railway building, and banking in the Transvaal, sometimes in association with Samuel Marks's firm. Marks, who was on friendly terms with Kruger, declared later that he demanded from Lippert a quarter share in the monopoly as the price of his support.[1]

The manufacturers of explosives in Europe sought to run their industry on the basis of monopoly. There existed at this time two combinations or rings, an Anglo-German (in reality mainly German) and a Latin or French ring. Lippert first offered his monopoly to two firms of the German ring, which turned it down on the ground that it was impossible to manufacture dynamite in the republic at the price Lippert was authorized to charge. He thereupon ceded his rights to a French company. This company set up a subsidiary in Pretoria, of which L. G. Vorstman became managing director in 1891, while Lippert was appointed salesman of the company's products at a commission of $12\frac{1}{2}$ per cent. Vorstman was the chief agent in the republic of the Netherlands Bank for South Africa and well known to Leyds. As for Marks, he was, according to his own testimony, taken on 'as part of the concession'.[2]

The mine-owners had at first no serious complaint to make about the price of dynamite, though in 1891 the Nobel dynamite trust company, which controlled the Anglo-German ring, offered to supply it at £4. 15s. 0d. per case instead of the £5. 2s. 6d. charged by the French company. What they did complain about in the early days of the monopoly was the quality of the dynamite. By 1891, however, this ground for complaint had been largely removed. It was at this stage that Nobels entered the field. They complained to the German and British governments about the exclusion of their dynamite

---

[1] Kotze, ii. 25; Botha, 253; Etheredge, 42–43; van Winter, i. 120; ii. 87, 92–96, 175; Williams, 171–2; Emden, 328; Backeberg, 103–6; Cd. 624, p. 136.

[2] Etheredge, 43; van Winter, ii. 84–85; Backeberg, 107; Cd. 623, pp. 70–71; Cd. 624, pp. 111–12, 136.

from the republican market. In September the British agent in Pretoria handed in the protest of his government against the monopoly. This was followed up by the German consul, who first broached the subject with Leyds in October, and in May 1892 delivered his government's protest. The republican government thereupon declared itself convinced that the French company had broken its contract by importing its dynamite instead of manufacturing it in the republic, and in August the state secretary informed the company that the contract had been cancelled. It was now the turn of the French government to protest, which it did through its consul in Pretoria. But the Pretoria government did not intend to face a 'show-down' with the French company, i.e. to eliminate the company without adequate compensation. It sought in fact for an agreed solution. Some time was to elapse, however, before that solution was found.[1]

As an interim measure the government sanctioned the importation of equal amounts of dynamite from France, Germany, and England. In August 1893 it asked the volksraad to agree to a state monopoly for the manufacture and sale of dynamite with the right of delegating it to agents. The raad accepted this in principle by a narrow majority. Negotiations with Nobels having failed, the government proceeded to set up its agency by means of a contract with the agent (Vorstman) dated October 1893. The agency proved to be in fact none other than the French company. There were further protests from the British and German governments, which now appeared to be acting in concert. Both the French company and Nobels sent representatives to the republic, and Nobels' agents got in touch with the chamber of mines. The chamber resolved to recommend to the mining companies that they should sign contracts with Nobels to buy two-thirds of their requirements from the Anglo-German ring, which would undercut the French company's price by 2s. per case down to a minimum price of 78s. Vorstman, with the support of the republican government, now embarked on a price war against Nobels, and the latter decided that it would be better business to abandon the mine-owners and come to an arrangement with the government and the French company. In February 1894 the French and German rings concluded their deal. Its terms were communicated to the chamber of mines in March. A new company was to be formed with a capital of £450,000 in £1 shares. The French and German rings were each to hold almost the same number of shares, but the management

[1] Etheredge, 44–56; Scholtz, i. 173–5; Backeberg, 151–2; Cd. 623, p. 70 (footnotes).

was to be controlled by Nobels. Lippert was to get 25,000 shares as well as a sales commission which would bring him in 8s. per case for the first three years and 6s. thereafter. Marks was to get a royalty of 2s. per case. The republican government was acquainted with these arrangements. The chamber of mines naturally enough objected to them, for the mining industry was now in the grip of a monopoly far stronger than the original one. Moreover, since the French shareholders had to be taken over by the new company, it would be heavily capitalized. This meant that, in addition to the large manufacturer's profits which Nobels expected to make, dividends would have to be found for the swollen body of the company's shareholders. As for the governments whose intervention had led to the formation of the second company, the German government was no doubt pleased, while the British and French governments acquiesced. The British government was aware that there were British manufacturers of explosives that did not belong to Nobels. It must have been aware also of the predicament of the mining industry under the new dispensation. But it made no further protest.[1]

In May 1894 the republican government made another contract with Vorstman, representing now the second dynamite company. The company was to take over the gunpowder or ammunition factory and to establish a dynamite factory. It had to pay the government 5s. for each case of dynamite sold as well as 20 per cent. of its 'surplus profits', which were defined as 'the balance remaining after deduction of all costs, wear and tear, the usual writings off and interest at 8 per cent. on the capital'. In making this contract the government was bound by certain regulations adopted by the volksraad in September 1893. One of these stated that the factory should be able to supply the needs of consumers in the republic before the end of April 1896. The government transgressed this regulation by making provision in the contract for the extension of the period within which the factory should meet all the requirements of the republic. Shortly after the signing of the contract it applied to the volksraad for such an extension, but the latter turned down the application. The factory did in fact fail to manufacture enough dynamite within the stipulated period and the government allowed importation to continue.[2] This went on until 1898, when the company

---

[1] Etheredge, 56–64; Scholtz, i. 175–6; van Winter, ii. 85 n.; Cd. 623, pp. 71–72; Cd. 624, pp. 111–13; Cd. 625, pp. 156–7.
[2] Cd. 623, pp. 72–80; Etheredge, 66.

was at length able to satisfy the needs of the mines from its own manufactures. By this time its factory at Modderfontein had become the largest establishment of its kind in the world.[1]

Enormous profits were made by Nobels and the second company on the manufacture of dynamite and its sale to the mines. Over 1,100,000 cases were consumed in the republic from June 1894 to September 1899 and the profit on the manufacture thereof was over 40s. per case, that is to say more than 100 per cent. The state received only 5s. per case as its share of the profits.[2] Such being the position, it is natural to ask how it came that the monopoly survived all the attacks made upon it. These attacks came from many quarters. The monopoly had in fact few friends. Most of the members of the volks-raad disliked it, though it proved impossible to obtain a majority in favour of outright abolition. President Steyn considered it to be inde-fensible.[3]

The Transvaal concessions commission appointed by the British government in 1900 ascribed the survival of the monopoly to bribery on the part of the second dynamite company.[4] But the evidence quoted by the commission does not justify this conclusion. What it does establish is: first, that Max Philipp, the chairman of the com-pany in Hamburg, who kept in close touch with his son and Vorst-man, its principal representatives in Pretoria, was convinced that he could further his ends by bribery.[5] Second, that Philipp paid out considerable sums of the company's money with the intention of bribing members of the volksraad and others. Who the persons were who actually pocketed this money we do not know, except perhaps in one case.[6] Third, that a few government officials had financial dealings with Philipp. Thus Leyds accepted from him a bank credit to speculate with and some dynamite shares. He made a few hundred pounds from the speculation and about £800 from the shares. J. Klimke, the state mining engineer, received some gold shares but was somewhat reluctant to take money. Finally, J. M. A. Wolmarans, one of Kruger's supporters on the executive council of the republic and a director of the company, accepted a gratuity of at least £500 from Philipp and an unspecified sum of money from Lippert.[7]

So much for the financial inducements that the company was

---

[1] African (South), 543, pp. 538–42, 548–9; 571, pp. 59–61, 253–4; Cd. 623, p. 82; Cd. 625, p. 152.
[2] Cd. 623, p. 81; African (South), 571, pp. 104–5.   [3] Van der Merwe, i. 184.
[4] Cd. 623, paras. 53, 107.   [5] Ibid., paras. 85, 87–88.
[6] Ibid., paras. 82, 92–94, 101–5.   [7] Ibid., pp. 84–88; Cd. 625, pp. 171, 198–9.

prepared to offer to individuals. That they played some part in the maintenance of its monopoly can hardly be doubted. But there were other factors involved. I do not believe that Kruger and Leyds, who supported the monopoly through thick and thin, were influenced by considerations of personal gain. The president defended the monopoly on the ground that it was 'the corner-stone of the independence of the republic'. He intended his listeners to interpret this statement as referring to the ammunition factory which the dynamite company had to operate in fulfilment of its contract.[1] But although the company did actually manufacture considerable quantities of ammunition, the state was nevertheless compelled to purchase most of its requirements abroad. Moreover, the government must have known that the company was importing all the cartridge cases it needed. Shortly before the war Kruger pressed Vorstman to find some means of making cartridge cases in the republic, which the latter declared to be 'no easy matter'.[2] Some observers thought that what Kruger really had in mind was the fact that the second company kept on hand a three month's supply of raw material, which formed some security for the mines against a coastal blockade. But they pointed out that if free trade in dynamite were allowed, the government could itself take steps to see that the supplies considered necessary were kept in reserve.[3] What seems more to the point is the suggestion that Kruger and Leyds considered it important to have 'capitalist' allies on whom the government could depend, as a counterpoise against those capitalists, including mining magnates, whom they regarded as the enemies of the republic. This is one of the reasons for the maintenance of the monopoly given by Dr. P. R. Botha, who was in close touch with Leyds after the latter's retirement.[4] He goes on to explain that the dynamite company and the Netherlands railway company were the government's only strong economic allies. A similar view was expressed by some of the mine-owners. They told the British agent in Pretoria that Kruger refused to get rid of the monopoly because *inter alia* 'he relies on the dynamite and railway companies as dogs to come to heel in any future financial embarrassment of [the] republic'. The government did in fact obtain direct assistance, financial and other, from these companies.[5]

[1] C. 9345, pp. 194 ff.; Scholtz, i. 325.
[2] Cd. 623, pp. 77–78; Cd. 625, pp. 153, 205; Breytenbach, 276–9.
[3] African (South), 543, pp. 628–9; 571, 187–9.
[4] Botha, preface and pp. 141, 202, 323.
[5] Ibid. 272; African (South), 572, pp. 6–7; Cd. 623, pp. 28, 77–78; below, p. 230.

There was another reason why the monopoly was not abolished. Kruger told Steyn in 1899 that this would have meant buying out the company at a high price.[1] It is true that the volksraad could have passed a resolution expropriating the company without compensation on the ground that it had infringed the regulations of September 1893. But this would have placed the government in a difficult position, since it had been a party to that infringement. The company might have appealed to Germany and France.[2] It would certainly have gone to law. The government had reason to fear an appeal to the courts on account of the revelations that were bound to follow. After the outbreak of war Steyn asked commandant-general Louis Botha how it came that he had in August 1899, as a member of a volksraad committee, signed a report advocating the continuation of the monopoly though he had formerly been strongly opposed to it. Botha's reply was that 'there was no other course open to him after he had examined the matter carefully and had seen how the government had allied the Transvaal to the concessionaires with that concession and other concomitant agreements. There was definitely no way out.'[3]

IV

The most important of the republic's concessions, measured by the amount of capital invested and the political and economic implications, was the one which granted the right to build railways in the Transvaal. In the Cape Colony and Natal the railways were state enterprises. Not so in the Transvaal. Her government was unwilling to add the responsibility for, and the odium of, railway management to the burdens of an inexperienced administration. The trunk lines of the republic were therefore to be built and run by private enterprise. The enterprise, furthermore, was to be Dutch. That was Kruger's will, for he held the Hollanders to be politically reliable.[4] In its final form the concession granted the holders the right to build and manage all railways connecting the republic with a seaport. The cost of construction was not to exceed £8,600 per mile unless the government agreed that a greater cost was justified. The state was to guarantee an interest of 6 per cent. on the share capital of the undertaking, and a somewhat smaller interest on its debenture capital.

[1] Van der Merwe, i. 184.   [2] Cd. 625, pp. 199–201.
[3] Van der Merwe, i. 192.   [4] See above, p. 15.

Eighty-five per cent. of the excess profit—that is to say the amount left after running costs and the interest on the share and debenture capital had been deducted from the earnings—was to go to the state. In addition, it would earn dividends on the 5,606 shares which it eventually acquired out of a total of 14,000.[1]

It proved impossible to form a company to take up the railway concession until the middle of 1887—about a year after the discovery of gold on the Witwatersrand.[2] Despite the fact that most of its initial capital was provided by a syndicate in which German bankers preponderated, the company was essentially a Dutch concern. Four of the seven members of the board of commissioners and both the managing directors were Netherlanders.[3]

The first railway constructed by this Netherlands company was the so-called Rand tram, which was built originally as a light railway along the Witwatersrand connecting Springs with Krugersdorp via Johannesburg—a distance of 51 miles. The mines required large amounts of coal for the production of steam-power and they found ox-wagon transport both expensive and unreliable, especially in the dry winter months. The volksraad decided, therefore, to grant a concession for the building and operating of a line connecting the mines with the coal-fields in the vicinity of Boksburg on the east Rand. The line was to carry passengers as well as coal and other goods. The applications considered by the volksraad were those of E. A. Lippert and the Netherlands company. In spite of the 'gifts' distributed by Lippert the majority of the members agreed to give the concession to the company, which completed the line early in 1891. Notwithstanding initial unco-operativeness on the part of the mine managements, the line soon established itself as a necessity for the industry. It became also a valuable milch cow for the company, for both its tariffs and its profits were high.[4]

The Rand tram was, nevertheless, a side line both from the company's and from the government's point of view. The real purpose of the creation of the company had been to connect the republic with the Portuguese harbour of Delagoa Bay and thus render it less dependent on the British ports in Natal and the Cape Colony. But before Delagoa Bay could be connected with Johannesburg two serious

[1] Van Winter, i. 68, 81–82, 255, 261–3; ii. 142.
[2] Ibid. i. 145, 167.
[3] Ibid. 161, 168–9.
[4] Ibid. 209–19, 264; ii. 114, 143, 200–1.

obstacles had to be overcome. The first was that presented by the railway company which was to build the line from Delagoa Bay to the republican frontier. The promoter and controller of this company was an American, Edward McMurdo, who proved to be a speculator interested in selling his concession at a high price rather than in building and operating a railway. He made it impossible for the Netherlands railway company to commence building by delaying the completion of his line to the frontier and by persistently refusing to come to an arrangement with regard to tariffs. In June 1889 the Portuguese government lost patience and expropriated McMurdo's company. Soon afterwards it concluded a tariff agreement with the Netherlands company and made arrangements for the completion of the line to the frontier. The company could at length start building its principal line.[1]

But now another obstacle presented itself. During the course of 1890 it became almost impossible to borrow money for the railway owing to the state of the money market in Europe and to a depression in the mining industry and consequent decrease of faith in the republic's financial viability. The company's need of funds led to an agreement with the Cape which will be mentioned presently. Kruger had at first wanted to prevent the railways from the British ports from entering his state until the Delagoa Bay line had reached Johannesburg. But by the end of 1889 he had come to realize that the Witwatersrand could not be kept waiting any longer and that at least a Cape line would have to be allowed entry. In June 1890 it had accordingly been settled that the railway through the Orange Free State which the Cape was to build and work should meet a projected Transvaal line to Johannesburg at Viljoensdrift on the Vaal river. Shortly afterwards the Netherlands company began work on the line.[2] In the meantime the Cape and the Orange Free State had entered into a customs union which the South African Republic and Natal refused to join, the former for political and the latter for economic reasons.[3] Kruger's refusal to join the customs union meant the continued subjection of the Transvaalers, and particularly the Uitlanders and their mining industry, to high customs duties. For they had to pay the duties levied on imported commodities at the Cape ports or at the Natal port of Durban and in addition the duties

---

[1] Ibid. i. 149–58, 174–85, 192–202; van der Poel (a), 35–37, 43–44.
[2] Van Winter, i. 232–3; ii. 114, 123, 128.
[3] Van der Poel (a), 34–35, 42–43.

imposed by the republic. The mainly agricultural products of the Cape and Natal paid, of course, only the republic's duties, while those of the Orange Free State entered duty-free. But these products could not meet the demands of the Witwatersrand for agricultural commodities. Goods entering the republic were taxed at the general rate of between 5 and 7½ per cent. *ad valorem*. In addition special dues, superimposed on the ordinary *ad valorem* taxes, were payable on a number of foodstuffs and beverages.[1]

The financial difficulties of the Netherlands company had become more acute than ever towards the end of 1891. In order to obtain money to meet the importunities of its creditors the company accepted a loan from the Cape government and agreed in return to carry the Cape–Orange Free State line on to Johannesburg within a year. Up to the end of 1894, so it was further stipulated in this so-called Sivewright agreement, the Cape should operate the whole line from her ports to Johannesburg and fix the rates on through traffic to that town. The Cape line reached Johannesburg in September 1892 and Pretoria at the end of the year.[2] The railway from the Portuguese frontier to Pretoria was now making good progress owing to the fact that the Netherlands company had at last been able to obtain all the money it needed to complete the line. During the course of 1892 confidence in the future of the mining industry revived and the credit of the republic consequently improved. In June the republic succeeded in obtaining from the London Rothschilds a loan of £2½ million, which was made available to the company. Its financial worries removed, it built to such purpose that it finished its principal line in October 1894.[3]

By this time a third railway—the Natal line from Durban—had been allowed to enter the republic. The Netherlands company had been opposed to the admission of another competitor with the line from Delagoa Bay. But Kruger judged otherwise. He saw that once the Cape–Orange Free State line was admitted it was no longer sound policy to exclude the Natal line. Durban was much nearer Johannesburg than the nearest Cape port, and the Natal revenues depended on the Rand traffic even more than those of the Cape. If he remained obstinately deaf to the appeals from Natal, she would seek an understanding with the Cape–Orange Free State combination, join her

[1] Van der Poel (*a*), 55, 63; van Winter, ii. 137; Scholtz, i. 249, 319.
[2] Van Winter, ii. 127–9, 135, 137, 151; van der Poel (*a*), 58–61, 69.
[3] Van Winter, ii. 137–9, 142, 164.

line to theirs, and by-pass his own south-eastern districts. His
Delagoa Bay line would then be confronted with the united opposition of the Cape, Orange Free State, and Natal. Far better to make
an ally of Natal. In August 1892 Kruger accordingly persuaded the
volksraad to agree to the survey of a line from the Natal frontier
to the Rand. Difficulties were raised, however, by both the Orange
Free State and Portugal, which had treaties with the South African
Republic entitling them to object to the extension of Natal's line, so
that the railway and customs convention with Natal was delayed
until February 1894. Its principal stipulations were the following:
the line from the Natal border to Johannesburg was to be built
jointly by the government of Natal and the Netherlands company
but operated entirely by the company; Natal was not to raise her
transit duties (adopted to undercut those of the Cape) beyond the
present level of 5 per cent. nor reduce them below the 3 per cent.
levied at Delagoa Bay; the railway traffic to the Rand from Durban
and Delagoa Bay was to be regulated in such a manner that neither
of the two lines was to have less than one-third nor more than one-
half of the total. Immediately after the conclusion of the agreement
the building of the railway was taken in hand and completed before
the end of 1895.[1]

The commercial alliances between the Cape Colony and the Orange
Free State, on the one hand, and the colony of Natal and the South
African Republic, on the other, cut across the political affiliation of
these states. For the two republics were political allies, while the
Cape Colony and Natal prized, in varying degrees, their membership
of the British empire. This divergence between the political and the
commercial affiliations of the South African states had its advantages
for a land that seemed bound to remain disunited for some time to
come. It was a factor that enhanced the chances of peaceful co-
existence.

The South African Republic could in theory dictate whatever
terms she chose to the lines that had entered the state from the Cape
and Natal. In practice, however, her freedom of action was limited.
That had been shown already by the agreement she thought it politic
to make with Natal. The question still to be decided was how
she would deal with the Cape–Orange Free State line when the
Sivewright agreement expired at the end of 1894. That she would seek
to deny to the Cape a share in the Rand traffic was unlikely, for this

[1] Ibid. 119, 132–3, 177–85, 206–8; van der Poel (*a*), 66–69, 76–78, 89.

would constitute an 'unfriendly act', which both the Cape and Britain
were sure to challenge. On her side the Cape might be expected to
recognize that, since two other railways were about to compete with
hers, her share of the trade with the Rand was bound to be drastically
reduced.

The negotiations with the Cape which began in June 1894 were
conducted by G. A. A. Middelberg, the managing director of the
Netherlands company in Pretoria. He was an able, reasonable, and
resolute man possessing Kruger's full confidence. Recognizing that
it would take some time before the Delagoa Bay line was able to
carry its full share of the Rand traffic, he proposed a temporary
arrangement fixing the tariff on goods transported to the Rand in
such a manner that the line from Delagoa Bay should carry them
somewhat more cheaply than the lines from the more distant Durban
and East London.[1] The tariff would be gradually adjusted until the
Delagoa Bay line carried about one-third of the traffic. If Durban
got a similar share, that would leave between one-quarter and one-
third for the Cape ports. The traffic to the Rand was increasing so
rapidly that the British high commissioner in South Africa believed
that it would soon be sufficient 'to supply full employment for all the
three lines of railway from the coast'.[2] Under these circumstances
Middelberg hoped that it would be possible to reach an amicable
settlement. The Cape government, however, decided to embark on
a tariff war by undercutting the other two lines. Middelberg's reply
was to raise the rates on the portion of the Cape–Orange Free State
line controlled by his company, i.e. the 51-mile section between the
Vaal river and Johannesburg. To side-step these high rates the Cape
government thereupon arranged that goods should be transported by
ox-wagon from the river to the Rand. It was a blunt weapon thus
resorted to by the Cape, and the ox-wagon could in any case only be
used in summer when the veld was green. But the republican government, following Middelberg's advice, chose to parry the thrust by
a provocative display of the power of the state. On 1 October 1895
it closed the drifts or fords across the Vaal to ox-wagon traffic by
presidential proclamation.[3] The Cape government now appealed to
Joseph Chamberlain, who had recently become colonial secretary in

---

[1] Delagoa Bay was 396 miles from Johannesburg, Durban 481 miles, and East
London (the nearest Cape port) 666 miles.

[2] African (South), 470, pp. 219–20.

[3] This prohibition, like Middelberg's increased railway rates, applied only to goods
from oversea.

Britain, and he sent Kruger a strong protest, at the same time urging the Cape ministers to be reasonable with regard to the division of the railway traffic. Neither C. J. Rhodes, the Cape prime minister, nor Chamberlain expected Kruger to ignore the British protest. Their diagnosis was correct, for on 7 November he withdrew his proclamation. The Cape could now resort to the ox-wagon once more until she had satisfied herself that it could not compete with the railway, expensive though the latter was.[1]

After 1895 the Cape's share of the traffic to the Rand decreased rapidly. In that year she claimed that this share was 85 per cent. But the returns for 1898 showed that it had declined to 28·4 per cent., as against Delagoa Bay's 37·06 per cent. and Durban's 34·54 per cent.[2] Owing to the tariff policy of the Netherlands company, consumers in the Transvaal paid high rates on goods carried from the seaports. On the other hand, owing to the competition for the Transvaal trade between the Cape and Natal, the customs duties levied at their ports on goods destined for the Transvaal were gradually reduced until in 1898 they reached the Delagoa Bay rate of 3 per cent.[3]

It has been pointed out already that the decision to entrust to a Dutch company the building and running of the republic's trunk lines, with the Delagoa Bay line as the first priority, was motivated by reasons of state. But while the decision could be justified on political grounds, a price had to be paid for it. The price was paid by the Transvaal consumers. By the beginning of 1897 the Netherlands company was making the following charges on the portions of the three railway lines to the Rand which it controlled:

	Amount per ton per mile in pence		
Line	Normal goods	Intermediate	Rough
Cape (51 miles in the republic)	7·7	7·7	7·7*
Natal (178 miles in the republic)	5·06	3·82	3·26
Delagoa Bay (341 miles in the republic)	4·27	3·69	2·54

* This high tariff was due, of course, to the tariff war with the Cape.

As against this the tariffs of the Cape, Natal, and Portuguese

[1] On the tariff war see van Winter, ii. 208–22; van der Poel (a), 79–89, and (b), 32–34, 39–41, 51; African (South), 543, p. 574.

[2] Van der Poel (a), 87; van Winter, ii. 220; African (South), 571, p. 203. The attractiveness of the Delagoa Bay line was to some extent promoted by tariff agreements concluded between the Netherlands company, the German East African shipping line, and the German railways in accordance with which through rates were established between German railway stations and Johannesburg. Van Winter, ii. 237.

[3] Van der Poel (a), 17–18, 66, 72, 104; van Winter, ii. 220 n.

administrations for goods carried to the republican frontiers were
as follows:

	Amount per ton per mile in pence		
Administration	Normal goods	Intermediate	Rough
Cape	2·78 and 2·33	2·0	1·3
Natal	3·04	3·04	1·94
Portuguese	4·07	3·53	2·44*

* *Selborne Memorandum* (reprint, 1925), 60; African (South), 536, pp. 4–11. See
also van Winter, ii. 206, 301.

So far as the Rand tram was concerned, it was at this time carrying
coal at the rate of 3*d*. per ton per mile after somewhat smaller rates
had been tried in 1896.[1]

It is not difficult to account for the company's high-tariff policy.
First and foremost, building costs had been high, especially the cost
of building the Delagoa Bay line.[2] This largely neutralized the competitive advantage which the proximity of Delagoa Bay to the Rand
conferred on the company's principal line. Second, the company
patriotically preferred to purchase the equipment for its railways
in the Netherlands, and failing the Netherlands in Germany.[3] That
meant that it did not necessarily buy in the best market. Third, its
policy of recruiting its personnel mainly in the Netherlands made the
acquisition of suitably qualified staff more difficult and increased
the running costs of the railways.[4] Lastly, the company wanted to
earn excess profits[5] in the interests both of the government (which
pocketed 85 per cent. thereof), and of its shareholders.

The company owned almost the whole of the Delagoa Bay line,
which was the shortest line to the Rand. It owned also 178 miles of
the Durban and 51 miles of the Cape line. The company's interests
(and the interests of the republic also) demanded that the Delagoa
Bay line should carry to the Rand as large a percentage of the goods
traffic as was practicable. Because of the relative shortness of its

[1] Van Winter, ii. 302; Fitzpatrick, 68.
[2] Van Winter, i. 214–15; ii. 156–8, 160–1, 171–4, 184–5, 188.
[3] Ibid. i. 168; ii. 361–4.
[4] Ibid. i. 216–17; ii. 195–9; *Hertzog-Annale*, July 1953, p. 55.
[5] See above, p. 34. The company's share capital amounted during the years 1896–8
to nearly £1,167,000, its debenture capital at the end of 1899 to over £7,200,000. On
the bulk of its shares—the A shares—it paid a dividend of 13½ per cent. in 1896,
13 per cent. in 1897, and 11¾ per cent. in 1898. The government received £329,882 in
1896, £265,978 in 1897, and £391,459 in 1898 by way of its 85 per cent. share of the
excess profits. Cd. 623, pp. 20–21. In taxing its customers for the benefit of the general
revenue of the republic, the company was following the example set by the state-owned
railways of the Cape and Natal.

principal and favourite line, the company might well have found itself
in a position to prescribe a downward trend in the tariffs on all three
lines to the Rand.[1] For the reasons I have mentioned its policy, as is
shown by the tariffs already quoted, actually had the opposite effect.
It is not surprising, therefore, that the company—to quote the words
of the Transvaal concessions commission—'aroused in an acute
form the resentment of the industrial and commercial community'
in the republic,[2] the British section of which disliked it in any case
because it was 'foreign' and identified with 'Krugerism'.

The company proved to be expensive also in the manner in which
it served the public. Its historian admits that some of the complaints
on this score were justified. During its early years, owing to inadequate personnel and insufficient rolling stock, the company could not
cope with the demands of its customers.[3] It is fair to add that by
1897 these teething troubles had been to a large extent overcome.
But the company had then only two more years to go.[4]

V

Very different in its outcome was the next railway concession
granted by Kruger's government. The first concession was worked
under the direction of railway men seeking profits for their company
from the actual running of railways. The second fell into the hands of
adventurers seeking quick returns from financial manipulation.

The second railway concession had, like that of the Netherlands
company, political as well as economic objectives. In this case
Kruger hoped to enlist the interest and sympathy of French capitalists
in favour of his state. His government therefore stipulated that the
headquarters of the second railway company should be in Paris and
that it should obtain its capital from French financiers.[5] The railway
to be built by the company was to serve the so-called Selati fields,
where there was said to be payable gold. Starting from a point close
to the Portuguese border on the Netherlands company's trunk line
to Johannesburg, its length was estimated at about 200 miles. In the

---

[1] See van Winter, ii. 169. [2] Cd. 623, p. 22.
[3] Van Winter, i. 217–19; ii. 147–9, 194–200, 214–15; van der Poel (a), 91–92.
Furthermore, at the harbour of Delagoa Bay and on the Portuguese section of the railway, there were deficiencies for which the Netherlands company was not responsible
but which impeded the proper functioning of its principal line. The harbour installa-
tions were defective, and the Portuguese railway administration fell down on its job.
Van Winter, ii. 214–15; van der Poel (a), 91; *Hertzog-Annale*, July 1953, p. 84. See
also below, p. 153.
[4] Van Winter, i. 218–19, 250; ii. 198–9 [5] Cd. 625, pp. 75, 81.

upshot none of the government's objectives was realized: the head-quarters of the company were transferred from Paris to Brussels; almost all the money actually raised for railway construction was obtained in England; and the railway itself petered out in a fever-stricken wilderness after only 74 miles of rails had been laid. The Selati project issued ultimately in lawsuits in the courts of three countries. Coupled as it came to be in the public mind with the dynamite concession, it did grave damage to the reputation of the Boer state.[1]

This in brief is the story of the Selati railway: in June 1890 there arrived in Pretoria Baron Eugène Oppenheim, a Frenchman in his early twenties, in quest of concessions in a rich land governed by simple-minded folk. It so happened that just at this time the Selati railway concession was under consideration in Pretoria. Kruger strongly advocated the construction of this railway, while Leyds opposed it.[2] The will of the president prevailed, and the government decided to support the application of a triumvirate, one of whom was B. J. Vorster, member of the volksraad for Zoutpansberg and an adherent of Kruger. Oppenheim persuaded Kruger that Vorster's concession, when ratified, should be assigned to him, and Vorster and company agreed to the cession—at a price.[3] Oppenheim, whose name, according to himself, was well known among financiers, posed in Pretoria as a man of great wealth. He entertained lavishly, and distributed largesse on a magnificent scale. Members of the volksraad received from him, through the agency of Vorster, carriages (spiders) and watches. He presented the state with a portrait in oils of Kruger. He made available several thousands of pounds for bribes to members of the executive council and the volksraad, as well as to the president's son-in-law (one F. Eloff).[4] Besides Oppenheim's expenditure, another £8,700 was spent by Vorster and his associates (or so they claimed), and refunded to them by Oppenheim.[5]

The volksraad did not confirm the concession immediately, and in August 1890 Oppenheim returned to Paris, where he became consul-general of the republic. During his absence a committee of the volksraad examined the draft concession, the scope of which had

---

[1] Cd. 623, pp. 38, 40, 47, 49–50.
[2] Nilant, 267 n. 9; Leyds, *Derde Verzameling*, Deel I, Voorrede, p. xxi; Coetzee, 129–30.   [3] Cd. 623, pp. 38–39, 45–46; Nilant, 266.
[4] Two members of the executive council and Eloff accepted cheques to the value of £500 each. It is impossible to establish conclusively how much money was accepted by members of the volksraad or who the members were that accepted money.
[5] Cd. 625, pp. 65–66, 69.

in the meantime been narrowed by the executive council. The committee narrowed it even more, so that in the concession ultimately sanctioned by the volksraad in July 1891, the length of the railway to be built was limited to about 200 miles instead of the 1,000 miles anticipated by the exuberant Oppenheim,[1] while the clause granting the concessionaire certain gold-bearing lands along the railway was omitted. Furthermore, the price to be paid to the original concessionaires was limited to £10,000, and Oppenheim was to hand over the concession gratis to the future operating company. According to Oppenheim, two of his agents were present while the volksraad committee discussed these limitations in Kruger's house. When they asked how their principal was to reap the profits to which he was entitled, they were told by one of the members of the committee, without dissent from the others, that 'he should make his advantage out of the cost of construction' notwithstanding the fact that the concession expressly prohibited such profit-taking. If Oppenheim is to be believed, he and his brother (and senior partner) Robert were quite satisfied with this oral declaration. They showed their satisfaction by making further large payments to prominent politicians in money as well as in shares in the prospective company. But the evidence which they submitted with regard to these transactions does not amount to proof.[2]

In so far as the payments were actually made, they may have been partly intended to promote another of the Oppenheims' schemes. In June 1891 Eugène Oppenheim visited Pretoria again, summoned this time by Kruger.[3] Part of his business concerned the railway concession, which was on the point of being finalized. But the president wanted to consult him also about a state loan which he was anxious to raise in order to assist the building operations of the Netherlands railway company and which Oppenheim had offered to place in France. Although both Leyds and Beelaerts van Blokland, the republic's diplomatic representative in Europe, took strong exception to Oppenheim's proposal, the government decided, nevertheless, to authorize him to procure a loan of between one and three million pounds from French bankers. His efforts failed dismally, but he succeeded in doing further damage to the republic's financial standing, already compromised on other grounds.[4]

---

[1] The concession provided for possible extensions beyond 200 miles, but only with the concurrence of the government and the volksraad.

[2] Cd. 623, pp. 38–39; Cd. 625, pp. 66–67, 75; Nilant, 121–2.

[3] Cd. 625, p. 67.　　　　　[4] Nilant, 313–22; van Winter, ii. 116, 119–20.

On this occasion the government managed to extricate itself by setting a term to Oppenheim's negotiations. It did not escape so lightly in the matter of the Selati railway. It had guaranteed to the company which Oppenheim was to form a dividend of 4 per cent. on a share capital of £500,000. It had agreed to guarantee also, direct to the holders, debentures to the amount of £1,500,000, with interest at 4 per cent. (All this at a time when the Netherlands company was having great difficulty in obtaining funds to build the trunk lines of the republic.)[1] When the Selati company was formed in February 1892, it consisted of only eight shareholders including the Oppenheim brothers, and only 10 per cent. of the shares were paid up. The money thus obtained was earmarked to defray preliminary expenses, including Eugène Oppenheim's bribes. There were, therefore, no funds available for the construction of the railway. The Oppenheims and their associates reckoned on obtaining these from the debentures to be guaranteed by the government. In order to convince the latter that the share capital had been duly paid up and spent in accordance with the terms of the concession, they had false entries made in the books of the company.[2] During the course of 1894 they obtained their debenture capital of £1,500,000. But the government, having commissioned an auditor to examine the company's books, had in the meantime become aware of the fraud perpetrated at its expense. Its suspicions thoroughly roused, it now accused the company of a further fraud in the shape of the deflexion of the railway line as originally sanctioned. The company thereupon stopped work on the line.[3]

Early in 1895 the Oppenheims and their associates sold about half their shares in London (having successfully concealed both the government's claim of £400,000 against them on account of their fraudulent book-keeping and the fact that work on the railway had ceased). This led during the following year to the assumption of control over the company by the British shareholders and the appointment of a British managing director in the place of Robert Oppenheim. The government, which had repudiated any further obligation to pay dividends on the company's share capital (though it continued to pay interest on the debentures), was now faced with the prospect of being mulcted in heavy damages for the stoppage of the railway.[4]

[1] Cd. 625, p. 75; van Winter, ii. 113–29.

[2] For this fraud the Oppenheim brothers were many years later sentenced by the Belgian court of appeal to three years imprisonment each.

[3] Cd. 623, pp. 42–47, 49.   [4] Ibid., pp. 47–49; Cd. 624, pp. 177, 214, 216.

There loomed also the possibility that the colonial office might intervene on behalf of the British shareholders, for it had begun to watch the affairs of the company. Towards the end of 1898 the Pretoria government made an unsuccessful attempt to buy a controlling interest in the company, presumably in order to liquidate it and, if possible, stop the lawsuits in which the company had involved the republic. The lawsuits continued, to the embarrassment of the government, for in the course of their pleadings the Oppenheims washed much dirty linen in public. The cases had not yet been concluded when the war broke out.[1]

The other railways constructed in the time of the republic may be dealt with briefly. In 1892 a concession was granted to Marks and Lippert for the building of a short branch railway connecting Barberton with the Delagoa Bay line. When these two men failed to carry out their contract, the work was taken over by the Netherlands railway company and completed in 1896. The company undertook also to extend the Rand tram from Krugersdorp via Potchefstroom to Klerksdorp, a distance of 97 miles, but the shrewd business men who directed its affairs, suspecting that the extension might not pay, saddled the government with any losses incurred on it. The last railway completed before the war was the line, 176 miles long, connecting Pretoria with Pietersburg in the north of the republic. It was built and worked by an English company in terms of a concession granted in 1895 to one H. J. Schoeman.[2]

[1] African (South), 536, no. 181; 543, pp. 353, 484–6, 571–2; 557, pp. 108–13, 115–16; Cd. 623, p. 50; Cd. 624, pp. 216–17; Leyds, *Derde Verzameling*, Deel II, Bijlagen P and Q; Nilant, 290.

[2] Van Winter, ii. 174–7, 186–9, 313; Cd. 623, pp. 58–59.

CHAPTER III

THE PRELUDE TO THE JAMESON RAID

I

In 1897 Rhodes told the Commons committee of inquiry into the Jameson raid, apparently at the suggestion of Joseph Chamberlain, that his participation in the plot against the Transvaal government was due largely to his fear of German interference in South Africa.[1] This statement, made by Rhodes in his defence after the event, must be treated with caution. To say this, however, is not to deny that there had been a *rapprochement* between the South African Republic and Germany in the years immediately preceding the raid. Leyds had convinced Kruger that in order to defend the interests and the independence of the republic against British pressure it was essential to secure the support of a great power, preferably Germany.[2] Their view was shared by influential Boers, including men in political opposition to Kruger.[3] In order to gain German political backing it seemed good policy to promote German economic activities in the republic.[4] This backing was needed as a counterpoise to several British pressures: but the one of greatest immediate urgency in the years 1890–5 seemed to be that of Rhodes and the British government on Delagoa Bay.[5] The republic considered the railway to Delagoa Bay to be her lifeline to the sea.[6] It was therefore of vital importance to her that this harbour should not fall into British hands. As for Rhodes, his idea was that if the Portuguese end of the railway were brought under British control the republic could be forced into a South African commercial union which should lead to a federation under the British flag. While his settlers were occupying Matabele–Mashonaland (later Rhodesia), he tried to bring under his control Gungunhana, the chief of Gazaland, whom Portugal claimed as a subject; and through the southern portion of Gazaland ran the railway from Delagoa Bay towards the Witwatersrand. Rhodes's plan was frustrated by the Anglo-Portuguese treaty of 1891, which assigned

---

[1] Van der Poel (*b*), 157–8, 201.   [2] Van Winter, ii. 236–8.
[3] Ibid. 90–92.   [4] Ibid. 237–8.
[5] Ibid. 227–39, 246.
[6] So did high commissioner Milner. Headlam, i. 267–8.

Gazaland to Portugal. But he seems, nevertheless, to have persisted in his efforts to establish his influence at Gungunhana's 'court'.[1] After the Anglo-Portuguese treaty Rhodes thought of another way of attaining his object. Portugal happened to be in grave financial difficulties, and it seemed to him that she might be willing to sell Delagoa Bay. (She had given Britain a pre-emptive right over the bay in 1875, and this had just been confirmed by the treaty of 1891.) During the years 1891–4 Rhodes made repeated efforts to buy the control of the harbour and the Portuguese end of the railway,[2] but in the end he had to admit defeat. The British government had not been enthusiastic in his support, and by September 1894 Germany had thrown her weight into the scale against him.[3]

Thus the Transvaal's persistent wooing at length received its reward. It is true that the strong language of the German ambassador was resented in Lisbon, but his warning against the acceptance by Portugal of financial assistance that might lead to the intervention of the British government in Portuguese East Africa could not be ignored.[4] During the course of the following months it became clearer to the British government that any attempt to alter the *status quo* either at Delagoa Bay or in the South African Republic to the disadvantage of the Boers would meet with strong German opposition. In September 1894 a Native insurrection in Gazaland—led by Gungunhana and ascribed at Berlin and Lisbon to Rhodes's 'intrigues'—moved the British consul at Lourenço Marques to have twenty blue-jackets landed 'for the protection of the Consulate'. The German government protested and dispatched a cruiser to Delagoa Bay in order to emphasize 'the large German interests involved both on the coast and in the Transvaal', to the delight of imperialist Germans and their press.[5] This public manifestation of German interest in South-East Africa touched British statesmen on the raw. Lord Kimberley, the foreign secretary, thought it necessary to speak to the German ambassador about the strength of the British navy.[6] Shortly afterwards Kruger, in a public speech, referred to 'the bonds of friendship . . . between Germany and this country' and added that

---

[1] Van der Poel (*a*), 53–54; van Winter, ii. 227–9.
[2] The South African Republic did likewise, in order to make sure of her access to the sea. Van Winter, ii. 227, 231, 234–6, 239.
[3] Van Winter, ii. 229–39; van der Poel (*a*), 61–62, 74; Williams, 198.
[4] Van Winter, ii. 238–9.
[5] *British Documents*, i. 323–4 (Tilley's memorandum); van Winter, 229, 234, 340–1; Lovell, 343, 349.
[6] Wolf, ii. 233.

'if one nation [Britain] tries to kick us [another version: tries to trample us under foot] the other [Germany] will try to stop it'. He also dwelt on the republic's desire to have 'bigger clothes' than those given her by the London convention of 1884,[1] with the obvious implication that Germany might help her to get them.[2] On Kimberley's instructions the British ambassador in Berlin drew the attention of the German foreign minister, Marschall von Bieberstein, to this speech and warned him that the republic, relying on Germany's 'unconditional support', might take a line 'incompatible with the Republic's international position'. Marschall's reply was that Germany aimed merely at maintaining the *status quo* in the republic and at Delagoa Bay, and that Kimberley had declared that this was his aim also. If so, there was no Transvaal question as far as Germany was concerned. But he warned Kimberley in his turn that the policy Rhodes was proclaiming was 'contrary to the *status quo*'. Why did Kimberley not check him?[3] Nine months later (October 1895) Marschall, in reply to the British ambassador, who had referred to the serious consequences of encouraging a hostile attitude to Britain on the part of the Boers, remarked that Germany was not to blame for the unfriendly attitude of the Transvaal: it was largely due to the *treibereien* of Rhodes.[4]

German diplomatic support of the South African Republic was resented by British statesmen as interference in a British 'sphere of influence'.[5] It was certainly a new development,[6] dating only from 1894. But then the German economic stake in the republic was new also. When Salisbury, the British prime minister, asked the German ambassador, Hatzfeldt, early in 1896 what Germany's interests in the republic were, he replied 'over 500 million marks[7] of German capital and . . . about 15,000 Germans'; which, declared Hatzfeldt, convinced Salisbury 'that we had to interest ourselves in the situation over there'.[8] It is clear, nevertheless, that this official interest in the

---

[1] Kruger particularly desired the cancellation of article IV, which forbade the republic to conclude treaties without the consent of the British government.

[2] 311—I (select committee on British South Africa), appendix no. 4; van Oordt, 609–10.

[3] *German Diplomatic Documents*, ii. 366–7.

[4] *Grosse Politik*, xi. 5–7.

[5] Lovell, 349. The technical term 'sphere of influence' was not applicable to the republic. See below, p. 49, n. 3.

[6] At any rate since 1885, when Germany agreed to keep clear of the coast south of Delagoa Bay.

[7] Over 300 million according to the Kaiser. Lovell, 347.

[8] Hatzfeldt to Holstein, 4 Jan. 1896. *Grosse Politik*, xi. 33.

republic was for Germany an incident in the game of European power politics: Britain must be made to feel that a policy of 'splendid isolation' was no longer practicable; that it was worth her while to consider what price she was willing to pay for German support, since otherwise she might find Germany thwarting her desires and helping her opponents in several parts of the world.[1] So far as the republic was concerned, this attitude meant that German friendship was unstable, and that she might find herself isolated if Britain agreed to a deal with Germany.

II

Since the days of the Great Trek it had been a persistent aim of the Boer leaders to have a seaport of their own. To this aim Kruger and his rival Joubert added the vision of a shipping company which would fly the republican flag on the high seas and thus enhance the republic's international status.[2] Because it was at least doubtful whether the republic would ever be able to acquire a foothold at Delagoa Bay, Kruger turned his attention to another possible harbour, viz. Kosi Bay on the coast of Tongaland—the only un-annexed portion of the South African coastline. But he could not get to Tongaland unless he managed to acquire rights in Swaziland and in certain other tribal lands lying beyond his eastern frontier. Here the London convention barred his way. For the convention stipulated that he could not make agreements with any chief to the east or west of his state without Britain's consent. He was left free, however, to make such agreements beyond his northern frontier.

In 1887 the republic made an agreement with Lobengula, the chief of the Matabele, which was intended to support a republican claim to a 'sphere of influence' in Matabeleland.[3] But Rhodes, who also had his eye on the north, now persuaded the high commissioner to take the necessary steps to achieve a British sphere of influence, which was formally proclaimed in July 1888. Though the republic protested, Kruger had no intention of opposing Rhodes's occupation of the north. But he did intend to obtain a *quid pro quo* in the east for his withdrawal from Matabeleland. He got some encouragement from the attitude of certain British officials. The high commissioner, Sir

[1] Brandenburg, 79; Lovell, 359, 362–3; van Winter, ii. 242, 244, 273.
[2] Van Winter, ii. 102–7; Scholtz, i. 146, 188–91; Kotze, ii. 186–8; Bryce, 168; Garson, 392 n., 397–8.
[3] To proclaim a sphere of influence meant to notify an intention to occupy tribal territory.

Hercules Robinson, wrote to him in 1888 that the British government had no objection in principle to the republic's legitimate ambition to reach the sea.[1] Early in the following year Herbert, the permanent under-secretary for the colonies, told the Dutch ambassador that it would be desirable, if parliament could be got to agree, 'to ... secure for the republic a free and independent access to the sea outside the Delagoa Bay railway'.[2] Shortly after he heard of this interview Kruger telegraphed to propose 'friendly settlement regarding Matabeleland and Swaziland—[the] Transvaal Republic to withdraw all claims to the north, and use influence to support British expansion in Bechuana-land and Matabeleland if Her Majesty's government withdraw from Swaziland, the territory of Zambane and Umbegesa, and Tongaland, including Kosi Bay'.[3]

The British authorities, who had for the past two years been evading a decision on the question of the republic's eastward expansion, continued their delaying tactics after the receipt of Kruger's 'friendly offer' of 3 May 1889.[4] It was not until March 1890 that Sir Henry Loch, the new high commissioner, conferred with Kruger at Blignaut's Pont. Loch was accompanied by Rhodes, who had meanwhile obtained a royal charter which permitted him to establish his power in the north. Kruger, on the other hand, in his anxiety to placate the British government, had weakened his bargaining position by bringing about the abandonment of a contemplated Boer trek across the Limpopo. Hence it was easier for Loch, following the instructions of the colonial office, to refuse to accept Kruger's offer as a basis for the negotiations. The president was told that his withdrawal from the north must be unconditional. He was not to have Swaziland nor the territories to the east of it, but he might obtain a railroad to Kosi Bay on condition that he entered the Cape–Orange Free State customs union and conceded free trade in South African produce and manufactures. A South African commercial union issuing in a political federation was Rhodes's cherished ambition, which the colonial office was prepared to back, while Kruger desired access to the sea precisely in order to frustrate such aims. Yet the mere idea of having his own port was so attractive to him at this time that he was prepared to contemplate a commercial union if he could get full access to the coast.[5]

[1] Garson, 301.   [2] Backeberg, 138.
[3] Acting high commissioner's summary. C. 6200, pp. 135, 153.
[4] Garson, 292, 299–302.
[5] Ibid., 398–9, 411–12, 416–17; Kotze, ii. 188–90; Hofmeyr, 394.

On his return to Pretoria Kruger found that Loch's proposals were not acceptable to the executive council. The high commissioner thereupon sent up J. H. Hofmeyr to continue the negotiations. The choice of this man to represent the imperial factor was significant. He was the leader of the Afrikaner bond, the political party of the Cape Afrikaners. Since 1881 every ministry at the Cape had been dependent on the support of the 'Dutch party', whose strength lay in the fact that it was the only group in parliament based on a permanent and widespread organization in the constituencies. Before Hofmeyr went to Pretoria it was already clear that he intended to oust the government in power at the Cape and to put in its place one headed by Rhodes.[1] It was a good stroke of business on the part of Loch (and presumably Rhodes) to send Hofmeyr to deal with Kruger and his executive council. He could speak with the men in Pretoria as a fellow Afrikaner, and could be trusted to do his best to further Rhodes's policy of northward expansion and a South African commercial union.

Hofmeyr seems to have gone to Pretoria with the belief that the situation was extremely grave. And, indeed, Loch asked the colonial office to send reinforcements to South Africa to provide 'for all eventualities'. He meant to compel Kruger to accept his proposals in their entirety. But when he talked of troops the colonial secretary[2] drew back. Loch had, therefore, to adopt a less high-handed attitude and to allow Hofmeyr to make some concessions. In particular he was authorized to promise an eventual reconsideration of any terms agreed to by the republic. This paved the way for the acceptance of the first Swaziland convention in August 1890.[3] It also paved the way for further negotiations.

In those negotiations Kruger showed himself anxious to deal with the destiny of Swaziland and the terms on which he would be permitted to reach the sea as entirely separate issues. He was in fact no longer prepared to achieve access to the sea on the conditions proposed by Loch. His dislike of a South African commercial federation had hardened, and he seems to have become convinced of the uselessness of Kosi Bay as a harbour. (Leyds had regarded the prospect of a railway to Kosi Bay as illusory from the beginning.)[4] Loch was

---

[1] Hofmeyr, ch. xxii; Williams, 185.
[2] Lord Knutsford. He was colonial secretary in Salisbury's Unionist government of 1886–92.
[3] Hofmeyr, ch. xxii; Garson, 321–3, 417–18.
[4] Garson, ch. iv and pp. 401, 403–4; van Winter, ii. 231; Scholtz, i. 139.

willing to settle the Swaziland question first, and this was ultimately accomplished by a convention signed in December 1894. Swaziland was to pass under the control of the republic subject to certain provisions safeguarding Native and British interests.[1] A great deal of lip service had been paid to the wishes and interests of the Swazis, but these counted for little in the decisions of the governments since 1887, when Swaziland became a 'question'. It was agreed in the convention of 1894 that the consent of Swazis to the republican acquisition of their country was unnecessary. They had in fact made it quite clear that they were strongly opposed to coming under Boer control in spite of the precautions taken by the republic. One of these was to buy the support of 'Offy' Shepstone, the resident adviser of the Swazis. But the tribesmen dismissed him from this office in July 1894.[2]

It had been agreed between Loch and Kruger that the question of republican access to the sea should be dealt with in a separate convention. Loch's conditions still stood, and he had recently added another—'a general agreement on South African railway tariffs'— which was even less acceptable to Kruger than the others.[3] It gradually became clear to the British authorities that the republic would be unlikely to accept their terms. In September 1894 Lord Ripon, the colonial secretary,[4] had already decided to annex the territories lying between Swaziland and the sea. Two months later he told his colleague, the foreign secretary, that the annexation would serve as a timely warning to Germany to 'keep their hands off' the republic. When the territories were actually annexed in April–May 1895 Kruger showed intense resentment. Though he had been unwilling to fulfil the conditions attached to his reaching the sea, he had not expected the road to be thus decisively barred.[5]

III

Swaziland and Kosi Bay were, however, side issues. The republic's main problems were internal ones. The mining industry demanded 'good, honest, intelligent government', as the president of the chamber of mines put it in 1894.[6] Among the general body of Uitlanders

[1] C. 7611, pp. 93–96. [2] Garson, 351–3, 355–61, and *passim*.
[3] Ibid. 338, 342–3.
[4] Ripon was colonial secretary in the Liberal government of 1892–5.
[5] Garson, 383–4, 421.
[6] 311—I, p. 591.

there was an important and vocal section who resented their political impotence.

When the Uitlanders began to enter the Transvaal in large numbers about the middle of the eighties they could obtain the republican citizenship together with the full franchise after five years' residence. But a high fee of £25 was demanded for this naturalization.[1] In 1887 Barberton petitioned for representation in the volksraad. The request was granted and before the end of the year both Barberton and the Witwatersrand were proclaimed electoral constituencies, each returning one member to the volksraad.[2] But Kruger was already becoming alarmed at the inrush of foreigners into the republic. By 1888 he had evolved a scheme whereby the Uitlanders would get a constitutional organ—the so-called second volksraad—to further their interests, without at the same time getting political power. When this scheme became law in 1890, it was accompanied by provisions extending the period of residence required to enable a new-comer to vote in elections for the volksraad proper,[3] the president, and the commandant-general. The residence qualification was raised from five years to fourteen, and the law laid down in addition that no Uitlander should henceforward acquire the full franchise until he had reached the age of forty. It was in order to give the Uitlanders some compensation for this loss of political privileges that the second volksraad was instituted. Foreigners who became naturalized at the reduced fee of £5[4] could obtain the franchise for this body two years after their arrival. After a further two years they became eligible for membership thereof. The raad had, however, a limited competence. It could deal only with certain specified matters such as the mining industry, and its legislation was subject to ratification by the volksraad proper.

In spite of its limited powers the second raad was not the cipher it has often been deemed. It took itself seriously, and so did the government and the first raad. Many of the measures it passed became law. But it failed to realize the aim of its founder. Kruger's aim had been a twofold one: to associate the new-comers with the government of the state and to wean them, particularly the British Uitlanders,[5] from

[1] Law 7 of 1882.
[2] In the nineties Barberton was represented by an English-speaking member.
[3] Known henceforward as the first volksraad.
[4] In 1894 it became £2.
[5] Under the term 'British Uitlanders' I include British settlers from the Cape Colony and Natal as well as settlers who came from Britain.

their former political loyalty. For if the Uitlanders became republican burghers they would no longer be able to appeal to their mother countries, particularly Britain, for support, and the danger of foreign intervention would be reduced. But the Uitlanders did not find the citizenship of the republic attractive, especially if it was divorced from the full franchise. The upshot was that only 2,087 of them were naturalized between the years 1890 and 1896.[1] It is idle to speculate what the outcome would have been if the second raad had functioned in accordance with Kruger's intentions. The Uitlanders were never in a position to work it and it never represented them. The old burghers remained the great majority of its electorate, and its constituencies remained the same as those for the first raad.[2]

At the instigation of the president, the volksraad legislated from time to time to grant the full franchise to groups of foreigners whose loyalty to the republic was considered to be above suspicion. Thus it agreed in 1895 to grant the franchise to foreigners who had taken part in recent commandos against Natives as well as in the expedition to take over Swaziland after the 1894 convention. But it added a rider to the effect that no foreigners should in future be enfranchised by special resolution unless two-thirds of the burghers of their ward had agreed to their enfranchisement. The great majority of the Uitlanders were, however, in no way affected by such legislation.[3]

The Uitlanders had, therefore, little representation in the central legislature. In the local government of Johannesburg they fared better. The town's sanitary board, created by the volksraad in 1887, exercised wider functions of local government than its name would indicate, though the central government had on paper the right to supervise it closely and granted concessions of a municipal character without consulting it.[4] From 1890 onward it consisted of fifteen members, three of whom were government nominees while the rest were elected by the White adult males of the town. One of the elected members acted as chairman. The principal government nominee was K. von Brandis, the popular *landdrost* of Johannesburg, who had to keep the government in touch with the board's administration. The board was empowered to levy local rates and to borrow money, the latter power being exercised under government supervision.[5]

These rights of local government did not satisfy the Uitlanders.

[1] Hugo, 34.
[2] For the second volksraad see Hugo, ch. iii and p. 51; Smit, 131–7; and *Notulen, Tweede Volksraad, passim.*
[3] Hugo, 48–56.   [4] See above, p. 24.   [5] Maud, 21–29.

Their spokesmen reasoned that given more political power they could make an effective contribution to the improvement of the central administration, which they held was not sufficiently alive to their interests. I have dealt already with the republic's administration.[1] But the policy of the government with regard to language and education was omitted from the discussion. The only official language of the republic was Dutch, and Dutch it remained until the end. All public business had legally to be transacted in that language. The Netherlands railway company followed the example of the state. This inconvenienced and irritated the immigrants, though in practice some allowance had to be made for the fact that most of them knew no Dutch. The government's education policy was designed to remedy this defect. During the term of the Rev. S. J. du Toit, the first superintendent of education after the retrocession, the volksraad had decreed that Dutch should be the medium of instruction in all state-supported schools. But his administration had been lackadaisical, owing partly to the lack (until 1889) of a paid inspectorate, and a number of schools teaching through the medium of English managed to obtain the state grant.[2] When in 1891 professor N. Mansvelt, a Hollander, succeeded du Toit, the scene changed. Mansvelt was a capable and energetic administrator: during his superintendentship, which lasted until the fall of the republic, education made a big stride forward. The state made more money available for the schools, the quality of the teachers and school textbooks improved, the inspectorate was enlarged, the republic began training its own teachers, and a gymnasium was established in Pretoria to prepare students for the university.[3]

In practice it was mainly the children of the Boers who benefited from Mansvelt's zeal, at any rate until the end of 1895. His strict application of the law enforcing the use of Dutch in the schools and his apparent preference for Hollander teachers and inspectors[4] antagonized not only the British Uitlanders but others as well. For the ministry of the *Nederduitsch Hervormde of Gereformeerde Kerk* (the largest Calvinist church in the republic), the Cape Afrikaner immigrants almost to a man, and a large minority among the Boers, also disliked Mansvelt's policy.[5] Shortly after he became superintendent a number of schools, some of them attended by Afrikaans-speaking

[1] See above, chs. i and ii.   [2] Malherbe, 265–6, 268; Basson, 91–93.
[3] Malherbe, 272, 274–8, 280–2; van Winter, ii. 70.
[4] Basson, 104–5; Lugtenburg, 205; van Winter, ii. 70–71.
[5] Lugtenburg, 188, 192–3; Ploeger, 111–24.

children, lost the state subsidy because they used English, either wholly or partly, as the medium of instruction. Most of these schools continued as private schools, and swelled the ranks of the private institutions, founded mainly by the English churches, which were already in existence.[1] In addition to the private schools teaching through them edium of English, other schools drawing the state subsidy were established for English-speaking children in terms of a volksraad resolution passed in 1892. These had to satisfy the authorities that Dutch was efficiently taught as a subject. The standard of proficiency demanded was one year below that of the Dutch-medium schools. The immigrants considered this standard too high, and by 1895 there were only five of these so-called *besluit* schools, teaching altogether 150 children.[2]

IV

As early as 1887 the Uitlanders had begun to organize in order to bring pressure to bear on the government. But until 1892 their political associations had been feeble and short-lived. In that year, however, a more powerful organization was formed. The immediate cause of its formation was the government's rejection of a request by the sanitary board of Johannesburg for wider municipal powers. The board thereupon convened a protest meeting which resolved to unite the Uitlanders for action. A week later, on 20 August 1892, another mass meeting approved the formation of the so-called Transvaal national union. The union's object was 'to obtain by all constitutional means equal rights for all citizens of this republic, and . . . the redress of all grievances'. Its leadership was in the hands of British settlers from the Cape, two of whom had held ministerial office. Among the leaders were the brothers Charles and J. W. Leonard, who had played prominent parts in the affairs of the empire league formed in the Cape in 1884 to support British intervention in Bechuanaland. The chamber of mines was strongly (though unofficially) represented on the committee of management set up on 20 August,[3] the Johannesburg chamber of commerce less strongly. Delegates of the mine employees' and mechanics' union, the first

---

[1] Lugtenburg, 172–3; Ploeger, 118; Basson, 102–3.
[2] Malherbe, 278–9; Basson, 114–15; Ploeger, 158.
[3] Early in 1893 an unsuccessful attempt was made to secure the election of J. Tudhope, the president of the national union, as president of the chamber of mines. Scholtz, i. 280.

trade union in the republic, sat there too, but were withdrawn before the end of 1893. From that time onward the committee consisted entirely of professional and business men.[1]

The national union tried to reach its objectives by several routes: it held public meetings to rouse and unite the Uitlanders; it sent the Boer authorities repeated and unsuccessful petitions, which rated the denial of the franchise to the immigrants as the first and foremost of their grievances; and it sought to make contact with the enfranchised burghers. Such contact was necessary if the national union was to achieve its aims by constitutional means. At the time of the formation of the union, presidential and volksraad elections were approaching, and a *rapprochement* took place between prominent supporters of Joubert, Kruger's rival, and the union. Thus Esselen, the chairman of Joubert's election committee, spoke from its platform in September 1892. When challenged with regard to this, Joubert found it politic to repudiate the union. He also repudiated his election committee. For its part the union set itself the task of dispatching an anti-Kruger manifesto to every farmstead in the republic.[2] Though the elections showed that Kruger's popularity was waning, they brought no benefits to the Uitlanders. The petitions they sent to Pretoria in 1893 received scant consideration, and in September Charles Leonard announced that the committee of the union had resolved to raise a fund in support of 'progressive' candidates in future elections. In May 1894 the union once more presented a petition in support of which it had managed to collect over 13,000 signatures. The volksraad's reply was to consolidate the franchise legislation of the last few years, making it somewhat stiffer in the process.[3]

The volksraad had acted in conformity with the president's expressed views. But it would appear that Kruger's prestige had continued to decline since the elections. Would the two groups in opposition to Kruger—the Boer opposition and the national union—now draw closer together? And how would the president react to sustained and increasing pressure?[4] The two opposition groups were already expressing similar views with regard to administrative reform, concessions, and the growing Hollander influence in the republic. In April 1894 Kruger made a characteristic and significant move: he

[1] Webb, 4–21, 27–29; Hofmeyr, 257, 260.
[2] Hugo, 58; Mouton, 126–7; Webb, 27; Scholtz, i. 279.
[3] Webb, 25–27, 29–30; law 3 of 1894.
[4] In spite of repeated assertions to the contrary by commentators, he was too shrewd a statesman to be 'immovable'.

took Esselen into his government as state attorney. In a letter to
Sir Henry de Villiers, the chief justice of the Cape, Esselen gave an
account of his appointment. His letter was a reply to one from de
Villiers expressing alarm at Rhodes's increasing power and arrogance.
Esselen began by expressing agreement with de Villiers 'with regard
to the policy Rhodes now seems to be following. It seems to me now
to be a threat and menace to the two republics.' He then continued
as follows:

I was very glad to get your letter expressing gladness at my meeting with
the president. Since the presidential and other elections, and especially after
the last session of the volksraad, I . . . came to the conclusion that some
steps had to be taken to prevent the personal, religious and family differences, caused by the election, from being extended and becoming permanent. Whilst still thinking about the best way out of the difficulty, Burgers
died suddenly.[1] The day we buried him . . . Koos Smit . . . told me that
as chairman of the election committee of Kruger he came to me as chairman of Joubert's committee to see whether I was ready and willing to
co-operate with him for the benefit of the country. He confessed that the
Kruger party could not do without us . . . admitted that there were grave
faults in their administration . . . and that important changes had to be
made in the constitution and government of the country. . . . He wanted
me to promise that I would accept the attorney-generalship should Kruger
offer it to me, saying that they would urge Kruger to offer me the appointment and if he refused they would leave him and come over to us. . . . Well,
I promised. The chief [justice][2] and Koos Smit called on the president . . .
and to their astonishment found, instead of opposition, approval, the old
man saying that he had thought of it himself. . . . Practically the only
question on which he wanted any assurance from me was that of an extension of the franchise. He thought, judging by what I had said at the
National Union meeting that I was in favour of immediately extending the
franchise universally. . . . I explained to him what I had said and my views
generally on the question. He admits that the present law is not good, but
he is in favour of this selective scheme[3] of his which I cannot agree with.[4]

Esselen did not remain long in the government. The latter had
agreed with the chamber of mines in 1894 on the establishment of
a special force of detectives, financed by the government and the
chamber, to check the theft of gold and gold amalgam on the mines.
One, Andrew Trimble, was appointed to command the force. On

---

[1] Burgers was the state attorney.   [2] J. G. Kotze.
[3] A scheme to grant the franchise to 'trustworthy' Uitlanders. See above, p. 54,
and Scholtz, i. 278.
[4] Walker (a), 241–4.

Trimble's dismissal towards the end of 1895 Esselen sent in his resignation.[1] This meant a weakening of the government at a time when the anti-Kruger element in the volksraad was increasing as a result of the elections held early in 1895.[2] The 'improvement' thus secured may have been partly due to the money spent to obtain a better raad by the national union and by Lionel Phillips, the president of the chamber of mines and the principal representative in Johannesburg of the Wernher–Beit firm.[3] The attitude of the raad on the franchise question was tested in August 1895 when the national union presented another petition, said to have been signed by over 32,000 persons. Lucas Meyer, one of the 'progressive' members, thereupon proposed that foreigners who had resided in the republic for five years and had reached the age of thirty-one should be enfranchised, subject to a reasonable property qualification. After a long and heated debate his proposal was rejected, but it obtained one-third of the votes.[4]

There is nothing noteworthy about the fact that the politicians who led the national union should have overstated their case against the government. But the temper of the Uitlander community, and particularly of its British section, does deserve some mention. James Bryce, who spent some time on the Witwatersrand shortly before the raid, said about the English-speaking immigrants: 'Hearing nothing but English spoken, seeing nothing all round them that was not far more English than Dutch . . . it was natural that the bulk of the Uitlanders should deem themselves to be in a country which had become virtually English, and should see something unreasonable and even grotesque in the control of a small body of persons whom they deemed in every way their inferiors.'[5] This attitude was reflected from time to time in the public speeches of leading Uitlanders. It was reflected also in the editorial columns of the capitalist-controlled *Star*, the newspaper most widely read among the Uitlanders. The *Star* was inclined to adopt a patronizing and supercilious tone towards the Boer authorities, and occasionally levelled personal abuse at the president himself.[6] Another noteworthy characteristic of the British community in the republic was its apparent eagerness to

[1] Etheredge, 88–90. Esselen was succeeded by a Hollander, Dr. H. J. Coster.
[2] Van Winter, ii. 253, referring to a letter written by Middelberg after a conversation with Leyds. See also the statement by R. K. Loveday quoted on p. 256 below.
[3] 311—I, p. 591; green book no. 2 of 1896, pp. 2–5; Fitzpatrick, 90.
[4] Hugo, 15, 64; *Notulen*, Eerste Volksraad, 1895, arts. 908–24.
[5] Bryce, 409.
[6] See Scholtz, i. 267 n., 269 n., 276, 281 n., 324; Fitzpatrick, 192.

display its political loyalty to Britain.[1] Such attitudes made more difficult the task of the progressives who sympathized with the cause of the national union.

V

Lord Ripon, the Liberal colonial secretary during the years 1892-5, like his Conservative predecessor, Knutsford, was averse to the idea of using force against the republic to achieve his aims, the most important of which was a South African federation under British hegemony. He was determined not to relinquish such controls over the republic as Britain possessed by virtue of the London convention, and he showed his dislike of the 'flirtations' between the republic and Germany. But he was cautious in his approach to the Transvaal's internal affairs. He understood the danger of being drawn into a public espousal of the Uitlander cause.[2] Yet he could hardly fail to take careful note of the situation on the Witwatersrand. As early as June 1891 Loch, the high commissioner, had suggested that the settlement of the Swaziland question in favour of the republic should be made conditional on the enfranchisement of the Uitlanders. But Ripon did not adopt this suggestion, though he authorized Loch to refer to the franchise issue during the course of the negotiations on Swaziland.[3]

On one celebrated occasion, however, he did sanction intervention inside the republic.[4] In May 1894 the government called up a number of British subjects to serve in a commando which was to take the field against a native chief called Malaboch. An agitation got under way immediately, and the national union promised financial assistance if legal proceedings were taken against those who disobeyed the order. A few of the commandeered men refused to go, were arrested, tried, and sent to the front. The national union appealed to the British government, and towards the end of June Loch went to Pretoria.[5] He had been instructed by Ripon to address a courteous remonstrance to the republican authorities. Ripon admitted that

---

[1] Examples in Scholtz, i. 268-9, 271, 286 n., 287, 296; van der Poel (b), 14; and C. 7212, pp. 153-4.

[2] Wolf, ii. 222-3, 225-6.

[3] Garson, 332, 336-7, 368, 371; C. 7933, pp. 92-93. Ripon was, of course, aware of the connexion between Uitlander enfranchisement and South African federation. See Garson, 420.

[4] For an earlier example see above, p. 29.

[5] He went there to discuss both commandeering and Swaziland.

British subjects could not claim exemption from commando duties 'on strict grounds of international law'. He asked for their exemption mainly on the ground that the subjects of certain other states were by treaty excused from serving on commandos. The British government, he concluded, 'consider that they can hardly be expected to acquiesce in a state of things under which Her Majesty's subjects, whose interests in the South African Republic are greater and more intimate than those of any other Power, should remain in a position of such marked disadvantage'. Loch succeeded in persuading the government of the republic to accede to Ripon's request. But the national union had not conducted the agitation merely in order to stop the commandeering of British subjects. It had hoped to procure much more comprehensive and decisive intervention on the part of the high commissioner. Loch's instructions, however, did not authorize such intervention, whatever his personal inclinations may have been.[1]

While Loch was in Pretoria he discussed the situation on the Witwatersrand privately with Lionel Phillips. The latter understood from Loch that he would intervene if the Uitlanders rose and had sufficient arms to hold Johannesburg for a few days.[2] The high commissioner had no sooner arrived back in Cape Town than he cabled Ripon that he wanted to come to London to confer with him. Since Loch had just returned to South Africa after a period of leave in England, the colonial secretary was taken aback by this request. Loch insisted, however, that he had certain proposals to make in view of the 'present grave situation in [the] South African Republic', and he got his way. In London he proposed that he should be authorized to use the Bechuanaland Protectorate police as first aid to a rising in Johannesburg prior to the intervention of the British garrison in South Africa, which should be increased by 5,000 men. But the colonial office rejected this plan. Sir Robert Meade, the permanent under-secretary, remarked that Loch's 'extremely dangerous proposal' would encourage the Uitlanders 'to make excessive demands', which would certainly be resisted by the government of the republic. He added that 'every nerve should be strained to prevent such a disgrace as another S. African war'. Ripon minuted his agreement with Meade on 12 September 1894.[3]

---

[1] C. 8159, *passim*; van der Poel (b), 13–16; Webb, 30–35.

[2] Van der Poel (b), 16, 18–19.

[3] Garson ,362, 369; Garvin, iii. 58, 63; van der Poel (b), 16–17; E. Drus in the *English Historical Review*, Oct. 1953, pp. 591–2.

The colonial office did, however, adopt Loch's suggestion that Kruger should be invited to a conference in London. At this conference Ripon intended to concede certain alterations in the London convention in return for the enfranchisement of the Uitlanders. 'I had little hope of success', he declared later, 'because I had so little to give.' And, indeed, the alterations he was prepared to make in the convention were of little significance. He never got the chance of confronting Kruger with his proposal, because the latter declined the invitation to come to London.[1]

After the high commissioner's visit to London it was clear that the Liberal government would be extremely hesitant to support an Uitlander rising for the purpose of overthrowing Kruger. It is true that Sydney Buxton, the parliamentary under-secretary for the colonies, was authorized to warn the consul-general of the republic in London that Britain could not look on unmoved in the event of a conflict with the Uitlanders.[2] But this did not commit the government to anything. If the leaders of the national union, who had hitherto been carrying on a 'constitutional' agitation, were to be brought to the point of contemplating armed insurrection, they would have to draw encouragement from sources other than the Liberal government. One such source was the mining magnates. Up to 1893 they had taken no part in politics. But the Macarthur–Forrest cyanide process[3] and the proving of the so-called deep levels appeared now to ensure a long life to the mining industry. There was also the prospect that a great iron industry might be established in the republic.[4] Some of the magnates began, therefore, to support the agitation of the national union. But it was not until August 1894, shortly after his interview with Loch, that Phillips, who from this time onward assumed the leading role among the Rand 'reformers', began to write to his principals in London about the desirability of procuring rifles. 'If the spending of money does not bring reform', he declared, 'the only alternative is force, and that will come in time. . . .'[5] Phillips converted some of the other capitalists to the idea of insurrection. But by no means all of them. Satisfactory evidence on this matter is naturally difficult to come by. But there is reason to believe that A. Goerz and G. Albu,[6] who operated mainly with German capital,

---

[1] Garson, 370–1; Wolf, ii. 254–5; African (South), 470, pp. 98–102.
[2] Garvin, iii. 58; Garson, 370 n.   [3] See above, p. 20.
[4] Van der Poel (b), 8; Younghusband, 14–16.
[5] Green book no. 2 of 1896, pp. 5–6.
[6] About Albu there is no doubt. Van der Poel (b), 80.

stood out. Nor would it appear that J. B. Robinson, Samuel Marks, and Barney Barnato were implicated in the insurrectionary movement.[1]

It was the accession of Rhodes and his Consolidated Goldfields company that gave the movement its greatest impetus. He had become impatient to get rid of Kruger, who continued to obstruct his aim of achieving the federation of South Africa. He decided, therefore, to get in touch with the disaffected capitalists on the Rand and to co-operate with them and the leaders of the national union. He undertook to place a force on the western border of the republic to give first aid to the insurgents, preparatory to the intervention of the high commissioner—the undertaking which Loch had been ordered to abandon. The high commissioner was now Sir Hercules Robinson, a man of advanced age who had already served a term in South Africa. Rhodes had strongly recommended him as Loch's successor. Ripon concurred with Rhodes on the ground that Robinson would be acceptable to the Afrikaners in the Cape and elsewhere. (It was one of the cardinal tenets of the colonial office that pains should be taken to conciliate Afrikaner opinion, especially in the Cape.) The prime minister, Lord Rosebery,[2] disapproved of the appointment and insisted on the sanction of the cabinet. Robinson embarked for South Africa in May 1895. He is said to have alleged after the raid that either Ripon or the foreign secretary, Kimberley, had promised him about 10,000 troops to support his intervention in the republic if the Uitlanders rose in revolt. But there are good reasons to disbelieve Robinson's story.[3]

[1] Ibid. 10, 112.
[2] Rhodes alleged that he told Rosebery about his plans. Rosebery denied this. For the present the matter must rest there. *English Historical Review*, Oct. 1953, pp. 592–3.
[3] Ibid., pp. 590–2.

CHAPTER IV

JOSEPH CHAMBERLAIN AND THE RAID

I

IN June 1895 Lord Rosebery's Liberal government resigned. Lord Salisbury became prime minister and Joseph Chamberlain took charge of the colonial office. In the general election that followed the Unionist administration obtained a majority larger than that of any government since 1832.

The new colonial secretary, now in his fifty-ninth year, had had a remarkable career. The eldest son of a small London shoe manufacturer, he went straight from school into his father's business. At the age of eighteen he was sent to Birmingham, where he soon became one of the principals in a screw factory in which his father had invested some capital. Owing mainly to Chamberlain's energy and initiative the business flourished exceedingly. Like Rhodes, though not on the same scale, he proved himself a great amalgamator, and in due course he achieved for his firm something like a monopoly. In 1874, at the age of thirty-eight, he retired from business a rich man, having resolved to devote himself henceforward entirely to politics.

He had already made his mark as a public man in and beyond his own city. As chief of the (nonconformist)[1] national education league, which demanded that primary education should be 'universal, compulsory, unsectarian and free', Chamberlain led the opposition against Forster's education act of 1870; and he showed to what lengths he could carry a fight by inciting his followers to refuse payment of an education rate imposed by the law. But it was his municipal achievement in Birmingham that set the crown on the first part of his public career. During his famous mayoralty of 1873–6 he transformed the town so that it became a model for others to follow: it was, in his own words, 'parked, paved, assized, marketed, Gas-and-Watered and *improved*'.[2]

In 1876 Chamberlain entered parliament as one of his town's Liberal members, and soon became a man of note in national politics.

---

[1] Chamberlain had been brought up in the unitarian creed.
[2] Garvin, i. 202. Chamberlain's improvement scheme involved the demolition and reconstruction of between 40 and 50 acres of slum property.

He had already become the prime mover in a campaign that was destined to transform the organization of political parties in Britain. If Chamberlain did not invent the idea of the 'caucus', it was he more than any other man that made it work, so that it became a mainstay of his power as a political leader. The plan of the caucus leaders was to organize the masses, especially the newly enfranchised workers of the towns, in the interests of Radical social reform. They began in Birmingham, and it was by means of the caucus that the town obtained its reforming council with Chamberlain in command. Chamberlain and his associates spread their new model of political organization far and wide. In 1877, with Gladstone's blessing, delegates from the local caucuses formed the national Liberal federation. Its headquarters were at Birmingham, Chamberlain was its first president, and his principal assistants became members of its executive body.[1]

With the federation at his back Chamberlain forced his way into the front rank of Liberal politicians. When Gladstone overthrew Disraeli in the election of 1880, he took the Radical leader into his cabinet as president of the board of trade. The 'new man' had achieved unexampled recognition: only two men of similar origin had sat in a British cabinet before him[2] and he had got there after only four years in parliament.

During the next five years Chamberlain's stature as a popular leader grew steadily. Conservatives, whether they belonged to the Conservative or to the Liberal party, came to look upon him as their most dangerous enemy. The Queen urged Gladstone to dismiss him from the cabinet. This happened during the struggle over the franchise bill of 1884, which extended the urban household franchise of the 1867 act into the countryside. The Lords threw out the bill after it had passed the Commons. During the recess Chamberlain stood out as the most powerful platform speaker against the Lords. In the end the opposition gave way and the bill was passed as an agreed measure. Then, in 1885, after the fall of the Gladstone government, Chamberlain made a memorable series of election speeches throughout Britain in support of his Radical programme of social reform. After that it seemed clear that he had established his claim to become Gladstone's successor.

It was not to be. In 1886 he destroyed his chances both of the premiership and of effecting far-reaching social reforms by splitting

---

[1] Ostrogorski, i, ch. iii. Garvin, i. ch. xiv.   [2] Ensor, 71, n. 1.

the Liberal party, as well as his own Radical following, on the Irish question. Refusing to accept Gladstone's policy of a separate parliament in Dublin (though he was a staunch advocate of large Irish reforms), he[1] helped the Conservatives to defeat Gladstone in the general election of 1886. This time he went to even greater lengths than in 1870–3 in opposition to a detested measure. His biographer tells us that he 'was deep in the Ulster movement' (1886–93), which intended to carry resistance to an Irish parliament to the point of rebellion. He does not say exactly how much encouragement Chamberlain gave in private to the Ulster leaders. But even in public he went so far as to say (in his biographer's paraphrase) that Ulstermen 'in the last resort would take up arms, and fight to the end'.[2]

Chamberlain did not take office in Lord Salisbury's Unionist government of 1886–92. During the time of this government and its Liberal successor (1892–5) he was engaged in strengthening his hold on the Unionist, and especially the 'Tory', masses in the great towns by appealing to both the reforming and the imperialist sentiment. But the most fruitful phase of his career as a social reformer was over. Though he continued to exert himself in the cause of reform and achieved some practical results, he had to pay his forfeits for alliance with the Conservatives. As an imperialist, on the other hand, he was at one with his allies: for on their banner Disraeli had inscribed the motto of imperialism.

Though the full opportunity to enter the lists as an imperialist came to Chamberlain only after his breach with the Liberals, imperialism had long been latent in this intense nationalist. (For what is imperialism, in one of its aspects, but nationalism writ large?) It first came to the surface when he was president of the board of trade in Gladstone's ministry of 1880–5. In 1882 his was perhaps the strongest influence—'Chamberlain almost the greatest Jingo', wrote Granville, the foreign secretary—behind the cabinet's decision to bombard Alexandria, which led to the British occupation of Egypt (against the inclination of most Liberals and, as Chamberlain himself believed, for a year or two only). He held that 'the honour and interests of England' justified intervention.[3] Three years later he broke with the Liberals on what was essentially a nationalist—or imperialist—issue. To Gladstone's policy of Irish home rule he offered relentless

---

[1] His own followers were supported by those of Lord Hartington, the leader of the right wing of the Liberal party. Together they formed the 'Liberal Unionists'.

[2] Garvin, ii. 540–3.

[3] Ibid. i. 446–56.

opposition because he was determined that 'the integrity of the Empire shall be a reality and not an empty phrase'.[1] 'I will never', he declared, 'recognise a separate political nationality in Ireland.'[2] His biographer thinks that this English nationalist, who believed 'in sentiment as the greatest of all the forces in the general government of the world',[3] never appreciated the strength of Irish nationalism.[4]

After his breach with the Liberal party Chamberlain's imperialism, and his influence in the country and the Empire mainly as a result thereof, grew from strength to strength. During the decade 1886–95 he defined his creed in a large number of speeches to enthusiastic audiences. The expansion of the British Empire he held to be imperative for several reasons. Other empires were expanding. A large empire meant power and prestige, provided it was effectively organized. To extend the Empire meant to expand the market for British manufactures, which were beginning to feel the effects of foreign tariffs and competition. The expansion of markets meant the possibility of employment for an expanding population. This appeal to economic advantage was potent in the manufacturing towns, both among employers and workmen. But it was not enough. The conscience of the people must be appeased. There were those who saw 'only wanton and unwise aggression in the constant growth and expansion of our Empire'.[5] Chamberlain maintained, on the contrary, that it was Britain's duty to extend her protectorate over 'those friendly chiefs and peoples who are stretching out their hands towards us. . . .'[6] He believed that the British 'race' was the greatest of all governing races,[7] and that the extension of the Empire could, and should, be as beneficial to the natives of annexed territories as to British trade. Of course, it would not be possible to defend and enlarge the Empire unless the navy in particular were strengthened. He accordingly supported the measures to this end adopted by Lord Salisbury's government of 1886–92.[8] And so we come to the year of the Queen's diamond jubilee (1897), when imperialist sentiment was advancing to its zenith in Britain, and Chamberlain

[1] Ibid. ii. 140.　　　　　　　　　　　　　　　　　　[2] Ibid. 514.
[3] Speech at imperial conference, 24 June 1897. Ibid. iii. 189.
[4] Ibid. i. 584; ii. 422. See also ibid. ii. 190.
[5] Chamberlain at Birmingham, 23 Jan. 1889. Ibid. ii. 486.
[6] Ibid. 465.　　　　　　　　　　　　　　　　　　　　[7] Ibid. iii. 27.
[8] Ibid. 467. In 1880 Chamberlain wrote to his sister: 'I walked back to the station with Mr. Gladstone, who said someone had told him I was like the statue of Pitt in Westminster Hall—and that there was certainly a resemblance.' Gladstone then went on to speak of Pitt, whom he called a great Reform minister in his earlier life carried away later by the miserable wars in which he was engaged. Ibid. i. 309.

proclaimed that he had no doubt 'that this great Empire of ours, powerful as it is, is nothing to what it will become in the course of ages when it will be in permanence a guarantee for the peace and the civilisation of the world'.[1]

As I have already indicated, a large empire was not, in Chamberlain's view, enough. Great organizer that he was, he held that the Empire should be better organized. That involved, so far as the self-governing British colonies in North America, Australasia, and South Africa were concerned, federation with Britain. His attention had apparently been directed to imperial federation by Seeley's book, *The Expansion of England* (1883), which left a deep impression on his mind. Seeley wrote that Britain was destined to be eclipsed by the United States and Russia unless a British imperial federation could be brought into being.[2] Imperial federation became almost an obsession with Chamberlain. But he considered that the federation of Australia and South Africa must come before imperial federation.

South Africa had been increasingly in Chamberlain's mind since 1880, when he became the cabinet's spokesman in the commons on South African affairs. In June 1880, six months before the Boers took up arms to reverse the annexation of 1877, he urged Gladstone to withdraw from the Transvaal. He believed that the annexation could not be justified. Four years later, when he realized that by their advance into Bechuanaland the Transvaalers had been violating the conventions of 1881 and 1884,[3] which gave them autonomy under certain conditions, his insistence powerfully influenced the dispatch of the Warren expedition and the resultant annexation of Bechuanaland. After the discovery of gold on the Witwatersrand his interest in South Africa became more intense. 'I mean some day to be Colonial Minister', he wrote to his future American wife in 1888, 'and deal with it.' Again, six weeks later: 'I am inclined to advocate a bold policy [in South Africa], fully recognising Imperial responsibilities and duty, but then I intend that it should be the policy of the Imperial and not of the Cape Government, and should be carried out by officials taking their instructions from the former.'[4] Accordingly, when in 1889 Sir Hercules Robinson, the high commissioner, declared on the eve of sailing to England on leave, that the imperial government ought to be 'a diminishing quantity' in South Africa,[5]

[1] Garvin, iii. 186.
[2] *The Expansion of England* (2nd edition), 344–50.
[3] Agar-Hamilton, *passim*.
[4] Garvin, ii. 347, 349.
[5] African (South), 380.

Chamberlain protested and received Lord Salisbury's assurance that Robinson would not return. It was about this time too that, with a pointed reference to the Transvaal gold-fields, Chamberlain put the question, which was to become of greater concern to him later, 'Who is to be the dominant power in South Africa?'[1]

'I mean some day to be Colonial Minister', Chamberlain had written in 1888. Seven years later he carried out that intention. That the principal apostle of imperialism in Britain should choose the colonial office is not surprising, in spite of the fact that it was not regarded as one of the major posts in the cabinet. 'I did not care a scrap for office or position', he reported himself as saying in 1888, 'although I admitted that I cared for power.'[2] He was bound to be a major figure in any cabinet which he joined, and any post which he held was bound to become a major post. The three outstanding men in the Unionist government formed by Salisbury in June 1895 were Salisbury himself, Balfour, who became the leader of the house of commons, and Chamberlain. In the shaping of cabinet decisions Chamberlain's influence was hardly second even to that of the prime minister. So far as his own department was concerned, there is little doubt that, once he had made up his mind about a colonial issue, he was strong enough to overcome any resistance in the cabinet. In the house of commons no one surpassed him as a debater. In the country at large, owing largely to a superb technique of public speaking calculated to appeal to 'the masses', his popularity was unrivalled. He knew also how to make use of the press, including the halfpenny popular press, to enhance his influence. The fact that he was at the same time the statesman most hated by his opponents helps to give us the measure of the man as a political fighter at home. He was to prove an equally formidable antagonist to any foreign statesman who crossed his path as colonial secretary.

In describing Chamberlain's character there are three expressions which his biographer uses again and again: 'a dangerous man'; a man of 'boldness' or 'audacity'; a man who had great power of 'incitement' over others.

In 1895, at almost sixty, he was still in his prime. His energy and drive were almost as great as they had ever been. After ten years 'in the wilderness', he was impatient, as his biographer puts it, 'to count

[1] Speech to the London chamber of commerce, 14 May 1888. *Foreign and Colonial Speeches*, 192, 193, 196, 200.
[2] Garvin, ii. 349.

in the world'. A few years later the German ambassador in London reported Balfour as saying 'that wanting to go too fast is Chamberlain's peculiarity'. Shortly after taking office he wrote: 'We have a chance now of doing something which will make this Government memorable.'[1] Whether or not the government as a whole fulfilled this hope, it certainly came true in the case of the colonial secretary, and nowhere more than in South Africa.

II

In November 1895 Mrs. Chamberlain wrote to America: 'The newspapers far and wide, and on all sides, are ringing with praise of the new life infused into colonial affairs by the policy of the Secretary of State, and it is a great encouragement after the years of abuse lavished on his devoted head. He feels the encouragement, and it helps his interest and energy. He says a "smash" must come. . . .'[2] And, indeed, before the year was out there occurred in South Africa an event which threatened to bring his career as colonial minister to an inglorious end.

In the evening of 29 December Dr. L. S. Jameson, the administrator of the British South Africa (B.S.A.) company in Rhodesia, invaded the South African Republic with a force of about 500 men, consisting mainly of Matabeleland mounted police and Bechuanaland border police. More than half of the latter had enlisted with the B.S.A. company on the disbandment of the force when the colonial office, in November, ceded to the company a portion of the Bechuanaland protectorate bordering on the republic. Jameson was placed on the republican frontier by Rhodes, prime minister of the Cape Colony; principal agent in Southern Africa of the B.S.A. company; controller of the diamond monopolist, the de Beers Consolidated Mines, and of the Consolidated Goldfields company; multi-millionaire. The plan was that the disaffected section among the Uitlanders of the Witwatersrand, who were being supplied with arms and money by Rhodes and Alfred Beit,[3] would rise in revolt against the republican government with the help of Jameson's force; whereupon the high commissioner, Sir Hercules Robinson, would hasten to the Transvaal[4] and decree that the destiny of the republic would be

---

[1] Garvin, ii. 643–4; iii. 268.   [2] Ibid. iii. 28.
[3] A partner in the Wernher–Beit firm and a director on the board of the B.S.A. company.
[4] 311 (select committee on British South Africa), Rhodes, Q. 264; Jameson, Q. 4513.

decided by the vote of the adult males[1] or by a constituent assembly representing them.[2] The conspirators agreed that the provisional date of the rising would be Saturday, 28 December, and that Jameson would set out from his camp at Pitsani two days before.[3] On second thoughts, however, it seemed better that he should move on the actual night of the rising.[4] On 23 December Rutherfoord Harris, Rhodes's agent, wired Jameson that Johannesburg would rise at midnight on 28 December and that he was to start four hours earlier.[5] But on 26 December colonel Frank Rhodes, the prime minister's brother, who was in charge of the military preparations in Johannesburg, telegraphed to Cape Town that it was 'absolutely necessary to postpone flotation'. Johannesburg was not yet ready to rise. There were not enough arms in the town. Among the principal men of the mining industry as well as among the Uitlander rank and file there was disunion. The insurrectionary leaders were paralysed by news that Rhodes and Jameson wanted the revolt to take place under the British flag. On the receipt of colonel Rhodes's telegram, Harris telegraphed to Jameson not to move until he got word from Cape Town. But he moved none the less, and on Thursday, 2 January surrendered to the Boers near Krugersdorp.

Rhodes refused to disavow Jameson's action and resigned as prime minister of the Cape Colony. A select committee was appointed by the Cape house of assembly in May 1896 to inquire into the circumstances—'as affecting this Colony'—under which the Jameson raid took place. The committee was assisted in its work by a republican green book[6] containing inter alia documents taken from the captured raiders and telegrams between the conspirators furnished by the telegraph department of the republic. An act of parliament enabled it to obtain from the Cape telegraph department a number of additional telegrams. The committee found that 'the whole movement' which ended in Jameson's fiasco 'was largely financed and engineered from outside' the South African Republic; and that the director and controller of the conspiracy was Rhodes. The house of commons committee which reported on the conspiracy in 1897 endorsed these findings.

---

[1] Ibid., Rhodes, Q. 290, 1348–9; A6 '96 (Cape committee on the Jameson raid), appendix, p. ccxliv.
[2] 311, Leonard, Q. 8010–15.
[3] Fitzpatrick, 125–6: A6 '96, appendix, p. xxii, no. 20.
[4] Fitzpatrick, 126; A6 '96, appendix, p. xxii, no. 19.
[5] A6 '96, appendix, p. lix, no. 68.   [6] No. 2 of 1896.

This committee of the house of commons had before it documents and witnesses not available to the Cape committee. It was able to examine *inter alios* Rhodes and his confidant, Harris, who had not appeared before its predecessor. It thus threw further light on the objects and activities, not only of the 'outside engineers', Rhodes, Beit, Harris, and their associates, but also of the Johannesburg leaders. It also passed judgement on the board of the B.S.A. company, which had given Rhodes *carte blanche* in South Africa. But it failed signally in its main duty, which was to examine how far the colonial office and the imperial representatives in South Africa were involved in Rhodes's plot. It is true that two officials—Sir Graham Bower, the high commissioner's or imperial secretary in South Africa, and F. J. Newton, the resident commissioner in the Bechuanaland protectorate —were found guilty, on their own admission, of withholding their knowledge of the plan from the high commissioner. But the innocence of the high commissioner and the colonial office was 'decisively' affirmed. In its examination of the knowledge of the high commissioner the committee may be acquitted of gross incompetence. Robinson denied point-blank that he knew anything about the plot, and he was confirmed by those who might have been expected to give him information. There were, nevertheless, certain unsatisfactory features about the examination of Robinson's complicity. He himself could not be summoned to appear because of the state of his health. But Bower was not questioned by the committee on the note he sent Robinson at 5 a.m. on 30 December 1895:

My dear Sir Hercules,

I hope you will come to town early. There is, I fear, bad news from Jameson. He seems to have disobeyed Rhodes, and to have taken the bit between his teeth.[1]

It did not occur to any of the members to ask how Bower could have thought that this was intelligible to a man who believed that Jameson's force was intended only 'to protect railway line and for economy as B.S.A. company troops could be kept there [at Pitsani] at half the expense'.[2] Rhodes, on being asked by Harcourt[3] why he had not taken the high commissioner into his confidence in this matter, replied as follows:

RHODES: You want an answer?

[1] C. 8063, p. 116.
[2] Robinson to Chamberlain, 10 Jan. 1896, C. 7933, p. 44; 311, Rhodes, Q. 96.
[3] For Harcourt see below, p. 73.

HARCOURT: Yes.

RHODES: I think you should get that answer from the High Commissioner. . . . I am sorry the High Commissioner is not here. I think he was aware there was trouble likely to occur in Johannesburg, and he knew there was this force on the border. But I do not like to say anything. I would prefer that the High Commissioner himself made his statement. He sent that statement there[1] and I accept it. It does not affect the question, I accept the statement that he has made.[2]

And Harcourt did not press Rhodes any further on this point.

The committee's failure to inquire thoroughly into 'the alleged complicity of the Colonial Office'[3] is a more serious matter. The committee was, of course, in a difficult position. For reasons of state it was undesirable to probe too far. A verdict of 'guilty' would undoubtedly have had some very unpleasant consequences. Kruger would have been justified in repudiating the London convention on the ground that it had been broken by the British government, and he would probably have sought the support of Germany. Whatever its motives, it is clear that the committee dealt in a most unsatisfactory manner with its main problem. That problem could, in fact, have been more satisfactorily investigated by a judicial commission.[4] The house of commons having agreed to a committee of politicians,[5] it was unfortunate that the colonial secretary was appointed one of its members. The Liberal opposition did not object to his inclusion; in fact his friend Harcourt, the leader of the opposition in the house of commons, wanted him to be chairman, partly in order that 'the resources of the colonial office should be at the disposal of the committee'. He failed to understand why Chamberlain should not regard himself as an 'impartial chairman' or why he should pay any attention to 'unfounded "insinuations"' as to his complicity.[6] His biographer declares that Harcourt's main object was 'the emphatic condemnation of Rhodes and of the Raid before the world. He had no desire to see the government, and least of all the colonial secretary, implicated in the adventure, for that would have rendered the condemnation of Rhodes futile, would have besmirched the honour of the country at its source, and would have made the future [in South

---

[1] The statement from which I have just quoted.
[2] 311, Rhodes, Q. 94–97.
[3] Labouchere's minority report, 311, p. lxii.
[4] Innes, 150; Viscount Cecil, 62–63.
[5] E. Drus in the *Bulletin of the Institute of Historical Research*, xxv (1952), 37–38; van der Poel (*b*), 160.
[6] Gardiner, ii. 394.

Africa] still more dark.'[1] Such considerations may explain why this acute lawyer, who played the principal part in the examination of the witnesses, failed to follow up a number of clues provided by the evidence.[2]

Let me now indicate a few of the unsatisfactory features about the committee's examination of 'the alleged complicity of the Colonial Office'. It was most remiss in the matter of the so-called 'missing telegrams'. These were cables which passed between Harris and Rhodes during the latter half of 1895, when the former was in England, negotiating with the colonial office for the cession of part of the Bechuanaland protectorate. On the demand of the committee some of the cables were produced by the Eastern Telegraph company,[3] but a number had been destroyed before it made its order. On being ordered to produce the cables (including the 'missing' ones), Hawksley, Rhodes's solicitor, refused. Thereupon the committee by a majority vote (11 against 2) decided not to carry the matter any farther on the mistaken grounds that Rhodes, who had returned to

---

[1] Gardiner, 343–5. 'I think we have accomplished all that was possible in getting a unanimous and uncompromising condemnation of Rhodes. If we had attempted anything more we should certainly have failed and given Rhodes a parliamentary triumph.' Harcourt to Ellis, 22 Oct. 1897. Ibid. 433. See also ibid. 393–5, 423–37.

[2] Sir Robert Meade told Bower early in 1897 that the committee was not the 'formidable thing the world supposed it to be. That Chamberlain and Harcourt were excellent friends and understood one another.' Reminiscences, 333.

[3] They are published in 311—I, appendix 14. On 5 June 1896 J. X. Merriman, one of the members of the Cape committee of inquiry, declared that Harris had sent cables to Rhodes about the protectorate and demanded their production. A6 '96, Q. 580. The next day Hawksley sent copies of the Harris–Rhodes cables to the colonial office at its request. Having read them Chamberlain offered Salisbury his resignation. Bower, Reminiscences, 304–5; Garvin, iii. 113. He was afraid that the Cape committee would get hold of them. But he was reassured by the acting imperial secretary at the Cape. (Bower, who was at this time in London, says that an inquiry on the subject was dispatched to the acting secretary in his name by the colonial office. The reply was addressed to him, but it was in cipher. One of the officials told him that the reply was satisfactory. Reminiscences, 304–5. Among Bower's papers are carbon copies of two cipher telegrams, dated 10 and 17 June 1896, which he believed to deal with this matter.) This was satisfactory as far as the Cape committee was concerned. But what would Rhodes do? According to Bower, George Wyndham—a friend of Rhodes and later a member of the house of commons committee—sailed with him in the same ship to South Africa in Aug. 1896 in order to secure a promise from Rhodes that the cables would not be produced; in return Chamberlain would guarantee the charter of the B.S.A. company. Reminiscences, 313. Chamberlain's biographer writes that he would have 'destroyed' the B.S.A. company, if Rhodes had published the cables. Garvin, iii. 113. The colonial secretary did, in fact, threaten Earl Grey, one of Rhodes's agents, with the destruction of the company. Ibid. 116. In reply (10 Dec. 1896) Grey intimated that Rhodes would follow Chamberlain's advice with respect to the cables. Ibid. 116. At the house of commons inquiry, therefore, neither Rhodes nor Harris would give the committee any information about these communications. And it took no decisive step in the matter until 7 May 1897—having begun its sittings on 5 Feb.—when it at length procured some of them.

South Africa, was the person to be proceeded against rather than his solicitor; and that he would have produced the cables if they shifted some of the responsibility for the plot against the Transvaal from him on to the colonial office.[1] The committee examined Hawksley towards the end of its sittings. The other witnesses who had knowledge of the Rhodes plot, including Rhodes himself, had been evasive and had suffered from lapses of memory, particularly on the subject of the complicity of the colonial office. Hawksley was comparatively willing to enlighten the committee. He read out two interesting communications between himself and the colonial office;[2] whereupon Chamberlain suggested that he had acted improperly in 'volunteering the information'. Hawksley was then asked why he only communicated the Rhodes–Harris telegrams to the colonial office five months after he had first informed it that he had them. But the committee refused to allow him to answer the question. When one of the members, Labouchere, subsequently moved that the witness be recalled for further examination, he was voted down by 11 to 2. Thus Hawksley could not be examined on the two letters he had read out, nor on Harris's statement that he was present when Harris explained to Fairfield, assistant under-secretary in the colonial office, why Rhodes was so anxious to obtain a portion of the Bechuanaland protectorate.[3]

Another witness who was let off lightly was Flora Shaw, colonial correspondent-in-chief of *The Times*, who admitted that she was a constant visitor at the colonial office. When Harris returned to South Africa at the end of November 1895 he gave the B.S.A. company's code to her so that she could communicate confidentially with Rhodes during the vital month before the raid. In her first examination she told the committee that she had received only three cables from Rhodes, one telling her the date of the Johannesburg rising, the second a purely formal one, and the third announcing Jameson's invasion of the Transvaal. But, when the Rhodes–Shaw cables were subsequently obtained from the Eastern Telegraph company, it transpired that there were among them two other communications from Rhodes, very important ones, which Miss Shaw had forgotten.

[1] For some of the 'missing' cables see below, pp. 80, 81 & n., 82, 88, 90.
[2] Hawksley wrote *inter alia*: 'Mr C[hamberlain] knows what I know, and can shape his course accordingly. You know, and I do not, what has passed between the High Commissioner or his secretary and the Colonial Office.' Hawksley to Fairfield, 5 Feb. 1896. 311, Q. 8752–3.
[3] 311, Harris, Q. 8687–8.

They were sent while Jameson was marching on Johannesburg and seemed to implicate Chamberlain in Rhodes's plot:

30th December. Inform Chamberlain that I shall get through all right if he supports me, but he must not send cable[1] like he sent the High Commissioner in South Africa. Today the crux is, I will win and South Africa will belong to England.

31st December. Unless you can make Chamberlain instruct the High Commissioner to proceed at once to Johannesburg the whole position is lost. High Commissioner would receive splendid reception and still turn position to England's advantage. . . .

Miss Shaw insisted that she was not aware that Rhodes was taking 'any active part' in the Johannesburg movement (though she knew that Jameson, Rhodes's administrator in Rhodesia, was in it);[2] and that, when she telegraphed to Rhodes, asking him to 'advise when will you commence the plans',[3] she meant by 'you' not Rhodes personally, but the British community in Johannesburg. Notwithstanding all this—and much more of a similar character—the committee's faith in Miss Shaw does not seem to have been shaken; for it declares in its report: 'Your Committee were satisfied that the statements and references contained therein [in the Rhodes–Shaw cables], and referring to the suggested knowledge of the Colonial Secretary and the Colonial Office,[4] had no justification [so Miss Shaw said in her evidence]. . . .'

III

So much for the way in which this 'Committee of No Enquiry'[5] tackled what should have been its principal task. We have now to consider our own verdict on the evidence available today. First, as to the complicity of the high commissioner. At the time of the inquiry

---

[1] A cable warning Rhodes not to 'force matters at Johannesburg' by an invasion of the Transvaal.

[2] 311, Shaw, Q. 8875, 9694. 'A point which we did not discuss but which is important, is that you should make it clear [to the committee] that you were not originally in the secrets of the conspirators; on the contrary that, from your knowledge of the situation in South Africa and of the general views of Mr Rhodes and others, you were able to make a shrewd guess of the kind of game that was being arranged, and so to worm the truth out of Dr Harris.' Buckle (editor of *The Times*) to Shaw, 24 May 1897. Bell, 187.

[3] 311, Shaw, Q. 9693.

[4] e.g. 'Have special reason to believe [Chamberlain] wishes you must do it immediately.' Shaw to Rhodes, 17 Dec. 1895.

[5] Cook, ch. viii.

it was sincerely believed, both in England and in South Africa, that he was innocent. Not even Kruger seems to have suspected him.[1] Yet the evidence against him is strong. First, there is Bower's note of 30 December 1895.[2] Then there is a statement published by Lady Milner in 1933, when there was no longer any need for concealment. Contrary to his evidence before the house of commons committee Jameson told her in 1900 (and she duly made a note of his statement): 'Rosmead [i.e. Robinson] had agreed to take action once we were there [in Johannesburg]. He knew every detail of the arrangements. . . . The night before I left for Mafeking . . . we went over the ground of our joint action again.' . . .[3] Finally, there are the Bower papers. In order (as he believed) 'to promote peace and goodwill between the two [White] races' in South Africa,[4] Bower decided to conceal from the committee what he knew about the complicity of the high commissioner and the colonial secretary in Rhodes's plans. In so doing he laid himself open to the charge of having withheld important information from his superiors: for he admitted that he was in Rhodes's confidence. He was accordingly censured by the committee, and was thereupon dismissed from the public service. In 1898 the colonial office re-employed him, but in an inferior post, whence he received no promotion during his remaining years in the service. Bower directed that his papers should remain sealed until 1 January 1946.[5] They contain a number of letters (including a long one addressed to Sir Montagu Ommanney of the colonial office and dated 11 May 1906) and his Reminiscences, which bear no date. The letter to Ommanney and the Reminiscences contain an account of occurrences connected with Rhodes's conspiracy. In judging the value of Bower's testimony I have borne in mind the fact that he felt himself to have been unfairly treated by his official superiors, including Robinson, and that he wished to justify himself to posterity. I have also taken due note of the fact that for parts of his story[6] he depended

---

[1] *Gedenkschriften*, 144–54.
[2] See above, p. 72.
[3] *National Review*, Sept. 1933, pp. 302–3. Lady Milner 'repeated the story in 1900 to Mr Chamberlain, who said "I believe that story to be substantially correct"'.
[4] Bower to Merriman, 28 Feb. 1898. (Merriman papers, no. 14 of 1898.) Before giving his evidence, Bower was told by Wyndham that if he implicated the colonial secretary or the high commissioner 'old Rosmead will be carried into the box in his bandages like the dying Chatham and will give you the lie. He will be backed by Chamberlain.' Reminiscences, 335.
[5] They are in the South African Public Library, Cape Town.
[6] But not for the whole of it. He had with him 'some manuscript memoranda of conversations etc. made years ago'. Bower to Ommanney, 11 May 1906.

on his memory. It seems to me, nevertheless, that his evidence against the high commissioner must be accepted. It is given in circumstantial detail, which is seen to be substantially accurate where it can be checked by information that has come to light since.[1] It explains Rhodes's reticence before the committee.[2] It answers this question about the alleged behaviour of Bower and Newton: how two experienced public servants could have got themselves, for reasons not satisfactorily explained,[3] into a thoroughly false position.[4] Bower's story solves this difficulty. It runs as follows: Rhodes told him about his plot in October 1895, and assured him that Chamberlain had been informed.[5] His reply was that the high commissioner must also be told. Rhodes agreed; and, continued Bower, 'I then conducted Rhodes myself into the High Commissioner's room and left the two men alone together',[6] whereupon Rhodes 'told him everything'.[7] Robinson never discussed the plot with Bower before the raid, believing apparently that such discussions would have to be regarded as 'official'.[8] But the imperial secretary had several indications of his knowledge from the high commissioner himself. For example, on the day after his interview with Rhodes, he remarked to Bower, 'The less you and I have to do with these damned conspiracies of Rhodes and Chamberlain the better.'[9] On 16 December Newton came down from Mafeking, where Jameson had told him of the plot, in order to discuss it with Robinson. But the latter refused to allow him to broach the subject, remarking to Bower: '. . . The whole thing is piracy,[10] I know nothing about it. I won't see Newton.'[11] And the poor man had to turn to Bower and Rhodes for comfort and advice.

---

[1] See below, pp. 87 n., 90, 92 n. It will be noticed that I have checked Bower's evidence as a whole, not merely the parts that refer to the high commissioner. See also E. Drus in *English Historical Review*, Oct. 1953, p. 588.

[2] See above, pp. 72–73.

[3] For the explanations of Bower and Newton see their evidence before the house of commons committee (311). Bower, Q. 2503–22, 2533, 2539, 2639–60, 2852–9; Newton, Q. 4639, 4641, 4646–50, 4758–9, 4768, 4697–4709.

[4] See above, p. 72.

[5] Reminiscences, 208–9. On 2 Aug. Rhodes had received a cable from Harris containing the following: 'Secretary of State for Colonies heartily in sympathy with C. J. Rhodes's policy.' See below, p. 80.

[6] Reminiscences, 210.

[7] Rhodes's subsequent statement to Bower. Ibid. 340.

[8] Ibid. 217.

[9] Ibid. 211.

[10] After the raid Robinson tried—unsuccessfully—to persuade Bower that the 'piracy' he was thinking of was 'Chamberlain's piratical attempt to jump the Transvaal as a consequence of the Revolution' and that he knew nothing of the use which the conspirators intended to make of the force at Pitsani. Ibid. 331–2.

[11] Ibid. 227–8.

IV

We come to the colonial office. What we want to discover is the part it played in the plot to foment a rising in Johannesburg and support it by rushing in troops from Bechuanaland. Chamberlain—and his biographer Garvin—sometimes tried to make it appear that the charge he had to meet was that of being implicated in Jameson's actual raid. To create such an impression is to draw a red herring across the trail. For the actual raid Jameson was, of course, alone responsible. But the Jameson raid, as W. T. Stead put it in 1899, wrecked the Jameson [or rather Rhodes] plan. What we are concerned with is the share of the colonial office in the plan.

In July 1895, when Chamberlain had been in office for about a month, Harris, Rhodes's agent, arrived in London in order to obtain from the new colonial secretary the fulfilment of his predecessor's promise to hand over at any rate part of the Bechuanaland protectorate to the B.S.A. company. On 1 August Harris had an interview with Chamberlain at which there was also present Lord Selborne, the parliamentary under-secretary for the colonies.[1] When this interview was investigated by the house of commons committee, there was a conflict between Harris's and Chamberlain's accounts of what had been said.[2] The two men agreed that the colonial secretary refused to hand over the protectorate, though, according to Chamberlain, he was willing to consider handing over 'a strip of land . . . sufficient for the making and the protection of the railway', which Rhodes was about to extend from Mafeking into the protectorate. According to himself, Harris

'then referred to the unrest at Johannesburg and added a guarded allusion to the desirability of there being a police force near the border', since 'it was present to my mind'—though he made 'no explicit statement' to that effect—'that in the event of a rising in Johannesburg, Mr Rhodes wished to be in a position to render assistance with the police forces of the B.S.A. company. . . . Mr Chamberlain at once demurred to the turn the conversation had taken. I never referred to the subject again.'

Later, on being pressed to repeat the exact words he had used, he replied that the words were: '"We shall be here [in the protectorate], and if a rising takes place at Johannesburg, of course we should not stand by and see them tightly pressed", or something to that effect.'[3]

[1] E. Drus in *Bulletin of the Institute of Historical Research* (1952), p. 43.
[2] Harris's statement is in 311, Q. 6220 and Chamberlain's ibid. Q. 6223.
[3] Ibid. Q. 8510.

Chamberlain's recollection of this part of the interview was different. He remembered that the position in Johannesburg had been discussed, but could not remember any 'guarded allusions' by Harris. The latter did say, however: 'I could give you some confidential information.'

I stopped him at once. I said: 'I do not want to hear any confidential information; I am here in an official capacity. I can only hear information of which I can make official use.'

Selborne corroborated his chief's statement.[1]

So far one must accept the word of Chamberlain and Selborne that if Harris did indeed make his 'guarded allusion' they had not understood it. But Harris was not the only person who spoke to Chamberlain about the protectorate on 1 August. When the latter stopped Harris's confidences Earl Grey, who had introduced him, intervened. (Grey was a director of the B.S.A. company; he was also a personal friend of Chamberlain[2] as well as of Rhodes, and, according to professor Basil Williams, 'a transparently honest man'.[3]) He 'took Harris out of the room, and returning alone . . . resumed the delicate topic, urging that he was ready to give private particulars and wished to give them'.[4] Chamberlain declared later that he refused to listen.[5] Grey, however, states: 'I told you privately that the . . . rising of the Uitlanders to secure for themselves the common rights of free men would shortly take place, and that being so it was desirable that an armed force should be stationed on the Transvaal border available for use if required.'[6] This is not all. On 2 August 1895 Harris sent Rhodes a cable which ran as follows:

We decided therefore to inform Secretary of State for Colonies guardedly reason why we wish to have base at Gaberones[7] and advisable our presence in Protectorate. Secretary of State for Colonies heartily in sympathy with C. J. Rhodes's policy but he would not on this ground alter decision with regard to Protectorate, but offered as alternate [alternative?] to justify residence B.S.A. Co. in Protectorate to consider favourable at once application for large land grant [in] Protectorate in exchange for Railway extension north. It is now [for] C. J. Rhodes to decide whether large grant township [and?] sale of stands is practicable during the month of October[;] appears only solution.[8]

---

[1] 311, Q. 9596.   [2] *Bulletin* (1952), pp. 47–48.   [3] Williams, 136.
[4] Garvin, iii. 38; *Bulletin* (1952), pp. 47–48. Selborne was not present at this interview, but Chamberlain declared later that he informed Selborne 'immediately afterwards of what had passed'. *Bulletin* (1952), pp. 43, 47–48.
[5] Chamberlain to Grey, 13 Oct. 1896. Garvin, iii. 38–39.
[6] Grey to Chamberlain, 10 Dec. 1896. Ibid. 39.
[7] Near the Transvaal frontier and about 50 miles north of Pitsani.
[8] *Bulletin* (1952), pp. 46–47.

This is the first of the 'missing telegrams', i.e. of the Rhodes–Harris cables that were withheld from the house of commons committee.[1] Its importance lies in the fact that it was sent, for the information of Rhodes, immediately after the Harris and Grey interviews with Chamberlain. Its contents do not contradict the subsequent statements of its authors,[2] but it adds the information—giving no doubt the impression left on Grey's mind by his 'private'[3] talk with Chamberlain—that the latter was in sympathy with Rhodes's 'policy'. This implies that, 'guardedly' though Chamberlain's interlocutors stated they had spoken, Grey was sure that the allusion to the use of an armed force, stationed in the protectorate, in connexion with the anticipated Johannesburg rising, had been understood by the colonial secretary (which is what he denied). Garvin is constrained to admit that Chamberlain did intend Rhodes's protectorate force to furnish 'the speediest means of intervention if made necessary by a revolt'. But, says Garvin, this intervention was to be *by the British government*.[4] If that was Chamberlain's intention he seems to have made no attempt to implement it. There is no evidence that either the high commissioner or Rhodes received any instructions as to the use of the force on the Transvaal border. And Rhodes, on the receipt of the cables of 2, 13, and 21 August, must have concluded that the perspicacious secretary of state, though naturally not wishing to know too much, had been given a plain enough hint, and had given him a free hand to go ahead with his plan. And the plan envisaged the action of the protectorate force, not at the behest of the secretary of state or his high commissioner, but at the behest of Rhodes.

At this point it is necessary to refer to two more of the 'missing telegrams'. Chamberlain summarized[5] them as follows:

October 28 and 29. In the first the sender at Cape Town [Rhodes]

---

[1] See above, p. 74.

[2] I assume that the cable was framed by Harris in consultation with Grey because of the latter's separate interview with Chamberlain. See also Hawksley to Maguire, 19 Feb. 1897 in W. T. Stead, *Joseph Chamberlain: Conspirator or Statesman?*, 91.

[3] 'Chamberlain will do anything to assist except hand over the adminisitraton protectorate provided he *officially* [my italics] does not know anything of your plan. He does consider Rhodes's ingenuity resource can overcome any difficulty caused by refusal protectorate now.' Harris to Rhodes, 13 Aug. 1895. 'Missing telegram' no. 2, Garvin, iii. 110. (On 13 Aug. Chamberlain had an interview with R. Maguire alone. *Bulletin* (1952), p. 52. Maguire was a fellow of All Souls College, Oxford, and Rhodes's proxy on the board of directors of the B.S.A. company.)

'You are aware Chamberlain states Dr Jameson's plan must not be mentioned to him.' Harris to Rhodes, 21 Aug. 1895. 'Missing telegram' no. 3, Garvin iii. 111. (On 20 Aug. Chamberlain had an interview with Harris and Grey. *Bulletin* (1952), p. 43.)

[4] Garvin, iii. 53, 56.   [5] See below, p. 82.

suggests that Lord Grey should see me privately to show the great importance of an immediate transfer of the Protectorate, and in reply from London it is stated, 'We dare not mention the reason'.

Chamberlain comments that this quotation 'proves that the sender was aware that up to that time at any rate, I had not been put in possession of the true reason'.[1] It proves nothing of the sort. If we read this extract in conjunction with 'missing telegrams' nos. 1, 2, and 3, the conclusion follows that what Harris meant was 'We dare not mention the reason again' or 'We dare not go any farther into our reasons'.

It has been suggested that Harris in his cables to Rhodes misrepresented the attitude of the colonial office towards Rhodes's plan.[2] Such misrepresentation must have been perpetrated either in collusion with Rhodes or on Harris's own responsibility (and that of his collaborators, Grey, Maguire, Beit, and Hawksley).[3] The first assumption has not been defended by any serious historian, though Garvin does hint, somewhat obscurely, that there may be something in it.[4] I do not propose, therefore, to discuss it. To accept the second assumption is to accuse Harris and his collaborators of deliberately deceiving Rhodes. Harris may have been 'an unmitigated liar';[5] but that is not the point. The point is whether he and his collaborators would have lied to *Rhodes* on a matter about which correct knowledge was vital to him.

Chamberlain's behaviour with regard to the 'missing telegrams' calls for some comment. The Rhodes–Harris cables—including the 'missing' ones—were sent to the colonial office in June 1896 'for confidential perusal and return'.[6] Thereupon Chamberlain made extracts from and comments on the incriminating ones. Eight of the 'missing telegrams' were treated in this manner.[7] During the course of his examination by the house of commons committee Chamberlain was asked: 'Do you think you could charge your memory at all with the substance of the contents of these [missing] telegrams that were shown to you?'[8] In reply Chamberlain did not plead inability to produce confidential information. His reluctance to comply with the request was due, he said, to the fear of being

[1] *Bulletin* (1952), p. 48.   [2] Garvin, iii. 39, 112–13.

[3] 'I need not say that very many of the cables, although sent by Harris, were settled in consultation.' Hawksley to Maguire, 19 Feb. 1897. W. T. Stead, loc. cit.

[4] Garvin, iii. 39, 113.   [5] Lovell, 330 n. 80.

[6] 311, p. xiv.

[7] *Bulletin* (1952), pp. 45–51.   [8] 311, Q. 9564.

'inaccurate in any description I may give of them from memory'.[1] But why 'from memory', since the relevant details were among his private papers? A little later he gave the false impression that the 'missing telegrams' did not add to the case against the colonial office.[2] Finally, he allowed himself to be prevailed on to give the committee, still 'from memory', two carefully selected extracts which seemed to support his plea of entire ignorance of the Rhodes plan.[3] If Chamberlain had been asked why he misled the committee in this matter of the 'missing telegrams', he would no doubt have repeated the words he used to Earl Grey with reference to the Rhodes–Harris cables as a whole: 'My first inclination was to insist on the immediate publication of these telegrams, together with my comments, but on reflection I came to the conclusion that, although I might be able completely to satisfy the House of Commons and English public opinion, yet that the disclosure would be used by the enemies of England, both on the Continent and in the Transvaal, and would seriously embarrass future action.'[4] This may be accepted as at any rate a partial explanation of the colonial secretary's motives. But whatever his motives, the fact remains that he deliberately misled the committee on a crucial issue. This cannot (I believe) be proved against Harris in his dealings with Rhodes on any issue whatever.

Garvin tries to make something of the fact that Chamberlain delayed until November 1895 the cession of the territory which Rhodes wanted in order to carry out his plan.[5] (The territory in question was, of course, the portion of the Bechuanaland protectorate that bordered on the South African Republic.) But Chamberlain was not entirely a free agent. It would have been impolitic—as the colonial office itself recognized[6]—to cede any part of the protectorate to the B.S.A. company without the consent of the chiefs concerned: for one thing, such cession would have evoked strong public protests in Britain.[7] On 5 September 1895 three protectorate chiefs arrived in London, accompanied by a missionary, to protest against the cession of any of their territory to the B.S.A. company. Chamberlain had perforce to hear what they had to say. After listening to them, he decided—very properly—that his first step

---

[1] Ibid., Q. 9565.   [2] Ibid., Q. 9582–3.
[3] Ibid., Q. 9591–2.
[4] Chamberlain to Grey, 13 Oct. 1896. Garvin, iii. 115–16.
[5] Ibid. 40.
[6] Robinson to Chamberlain, 9 Aug. 1895; Chamberlain to Robinson, 20 Sept. 1895. C. 7962, pp. 7, 13.
[7] Garvin, iii. 40; 311—I, appendix no. 14, telegrams no. 2, 18, and 30.

should be to bring the company's representatives and the chiefs together.[1] Let them try to come to some arrangement while he was away on holiday at San Sebastian in Spain. If they had failed to agree on his return early in November, it would be time enough for him to intervene.

Though Chamberlain couldn't at once give Rhodes the desired territory, he did not remain entirely inactive. On 20 August, the day on which he had his second interview with Harris and Grey,[2] he cabled the high commissioner to obtain a grant of land for the B.S.A. company from Bathoen, one of the three protectorate chiefs who were about to embark for England. Gaberones, which Rhodes had in mind as his military base against Kruger,[3] was situated in Bathoen's territory. When the high commissioner failed to obtain Bathoen's consent to the cession, Rhodes took other steps. Two Bechuana chiefs who had not gone to London were persuaded to agree that their 40 square miles of land in the protectorate might come under the company's jurisdiction, and on 18 October the high commissioner, with Chamberlain's consent, issued a proclamation handing over this territory to the company. It was here that Rhodes's agents now proceeded to prepare the military base. Immediately after the issue of the high commissioner's proclamation, company police began to move from Bulawayo to Pitsani in the newly acquired territory.[4]

By 2 November Chamberlain was back in England. He was now prepared to impose a settlement on the three Bechuana chiefs,[5] and they were prepared to accept it.[6] It was just in time. Rhodes had fixed 7 November as the last possible date for a decision.[7] On 4 November Harris saw Fairfield,[8] who, according to Harris, already knew as much as Chamberlain about the Rhodes plan,[9] and 'spoke open' to him.[10] Immediately after the interview Fairfield wrote as follows to his chief, who was spending a few days at Birmingham:

You will see that events are moving rapidly in South Africa. Rhodes, having accepted the responsibilities imposed on him, is naturally very keen

---

[1] Meade to the chiefs Khama, Sebele, and Bathoen, 7 Oct. 1895. C. 7962, p. 17.
[2] See above, p. 81, n. 3.   [3] See above, p. 80.
[4] C. 7962, pp. 1–3, 26–28; van der Poel (b), 31, 33, 39; E. Drus in *English Historical Review*, Oct. 1953, pp. 584–5.
[5] 311—I, appendix 14, telegram 2.
[6] Fairfield to Chamberlain, 4 Nov. 1895, 311, Q. 8579.
[7] Garvin, iii. 111, 'missing telegram' no. 4; 311—I, appendix 14, telegram no. 21.
[8] An assistant under-secretary in the colonial office who specialized in South African affairs.
[9] 311, Q. 8584–6, 8705–6.
[10] 311—I, appendix 14, telegram no. 7.

to get the Protectorate question settled and has been telegraphing all day to this end. . . . The result of all this [the contemplated protectorate settlement] will be that the chiefs and our Commissioners will be in cotton-wool, having no frontier, the Company being on each side of us. There will be no occasion to keep up the Bechuanaland Border Police, but only a small body-guard for the Commissioner, and a native police (very cheap) of about 60 to keep down the drink traffic. Rhodes wants you then to authorise the Bechuanaland Border Police to enlist with the Company. . . . He is urging a speedy settlement and the Company want to beg you to see the Chief[s] and polish off the business on Wednesday. I said I would lay this before you; in fact, Rhodes very naturally wants to get our people off the scene as this ugly row [that, of course, refers to the drifts][1] is pending with the Transvaal. That, I think, is also our interest. . . . I do not think that there can be any doubt but that the Transvaal will give way on the immediate question of the drifts; but that will not end the political 'unrest'. They will have in their hands to-night or to-morrow morning a letter from Montagu White[2] written after Lord Salisbury's message to him,[3] warning them that the British Government is in deadly earnest [about the drifts].[4]

This letter, which Chamberlain read to the house of commons committee at a moment of the inquiry when the colonial office was in a tight corner, clinches the argument as to his complicity in the Rhodes plan. The letter will repay careful examination. It has been suggested that the 'responsibilities' which Rhodes 'accepted' were those 'imposed' in connexion with the so-called drifts crisis.[5] But that cannot have been Fairfield's meaning. It is impossible to understand how the settlement of the protectorate question could have helped Rhodes to discharge his responsibilities, if Chamberlain's note on the drifts issue, which had just been handed to the South African Republic, resulted in war. (That it must do, or else the republic must climb down and the drifts 'crisis' would be over.) On the other hand, if the 'responsibilities' are those in connexion with the Johannesburg rising,[6] which Rhodes had undertaken to support, then the relevance

---

[1] Chamberlain's interpolation.
[2] Consul-general in London of the South African Republic.
[3] See Chamberlain to Robinson, 16 Oct. 1895. C. 8474, no. 5.
[4] Fairfield to Chamberlain, 4 Nov. 1895. 311, Q. 8579.
[5] On 1 Oct. 1895 Kruger closed the fords (drifts) across the Vaal river to overseas goods, notwithstanding the protest of the Cape government. Chamberlain agreed to intervene on condition that Rhodes as prime minister should, on behalf of his ministry, guarantee full Cape support if Britain went to war on the question. The guarantee was received by the colonial office on 4 Nov. On 3 Nov. the high commissioner dispatched a peremptory 'message' to the South African Republic, which agreed, on 7 Nov., to comply with its terms and reopen the drifts. See also p. 38 above.
[6] Was the term Rhodes's 'responsibilities' a set expression well understood by those

of the settlement of 'the Protectorate question' is obvious. This brings us to the much-discussed words 'this ugly row': 'I said I would lay this before you; in fact, Rhodes very naturally wants to get our people off the scene as this ugly row is pending with the Transvaal. That, I think, is also our interest.' When Chamberlain read out this passage, he explained to the committee that 'this ugly row' referred to the drifts question. The explanation must be rejected for three reasons: first, Fairfield had no doubt that the republic would give way and no 'ugly row' on that issue could, therefore, be 'pending'; second, if an 'ugly row' (i.e. an armed conflict) broke out on the drifts question, Britain, the Cape, and the B.S.A. company would be fighting, side by side, an officially declared war, and Rhodes would welcome the co-operation of 'our people' instead of 'very naturally' wanting to get them 'off the scene'; third, in the case of conflict on the drifts issue, it would *not* be in 'our [Britain's] interest' to get Britain's police and officials out of the way. But if Rhodes, with his eye on 'the political unrest' in Johannesburg, was preparing for a type of intervention of which the colonial office wished to profess ignorance, then indeed it was 'our interest' to 'get our people off the scene'—unless, of course, they chose 'to enlist with the Company'.

How can one resist the conclusion that Chamberlain's explanation of the words 'this ugly row' was disingenuous? Yet the committee swallowed the explanation without the slightest apparent difficulty. They had no questions to ask about Fairfield's letter—not even after the day's proceedings had been circulated in print.[1]

On 6 November—one day within Rhodes's time limit—Chamberlain settled the protectorate question. The chiefs were to have reserves marked out for them, and the rest of the country was to go to the B.S.A. company, including the important strip running along the western border of the republic right up to the Rhodesian frontier.[2] On 7 November Chamberlain sent the high commissioner

---

who used (and read) it to refer to the Rhodes plan? In a letter to Sir Robert Meade dated 18 Dec. 1895 Chamberlain referred to the 'responsibility' for the Johannesburg rising as resting with Rhodes. Garvin, iii. 72. On 20 Aug. 1896 Hawksley, Rhodes's solicitor, wrote to Fairfield 'that responsibilities were undertaken ... with the approval of the Imperial Authorities. . . . I very respectfully submit that on reconsideration Mr Chamberlain will recognise that reasons other than the ostensible ones were intimated to him why the acquisition by the Chartered B.S.A. Company of the Bechuanaland Protectorate was urgently necessary.' Ibid. iii. 114. In 311, Q. 8875, Flora Shaw spoke about 'the responsibility for having a force ready' taken by Jameson (Rhodes's agent).

[1] It was the practice to print each day's evidence for immediate circulation among the committee and the witnesses examined.

[2] C. 7962, pp. 21–26, 29–30.

a cable which outlined the settlement and authorized him to 're-
lease from their engagement as many of the officers and men of
Bechuanaland Police as may be willing to transfer their services to
[B.S.A.] Company'.[1]

V

The evidence dealt with so far leads irresistibly to the conclusion
that, when he handed over the border region of the protectorate to
Rhodes, Chamberlain intended to give him *carte blanche* to use as
he saw fit any force that he might organize there, in connexion with
the impending Johannesburg revolt.[2] But the colonial office was not
content to play the part of a mere sleeping partner to Rhodes. While
Chamberlain was on his Spanish holiday he wrote the high commissioner a private letter about the Johannesburg rising. The letter
made a strong impression on the high commissioner's secretary,
Bower. He remembered that it was fairly long and that it asked for
the high commissioner's views on a Johannesburg rising 'with or
without assistance from outside'.[3] The secretary tells us that he,
Rhodes, and Robinson collaborated on the high commissioner's
reply.[4] This reply[5] showed—not unnaturally under the circumstances
—that Robinson's views on what should be done when the rising
took place bore a close resemblance to the plans of Rhodes and his
fellow conspirators. The high commissioner expected (what Rhodes
knew)[6] that a provisional government would be proclaimed in
Johannesburg. He would then 'issue a Proclamation directing both
parties to . . . submit to his arbitration', and go at once to Pretoria,
where he would 'order the election of a Constituent Assembly—such
Assembly to be elected by every adult white male in the country. . . .
If the Convention [i.e. Assembly] were to represent fairly the wealth,
intelligence and various nationalities of the population, a large
majority would be English.'[7] When the high commissioner had issued

---

[1] Ibid., pp. 23–24.
[2] For a discussion of Chamberlain's motives see van der Poel (*b*), 51.
[3] Bower quotes these words as Chamberlain's own. Reminiscences, 211. One's confidence in Bower's memory is strengthened by the fact that he gives an accurate account
of the high commissioner's reply, which was not published by Garvin until after his
death. Ibid. 212–14.
[4] Ibid. 212–14.
[5] Robinson to Chamberlain, 4 Nov. 1895. Garvin, iii. 59–62.
[6] 311, Q. 1346.
[7] Compare this with the plans of the conspirators—p. 70 above.

his proclamation, the British government should state that it stood behind him, 'and it might be announced in the Home press that a large force had been ordered to hold itself in readiness to proceed to South Africa'. Like Rhodes, Robinson hoped that these measures would ensure a successful and bloodless 'revolution'. On the other hand, if the South African Republic did not capitulate, these measures meant war.

If the revolt succeeded Robinson expected, like Rhodes, that the immediate result would be 'an Anglicised and liberalised Republic' which would enter a South African customs and railway union. But Chamberlain wanted the Transvaal to be a British colony.[1] Early in November the colonial office got Rhodes to agree—undoubtedly against his better judgement—that 'results [of] Dr Jameson's plan include British flag'.[2] A month later Chamberlain again referred to the flag. He had received Robinson's letter, and was sending him secret instructions[3] with regard to the Johannesburg rising. According to Garvin Chamberlain telegraphed:

'Agree generally with your idea in private letter of Nov. 4th. . . . I take for granted that no movement will take place unless success is certain, a fiasco would be most disastrous.' [Note the implication that the high commissioner was, or would put himself, in touch with leaders of the conspiracy.] In further agreement with the High Commissioner he expressed his hope that one result of the revolution would be the acceptance of the British flag.[4]

According to Bower he did rather more than this. On 6 December, he writes, a cipher telegram arrived from Chamberlain 'marked private and personal', which approved of the High Commissioner's proposals 'but went on to say that, if the Johannesburgers would agree to accept the British flag, they would be allowed to elect their own Governor'.[5] Was it this cable that caused Bower to write to his wife on 13 December, 'I have not yet got over my worries about Chamberlain. That man makes me anxious.'[6]

A few days later that man was called upon to make an important decision. On 17 December President Cleveland of the United States,

[1] Garvin, iii. 112.
[2] 'Missing telegram' no. 6. Ibid. 75, 112.
[3] Chamberlain to Salisbury, 26 Dec. 1895. Ibid. 78. Garvin writes that Chamberlain consulted 'Salisbury and other principal members of the Cabinet' before sending off these instructions. He gives no evidence in support of this statement, and Chamberlain's letter to Salisbury (of 26 Dec.) does not bear him out.
[4] Ibid. 63.
[5] Reminiscences, 220.
[6] Bower to Lady Bower, 13 Dec. 1895. Bower papers.

in a message to congress, threatened Britain with war on the British Guiana–Venezuela boundary question. That threat led to a consultation between Chamberlain (at Birmingham) and his permanent under-secretary:

Meade to Chamberlain, December 18.—I propose to hold over the telegram to Robinson as to Dr Leyds's supposed intrigues until I hear again from you, as, when you directed it to be sent, you had not seen President Cleveland's Message. Perhaps as we shall have to face German opposition you may wish the Uitlander movement to be postponed for a year or so. Fairfield thinks he could get this done through Maguire . . .[1] but if the movement is to be postponed it must be done at once. Fairfield is confident he could do this without compromising you—should you wish it to be done. He thinks that there are not many of the important men who are heartily in favour of this movement, though if rushed by Rhodes they will no doubt join actively. If it takes place there will probably be a 'slump' in the South African mining market, which joined on to a more general 'slump' on account of an apprehended quarrel with the U.S. may produce a serious crisis in the City. . . .

Chamberlain replied the same day:

Thanks for your letter. The question is a serious one to decide. It must be noted that the American affair cannot become serious for some time. . . .

Now as to Transvaal. Might it not come off just at the critical time if it is postponed now? The longer it is delayed the more chance there is of foreign intervention.

It seems to me that either it should come *at once* or be postponed for a year or two at least. Can we ensure this?

If not we had better not interfere, for we may bring about the very thing we want to avoid.

If Fairfield can make the situation clear to Maguire I should like him to do so—then the responsibility must rest with Rhodes and we had better abstain even from giving advice. I again repeat, the *worst* time for trouble anywhere would be about six months hence. I cannot say that any time would be a good one, but can the difficulty be indefinitely postponed?[2]

On the receipt of this letter Fairfield summoned Maguire to the colonial office and gave him Chamberlain's message. What was that message? Meade (apparently with the concurrence of Fairfield) had suggested that the revolt be postponed. Fairfield could have drawn only one conclusion from his chief's reply, which was that the balance of advantage lay in its coming off at once. The phrase 'we had better

---

[1] For Maguire see above, p. 81, n. 3.　　　　　　[2] Garvin, iii. 71–72.

not interfere' obviously means 'we had better not interfere for the purpose of postponing action'. After the interview with Fairfield, Maguire[1] cabled Rhodes that the sooner the revolt came off the better.[2] The precise words of this cable have never been revealed. It was among the telegrams which Hawksley sent to the colonial office in June 1896 'for confidential perusal'.[3] Bower, to whom Rhodes showed the cable, writes that it 'reported a conversation with Fairfield who had told them [Maguire and Grey] to hurry up on account of approaching trouble with Venezuela'.[4] When the colonial office was preparing its defence in view of the coming inquiry, Fairfield wrote to Chamberlain that he said to Maguire that if an early Uitlander outbreak was inevitable, 'the sooner it came off the better', but only after 'I [had] used every argument I could think of to secure indefinite postponement'.[5] If Fairfield did indeed argue to this end, he was not carrying out his chief's instructions. In his report to Chamberlain immediately after the interview he makes no reference to his having urged 'indefinite postponement', though he does say that he ascertained that 'it is now too late to defer action for a year'. He continues: 'Maguire and his friends here were already [i.e. before Fairfield gave Chamberlain's message] impressed with the disadvantages of postponing action for a few months, and are urging early action. . . .'[6] There follows this sentence, omitted by Garvin: 'They did not base this view on the possible development of the American question, but Maguire agreed with what I put to him on that point.'[7] Six months after this Bower spoke to Fairfield in London: 'He [Fairfield] told me he had written[8] to Birmingham to Mr Chamberlain suggesting that the Revolution should be damped down. Mr Chamberlain had replied telling him to hurry it up on account of the Venezuela dispute. He had therefore instructed Lord Grey and Mr Maguire accordingly. . . .'[9]

The 'flag telegrams'[10] and the Chamberlain–Meade–Fairfield correspondence underline the complicity of the colonial office in the conspiracy against the South African Republic. The former prove that the office intervened in the conspiracy with the object of ensuring

---

[1] And Grey (according to Bower). Reminiscences, 231–2.
[2] Garvin, iii. 73.　　　　　[3] See above, p. 82, and *Bulletin* (1952), p. 49.
[4] Reminiscences, 231–2. Bower declares that, on his advice, Rhodes showed this cable to the high commissioner. Ibid. 231, 234–5.
[5] Garvin, iii. 73; see also *Bulletin* (1952), pp. 49–50.
[6] Garvin, iii. 73.　　　　　　　　　　　　[7] *Bulletin* (1952), p. 35.
[8] Actually the writer was Meade. The error is immaterial.
[9] Reminiscences, 238–9.　　　　　　　[10] See above, p. 88.

that one of the results of the Johannesburg revolt would be the hoisting of the British flag in the Transvaal. The correspondence between Chamberlain and his officials contains the colonial secretary's own admission that he was aware that Rhodes was a leader of the 'Uitlander' conspiracy—'then the responsibility must rest with Rhodes'.[1] It shows also that Chamberlain was so far from being merely, as he pretended, an interested spectator of the unrest on the Witwatersrand (though, of course, preparing his own independent plan of intervention against the time when the Uitlanders, of their own motion, rose against their oppressors), that he advised the principal conspirator, who was not a Johannesburg Uitlander at all, when the fomented rising should start.

On 26 December Chamberlain wrote to the prime minister that a rising in Johannesburg would probably take place in the next few days: 'The War Office has arranged that two regiments, one from Bombay, and one from Barbadoes, shall call at the Cape about the middle of January. . . . We have, of course, our usual garrison at the Cape, and Rhodes has the Bechuanaland Police. . . . If the rising is successful it ought to turn to our advantage.'[2] But things went wrong.[3] On 29–30 December,[4] at Birmingham, he received two communications: one, a cable from the high commissioner stating that the Johannesburg movement had 'collapsed'; the other, a letter from Fairfield reporting a conversation with Hawksley: 'He seemed to think that Rhodes . . . might be driven into an attitude of frenzy and unreason [by the failure of Johannesburg to rise], and order Dr Jameson to "go in" from Gaberones with the Company's police and manipulate a revolution. . . . Were the Company's police to go in filibustering it would be a breach of Article 22 of their charter. . . .'[5] As a result of Hawksley's forebodings Chamberlain telegraphed to Meade: 'Affair is evident fiasco. Think it would be well to telegraph

---

[1] Chamberlain's words to Meade.

[2] Chamberlain to Salisbury, 26 Dec. 1895. Garvin, iii. 78.

[3] See above, p. 71.

[4] Chamberlain got his first news of the collapse on 27 Dec. On the following day a cable from *The Times* correspondent in Johannesburg confirmed the news. Garvin, iii. 79; *History of 'The Times'*, iii. 175.

[5] Garvin, iii. 81. Chamberlain later told the house of commons committee that he thought Fairfield was 'put upon the scent' of this story 'by something which he saw in an article' in a financial paper (311, Q. 9562). If, as seems to be the case, Chamberlain misled the committee—for he had Fairfield's letter among his papers—the explanation must be his belief that the less there was revealed of the constant communication between the colonial office and Rhodes's agents in the weeks before the raid the better. For evidence of this constant communication see above, pp. 75–76, 89, and Garvin, iii. 70–73, 81.

Robinson to remind Rhodes if necessary, but not otherwise, of articles 22 and 8 of Charter. Also you might send for representative of South African Republic and suggest that Kruger would do well to ask advice or intervention of Her Majesty's Government.'[1] Whereupon Meade sent off the following cable in Chamberlain's name:[2]

There seems to be a fiasco at Johannesburg owing probably to Rhodes having misjudged the balance of opinion there.

It has been suggested, although I do not think it probable, *that he and Jameson might endeavour*[3] to force matters at Johannesburg to a head by *Jameson or* some one *else* in the service of the Company advancing from the Bechuanaland Protectorate with police.

In view of Articles nos. 22 and 8 of the Charter I could not remain passive were this to be done. Therefore, if necessary, but not otherwise, remind Rhodes of these Articles, and intimate to him that, in your opinion, he would not have my support, and point out the consequences which would follow *to his schemes were I to repudiate the action.*[4]

When it became clear that Jameson had indeed 'taken the bit between his teeth',[5] Robinson acted in the spirit of Chamberlain's message. He 'repudiated' Jameson's invasion of the South African Republic and ordered him to return. Before midnight on 30 December Chamberlain endorsed the high commissioner's action. He later tried to make a virtue of his repudiation of Jameson's raid—as if he was thereby exonerated from complicity in the Rhodes plan.[6] Actually it must have been clear to him that Jameson had wrecked the plan. For the information he had both from the high commissioner and from Rhodes's agent was clear: the movement in Johannesburg had collapsed.[7] It is true that after the midnight cable (30 December) had been dispatched,[8] the colonial office learned from Flora Shaw[9] 'that an invitation[10] to come in was sent to Dr Jameson from

---

[1] C.O. 537/129.

[2] The italicized passages were omitted in the version published in C. 7933, no. 2. Bower correctly reports the gist of the first passage omitted. Reminiscences, 249.

[3] The published version reads 'that an endeavour might be made'.

[4] C.O. 537/129.

[5] Bower to Robinson, 30 Dec. 1895. C. 8063, p. 116.

[6] 311, Q. 9559; Garvin, iii. 122–3.

[7] 'If the Government of the South African Republic had been overthrown, or had there been anarchy in Johannesburg, there might have been some shadow of excuse for this unprecedented act.' Statement by Chamberlain in C. 7933, p. 5.

[8] See Flora Shaw's evidence in 311, Q. 9604–7.

[9] 311—I, appendix 16, cable no. 1557.

[10] The notorious 'letter of invitation'—undated—which Jameson got the Johannesburg leaders to give him in November. Fitzpatrick, 124–5. Harris cabled the letter—dated 28 Dec.—from Cape Town on 30 Dec., and Miss Shaw published it in *The Times* on 1 Jan.

Johannesburg'.[1] Chamberlain, in some doubt, cabled the high commissioner whether this was so. The latter replied on 1 January that, according to his information, the Johannesburg leaders repudiated Jameson and added: 'Jameson's action is condemned throughout all South Africa; not a voice is raised in his support.'[2]

In a letter written at the time Chamberlain gave convincing reasons for his repudiation of Jameson's raid:

... This is a flagrant piece of filibustering, for which there is no justification that I can see in the present state of things in the Transvaal. If it were supported by us, it would justify the accusation by Germany and other Powers that having first attempted to get up a revolution in a friendly State and having failed, we had then assented to an act of aggression[3] and, without any grievance of our own, had poured in British troops.[4] It is worth noting that I have no confidence that the force now sent, with its allies in Johannesburg, is strong enough to beat the Boers—and if not we should expect that a conflict would be the beginning of a race war in South Africa. . . .[5]

This letter requires no comment except for the last sentence, in which Chamberlain says he does not believe that Jameson can beat the Boers, even if he succeeds in 'manipulating' a revolt in Johannesburg. This proves that one of Chamberlain's statements to the house of commons committee contains a clear *suggestio falsi*. In explaining why it was incredible that he should have had 'any fore knowledge of . . . the raid, or of the preparations for the raid' he made this statement: '. . . when the raid took place . . . we took every possible step to defeat it, and we did so at a time when all the information that was tendered to us was to the effect that *if we would hold our hand the raid would succeed*.'[6] The last (quoted) sentence of Chamberlain's letter also indicates that he looked upon the intervention (or threat of intervention) of the reinforced British garrison in South Africa[7] as essential to the success of the Johannesburg rising. Such intervention would, of course, have constituted a powerful argument in support of his view with regard to the future of the Transvaal.[8]

[1] Chamberlain to Robinson, 31 Dec. 1895. C. 7933, p. 5.
[2] C. 7933, p. 11. There was, in fact, widespread sympathy with Jameson, especially among the British section of the population.
[3] i.e. the raid.   [4] See above, p. 91.
[5] Chamberlain to Salisbury, 31 Dec. 1895. Garvin, iii. 90.
[6] My italics. 311, Q. 9559. See also Garvin, iii. 122.
[7] See above, p. 91.
[8] See above, p. 88. According to Bower, Chamberlain told Rhodes's correspondents in London, presumably in Nov. 1895: 'The future constitution of the Transvaal will be dictated from this office', meaning the colonial office. Reminiscences, 224.

VI

This concludes the discussion of the evidence relating to Chamberlain's complicity in the Rhodes plot. It remains to recapitulate the conclusions we have reached. There are three counts in the indictment against the colonial secretary.[1] The first two concern the projected Johannesburg rising, considered (for the purpose of the indictment) by itself and apart from Jameson's force on the Transvaal frontier. The first charge is that Chamberlain, being aware that Rhodes, prime minister of the Cape Colony and managing director of the B.S.A. company, was playing a principal part in the Johannesburg insurrectionary movement against the government of the South African Republic[2] and that such action on Rhodes's part constituted a breach of international good conduct, not only did nothing to stop him (as was his duty, being the responsible official under the Crown) but actually collaborated with him to the extent of giving him advice as to the date of the rising.[3] To this charge he must, on the evidence of his own correspondence, plead guilty. The second charge, on which the verdict is also 'guilty', is that he intervened, before the rising took place, in order to ensure that the British flag would be hoisted in the Transvaal;[4] and that the intervention he envisaged when the rising should have taken place[5] ran a serious risk of provoking war. His high commissioner in South Africa was by no means prepared to rule out the possibility of a 'race war'. All he allowed himself to say was that, if Chamberlain sanctioned his plan[6] of intervention, he 'would probably receive the support of both races'.[7] Let me recall that the high commissioner's plan, sanctioned by the colonial secretary, was to dictate a settlement which, in the former's judgement, involved the immediate termination of Boer control of the South African Republic.[8] The third and final charge is that Chamberlain was aware of the reason why Rhodes wanted to secure an immediate transfer of the borderlands of the Bechuanaland protectorate to the B.S.A. company; that, being acquainted with Rhodes's object, he did in fact facilitate the transfer of the territory Rhodes needed, as well as a portion of the territory's police; and that he deliberately left Rhodes a free hand to use his troops in the transferred

---

[1] The words 'count', 'indictment', 'charge' and 'guilty' are, of course, used in this paragraph as they would be used in a court of law.
[2] See above, pp. 89, 91.   [3] See above, pp. 89–91.
[4] See above, p. 88.   [5] See above, p. 93.   [6] See above, p. 87.
[7] Robinson to Chamberlain, 4 Nov. 1895. Garvin, iii. 61–62.
[8] See above, p. 87.

territory as he thought fit in support of the Johannesburg rising.
Both Chamberlain and his parliamentary under-secretary, Selborne,
repudiated this charge on oath before the committee of the house of
commons. I have shown that Chamberlain's word on matters touch-
ing his complicity in the Rhodes plot is worthless.[1] What is the value
of Selborne's evidence? It was given in the form of a written statement which he read to the committee and he was asked only two
questions bearing on his evidence.[2] In his statement he declared:

> I believe I did not miss a single one of those [i.e. Chamberlain's appoint-
> ments] which concerned the transfer of the Bechuanaland Protectorate to
> the British South Africa Company. I was also in the most constant com-
> munication with Mr Chamberlain, Sir Robert Meade, and Mr Fairfield[3]
> throughout the autumn of 1895, and I believe I knew absolutely everything
> that passed in the Colonial Office at that time. . . . Neither then [at the
> time of Harris's first interview with Chamberlain] nor at any subsequent
> period prior to the raid did we know of what is now called 'Jameson's
> [i.e. Rhodes's] plan', nor that the revolution in Johannesburg was being
> largely controlled and financed from Cape Colony and Rhodesia.[4]

The last part of the last sentence impairs Selborne's evidence. For
we have seen that the colonial office did know that the 'revolution'
was being, if not largely controlled and financed, then at any rate
largely controlled from Cape Colony and Rhodesia (i.e. by Rhodes).
It follows either that Selborne was ignorant of what Chamberlain,
Meade, and Fairfield knew[5] (in which case what becomes of his
claim to omniscience?) or that we have to do with another *suggestio
falsi* by a member of the colonial office. I do not see how Selborne's
evidence can stand against that of Harris, Grey, and Bower, the
Harris cables, and Fairfield's letter of 4 November 1895.[6] And so to
the third charge also Chamberlain must plead guilty.

---

[1] See above, pp. 82–83, 84–86, 93.
[2] 'Mr Chamberlain asked me to send you these copies of his evidence before the
Committee. . . . He said he hoped and believed that the questions would be of a kind
which would enable you keep within the four corners of his own statements. . . . As
regards the Hawksley telegrams [see above, p. 74] the S. of S. would like your answers
to be as general as possible—as his own were—but he does not think that anyone—
except Labby [Labouchere]—is at all likely to press the point of their contents.'
H. F. Wilson (Chamberlain's private secretary) to Selborne, 3 June 1897. *Bulletin*
(1952), p. 41.
[3] Meade and Fairfield were unable to give evidence before the committee. On their
attitude and Selborne's see *Bulletin* (1952), pp. 40–44, and *English Historical Review*,
Oct. 1953, pp. 588–9.
[4] 311, Q. 9596.   [5] See above, pp. 89–91.   [6] See above, pp. 77–82, 84–86.

CHAPTER V

THE AFTERMATH

I

THE Jameson raid increased political tensions throughout South Africa. The South African Republic, where Kruger's hold on his own people was greatly strengthened by the raid, feared further British attempts on her independence.[1] Having already begun to arm in 1895, presumably in response to the growing excitement among the Uitlanders, she now stepped up the process. The Orange Free State, in pursuance of a treaty of 1889 with her northern neighbour, had sent a commando to the Vaal as soon as her government received the news of Jameson's invasion. Under her new president, M. T. Steyn, she now drew closer to the sister republic. While her customs union with the Cape Colony remained intact, she took the management of her railways out of the colony's hands, and Steyn arranged with the Netherlands railway company for co-operation in case of war.[2] In the Cape the alliance between Rhodes and the Afrikaner bond was shattered. Throughout South Africa the Afrikaners and the British colonists began to draw apart into opposing political camps.

The fact that neither Chamberlain nor Rhodes was eliminated from South African politics after the raid increased the difficulty of solving the Uitlander problem. Kruger's belief that it was Rhodes's policy to put an end to the independence of his republic was confirmed by the revelation of the details of the 'Jameson plan'. It is true that Rhodes lay low for a time. But before very long he was back in Cape politics, this time as the leader of a British party. As for Chamberlain, his position in the Unionist government became stronger after the raid. But Kruger and the Transvaal Boers were firmly convinced of his complicity in Rhodes's plot[3] (which to their minds involved the corollary that his interventions after the raid were those of an enemy of their independence). And other Afrikaners too. Had not the high commissioner, discussing the raid with

---

[1] C. 8063, part I, no. 24.
[2] Van Winter, ii. 266; van der Poel (a), 93.
[3] C. 7933, no. 14; C. 8063, part I, no. 24; Butler, 426; high commissioner to Chamberlain, 2 Feb. 1897 (C.O. 537/131).

Hofmeyr, the Cape Afrikaner leader, remarked: 'I am afraid Pushful Joe is in it'?[1]

II

Soon after the high commissioner learned that Jameson had crossed the Transvaal frontier, he sent messages to turn him back. In Hofmeyr's opinion, however, that was not enough. On his insistence Robinson, after some hesitation on the score of Chamberlain's presumed attitude, agreed to publish a proclamation repudiating Jameson and forbidding British subjects to support him.[2] The proclamation was telegraphed to de Wet, the British agent in Pretoria, who immediately published it in the Transvaal press.[3] On the same day (6.30 p.m., 1 January 1896) Chamberlain cabled Robinson: 'Are you of opinion that the time is at hand when you might usefully intimate to President Kruger your intention of proceeding to Pretoria as peacemaker and with a view to a reasonable settlement of grievances? Have you considered that Dr Jameson's movements may be only a feint to draw off the Transvaal forces while the English rise and seize Johannesburg or Pretoria?'[4] In other words, might not something yet be saved from the wreck of Rhodes's plan? (That morning Flora Shaw had received Rhodes's message, 'Unless you can make Chamberlain instruct the High Commissioner to proceed at once to Johannesburg the whole position is lost. High Commissioner would receive splendid reception and still turn position to England's advantage. . . .'[5]) But the initiative now lay with Kruger, and Robinson had to wait for an invitation from him. Before receiving Chamberlain's message he had already approached the president on the advice of Hofmeyr and others. Avoiding the use of the word 'grievances' he asked Kruger 'if he would wish me to come up to Pretoria to co-operate [with] him in endeavouring to bring about a peaceful settlement'. Hofmeyr wired to Pretoria urging acceptance of the high commissioner's offer, and Kruger thereupon asked him to come.[6]

---

[1] Hofmeyr, 490. According to Bower, Robinson remarked when he heard of Jameson's invasion: 'But perhaps Chamberlain has sent him in, or may approve his going. He is such an extraordinary fellow, he is capable of anything.' Reminiscences, 247–8.
[2] Hofmeyr, 490.
[3] C. 8164, p. 4.
[4] Van der Poel (b), 102. The second sentence of this cable was omitted in C. 7933, no. 24.
[5] 311—I, p. 599, no. 1877; 311, Q. 9616.
[6] C. 7933, no. 28; Hofmeyr, 492.

While the high commissioner was on his way to Pretoria, the Kaiser, who seems to have believed, in common with his advisers, that the British government was implicated in the raid,[1] sent off the famous Kruger telegram congratulating the president on the capture of Jameson's men. Towards the end of 1895 Herff, the German consul in Pretoria, had reported that trouble appeared to be imminent on the Witwatersrand. In reply he was instructed to inform the Boer authorities that Germany had given another warning to the British government;[2] and at the same time to impress upon them that they should 'strictly avoid all provocation if they wished to retain German goodwill'.[3] Then came the news of Jameson's invasion. It roused the anger of the German people[4] and called forth a sharp reaction from the German government. 'For two years now', wrote Marschall to the Kaiser, 'we had called the British Government's attention to the dangers threatening in those parts from Sir Cecil Rhodes's gestures, but had never received a clear answer as to the British Cabinet's attitude towards those doubtful methods.'[5] If the cabinet approved of the invasion, the German ambassador was instructed to ask for his passports. Salisbury and Chamberlain declared that they did not approve.[6] But Jameson, nevertheless, marched on. Marschall believed that if he reached Johannesburg the British government intended to pluck the fruits of his invasion and instructed Hatzfeldt to deliver a strong note to Salisbury.[7] Soon afterwards there arrived the news of Jameson's surrender. 'Gottlob', exclaimed Marschall,[8] and told the ambassador not to deliver the note.[9]

As soon as he heard of the raid, Kruger had told Herff that he counted on the intervention—meaning apparently the diplomatic intervention—of Germany and France. At the consul's request Marschall authorized him to requisition a small landing party from a German cruiser in Delagoa Bay to protect German interests in the republic. The idea had, however, to be given up: the Portuguese government failed to give permission for the men to land, and Kruger indicated that he did not wish them to cross his border 'so as not to complicate the situation'.[10]

[1] Van Winter, ii. 246–7; *German Diplomatic Documents*, ii. 379, 382; Bixler, 83.
[2] For previous warnings see above, p. 48.
[3] *Grosse Politik*, xi. 15–16.
[4] Ibid. 26; Lovell, 371.
[5] *German Diplomatic Documents*, ii. 380.
[6] Ibid. 377–8.   [7] Ibid. 382–4.   [8] Lovell, 362, 368.
[9] *Grosse Politik*, xi. 28–29.
[10] *German Diplomatic Documents*, ii. 370–1, 378–9, 383; van der Poel (*b*), 134.

The day after Jameson's surrender the Kruger telegram was sent off and published. This demonstration is the high-water mark of Germany's support of the Transvaal. I have already indicated that the ulterior motive behind this support was the desire to persuade Britain to come to terms with Germany.[1] By raiding the Transvaal Jameson had dealt the German government a strong card.[2] But it then proceeded to overplay its hand. The publication of the Kruger telegram produced a great outburst of popular indignation in England.[3] The German government, taken aback by the unexpected result of its demonstration, and baulked in its efforts to form a continental *bloc* against Britain, decided that it was politic to withdraw from the position it had taken up at the side of the Transvaal.

One of the expressions in the telegram which angered the British press and public was that Kruger had preserved 'the independence of the country' against attacks from outside.[4] Garvin writes that the anger was due partly to the fact that all Britain believed that this statement was intended as an attack on the convention of London,[5] which imposed certain limitations on the sovereignty of the republic. That may be so. But there is no evidence that the German government intended any such thing. What is certainly true is that the British press, or an influential section thereof, claimed that there existed a British suzerainty over the republic.[6] The Kruger telegram implied a rejection of that claim. As Marschall put it to the British ambassador, 'Germany had a right to speak of the independence of the South African Republic, since that had been recognized in the [London] convention . . . except for the minor [*sic*] restriction of article 4'.[7]

After the publication of the Kruger telegram the German foreign office discouraged the Transvaal from pursuing what it considered to be dangerous courses. The Kruger government wanted to exploit the raid and the defeat of the raiders to the full. On 4 January Herff cabled Kruger's programme: unconditional submission of Johannesburg; annulment of the London convention; dismissal and punishment of Rhodes; dissolution of the B.S.A. company (thus 'breaking Rhodes's power in South Africa permanently'). 'In pursuing these aims', continued the consul, 'the Transvaal government foresees the

[1] See above, p. 49.
[2] See the opinion of *The Times* quoted in Lovell, 374.
[3] *German Diplomatic Documents*, ii. 389, 394; Garvin, iii. 93; Langer, 240–4.
[4] *Grosse Politik*, xi. 31–32.
[5] Garvin, iii. 92–93.
[6] *Grosse Politik*, xi. 40. For the suzerainty see below, pp. 195–200.
[7] Ibid. 40. For article IV see above, p. 48 n. 1.

possibility of war with England'; what was the attitude of Germany and the other interested powers towards those aims? In reply Marschall warned the republic strongly against the adoption of a provocative policy. He advised instead that she should take the initiative in proposing a conference of the powers in order to secure the republic's position in the future.[1] Leyds, who was in Berlin at the time of the raid, supported this plan. But his government was hesitant. At first it decided that there must be no approach to the powers unless Britain refused the demands which the republic intended to make. Later, on Leyds's insistence, he was authorized to propose a conference if he was sure that it would achieve 'full independence' for the republic. But he soon found that there was no hope of co-operation among the powers on the Transvaal question.[2] That was a disappointment also for Germany, and it spelt the end of her intervention in South-East Africa except for a famous occasion in 1898 when Britain succeeded in buying her off.[3]

III

We left the high commissioner on the train *en route* for Pretoria. In order to understand the situation which confronted him on his arrival, it is necessary to sketch the course of events in Johannesburg at the turn of the year 1895. On 26 December Charles Leonard, the new president of the Uitlander national union, published a manifesto demanding drastic reforms. The mass meeting which was to have been held on 27 December to press for these reforms was postponed until 6 January, on which day the people were to tell the leaders plainly how the reforms were to be obtained.[4] One of these leaders was Leonard, who practised as an attorney. The others—Lionel Phillips, colonel Frank Rhodes, J. H. Hammond, G. Farrar, and J. P. Fitzpatrick—were representatives of companies interested in mining profits. But during the latter months of the year, with the approach of the date of the contemplated rising, the leaders had realized the need of taking into their confidence a number of other

---

[1] *Grosse Politik*, xi. 31, 35.
[2] Ibid. 31 n.; van der Poel (*a*), 136–7. It is doubtful, to say the least, whether Germany would have supported the republic's claim to 'full independence' at the conference table. German policy seemed to envisage merely a guarantee of the *status quo*. *Grosse Politik*, xi. 47, 49, 52.
[3] See below, p. 215.
[4] C. 7933, no. 1.

Uitlanders.[1] When James Bryce visited the Transvaal in November many people were discussing the 'revolution':

> People have talked of a conspiracy, but never before was there, except on the stage, so open a conspiracy. . . . The visitor had hardly installed himself in an hotel at Pretoria before people began to tell him that an insurrection was imminent, that arms were being imported, that Maxim guns were hidden, and would be shown to him if he cared to see them. . . . In Johannesburg little else was talked of, not in dark corners, but at the club where everybody lunches, and between the acts at the play.[2]

Towards the end of December a burgher questioned Kruger at a gathering not far from Pretoria about certain rumours which had reached his ears. The president replied that he had heard of the threatened rising, and proposed to wait until the Uitlanders took action.[3] But actually Johannesburg was neither psychologically[4] nor materially in a condition to fight the Boers. There were few men in the city trained to the use of arms,[5] when Johannesburg rose only a few thousand rifles and a few Maxims had been smuggled in. That is why the leaders relied upon the help of Jameson's force. But Jameson's force would not be enough to ensure success. The factor that would do that was the intervention of the high commissioner in the name of the British government.

By the time Leonard issued his manifesto the majority of the leaders seem to have decided that Jameson was an undesirable ally owing to his impatience for the revolt to start and his presumed intention of marching in under the British flag; and that it would be better to 'act' without his help.[6] Before the raid a beginning had

---

[1] Garrett, 48–50, 63, 83.
[2] Bryce, 423. See also Younghusband, 64.
[3] Fitzpatrick, 134.
[4] Garrett, 63, 125–9; *History of 'The Times'*, iii. 171, 176. Dr. A. P. Hillier, who was reputed to have shared some of the secrets of the 'inner circle', told the governor of Natal that 'except as regards education, the "grievances" had not really caused a very strong feeling in the mass of the population of Johannesburg. The capitalists, and such of the higher employés in the mines as had an interest in profits, were the real revolutionaries. The clerks and artizans, although they growled, received high wages and made a good living.' Hely-Hutchinson to Chamberlain, 11 Apr. 1896. Chamberlain papers, H. Similarly F. E. Younghusband, who had been sent to Johannesburg by *The Times* to report the 'revolution' wrote: 'But the great mass of the people were not at that time discontented. . . . The ordinary miner, the business employé and the clerks were all getting very high wages. . . .' Younghusband, 69.
[5] Garrett, 125; Bryce, 427.
[6] Fitzpatrick, 129–30. Younghusband, who possessed the confidence of the Johannesburg leaders, wrote on 11 January 1896: 'They were not really game for the business and if he [Jameson] had not crossed the border would never have taken up arms. The great mistake made was trying to run races with cart horses.' *History of 'The Times'*, iii. 213 n. 1. See also ibid. 173–4; Williams, 267. Chamberlain wrote more bitterly, no

already been made with the issue of arms to the populace and men had begun openly to drill. The leaders wished to find out how much the government would concede to a threat of force.[1] A number of concessions were in fact foreshadowed by the government on 30 December, the day on which it became known in Pretoria that Jameson had crossed the border. The executive council abolished at once the special duties on foodstuffs pending confirmation by the volksraad.[2] It agreed also to recommend to the volksraad that English-medium schools should henceforward receive the government subsidy on easier terms than in the past; that railway fares to the mines should be reduced for Native labourers; and that the franchise should be granted to all those who supported the state during the present crisis.[3]

The news of Jameson's crossing brought the rising excitement in Johannesburg to its climax. But the enthusiasm was of the effervescent kind.[4] A reform committee of sixty-four of the leading men was formed to take charge of the town, and the government withdrew its police in order to avoid a clash with the citizens.[5] Johannesburg now assumed the air of a town in revolt.[6] The arms which had been smuggled in were all distributed among the people, and bodies of armed men were posted on the outskirts of the town.[7] The reform committee's first reaction to Jameson's move had been to repudiate it.[8] But as the excitement among the people rose and the belief became general that he would soon be in Johannesburg, the committee prepared to welcome him as a hero and liberator. The high commissioner's proclamation of 31 December repudiating him does not seem to have produced much effect.[9] By the time its contents were known in Johannesburg, a telegram had come from Garrett, the editor of the *Cape Times*, which was known to be in sympathy with

doubt because he felt that he had been let down: 'The latter [the Uitlander leaders] are a lot of cowardly, selfish, blatant speculators who would sell their souls to have the power of rigging the market.' 'A Statement of Policy in 1896', 5 Apr. 1896. Chamberlain papers, C.

[1] Garrett, 128, 130, 134–6; Rose, 99; Fitzpatrick, 140.
[2] The volksraad subsequently confirmed this decision. For the special duties see above, p. 36.
[3] Memorandum by G. V. Fiddes in Chamberlain papers, C, quoting the *Standard and Diggers' News* of 4 Jan. 1896; van Oordt, 693; Fitzpatrick, 136.
[4] Garrett, 135–6, 164–5, 170–1, 174.
[5] Ibid. 137, 169; Fitzpatrick, 141–3.
[6] Younghusband, 77–78.
[7] Fitzpatrick, 150, 156; Garrett, 163–4, 201; Phillips, 153.
[8] Garrett, 161.
[9] Ibid. 177–9, 182, 201, 206; Fitzpatrick, 163, 165, 180–1; S.A.R. green book no. 2 of 1896, no. 95.

the reformers and whose assistant editor had arrived on Christmas day to report the rising.[1] It was addressed to the *Star*, the unofficial organ of the reform committee,[2] and made the following comment on the proclamation, which Garrett himself had helped to frame:

You must expect and not misunderstand a proclamation putting Jameson formally in the wrong. Imperial authorities have no other course; don't let this weaken or divide you, this merely for your information.[3]

On 1 January the *Star* wrote:

The British Government as in duty bound, may formally repudiate and denounce the great dash [of Dr. Jameson] . . .; but . . . the assistance of the column must be accepted in defiance of all considerations. . . . What was initially a grave crime on the part of Dr Jameson, his gallant officers and brave men, becomes by sheer stress of events a magnificent achievement. Its success will silence all criticism of his conduct. It will be justified by the event. He may fairly claim, if he gets through after repulsing every commando sent to stay his advance, to be the saviour of the situation; because we ardently believe that his presence here, his junction with our own forces, will end the campaign. It will compel an unconditional surrender. The Boer Government will go down, to be replaced by one of our own creation under the same flag.

The leading members of the reform committee did their best to give the government and their own supporters the impression that they controlled formidable armaments. They let it be known that there were more than 20,000 rifles in the town, and they had mining machinery—covered with tarpaulins—which was taken to be cannon, towed through the streets.[4] At the same time they sent appeals to the high commissioner to come to their assistance.[5] Meanwhile, they had dispatched a deputation to Pretoria at the invitation of the government. The deputation declared that they would be satisfied with 'a reasonable instalment' of reforms. But all they obtained was the following official statement,[6] which was handed to them at the close of the discussions: 'The High Commissioner has offered his services with a view to a peaceful settlement. The Government of the South African Republic have accepted his offer. Pending his arrival, no hostile step will be taken against Johannesburg provided

---

[1] Garrett, 123–4. [2] Ibid. 161.
[3] S.A.R. green book no. 2 of 1896, no. 92; Garrett, 187, 192–3.
[4] C. 8063, p. 41; Hammond, i. 339; Bryce, 423 n. 1.
[5] C. 8063, part II, no. 42.
[6] For the executive council resolution on which this statement was based, see van der Poel (*b*), 120.

Johannesburg takes no hostile step against the Government. In terms of a certain proclamation recently issued by the State President the grievances will be earnestly considered.'[1] The deputation had in fact allowed themselves to be fobbed off with promises that did not commit the government to any reform whatever. The government, on the other hand, had succeeded in its aim of spiking the guns in Johannesburg while it dealt with Jameson. It was clearly in its interest to obtain the submission of the rebels without firing a shot.[2] The shooting down of Johannesburgers would have stirred up excitement both in South Africa and in Britain and might have led to the armed intervention of the British government.[3]

Jameson's surrender was reported in Johannesburg during the afternoon of 2 January, and the reform committee in their head-quarters—the building of Rhodes's Goldfields company—experienced the 'blood-curdling roar of an angry mob'[4] which threatened violence against the leaders for leaving Jameson to his fate. They calmed the agitated populace with soothing assurances: all that was possible had been done for Jameson; the preparations for the defence of the town were complete; the high commissioner would arrive within two days.[5] The committee realized, however, that it was time the people got back to their jobs. The mines, many of which had closed down after Jameson's crossing, resumed work. A beginning was made with the disarming of men not needed for police and outpost duties. Government officials began gradually to take control. On 4 January, the day on which the high commissioner arrived in Pretoria, the government sent an armed detachment of Boers into Johannesburg and created a civic bodyguard from among the loyalists in the town.[6]

IV

Sir Hercules Robinson had never liked the Rhodes plan. And now Jameson's move had brought about that fiasco which Chamberlain had warned him would be 'most disastrous'. According to Bower, Robinson exclaimed on learning of the raid: 'But good God

---

[1] Fitzpatrick, 156–8; Garrett, 175–6.
[2] For a contrary opinion by leading reformers see Fitzpatrick, 141; Hammond, i. 339; Phillips, 158.
[3] For the proceedings in Johannesburg of the government's 'peace committee', see van der Poel (b), 115–16.
[4] Phillips, 161.
[5] Ibid.; Hammond, i. 348–9; Garrett, 207–9; Fitzpatrick, 200–1.
[6] Fitzpatrick, 142–3; Garrett, 213–17; C. 8063, part II, nos. 8 and 10.

he has not gone in without a rising? If so you never told me.'[1] He seems to have now experienced a revulsion from the policy which had brought South Africa to the brink of war. But he was an old man suffering from heart trouble,[2] and it would appear that his first impulse was to let Chamberlain deal with the situation. Robinson, writes Bower, who accompanied him to Pretoria, 'urged that he was only a Post Office' transmitting Chamberlain's and Kruger's correspondence. He did, in fact, send on to the president Chamberlain's long telegram of 4 January giving the British government's views on Uitlander grievances.[3] But Bower, according to himself, soon convinced his chief 'that he was a great deal more than a Post Office';[4] whereupon for seventeen critical days Robinson took control of Britain's Transvaal policy.[5]

During Robinson's stay at Pretoria Chamberlain kept in touch with him by cable. He began by sending him the long message of 4 January in which, after being permitted to exercise his own discretion, the high commissioner was instructed to press for the removal of the main Uitlander grievances.

Danger from which they [the government of the republic] have just escaped was real, and one which, if the causes which led up to it are not removed, may recur, although in a different form. . . . They must fully admit the entire loyalty of yourself and of Her Majesty's Government to the terms of the London Convention, as shown by their recent intervention, and they must recognise that their authority in crisis through which they have passed could not have been so promptly and effectively asserted without that intervention.[6]

It is clear that in spite of the alleged discretion Chamberlain was prepared to allow the high commissioner, he expected him, 'as the Representative of the Paramount Power', to obtain from Kruger definite promises as to reform.[7] That would be tantamount to giving Britain a *locus standi* in the internal affairs of the republic—a matter on which the president held very decided views. He might be expected, therefore, to refuse to discuss Uitlander grievances. What was the

---

[1] Reminiscences, 248.

[2] Both Bower (Reminiscences, 256–7) and Garrett (238) say that Robinson was ill on the train and after arrival in Pretoria. Judge E. J. P. Jorissen, who was present at the interview with Robinson on 6 Jan. (see below, p. 107), writes that he was 'thankful for the sofa' placed at his disposal, and that 'in morale also there was something of a broken man about him'. Jorissen, 137–8.

[3] C. 8063, p. 40, para. 27.   [4] Reminiscences, 264.

[5] Bower suggests that he was the author of Robinson's policy. Ibid.

[6] C. 7933, pp. 19–20.   [7] Ibid., pp. 51, 55, 88.

high commissioner then to do? There are a number of indications of what Chamberlain had in mind. He expected Robinson to use 'firm language'.[1] And he was prepared to back up this firm language with a show of force. On 13 January the high commissioner was told that, since the republic might rely on Germany 'in resisting the grant of reforms or in making demands upon Her Majesty's Government', he (and presumably Kruger too) should know that the British government has commissioned 'a Flying Squadron of powerful men-of-war . . .'.[2] A week earlier the war office, at Chamberlain's request, had instructed the officer commanding at the Cape to send troops to Mafeking on the pretext of preventing further raids on the republic. Robinson at once countermanded the order on the ground that troop movements would fan the excitement which was gradually subsiding.[3] On 7 January he foreshadowed the unconditional surrender of Johannesburg, to Chamberlain's 'bitter chagrin', says his biographer.[4] If there is warrant for this diagnosis, it means that the colonial secretary had still been clinging to the Rhodes plan, modified to suit the altered circumstances. He had wanted the high commissioner to extort reforms from Kruger at the point of the bayonets of Johannesburg, with imperial troops on the frontier to take Jameson's place. Now Johannesburg was going to lay down its arms. The high commissioner might, however, still have the troops: 'large forces including cavalry and artillery' would be sent to the Cape if he would only ask for them. But once again he declined the offer.[5] 'Months afterwards', writes Bower, 'Mr Chamberlain reproached me with not taking a hint, and with spoiling his policy at Pretoria.' When Bower referred to Britain's military weakness in South Africa and the danger of European complications, Chamberlain replied, 'That was my business, not yours.'[6]

Chamberlain's general inclination seems to have been to believe that in a crisis, 'facing the risk [of war] would remove it'.[7] So far as the Transvaal problem was concerned, he thought it probable, to quote his biographer once more, 'that Kruger when firmly summoned

[1] C 7933, no. 153.
[2] Ibid., no. 140.
[3] Ibid., nos. 77, 82, 84, 9 0,93, 94 (extract), 101.
[4] Garvin, iii. 99.
[5] Chamberlain to Robinson and to Mrs. Chamberlain, 7 Jan. 1896, ibid.; C. 7933, nos. 91, 103, 105; C. 8063, pp. 40–41, para. 29. Nos. 91 and 105 (of C. 7933) respectively omit Chamberlain's reference to 'large forces' and the refusal of them by Robinson.
[6] Reminiscences, 264.
[7] Garvin, iii. 251–2. See also ibid., chs. lv and lvi.

would always climb down'.[1] Robinson and Bower judged otherwise. They had long experience of South African affairs. At Pretoria they became aware of the deep anger of Kruger's burghers at the raid and the simultaneous Uitlander rebellion. Though Robinson had told Chamberlain that he would raise the question of Uitlander grievances as soon as Johannesburg had surrendered,[2] he subsequently changed his mind. He decided that it was too much to expect Kruger to promise immediately a more liberal franchise to the Uitlanders: for that was the reform on which the colonial secretary at this time laid most stress.[3]

Nearly all leading Johannesburg men [he told Chamberlain] are now in gaol, charged with treason against the State, and it is rumoured that government has written evidence of a long-standing and widespread conspiracy to seize Government of country. . . . The truth of these reports will be tested in the trials to take place shortly in the High Court, and meanwhile to urge claim for extended political privileges for the very men so charged would be ineffectual and impolitic. . . . The present moment is most inopportune [for advocacy of Uitlanders' claims], as the strongest feeling of irritation and indignation against the Uitlanders exists both amongst the Burghers and Members of Volksraad of both Republics; any attempt to dictate in regard to the internal affairs of South African Republic at this time would be resisted by all parties in South Africa, and would do great harm.[4]

About the surrender of Johannesburg a few words will suffice. On 5 January the high commissioner was informed by an envoy of the reform committee that the town could not resist an attack by the 8,000 Boers who were said to have surrounded it.[5] The following day Kruger told Robinson that the town must surrender unconditionally within twenty-four hours. After the townsmen had been told, on instructions from Robinson, that the lives of Jameson and his officers depended on compliance with the government's terms, those terms were accepted.[6] Thereupon the government granted an amnesty to all the rebels except the reform committee, provided the arms smuggled into Johannesburg were given up within a stipulated time; and the president issued a proclamation which held out to the townsmen the prospect of an elected municipal council.[7]

[1] Ibid. 44. Chamberlain's own words fifteen months later support Garvin's statement. See below, p. 157.
[2] C. 7933, nos. 89, 98, 105, 108; C. 8063, part II, no. 47, and appendix no. 179.
[3] C. 7933, nos. 49, 140. [4] Ibid., nos. 154, 168.
[5] Ibid., no. 89; C. 8063, part II, no. 47; Garrett, 177, 218–19, 237; Fitzpatrick, 166.
[6] C. 7933, nos. 89, 98; C. 8063, part II, appendix no. 236, enclosure II; C. 8164, no. 1, enclosure 10; Garrett, 218–23.
[7] C. 7933, no. 118; C. 8063, part II, no. 49; S.A.R. green book no. 1 of 1896, no. 92.

Immediately after the issue of the ultimatum to Johannesburg the fate of Jameson and his officers was decided—but not until Kruger had surmounted one of the crises of his career. With one accord the commandos demanded the execution of the raid leaders. The shrewd old president knew that such a course would jeopardize the peaceful settlement which he was doing his utmost to secure. His plan was to hand over the captives to the British government, which the burghers believed to have been behind Jameson. First he had to convince the executive council, and thereafter the commandants assembled in Pretoria, who would have to explain to the burghers in due course why he had been right. He struggled for four hours before he had his way with the commandants.[1] And even then he was not yet out of the wood. Johannesburg surrendered only a small proportion of the arms which the leaders had boasted they possessed. The commandos wished to seize the opportunity to punish Babylon for her sins, but Kruger once more stood in the breach.[2] 'Old Kruger is behaving splendidly', wrote Bower to his wife,[3] 'and we have every reason to be grateful to the old man.'

After the pacification of Johannesburg and the handing over of the raid prisoners, the republican government wished to be rid of the high commissioner, who accordingly left Pretoria on 14 January.[4]

V

Before the end of January Chamberlain once more took control of British policy towards the republic. He received information from Samuel Marks[5] and Sir James Sivewright, a member of the Cape ministry, that the president would accept an invitation to come to London to discuss 'pending questions'.[6] The colonial secretary saw at once that here was his opportunity of resuming the initiative which had passed to Kruger after Jameson's fiasco. Sanguine as usual, he gave rein to desires that were not destined to be fulfilled. He told the prime minister about his plans and confided to his wife: 'I am hoping

[1] C. 7933, nos. 105, 151; Bower, Reminiscences, 256–62; Jorissen, 137–41; van Oordt, 717–20.
[2] C. 7933, nos. 108, 110.
[3] 10 Jan. (Bower papers).
[4] C. 8063, part II, appendix no. 342; C. 7933, no. 152.
[5] Contrast Garvin, iii. 127.
[6] Marks to Lewis, 17 and 25 Jan. 1896; Sivewright to Chairman, 22 and 23 Jan. 1896 (C.O. 537/130); C. 8063, part I, no. 1.

to make a great coup and get Kruger over here . . . if he will walk into my parlour it will be very nice of him.'[1]

Both Marks and Sivewright urged Chamberlain to send the invitation to Kruger without delay in order to check 'foreign intrigue' in the Transvaal. The high commissioner, on the other hand, advised caution. He warned his chief that the two objects the president had most at heart were, first, the abrogation of article IV of the London convention,[2] and second, the recognition of his republic's claim to Tongaland and the territory of the chiefs Zambaan and Umbegisa recently annexed by Britain.[3] These two points should be ruled out in advance. 'It would be I think better', continued the high commissioner, 'that he [Kruger] should [first] offer a visit and that we should [then] express great pleasure to receive him subject to reservation as to . . . two points stated, than that we should write [first] with reservation. I think that if you approve I could manage this.'[4]

Chamberlain ignored the high commissioner's advice. He preferred to rely on Marks and Sivewright, who had assured him that Kruger was prepared to come to England notwithstanding Chamberlain's express proviso[5] that article IV of the London convention could not be modified. On receiving the high commissioner's telegram he wrote the following minute:

[There may be something in Robinson's advice], 'but the effect, the "coup" will be manqué unless the visit is clearly part of *our* policy and appears to be the result of our initiative. If we invite him [Kruger] public opinion here and abroad will say "They are going to get something out of him". If however he proposed [the visit] himself they will think "He is going to get something from them".

If Robinson has carried out my previous instructions[6] Kruger knows that we will not modify Article IV. Besides he has been warned by both Sivewright and Marks about this.

I did not think of the territories recently annexed and it may be awkward now to make a further reservation. But if he comes and asks for them we can point to our previous flat refusal,[7] although we shall be obliged to allow him to open the question. . . .'[8]

---

[1] Garvin, iii. 127. [2] See above, p. 48 n. 1.
[3] See above, p. 52.
[4] Robinson to Chamberlain, 25 Jan. 1896 (C.O. 537/130).
[5] Lewis to Marks, 23 Jan. 1896 (C.O. 537/130).
[6] This presumably refers to certain instructions sent to Robinson during his visit to Pretoria after the raid. Robinson had replied that he did not consider it desirable to transmit them to Kruger. C. 7933, nos. 140 and 154.
[7] Before the raid.
[8] Chamberlain's minute dated 26 Jan. 1896 (C.O. 537/130).

On 27 January Chamberlain, without confirming his private information through the Queen's official representatives in South
Africa and ascertaining fully what was in Kruger's mind, sent him—
and soon afterwards published[1]—a formal invitation to confer on all
matters of common interest with the exception of article IV.[2] The
outcome was misunderstanding[3] and recrimination, for Chamberlain
expressed the view that by negotiating for months about the invitation Kruger was slighting the British government.[4]

It soon became clear that the principal gain which the president
hoped to achieve by a visit to England was the abolition of the
London convention, and especially article IV. That article had been
a thorn in his flesh from the beginning. The Jameson raid, which, he
claimed, constituted a breach of the convention,[5] gave him his best
opportunity so far of getting rid of that instrument. He knew that
he could not count on German support for a unilateral repudiation.[6]
Accordingly, a few days before Chamberlain sent his invitation,
Kruger wrote a private letter to the high commissioner, vainly hoping
to enlist his help in the approach he proposed to make to the British
government regarding the abolition of the convention.[7]

Kruger's reply to the British government showed that he did not
intend to accept the invitation on Chamberlain's terms. He wished
that an understanding should first be reached on the matters that
would be discussed; in particular he wanted article IV to be included
in the agenda.[8] That did not sound very hopeful. Moreover, Chamberlain had already taken a line which rendered the prospect of a
conference even more remote. On 7 February, weeks before it reached
Pretoria, he published in the *London Gazette* a lengthy dispatch on
the Transvaal,[9] of which he sent Kruger a short telegraphic summary.[10]
The latter, who harboured strong feelings on 'the dignity of an

---

[1] *Parliamentary Debates*, 4th series, vol. xxxvii, col. 330 (13 Feb. 1896).
[2] C. 8063, part I, no. 3.
[3] Chamberlain to Robinson, 27 Apr. 1896. C. 8063, part I, no. 32.
[4] White to secretary of state, S.A.R., 24 or 25 Mar. 1896. Quoted in Breytenbach,
131–3.
[5] C. 8063, p. 13; Breytenbach, 88.
[6] See above, p. 100.
[7] Breytenbach, appendix B.
[8] Kruger to Robinson, 8 Feb. 1896. C. 8063, part I, no. 9. Fairfield minuted on
11 Feb. 1896: 'I think it probable that Sir James Sivewright and possibly other friends
on the spot held out hopes to him [Kruger] that the difficulty about discussing Article IV
might be got over.' C.O. 417/179.
[9] C. 7933, pp. 83–91. Dispatch dated 4 Feb.
[10] C. 8063, pp. 2–3. Telegraphic summary transmitted to Kruger in a letter dated
8 Feb. from the British agent in Pretoria.

independent Republic',[1] could hardly fail to resent this action as a slight. (He retaliated by publishing his reply forthwith.) His second and more serious objection to the publication of Chamberlain's dispatch was that he deemed it 'undesirable and inadvisable to give publicity beforehand to the position which the British cabinet intends to be able to take up' at the proposed conference: 'The position of affairs has been greatly complicated thereby.'[2] It would appear that the colonial secretary was deliberately taking risks with Kruger in order to justify himself to public opinion at home and give it a lead; for the house of commons was about to discuss Britain's policy towards the Transvaal. He sought to silence those who suspected the colonial office of being implicated in the raid and the Johannesburg rising; as well as those others (of his own party)[3] who believed that it was he—and not the high commissioner—who had let the Uitlanders down.[4] He had also to consider Rhodes, who, unless carefully handled, might reveal explosive secrets.[5] 'Through the Chartered [B.S.A.] company in London, he had [immediately after the raid] bombarded the Colonial Office with telegrams, insisting almost in the tone of a superior giving orders that Chamberlain must force reforms at Johannesburg. . . .'[6] In addition the formidable *Times*, which was among Rhodes's collaborators,[7] had expressed the hope that 'by disowning the Raid and saving the Boer Government, Chamberlain had taken moral responsibility for the reform of the Boer administration'.[8] At the beginning of February Rhodes arrived in England, and on the 5th his solicitor prodded the colonial office to 'hurry up the publication of the despatch about the Uitlanders'.[9] On the 6th Reginald Brett, later Viscount Esher, who was acting as intermediary between Rhodes and Chamberlain, reported to the latter that at the interview which was about to take place Rhodes would press strongly '(I) the hard lot of the [reform] prisoners (II) the Uitlander grievances (III) the position of the Chartered Company and *not* refer much

---

[1] Ibid., p. 13.   [2] Ibid., p. 5.
[3] Garvin, iii. 129.
[4] The effect of the dispatch was enhanced by the publication—some hours before Chamberlain spoke in the house on 13 Feb.—of the telegraphic correspondence between the high commissioner and himself. *Parliamentary Debates*, 4th series, vol. xxxvii, cols. 308, 314.
[5] Garvin, iii. 108–9.
[6] Ibid. 104. See also van der Poel (*b*), 145–6.
[7] *History of 'The Times'*, iii, chs. vii and ix.
[8] Ibid. 212; see *The Times*, 2 Jan. 1896.
[9] Hawksley to Fairfield, 5 Feb. 1896. 311, Q. 8753. Chamberlain's statement to Kruger that Rhodes was 'not aware' of the dispatch 'till after publication' is inaccurate. C. 8063, p. 6. See also van der Poel (*b*), 158–9.

to past events'.[1] The interview between Rhodes and Chamberlain, which lasted almost two hours, was according to Selborne, who was present, 'most satisfactory', since Rhodes showed 'a great amount of common sense'.[2]

Chamberlain's dispatch[3] dealt at great length with the position of the Uitlanders. He described the list of their grievances as 'formidable in length and serious in quality'. Once again he dwelt on the question of the franchise. If, however, he concluded, Kruger remained convinced that the enfranchisement of the Uitlanders would endanger the stability of the republic, would he consider a scheme whereby they might achieve 'home rule'[4] or local autonomy within their district—the Witwatersrand—in return for surrendering their claim to the franchise?

Chamberlain supplemented this dispatch by a speech delivered on 13 February in the house of commons. He spoke at some length on Rhodes and the B.S.A. company. Rhodes would retain his position as the company's managing director in South Africa.[5] The Johannesburg leaders—notwithstanding the 'letter of invitation'[6]—and Rhodes were, he believed, ignorant 'of the intention or action of Dr Jameson'. 'I say it would be an act of ingratitude if we were, even now, when suspicion hangs over him [Rhodes], to forget the great services he has rendered. I believe he is capable of great service still. . . . I believe his right place is in Africa. . . .' He announced one important concession to Kruger's wishes: the B.S.A. company would be 'disarmed'.[7] But he was not in favour of the cancellation of its charter. His policy with regard to its governmental rights in Rhodesia would depend on the outcome of the inquiry he had promised. 'But if there is to be an Inquiry . . ., what object is to be effected? With a vindictive object, in

---

[1] E. Drus in *Bulletin of the Institute of Historical Studies* (1952), 38. See also van der Poel (*b*), 157–8.

[2] Garvin, iii. 104.

[3] The first draft of this dispatch was composed by G. V. Fiddes, an official of whom more will be heard later. Chamberlain was very pleased with it. Minute, 26 Jan. 1896. C.O. 417/177.

[4] As the scheme was soon not inaptly described. *Parliamentary Debates*, 4th series, vol. xxxvii, cols. 329, 331. Hofmeyr at once described the scheme as impracticable. In March Chamberlain told the high commissioner that his proposal of limited autonomy for the Rand 'does not appear to have met with favour in any quarter', and that he did not desire 'to press it further'. Memorandum by Hofmeyr dated 11 Feb. 1896 and enclosed in Robinson to Chamberlain, 25 Feb. 1896; Chamberlain to Robinson, 17 Mar. 1896. Chamberlain papers, K.

[5] He did not resign until June—apparently on Harcourt's insistence—after the details of his plot against the Transvaal had been revealed. Williams, 285 n. 1; Gardiner, 389–91, 393–4.

[6] See above, p. 92 n. 10.   [7] Garvin's word.

order to punish individuals? No, that is not the object of anyone in this House. The object is to see whether the Company are fit and proper persons to continue to be entrusted with the administration of this territory.'[1]

Kruger knew of the interview between Rhodes and Chamberlain.[2] The latter's speech, with its tender references to Rhodes, made it clear that he was not to be punished if the colonial secretary could help it; and that his power in South Africa, though it had been diminished, was not to be broken.[3]

Professor E. A. Walker writes that 'at first he [Kruger] was ready to go to a conference. . . . But in the latter part of March 1896 the president turned right round.'[4] The first part of this statement seems to be based on a telegram which the high commissioner sent to Chamberlain on 16 February: 'I have a private and very friendly letter from President of the South African Republic, written since receipt by him of your message of 6th February [the telegraphic summary of the Uitlander dispatch], in which he writes as if he had quite determined to visit England. I am told that the Hollanders about him[5] are averse to his acceptance of your invitation, but that he himself strongly wishes to go. . . .'[6] But in the private letter apparently referred to,[7] Kruger repeated his wish to have article IV discussed at the conference and concludes as follows: 'I hope with all my heart that England would indeed desire that conference, after I have set out the matter also on other points in my official letter that is to come.' As regards 'the Hollanders', Kruger later denied that his decision on the conference had been altered by them.[8] Nor was it influenced by the advice tendered to him from Cape Town by Kotze, his chief justice, and Hofmeyr that he should go to London.[9]

In his 'official letter', dated 25 February, Kruger laid great stress on his desire to have the London convention, including article IV, superseded 'by a treaty of peace, commerce and friendship'. In return he was prepared 'to give . . . assurances' that he would never

---

[1] *Parliamentary Debates*, 4th series, vol. xxxvii, cols. 308–32.
[2] C. 8063, p. 6.   [3] See above, p. 99.   [4] *C.H.B.E.* viii. 569.
[5] See also Walker (a), 270.   [6] C. 8063, part I, no. 13.
[7] Dated 8 Feb. and quoted in Breytenbach, 93–94.
[8] C. 8063, p. 18. Leyds, the most influential of Kruger's Hollanders, had been telegraphing him from Europe since 4 Feb. not to go to London unless he got a promise that article IV would be abrogated. But Kruger had already before 4 Feb. shown the importance he attached to the abrogation of article IV. See above, p. 110.
[9] Breytenbach, 113–14; Hofmeyr, 507.

seek 'the protection of a foreign Power'. With his eye on the Uitlander dispatch, he declared that he could allow no interference in his internal affairs and, therefore, no official discussion of Uitlander grievances; but that he would give consideration to 'private hints'. Like Chamberlain[1] he invited the support of the Cape Afrikaners: 'I declare myself prepared, if it is made possible for me, not for a forced but for a voluntary and hearty co-operation, and I am of opinion that . . . in this I am the interpreter of every true Afrikaner.'[2] The correspondence that followed revealed the wide gulf that separated the two negotiators. Kruger proposed to go to London as the wronged party, seeking redress and compensation. Chamberlain was prepared to offer monetary compensation for the raid and a guarantee against aggression, both of which Kruger claimed as of right. In return he asked that the president should submit proposals regarding the Uitlanders for discussion. Chamberlain, in fact, envisaged the conference as primarily one on Uitlander grievances. But Uitlander grievances Kruger persistently refused to discuss. He was determined to avoid even the appearance of giving the British government a foothold in his internal administration. The correspondence concluded with a statement by Chamberlain that 'Her Majesty's Government are, as representing the paramount Power in South Africa, specially interested in its peace and prosperity, and they cannot be blind to the danger which threatens its future if legitimate causes of discontent continue to be ignored by the Government of the South African Republic'; to which Leyds, who had recently returned from his visit to Europe, replied that his government 'notes with satisfaction that Her Majesty's Government is solicitous of the interests of South Africa as a whole. These interests are also treasured by this Government, and the State President can justly appeal to the fact that he knows and represents a considerable section of the public opinion of South Africa.'[3]

VI

For months after the raid the relations between Britain and the South African Republic continued to be strained. In South Africa a number of newspapers, both British and Afrikaner, fed the fires of the

---

[1] House of commons, 13 Feb. *Parliamentary Debates*, 3rd series, vol. xxxvii, col. 332.
[2] C. 8063, pp. 12–14.
[3] Chamberlain's statement, 26 Mar.; Leyds's, 18 Apr.; invitation to Kruger withdrawn, 27 Apr.: C. 8063, part I, nos. 23, 32; C. 8423, no. 18.

rival nationalisms.[1] In Britain an influential section of the press, led by *The Times*, demanded the dispatch of troops to South Africa in order to force Kruger's hand, on the ground that the Transvaal was arming.[2] A succession of 'alarming reports'—to use Chamberlain's words—regarding the arrogance and warlike intentions of the Boers kept the excitement alive.[3]

Until April Chamberlain worked hard to secure the acceptance of the invitation he had so hurriedly sent to Kruger. He continued sending messages to the president through private persons, though he probably made it clear to his correspondents that the authorship of those communications was not to be divulged. The trend of the messages was to threaten Kruger with war unless he came to London. Thus Chamberlain got in touch through a certain Puleston with J. B. Robinson, the Johannesburg mining magnate, who knew Kruger well. Robinson sent letters and cables to his representative in Johannesburg stressing *inter alia* the influences driving Chamberlain to war, such as the bellicose attitude of the English press and people. Later, towards the end of March, after a 'hurried interview' with Chamberlain, he telegraphed his representative to warn Kruger, 'England determined. Position serious.'[4] On 25 April one Sydney Woolf wrote from Johannesburg acknowledging a letter from Chamberlain and informing him that since his (Woolf's) last letter he had had several interviews with Kruger and commandant-general Joubert, in one of which he told them that Kruger's decision 'to finally refuse or accept your invitation had come to be looked to as the definite intimation from the Transvaal burghers and their government whether they deemed a peaceful settlement possible or impossible'.[5]

Before the end of March Chamberlain decided that the time had now come to increase the garrison at the Cape. Less than three months before the high commissioner had turned down his proposal to that effect.[6] Now he tried again. He had recently learnt 'with feelings amounting almost to dismay'[7] that Kruger would not come

---

[1] Breytenbach, 153–5, 157; Hofmeyr, 504–5; Garrett, 254; C. 8063, part I, no. 24; Hely-Hutchinson (governor of Natal) to Chamberlain, 1 Feb. 1896 (Chamberlain papers, K).　　　　　　　　　　　　　　　　[2] Breytenbach, 146–52.

[3] Garvin, iii. 99; Breytenbach, 146, 149, 158; Garrett, 254; C. 8063, pp. 15, 27–28; Hely-Hutchinson, 'note of an interview with Sir J. Robinson', prime minister of Natal, 9 Apr. 1896 (C.O. 537/130).

[4] Correspondence between Puleston and Chamberlain in Jan., Feb., and Mar. 1896; J. B. Robinson to Chamberlain, 30 Mar. 1896. Chamberlain papers, C.

[5] Woolf to Chamberlain, 25 Apr. 1896. Chamberlain papers, C.

[6] See above, p. 106.

[7] Was his dismay due partly to the fact that without an early settlement with Kruger

to England for at least six months.[1] On 29 March the *Observer* advocated the dispatch of a large force to South Africa on the pretext of the Matabele rebellion which had just broken out in Rhodesia.[2] Two days later Chamberlain telegraphed to Robinson: 'Do you consider that in view of the Matabele rising' [and bearing in mind the fact that the Transvaal was arming] 'it would now be a good opportunity to increase the garrison of the Cape?' (And of Natal, he added a week later.) 'If you think this should be done make the proposal to me officially in a telegram informing the President at the same time that you have done so and the reasons. . . .'[3] Robinson's reply was an uncompromising 'No': 'I think that it would be most impolitic to increase the garrison of the Cape Colony at the present moment. . . . Such a transparent excuse as the Matabeleland rising would only confirm the burghers in their belief that we have designs on their independence and in their present suspicious temper, the increase might precipitate action on their part which would involve us in a war. . . .'[4] Then Chamberlain tried a somewhat different approach. The Matabele rebellion, he telegraphed, was giving the British government 'great anxiety'. Was Robinson absolutely certain that he had enough troops to put it down? He should bear in mind that if any disaster occurred the responsibility would be fixed on the British government and on himself. But still the high commissioner would not budge.[5]

At this time there was on its way to Robinson a long private letter in which Chamberlain revealed his state of mind and the policy that he thought should now be pursued. On the colonial secretary's instructions G. V. Fiddes, a member of his staff, had been working for some weeks on the preparation of a memorandum entitled 'The Case against the South African Republic'.[6] In the letter to Robinson Chamberlain adopted the tone of a man contemplating an ultimatum. After referring to the pressure upon him of public opinion to obtain 'definite assurances' from Kruger and the irritation caused in England by the arrest and trial of the Johannesburg reformers, he continued:

which would include 'letting bygones be bygones', he would have to face an inquiry into the raid with all its ugly possibilities?

[1] Chamberlain to Robinson, 17 Mar. 1896. Chamberlain papers, K.

[2] Breytenbach, 150.

[3] Chamberlain to Robinson, 31 Mar. 1896. C.O. 537/130.

[4] Robinson to Chamberlain, 1 Apr. 1896. C.O. 537/130.

[5] Chamberlain to Robinson, 9 Apr. 1896; Robinson to Chamberlain, 11 Apr. 1896. C.O. 537/130.

[6] Minute by F. Graham, 14 Mar. 1896. C.O. 417/180. The memorandum was printed in July 1896 as a white book, no. 518, African (South), for the use of the colonial office.

'You will have seen by my speeches and answers in the House of Commons that I have endeavoured to quiet the angry feeling which largely prevails, but I admit that my patience is nearly exhausted.' If Kruger would not 'decide at once to come to England', he would have to consider whether he should proceed immediately to make representations the neglect of which would undoubtedly lead to strained relations.

It may be desirable in view of possible eventualities, to strengthen the garrisons of the Cape and Natal. . . . Meanwhile I must impress upon you that I regard the situation as urgent and serious. You may, if you think fit, convey this impression to President Kruger, and in this, or in every other way that your experience suggests, you may warn him of the complications that will certainly arise if an early attempt is not made to come to an agreement with Her Majesty's Government.[1]

In reply to this letter Robinson telegraphed his most outspoken warning yet:

The feeling of the Dutch African inhabitants of the Cape Colony has undergone a complete change since Jameson's raid and they would now neither sympathize with nor support any forcible measures undertaken by Imperial Government to secure redress of Uitlanders' grievances. The situation at present is this. Kruger refuses to discuss alleged grievances relating to certain internal matters and sooner than do so . . . [he] would, I believe, if necessary face hostilities. We have now only the choice of making such a refusal a casus belli or contenting ourselves with the private suggestions as to the interests of British subjects which he states he is willing . . . to consider in a friendly spirit. Before Her Majesty's Government come to a decision on this question I think it my duty to point out that in event of hostilities growing out of the Jameson raid the South African Republic will be openly assisted by the Orange Free State [and, at all events covertly, by] a large number of Dutch both in the Cape Colony and in Natal.

Such a war, continued the high commissioner, would require a force of 30,000 to begin with. It would have to be prosecuted to the end, even if it required the whole strength of the Empire to defeat the Boers. And after the defeat of the Boers

there will remain the question of Government of a people embittered by race hatred and torn asunder by internal dissensions which will for generations require the maintenance of a large permanent garrison.

[1] Chamberlain to Robinson, 17 Mar. 1896. Chamberlain papers, K. It would appear from some passages in this letter that an ultimatum to Kruger would actually have been based on alleged breaches of the London convention. But its real reason would have been Kruger's refusal to discuss Uitlander grievances.

My own opinion is that our best course is to sit still and wait patiently to see what measures of redress the President himself will propose. . . .

If his concessions should prove insufficient private representations and official remonstrances from Her Majesty's government might then be renewed and by the publication of these public opinion both in South Africa and in England might be brought to bear on the Government of the Republic.

This is an influence to which they are not insensible.[1]

Though Chamberlain described this reply as 'wholly inadequate',[2] Robinson's grave words nevertheless struck home. For they strongly reinforced the warnings of others. Fairfield had already dwelt on 'the serious risks of a conflict with the S.A.R.'[3] Bower, too, had recently spoken to the colonial secretary in similar strain. According to Montagu White, the consul-general of the republic in London, who spoke with Bower during the course of his brief visit, the latter had been deputed by Robinson to urge moderation and patience.[4] Bower himself reports part of his conversation with Chamberlain as follows:

> BOWER: I would not advise you to join the Burlington Hotel party [i.e. Jameson and his officers]. . . . If you adopt that policy [a warlike policy] you will have to get another High Commissioner.
> CHAMBERLAIN: I know that.[5]

There came from South Africa further warnings besides those of Robinson and Bower. The Natal ministry deprecated the dispatch of an ultimatum to Kruger. So did the prime minister of the Cape. 'This is not the time', he telegraphed, 'for an ultimatum and troops, the resources of diplomacy are not yet exhausted. . . .' Even the *Cape Times*, a staunch supporter of British supremacy in South Africa, joined the anti-ultimatum chorus.[6]

Chamberlain had perforce to realize that the time for vigorous action was not yet ripe. Three speeches delivered by him in April and May mark his retreat from the policy of interference in the internal affairs of the republic and inaugurate a new phase in Anglo-Boer relations.

[1] Robinson to Chamberlain, 27 Apr. 1896. C.O. 537/130.
[2] Minute dated 28 Apr. 1896. C.O. 537/130.
[3] Chamberlain, 'A Statement of Policy in 1896', 5 Apr. 1896. Chamberlain papers, C.
[4] Breytenbach, 164–5; minute by Fairfield, about 21 Apr. 1896 (C.O. 537/130).
[5] Bower, Reminiscences, 291.
[6] C. 8063, part I, no. 26; Tennant (Cape agent-general in London) to Chamberlain, 7 Apr. 1896 (C.O. 537/130); Garrett, 254–5.

In these speeches he attempted to placate Afrikaner sentiment. He did not, it is true, budge an inch from the position he had taken up regarding British paramountcy in South Africa—'it matters not whether we call ourselves suzerain or paramount'—which involved *inter alia* the right of making 'friendly representations' regarding the Uitlanders. Nor did he refrain from criticizing the republic for alleged breaches of its conventions with Britain and for its 'defective and corrupt' administration.[1] But he laid great stress on the necessity of Britain's exercising patience in her dealings with Kruger. Time must be given for the wounds inflicted by the raid to heal. 'As a Dutch Government ourselves, as well as an English Government, it ought to be our object, in endeavouring to secure the redress of these [Uitlander] grievances, to carry with us our Dutch fellow-subjects.' In that case the republic would not be able to resist the steady pressure of South African public opinion in favour of reform. He quoted with approval from an address in which members of the Cape parliament representing Afrikaner constituencies had urged 'moderation and conciliation', and rebuked those newspapers and members of parliament—of his own party—who were urging immediate action.[2]

In some quarters [he told the house of commons in a passage which was not without its piquancy in view of what had gone before] the idea is put forward that the Government ought to have issued an ultimatum to President Kruger, an ultimatum . . . which must have led to war. Sir, I do not propose to discuss such a contingency as that. A war in South Africa would be one of the most serious wars that could possibly be waged. It would be in the nature of a civil war. It would be a long war, a bitter war and a costly war, and . . . it would leave behind it the embers of a strife which I believe generations would hardly be long enough to extinguish. Of course there might be contingencies in which a great Power has to face even such an alternative as this . . . but to go to war with President Kruger in order to force upon him reforms in the internal affairs of his State with which successive Secretaries of State, standing in this place, have repudiated all right of interference—that would have been a course of action as immoral as it would have been unwise.[3]

[1] House of commons, 8 May: *Parliamentary Debates*, 4th series, vol. xl, cols. 907–11, 915; constitutional club, 22 Apr.: *Foreign and Colonial Speeches*, 205–6; Breytenbach, 160, 167.
[2] Constitutional club, 22 Apr.: *Foreign and Colonial Speeches*, 205–8; house of commons, 8 May: *Parliamentary Debates*, 4th series, vol. xl, col. 917; South African dinner, 21 May: *Foreign and Colonial Speeches*, 217–19.
[3] House of commons, 8 May: *Parliamentary Debates*, 4th series, vol. xl, cols. 914–15.

There was another question on which Chamberlain had at this time to make up his mind. The republican government had just handed to the press a number of documents revealing the nature of Rhodes's responsibility for the raid. It was impossible for Chamberlain any longer to keep up the pretence that Rhodes had been ignorant 'of the intention or action of Dr Jameson'.[1] The question he had now to answer was whether Rhodes should take his place in the dock by the side of Jameson. The latter was shortly to be tried for the infringement of section 11 of the foreign enlistment act.[2] Kruger's documents constituted a strong prima facie case against Rhodes as another offender—if not the principal offender—under the act.[3] But Chamberlain obscured the issue by talking of the vindication of the law as vindictiveness.[4] 'But for Englishmen like Mr Rhodes', he told the house of commons on 8 May, 'our English history would be much poorer—[loud ministerial cheers]—and our British dominions would be much smaller. [Renewed cheers.][5] It was not, in fact, politically feasible to bring Rhodes to trial. For one thing, his friends hinted that, if provoked, he might publish the compromising cables sent him by his agents in London.[6] Another consideration, which probably weighed more heavily with Chamberlain, was Rhodes's popularity with large sections of the British[7] and South African public. He explained the South African aspect of the matter to the house of commons: it was necessary 'to pay some attention to the views of that section of the population who, at all events, are well-wishers to the British rule'.[8] And Garrett, the editor of the Cape Times, wrote some months later that the imprisonment of Rhodes would cause 'sullen feelings' throughout British South Africa.[9] Thus when the republican government sent a pressing request that Rhodes, Beit, and Harris should be brought to trial and that the

---

[1] See above, p. 112.
[2] Section 11 reads: 'If any person within the limits of Her Majesty's Dominions and without the license of Her Majesty,
'Prepares or fits out any . . . military expedition to proceed against the dominions of any friendly State . . .:
'(1) Every person engaged in such preparation or fitting out, or assisting therein . . . shall be guilty of an offence under this Act. . . .'
[3] Contrast Williams, 277.
[4] See above, p. 112; *Parliamentary Debates*, 4th series, vol. xl, col. 919; Breytenbach, 168.
[5] *Parliamentary Debates*, 4th series, vol. xl, col. 920.
[6] Garvin, iii. 109, 113–14. Early in June Chamberlain spoke to Montagu White about 'the terrible influences that exercise pressure on him'. Breytenbach, 167.
[7] Williams, 274, 285.
[8] *Parliamentary Debates*, 4th series, vol. xl, col. 920.
[9] Garrett, xxx.

administration of Rhodesia should be transferred from the B.S.A. company to the British government, Chamberlain reacted sharply. The government, he replied, did not need to be reminded of its duty.[1] An inquiry would be held into the company's administration. As for Rhodes and his two collaborators, the government 'can only act in this matter on the advice of the Law Officers of the Crown. . . '.[2] Rhodes was in due course condemned by parliamentary committees both at the Cape and in Britain,[3] but he never underwent a judicial trial.

In May 1896, when the case against Rhodes had become clear, the rumour was circulated that Hawksley, his London solicitor, had documents[4] proving that Chamberlain also had been 'in it up to his neck'. On 6 June the colonial office called upon Hawksley to produce the documents. Having read them, Chamberlain offered his resignation to the prime minister, who refused to accept it.[5] It was at this moment that the high commissioner arrived in England for consultations with the colonial office. He found the colonial secretary 'a little under the influence of the war party in London which is composed of society fools and knaves'.[6] But he expressed himself as 'quite satisfied with the frame of mind' in which he left Chamberlain on his return to South Africa in August.[7]

VII

Chamberlain's decision to refrain from pushing Kruger towards internal reform eased the tension between Britain and the republic.

[1] To Montagu White he said that the republic's request proved that its attitude was hostile and challenging. Breytenbach, 173–4. It was a severe warning.

[2] C. 8423, nos. 33 and 36. Chamberlain had in fact received the following opinion—dated 5 May 1896—from the attorney-general and the solicitor-general, who were, of course, members of the government: 'Upon the materials now before us there is not in our opinion sufficient evidence to justify the institution of criminal proceedings against Mr C. J. Rhodes.' Chamberlain papers, C. In the absence of information as to the grounds on which this opinion was based, not much value can be attached to it. There is no evidence that the law officers were again consulted after the report of the Cape committee of inquiry into the raid in July 1896.

[3] See above, p. 71.　　　　　　　　　　　　　　[4] The cables.

[5] Garvin, iii. 109, 113.

[6] The description lacked comprehensiveness.

[7] Walker (a), 276–7. On 20 Aug. the prime minister wrote to the Queen: 'Mr Chamberlain wrote to me that according to the view of the doctors, Sir H. Robinson could not return [to South Africa]. I took it as meaning that he did not intend to return. I accordingly submitted it to Your Majesty. Sir H. got well unexpectedly and insisted on going back. Mr Chamberlain could not have dismissed him without exposing himself to serious imputations in the present excited state of feeling in South Africa. But Sir H. promised faithfully to resign in the Spring at latest.' Royal archives, Windsor, vol. O. 45. Robinson returned to South Africa as Lord Rosmead.

But not for long. Before we come to the new causes of tension, there is a point on which it is desirable to obtain clarity. I wrote earlier in this chapter that Kruger was determined to resist British interference in his internal affairs. That statement needs to be qualified. The president could not correctly resist Britain's exercise of her right under international law to protect her subjects against maltreatment in his state; nor could he resist such interference in his internal affairs as was justified by the provisions of the London convention. When Chamberlain renounced the idea of pressing internal reforms upon the republic, he did not, of course, intend to surrender Britain's legal or conventional rights.[1] The renewed tension between Britain and the republic was due to his insistence, during the second half of 1896, that the latter had broken the convention not only in her external relations but also in her internal legislation.

In view of Kruger's expressed desire to get rid of the convention it was to be expected that Chamberlain would be on his guard against any action by the republic that might tend to impair British rights under that instrument. In October 1894 Leyds had told the German consul in confidence 'that the Republican Government was striving to evade the article in question [apparently article IV] of the London Convention as much as possible and to render it of no effect in practice'.[2] Yet by 1896 he apparently favoured a different policy, for he wrote privately to a friend that 'the South African Republic must seek her strength in her *right*', including her rights under the convention.[3]

The first matter in dispute between Britain and the Transvaal during the latter half of 1896 related to the republic's treaty-making rights. The actual treaties which led to the dispute—extradition treaties with Portugal and the Netherlands—were of small account. But the issue seemed to gain significance from the fact that it was argued concurrently with other questions, of more serious import, arising out of conflicting interpretations of the convention. The correspondence in connexion with all these disputes was published by Chamberlain in April 1897[4] in order to obtain public support for the action he had decided to take.

---

[1] Conventional rights were those derived from the London convention.
[2] Van Winter, ii. 248 n. 4.
[3] Leyds to J. P. Moltzer, 5 Aug. 1896; Leyds's interview with Marschall, 11 Jan. 1896. Leyds, *Tweede Verzameling*, ii. 12–14. For Chamberlain's attitude to the convention see below, p. 125.
[4] C. 8423.

Article IV of the convention reads as follows:

The South African Republic will conclude no treaty or engagement with any State or nation other than the Orange Free State, nor with any native tribe to the eastward or westward of the Republic, until the same has been approved by Her Majesty the Queen.

Such approval shall be considered to have been granted if Her Majesty's Government shall not, within six months after receiving a copy of such treaty (which shall be delivered to them immediately upon its completion), have notified that the conclusion of such treaty is in conflict with the interests of Great Britain or of any of Her Majesty's possessions in South Africa.

This article gave rise to conflicting interpretations because the meaning of the concept 'completion of a treaty' had not been defined. It would seem that the article intended to draw a distinction between the 'conclusion' and the 'completion' of a treaty, since approval had to be obtained before its 'conclusion' and after its 'completion'. The republic argued that a treaty was not 'completed' until it had been sanctioned by the constitutional authorities of the contracting parties.[1] Chamberlain's view—that 'the word "completion" ... refers to the stage at which a treaty first assumes a complete shape, viz., the signature of the Plenipotentiaries or other negotiators'[2]—seems to be more reasonable. But the fact remains that article IV was badly drafted. Sir Alfred Milner, though he endorsed Chamberlain's interpretation, considered that the article was 'somewhat ambiguous' with regard to the stage at which treaties should be submitted for the Queen's approval.[3] The librarian of the foreign office, from which the colonial office sought confirmation of its view, could find no support for Chamberlain's interpretation of the word 'completion'. He stated that the word was seldom or never used with reference to treaties, but if it was so used it must be taken to have the same meaning as 'conclusion'.[4] A few months later the permanent under-secretary (colonial office) declared that he preferred the republican interpretation of article IV to that of Chamberlain and the law officers.[5]

At one stage during this protracted controversy the government of the republic took a false step. It did not submit its extradition treaty with the Netherlands for approval until the ratifications had been

[1] C. 8423, no. 10.
[2] Chamberlain told the law officers that he would like to take up this position, if possible, and they concurred. Law officers to Chamberlain, 27 Apr. 1896 (C.O. 417/187); C. 8721, no. 7.
[3] Milner to Chamberlain, 11 May 1897. Chamberlain papers, D.
[4] Foreign office to colonial office, 4 May 1897 (enclosure). C.O. 417/228.
[5] Minute by E. Wingfield, 7 July 1897. C.O. 417/217.

exchanged and the treaty had been published in the Netherlands *Gazette*. In reply to Chamberlain's protest it seemed to admit that 'the practice generally followed by it in other cases has been departed from';[1] but later on it maintained that there was no obligation to submit treaties to the Queen until they had been ratified.[2] The dispute dragged on until the end of 1898, when Chamberlain imposed the compromise he had suggested earlier, viz. that the treaties of the republic might be approved by the constitutional authorities of the contracting parties before being submitted to the Queen, provided they contained a declaration that they would not come into force until her sanction had been obtained.[3]

Chamberlain's claim that certain republican laws constituted a breach of the convention was a more serious matter. In response to a number of burgher memorials the volksraad resolved in 1895 that the government should frame and publish a bill dealing with persons who were a danger to the internal peace of the state.[4] After the Jameson raid further memorials were presented, in the name of over 2,000 burghers, reiterating the previous request.[5] The government thereupon introduced into the volksraad a bill providing that an alien who was considered by the president and the executive council to be 'a danger to the public peace and order' might be summarily expelled from the republic. The acting British agent in the Transvaal was 'credibly informed' that the measure would be rejected.[6] When this prediction proved false within a month,[7] he explained that the volksraad's action was largely due to 'the speeches of Dr Hartley at Johannesburg and the establishment of a branch of the [South African] League there'.[8]

It is probable that, had the British government not protested against the aliens expulsion act, this law would have had a depressing effect on Uitlander political activity, which was beginning to revive after

---

[1] In the case of several treaties concluded by the republic during the 1880's the approval of the foreign constitutional authorities had been obtained after the signification of the Queen's consent. Nilant, ch. ii; C. 8423, no. 82; African (South), 505, no. 298.

[2] C. 8423, nos. 51 and 67; C. 8721, no. 3.

[3] C. 8721, no. 7; C. 9507, nos. 6 and 7.

[4] *Notulen*, Eerste Volksraad, 1895, arts. 831–2.

[5] Ibid., 1896, arts. 886–8.

[6] C. 8423, nos. 46 and 59.

[7] Bill passed by volksraad on 28 Sept. 1896. *Notulen*, Eerste Volksraad, 1896, arts. 1780–95, 1818–19.

[8] For the league see below, p. 161. Dr. Hartley was the leader of the league in the Cape Colony. The latter part of the British agent's telegram, referring to Dr. Hartley and the league, was omitted in C. 8423, no. 61. The telegram as dispatched is in C.O. 417/184.

the setback of the raid.[1] (The members of the reform committee had been convicted of treason, fined, and released after promising to take no part in politics for three years.[2])

The question immediately arose whether the aliens expulsion law was a breach of article XIV (*a*) of the convention, which states:

All persons, other than natives, conforming themselves to the laws of the South African Republic (*a*) will have full liberty, with their families, to enter, travel or reside in any part of the South African Republic.

The law officers declared that it was.[3] Meade and Fairfield were of the opposite opinion. In February 1896 Chamberlain had written, on the subject of the republic's treaties with foreign powers:

If we are dealing with the S.A.R. *after* a settlement which had placed our relations on a permanent and friendly basis I should not be disposed to take any technical objections. But the situation is exceptional and indeterminate and I think our policy should be to press the Convention Art. IV for all it is worth. Kruger tells us in offensive language that we have no right to meddle in his internal affairs. This is substantially true but if he rejects our friendly suggestions in these matters we must show him that we have rights under the Convention which may be used to annoy and embarrass him if he takes up the position of an enemy. The present is not a big matter, but I cannot help thinking that it may be a 'peg' on which we can extend our suzerain rights.[4]

He now declared in reply to Meade and Fairfield: '. . . I do not . . . express any view on the legal points raised but I have a very strong feeling on the question of policy. I am anxious to maintain the most stringent possible interpretation of the Convention and of all that remains to us of our Suzerainty over the Transvaal.' British influence over the republic, he continued, had been steadily whittled away since 1881, *inter alia* by 'the [Transvaal's] secret intrigues with Germany and France. We ought to keep our hands clenched on what remains, and if possible magnify it by any plausible interpretation of the Convention.' The Boers and 'the Hollanders by whom they are led' will, unless they are checked, 'use their new powers to persecute all who are obnoxious to them. . . .' Meade, continues the minute, compares article XIV of the convention with analogous articles in treaties of commerce between Britain, on the one hand, and Switzerland and the United States, on the other. But 'I consider that the

---

[1] See below, p. 162. [2] Van der Poel (*b*), 168.
[3] African (South), 516, no. 340.
[4] Quoted in Wilde, 48. For the suzerainty see below, p. 195.

Convention is ab initio different in character and intention from any treaty between two independent Powers. It is either the consideration for which independence was given, or, as I prefer to think, it is the terms imposed when independence was given. If so, any breach of the Convention forfeits independence, and the terms imposed must be construed much more strictly than in an ordinary treaty.'[1] In other words, on the ground that when the convention was concluded the Transvaal was a dependent state under the suzerainty of the Queen, Chamberlain was prepared to argue that the provisions of the convention might be interpreted in a different manner from those of a treaty between two independent powers: that is to say, the meaning of words in a treaty (or convention) depended on the status of the contracting states, and precisely the same formula might mean one thing in a treaty between Great Britain and the United States but something different in a convention between Britain and the Transvaal. Significantly enough it did not occur to any of the international jurists consulted by the republic[2] that different rules of interpretation could possibly be applied to the London convention from those which governed the interpretation of treaties in general.

On 15 December 1896 Chamberlain instructed the high commissioner to inform the government of the republic that 'Her Majesty's Government cannot, in view of Article 14 of the London Convention, admit that Government of the South African Republic has a right of expelling or restricting foreigners who are not shown to have failed to conform to the laws of the Republic'.[3]

The republic asked three authorities on international law—the Englishman Westlake, the Netherlander Asser, and the Frenchman Clunet[4]—whether the aliens expulsion law was a breach of the convention. Westlake supported the law officers' view; Asser and Clunet contradicted it. Westlake[5] held that the law was contrary to the convention

First, because it makes aliens subject to expulsion although they have not failed to conform themselves to the laws of the Republic;

Secondly, because it refers to the Government, and not to a Court of Justice, the decision whether an alien is liable to expulsion.

---

[1] Chamberlain's minute, dated 22 Nov. 1896, on the law officers' opinion with regard to the aliens expulsion law. C.O. 417/187.

[2] See below.

[3] C. 8423, no. 78.

[4] For their opinions see Botha, appendix H.

[5] He was professor of international law at Cambridge.

He continued:

It is argued that the Law ... is one of police and as such is not excluded
by Article 14.

This I take to mean that similarly indefinite powers of expelling aliens
are possessed by many Governments, and that their exercise, when not in
excess of what the safety of the country in question may reasonably be
thought to require, is not considered to be a breach of a treaty conceding
the right of residence to the subjects of another State.

That is true when, as is usually the case, the treaty concedes the right of
residence in terms so general that reason requires some exception to be
tacitly understood. But in the present instance the treaty excludes tacit
understanding by itself defining the condition under which the right of
residence is to be enjoyed, namely, that the alien shall conform himself to
the laws of the South African Republic.

The validity of this opinion depends on the correctness of the statement that treaties conceding the right of residence 'usually' do so
'in terms so general that reason requires some exception to be tacitly
understood'. But do they? Clunet did not agree. According to him
article XIV, including the phrase 'conforming themselves to the
laws of the Republic', followed a formula commonly used in treaties
guaranteeing the right of residence to foreigners, and the formula
could not be, and was not in practice, interpreted to mean that the
government of a state which had granted such a right was thereby
debarred from summarily expelling aliens. The law officers' view of
the aliens expulsion law may, therefore, have been mistaken.

The second piece of legislation that led to controversy between the
British and republican governments was the immigration law. The
purpose of this law, which came into force on 1 January 1897, was
to check the influx of undesirable foreigners[1] into the republic and
to secure the registration of such foreigners as had been admitted.
An alien entering the Transvaal either as a traveller or as a settler
had to be provided with a passport—viséd by a consular official of
the republic—which showed that he had means or the ability to
support himself. He might also be admitted without a passport if he
could satisfy the authorities that he was able to make a living. On
admission he was given a 'travelling and residing' passport, which
had to be renewed periodically.

Whether or not the Boer authorities were wise[2] to pass the immigration law, they do not appear to have exceeded their rights. In other

[1] The undesirable foreigners were principally Indians.
See Botha, 755, 761.

words, the view of Chamberlain and the law officers that the law infringed article XIV (*a*) of the convention[1] is open to grave question.

In transmitting to Chamberlain their view that the immigration law infringed article XIV of the convention the law officers advised him to think carefully before he acted on this opinion. As there are provisions, they wrote,

similar . . . to this article in some treaties concluded by England with foreign powers . . . it may be necessary to consider whether the considerations governing the construction [that is to say, the interpretation] of such an article in the case of a treaty between two independent Powers . . . are the same as those which apply in the case of a Convention like the present defining the terms upon which a qualified independence had been granted to what was previously a British territory. . . . The question how far any possible legislation as to immigrants into the United Kingdom might be affected in the light of Treaties with Foreign Powers by any action taken with reference to this law of the South African Republic deserves consideration. The subject is of such great importance that we think it right, at present, only to indicate these considerations and to suggest that before any step is taken, it should be considered in all its bearings.[2]

Chamberlain brushed aside this advice. He wrote to the foreign office that no further consideration seemed to be necessary. The matter brooked no delay.[3] Unless Salisbury[4] objected he proposed to dispatch the British government's protest against the immigration act forthwith.[5] Salisbury did not take long to make up his mind. He replied the next day and authorized Chamberlain to go ahead with his protest. After declaring that he had duly considered the points raised by the law officers he continued: 'The precise relation now existing between the Transvaal and Great Britain has never occurred in historical experience before this time, and . . . therefore there can be no precedents' to guide the British government. They must act upon such an interpretation of the London convention as

suits British interests best, if it is a reasonable construction under the circumstances of the case. Lord Salisbury would therefore be disposed to

---

[1] See above, p. 125.

[2] Law officers to Chamberlain, 9 Dec. 1896. C.O. 417/187.

[3] The reason for the hurry appears to have been that, in view of the forthcoming parliamentary session and the expected reappointment of the committee of inquiry into the Jameson raid, Chamberlain wished to score a point and/or to publish a case against the republic as soon as possible. On 28 Feb. 1897 he minuted: I desire 'to publish as early as I possibly can' some more papers regarding the republic. Minute on Rosmead to Chamberlain, 27 Jan. 1897. C.O. 417/214.

[4] He was foreign secretary as well as prime minister.

[5] E. Wingfield (for Chamberlain) to under-secretary, foreign office, 12 Dec. 1896. C.O. 417/187.

contend that a convention between a suzerain and a dependent state is not 'ejusdem generis' with a treaty between two independent powers. Consequently any signification assigned by Her Majesty's Government to the provisions of the convention cannot affect the interpretation which they would accept in construing a treaty concluded with powers who, at the time when it was concluded, stood in a totally different relation to Britain from that which existed at a similar period between Great Britain and the South African Republic.[1]

The three authorities consulted by the republican government[2] declared that the immigration law was not an infringement of the London convention.[3] One of them, Westlake, gave his opinion in these words:

... Article 14 of the Convention of London expresses that all persons, other than natives, conforming themselves to the laws of the South African Republic shall have ... liberty to enter the State and reside in it.

This has been read as if the laws to which aliens had to conform were only those which would apply to them as already admitted or resident, so that laws attaching conditions to their admission or residence would be excluded.

I am unable to agree to such a limitation of the very general terms in which the laws to be observed by aliens are mentioned. The only limitation which in my opinion can be put on those terms is that the laws in question must be reasonable.

I cannot deem the Law No. 30 of 1896[4] to be unreasonable either in its policy or in the general nature of the machinery by which it gives effect to that policy. That the admission and residence of aliens should depend upon their possessing means of subsistence or being able to procure such by their labour is a policy in force in the United States of America, and the adoption of which in the United Kingdom is advocated by many serious politicians.

To forbid it to the South African Republic would be to assert that the Republic accepted by the Convention the duty of maintaining all the helpless or idle British subjects who might throw themselves on it, and it would be difficult to find in the convention any words on which such an assertion could be based.

In September 1896 the volksraad passed a press law, which *inter alia* empowered the executive council to prohibit the distribution of printed publications whereof the contents were in its opinion 'in conflict with public morals or dangerous to the order and peace of the Republic'. Towards the end of December the president, in alleged

---

[1] Foreign office to colonial office, 13 Dec. 1896. C.O. 417/194.
[2] The same men as were consulted on the aliens expulsion law.
[3] Botha, appendix J.   [4] The immigration law.

conformity with the law, issued an order suppressing a Johannesburg weekly, the *Critic*, for six months on the ground that it was a danger to public peace and order. Its proprietor, one Henry Hess, had been for some time a thorn in the side of the republican authorities. In 1895 he had been convicted of libelling one of the judges.[1] He had furthermore shown an interest in the dangerous topic of republican Native policy.[2] Notwithstanding the presidential order, Hess continued to publish his journal under the new name of the *Transvaal Critic* and appealed to Chamberlain for redress. In the opinion of the British agent in the republic, the 'paper was not ... dangerous to public peace. It attacked public men, officials, bogus companies, drink-shops etc., indiscriminately and severely, but not more so than similar paper would do at home.'[3] The law officers advised the colonial office that the president should be asked to explain his reason for suppressing the *Critic*, and continued: 'If the accounts supplied to the Colonial Office of the character of the *Critic* can be relied on, there has been a gross abuse of the powers of the [Press] Act, which would justify Her Majesty's Government in insisting upon compensation.'[4]

It is worth noting that the law officers did not suggest that Hess should be advised to appeal, in the first instance, to the courts of the republic. Yet this was the advice given—to the knowledge of the colonial office—by the British agent and the high commissioner, as well as by three barristers consulted by Hess's solicitors.[5] Chamberlain decided to act on the opinion of the law officers—up to a point. He did not try to find out from Kruger why the *Critic* had been suppressed, apparently on the ground that too much time had elapsed since the president's order.[6] The protest to the republican government as drafted by the secretary of state was considerably watered down by his staff, on whose advice the words 'we trust that the President will at once recall the mandate' suppressing the *Critic* were omitted.[7]

---

[1] His sentence of two months' imprisonment was later quashed on a technicality. Webber and Kotze, ii. 112–29.

[2] African (South), 470, pp. 250, 283–4. On republican Native policy, see below, p. 183.

[3] African (South), 516, no. 444. Similar views were expressed by two of Chamberlain's staff, H. Lambert (24 Feb., on Rosmead to Chamberlain, 30 Jan. 1897—C.O. 417/214) and J. F. Perry (5 Jan. on law officers to Chamberlain, 4 Jan. 1897—C.O. 417/226).   [4] Law officers to Chamberlain, 8 Feb. 1897. C.O. 417/226.

[5] Rosmead to Chamberlain, 30 Jan. 1897 (C.O. 417/214); C. 8423, no. 95 (enclosure): opinion of H. H. Asquith, E. Carson, and F. Mackarness dated 13 Jan. 1897.

[6] Minute by J. Bramston, dated 10 Feb. 1897, on law officers to Chamberlain, 8 Feb. 1897. C.O. 417/226.

[7] Original draft of protest in Chamberlain's minute, dated 13 Feb. 1897, on law officers to Chamberlain, 8 Feb. 1897 (C.O. 417/226); protest as dispatched in C. 8423, no. 109.

On 24 March 1897, at a moment of great political excitement in the republic,[1] the Johannesburg daily, the *Star*, was suppressed on the same ground as the *Critic*.[2] Like the latter, the *Star* continued publication under the name of the *Comet*, though the Argus company, which owned the *Star*, gave the journal a new editor. Among the reasons for its suppression, in the opinion of the managing director of the Argus company,[3] was a leading article on a speech which Kruger had made at Bloemfontein.[4]

The president, it stated, has been compared to Gladstone. But Gladstone's utterances 'are those of a giant and cultured intellect while those of the under-study are the merest drivel. . . . Retention of power by men of his stamp to-day is a ludicrous anachronism. . . .' The article went on to refer to the 'monotony of his pious patter'. Kruger acts 'conjointly as Predikant and President. From an archaeological point of view this is an interesting role, but it does not fit in with nineteenth century notions. . . .' What the President has so far said at Bloemfontein is 'unmitigated and reiterated twaddle. . . . It is really to be hoped that at to-day's banquet he will disprove the aspersion cast on him by Mr Rhodes that he drinks nothing but water, and give his brain at least sufficient artificial stimulus to infuse into his post-prandial homily a few dashes of commonsense; would that we could also add a little humour, but we fear that no amount of Drakenstein could imbue Paul Kruger with so much saving grace as that. . . .'[5]

'Ridiculous to be so thin-skinned', commented the permanent under-secretary in the colonial office, 'but the Bloemfontein article is coarsely offensive.'[6] In addition to this article, there were two cartoons. The first, entitled 'The Science of Swollen Heads', shows Doctor Chamberlain diagnosing many evil qualities, duly listed, in Kruger.[7] The second, though it did not indulge in personal abuse, was perhaps even more offensive to Boer susceptibilities. It shows Kruger, asked by Chamberlain to play the republican national anthem, playing *Rule Britannia* instead, while Chamberlain remarks: 'That shows the Spirits are working.'[8]

---

[1] See below, p. 145.
[2] For the *Star* see above, pp. 59 and 103.
[3] Rosmead to Chamberlain, 31 Mar. 1897, enclosing Greene to Rosmead, 26 Mar. 1897. C.O. 417/216.
[4] Kruger's visit to Bloemfontein was in connexion with the treaty of alliance dealt with on pp. 147–8 below.   [5] The *Star*, 11 Mar. 1897.
[6] Minute by E. Wingfield, dated 19 Apr. 1897, on Rosmead to Chamberlain, 31 Mar. 1897. C.O. 417/216.   [7] The *Star*, 27 Feb. 1897.
[8] Ibid., date uncertain. The cartoon arrived in the colonial office on 17 Apr., and was probably published not long before 24 Mar., the date on which the paper was

Such then, it would appear, were the grounds for the suppression of the *Star*. But while it is true that the journal had behaved offensively, it is difficult to see how this behaviour was 'dangerous to peace and order in the Republic'.[1] The proprietors of the paper took the correct course of appealing to the high court of the republic, which pronounced the suppression illegal on the ground that the president had no power to prohibit the publication of matter not yet printed.[2] Chamberlain thereupon returned to the charge on behalf of the proprietor of the *Critic* and claimed compensation from the republic. But he was told in reply that Hess must seek redress in the republican courts, a reply which was stated in the colonial office to be difficult to answer.[3]

The press law had little effect on the conduct of the Transvaal newspapers, whose editors apparently believed that the *Star* judgement had rendered the law harmless.

VIII

During the session of 1896 the volksraad also legislated to improve the state of education on the proclaimed gold-fields and to grant a minor extension of the franchise.

The education law, which was passed in August 1896, was mainly the work of Leyds and Mansvelt, the superintendent of education.[4] The law inaugurated a system of almost fully state-financed and state-managed schools on the gold-fields. It authorized the government—in practice the superintendent of education—to appoint teachers and draw up curricula. Its purpose appears to have been twofold: first, to implement the government's promise[5] to make more satisfactory provision for the education of Uitlander children—it constituted in fact the only attempt to carry out that undertaking; second, and more important, to checkmate the recently created Witwatersrand council of education.[6] This body had been formed by the political leaders of the Uitlanders, including Lionel Phillips and other mining magnates,

suppressed. I have not been able to find either of the cartoons in the Johannesburg Public Library. For further examples of the provocative tone adopted by the *Star* about this time see Scholtz, ii. 160–2.

[1] *Officieele Rapporten—Hooggerechtshof*, Deel IV, Afl. I, 1897, p. 170.

[2] Ibid., p. 175.

[3] C. 9345, nos. 12, 14, 16; minutes on Milner to Chamberlain, 13 May 1897, by F. Graham, 28 June, and E. Wingfield, 9 July (C.O. 417/218). See also African (South), 536, pp. 265, 328; 600, pp. 124, 458–9.

[4] Ploeger, 156–7, 160–2, 176–7, 179–80, 183–5.

[5] See above, p. 102.   [6] Ploeger, 156, 161, 177, 183, 185.

some eight months before the raid. Owing to its inability to raise the money it had reckoned on, the council's bark proved to be worse than its bite.[1] But this the government could not know when it framed its education law in the early months of 1896.

With regard to the English-speaking children attending these state schools, Mansvelt's plan was that they should be educated through the English medium in the lowest standards but that it should be gradually supplanted by Dutch as the child's education progressed.[2] In October 1898 the executive council agreed that the Dutch medium should be introduced as follows: one hour per day in standards I and II; one and a half hours per day in standard III; two and a half hours in standard IV; three hours in standard V; and two-thirds of the school time in standard VI.[3] The principals of the state schools were Hollanders to a man.[4] By 1899 there were thirteen such schools attended by about 1,500 pupils, the majority of whom were English-speaking. Of the 51 teachers, 24 were of British origin. In 1898 the government spent altogether £226,291 on education. Of this total the education of both English- and Afrikaans-speaking children on the gold-fields in government-subsidized as well as state schools cost £36,503.[5] Among the schools subsidized by the government were included the *besluit* schools for English-speaking children.[6] These had not grown more popular with the years. By 1898 they were attended by 350 pupils.[7]

The state schools on the gold-fields began to get into their stride only during the course of 1898.[8] They did not have the time, therefore, to show their viability. On the other hand, Mansvelt had fair warning that unless he relaxed his language requirements his schools would run into difficulties. The 'English' school at Barberton had been opened with something of a flourish in the new year of 1897. It had an influential and active school board, a Dutch principal who had just spent four months in England, and three assistant teachers. But disillusionment came soon enough. In 1898 the inspectors reported that only 'working class' children attended the school, while even members of the school board sent their children to private schools. As for the medium of instruction in the school, the parents

---

[1] Ibid. 102–10, 205–8; Malherbe, 291–5; Lugtenburg, 243–9; C. 9345, p. 77.
[2] Ploeger, 177, 185, 216; C. 8423, p. 95.
[3] Malherbe, 289; Ploeger, 203, 226.
[4] Ploeger, 205, 216, 224.
[5] Ibid. 225–6.   [6] See above, p. 56.
[7] Ibid. 191, 226; Lugtenburg, 209.
[8] Malherbe, 279; Ploeger, 226.

desired that it should be English throughout. On the Witwatersrand Mansvelt's system had a serious setback at the very outset. In November 1896 the executive council agreed to the creation of a nominated school board for the Rand gold-fields. On the recommendation of the mining commissioner of Johannesburg, J. L. van der Merwe, ten members were appointed to the board to represent the Afrikaans-speaking, British, Dutch, German, and American communities.[1] The government appointed a salaried secretary, who had soon to be dismissed on the score of incompetence. A difference of opinion arose between the board and the government on the question of his successor. The government decided that applicants had to be either fully enfranchised or naturalized burghers. This decision the board refused to accept, and it was ostensibly on this issue that the members resigned in September 1897. Actually the board had come to the conclusion that its views on more important questions, such as the medium of instruction and the appointment of teachers, carried no weight with the superintendent of education and the government. After the resignation of the board Mansvelt carried on alone.[2]

Like the education law, the franchise resolution of 17 August 1896 was passed by the volksraad in order to give effect to a government promise.[3] The resolution granted the full franchise to those who had shown themselves willing to defend the republic at the time of the raid. The administration's subsequent handling of this matter brought it into hot water with the volksraad. During the session of 1897 some members alleged that Uitlanders had been given the franchise carelessly and indiscriminately. An attempt to repeal the resolution of the previous year was narrowly defeated after an earnest plea by the president. In 1898 the volksraad took up the matter once more and appointed a committee to carry out a thorough investigation. The report of the committee showed that serious irregularities had been perpetrated for which not only minor officials like the field-cornet of Johannesburg but the executive council itself, were to blame. The volksraad thereupon resolved, in May 1899, that those of the 'Jameson raid burghers' who could not substantiate their claim to the franchise within three months should be struck off the roll. But the government was unwilling to face the odium of

---

[1] Van der Merwe was chairman, and among the members were George Albu, George Farrar, and H. H. Webb, an American, who was the acting chief engineer of the Consolidated Goldfields company.

[2] Ploeger, 194–5, 211–19, 318.   [3] See above, p. 102.

disfranchising men who had given up their previous citizenship to become full burghers of the republic.[1] It accordingly induced the raad to amend its resolution in such a manner that only those whom the government suspected of having obtained the franchise fraudulently should be called upon to prove their claim. Thus ended an episode which contributed its share towards bringing the republic into disrepute.[2]

When Johannesburg surrendered to the Boer government in January 1896, Kruger had expressed the intention of converting the sanitary board of the town into a municipal council.[3] A bill to this effect was published by the government in 1896, but it did not become law until September 1897. It established an elected *stadsraad* (city council) for Johannesburg, which was to consist of not more than twenty-four members, one-half of whom were to be elected by the comparatively small number of born and naturalized burghers living in the town. The council had wider powers of local government than the board which it replaced, though the central government could still keep a close watch upon its proceedings. The government also appointed the burgomaster, who was *ex officio* chairman of the council and its principal executive officer. The first and only burgomaster was J. Z. de Villiers, formerly *landdrost* of the Lydenburg district, who succeeded in maintaining friendly relations with the council except on one notable occasion. This was when the government late in 1898 granted a concession[4] for sewering the town to E. Mendelssohn, part-owner of the government-subsidized newspaper, the *Standard and Diggers' News*. The burgomaster refused to authorize the council to test the validity of the concession in the courts, and that body thereupon threatened him with legal proceedings. Shortly afterwards the government withdrew the concession. The council's prestige was further enhanced when, in the last session before the war, the second volksraad passed a measure extending its right to levy local taxes.[5]

[1] Schalk Burger, a member of the executive council, asserted that 3,437 persons had been enfranchised. The British agent put the number at 1,800.
[2] Hugo, 80–86; *Notulen*, Eerste Volksraad, 1899, arts. 183, 190; African (South), 516, pp. 526–7; 536, pp. 45, 330–1; 543, pp. 167–8; 557, p. 104; 600, pp. 16–19, 157–8. Walker's brief statements on the 'raid burghers' in *C.H.B.E.* viii. 592 and in Walker (*b*), 480 do not indicate the provocation the volksraad had received from the administration.
[3] See above, p. 107.
[4] The *stadsraad* already held the concessions to supply the town with gas and electricity, the sanitary board having acquired them from the concessionaires in 1895.
[5] C. 8423, p. 94; C. 9345, pp. 65–70, 75–76; Cd. 623, p. 134 n.; *Notulen*, Tweede Volksraad, 1899, arts. 92, 807–28; Maud, 44–46.

CHAPTER VI

THE CRISIS OF APRIL 1897

I

TOWARDS the end of the year 1896 two of Chamberlain's senior officials retired from the colonial service: Fairfield, the expert on South African affairs, and Meade, the permanent under-secretary. Like Robinson and Bower, who were also soon to retire, they had favoured, since the raid, a rest cure for South Africa with a minimum of imperial intervention. They were much friendlier to the South African Republic than their successors Graham and Wingfield, and a check on Chamberlain's tendency towards reckless or provocative proceedings. At about the same time another change of personnel took place. The experienced—but old and ailing[1]—de Wet was succeeded as British agent in the republic by Conyngham Greene, who had held a post in the British embassy at The Hague. Greene was described by the diplomatic representative of the republic in Europe as 'a sound and cultivated man, who understands and speaks Dutch with ease'.[2]

On his arrival at Pretoria early in December 1896 Greene reported, in somewhat alarmist terms, that the republic was 'paralyzed' by rinderpest, drought, locusts, and famine.[3] In addition, a depression in the 'Kafir' share market had set in, which continued throughout 1897 and most of 1898.[4] But the effect of this depression on the internal stability of the republic must not be exaggerated. The great bulk of the share and other capital of the mining industry came from abroad. Of course, if the loss of confidence had been so serious as to put a virtual stop to the inflow of capital, serious internal difficulties must have developed. But such a situation did not arise. In spite of all retarding factors[5] the output of gold and the profit per ton of ore milled continued to rise throughout the 1890's until shortly before the outbreak of war.[6] Notwithstanding the slump in the share

[1] Minute by F. Graham, 20 Jan. 1896. C.O. 417/177.
[2] Beelaerts van Blokland to Leyds, 25 Sept. 1896. Quoted in Nilant, i. 23 n.
[3] Greene to Rosmead, 10 Dec. 1896 in Rosmead to Chamberlain, 15 Dec. 1896. C.O. 417/185.
[4] C. 9093, pp. 7–8.
[5] See above, pp. 31, 39, and below, p. 187.   [6] Bryce, 301–2; C. 9093, p. 9.

market White salary- and wage-earners on the Witwatersrand continued to draw good pay throughout 1897 and there was little unemployment among them,[1] though some may have left the republic. The value of real property in Johannesburg remained very high until about September. On the other hand, the volume of business began to shrink before the end of the first quarter, and by July it became clear that imports were falling off. A crop of insolvencies during the last quarter of the year indicated that the depression had deepened.[2]

Early in December 1896 Hely-Hutchinson, the governor of Natal, sent Chamberlain an extract from a letter of a 'well-informed' Johannesburg correspondent. The writer believed that the slump in gold shares had been deliberately engineered by the representatives of Wernher, Beit, and company, the largest investors in the gold-mining industry, in order to force the republican government to alter its policy towards the industry so that the cost of production might drop. 'If labour keeps coming in, and mines keep closing down . . . and prices of food keep mounting up as rinderpest spreads . . . genuine discontent will be the result. My reading of recent market operations is that certain people, headed by the house of Eckstein [Wernher, Beit, and company] have determined to try and get the reforms in another way, which they failed to get by their muddle-headed revolution last year.'[3] Though this diagnosis of the slump was probably mistaken, Chamberlain considered it 'interesting'.[4] Lionel Phillips happened to be in London at the time. Chamberlain immediately wrote him a letter, which in its cool audacity is remarkable even for him. Shortly after the raid he had let it be publicly known that he deprecated the idea of closing down mines on the Rand in order to bring about a crisis.[5] Now he took a different line.

Is it probable [he asked Phillips] that any considerable number of mines will be shut down? What effect would this have on the labour market, and what would be the general result on the population of Johannesburg if want of employment made itself felt? Would not any serious depression in the mining industry affect the Revenues of the Transvaal Government? If so, would not this be a legitimate means of bringing pressure to bear to

---

[1] Middelberg mentions some unemployment in Aug. 1897 and 'many unemployed' in Mar. 1898. Middelberg letters (*Hertzog-Annale*, July 1953, pp. 100–1, 130).
[2] C. 9093, pp. 35–39, 43; African (South), 536, p. 297, no. 323; 543, pp. 95–96. There were 108 insolvencies in the republic in 1897 as compared with 38 in 1896. C. 9093, p. 37.
[3] Hely-Hutchinson to Chamberlain, 5 Dec. 1896. Chamberlain papers, H.
[4] Minute, 29 Dec. 1896.
[5] B. F. Hawksley to Fairfield, 1 Feb. 1896 (C.O. 417/201); *Bulletin* (1954), p. 164.

secure the reasonable reforms which are required in order to maintain the prosperity of the Rand? It has been represented to me that the mining magnates of Johannesburg could, if they chose, bring matters to a satisfactory issue by closing the mines, and that in this case the Transvaal Government would be obliged to make concessions in order to secure their revenues.

The letter then proceeded to put questions on other topics, which do not concern us here. Phillips answered that 'in view of the extremely important nature of the questions put, and the paramount necessity for me to use the utmost care in treating these subjects I must beg your indulgence for a little time to frame my reply'.[1] This reply, if it was ever sent, is not now to be found among the Chamberlain papers. We do know, however, that Phillips's firm did not act on the hint of the colonial secretary.

Shortly after the opening of the parliamentary session Chamberlain made a speech in the house of commons which angered Kruger and his supporters[2] and embarrassed some at any rate of the mining magnates. The occasion for his speech was a motion for the reappointment of the committee of inquiry into the raid. He said *inter alia*: An inquiry into the origin of the raid would be a sham unless it went carefully into Uitlander grievances. Kruger 'has again and again promised to give full and favourable consideration' to requests and friendly representations on the subject of reform, and those promises had not been kept.[3] It must have seemed to Kruger that the colonial secretary was preparing the ground for that intervention in the republic's internal affairs which he had forsworn nine months before.[4] He angrily challenged Chamberlain to state the precise promises to Uitlanders which he had not kept.

Chamberlain soon got confirmation as to the effect of his speech on the republican government. He had already learnt that, whatever the attitude of the Wernher, Beit firm might be, other mining

[1] Chamberlain to Phillips, 1 Jan. 1897; Phillips to Chamberlain, 4 Jan. 1897. Quoted by E. Drus in *Bulletin* (1954), pp. 165–6.
[2] They had already been deeply disturbed by the tumultuous reception of Rhodes, by English-speaking citizens mainly, when he journeyed through the Cape Colony from Rhodesia in the last days of 1896 in order to embark for England. He was to appear before the committee of inquiry into the raid. Walker (*a*), 285.
[3] See above, p. 102; *Parliamentary Debates*, 4th series, vol. xlv, cols. 804–6 (29 Jan. 1897).
[4] See above, p. 119. Chamberlain wrote later: 'I wish I knew what was telegraphed them [about the house of commons speech]. There was really nothing . . . to rouse their feelings.' Minute, dated 24 Feb. 1897, on Rosmead to Chamberlain, 23 Feb. 1897. C.O. 537/131.

magnates were hopeful of the outcome of a friendly approach to the Transvaal authorities. Thus, for example, Hely-Hutchinson's informant stated that the representative of 'a very powerful French group' told him that if Wernher, Beit attempted 'to starve the Government' by closing mines they would fail, 'as many groups, his own included, would bring out a Transvaal loan . . . '.[1] Again, Sapte, the manager of the Consolidated Goldfields company (Rhodes's company)[2] told the assistant military secretary to the G.O.C., South Africa, that

Kruger and his Executive have of late shown marked signs of a conciliatory attitude towards the Uitlanders, and he [Sapte] particularly instanced the Sunday labour and mining titles questions,[3] in both of which they listened with readiness to the objections raised by the representatives of the mining community, and altered the proposals which would have materially affected their interests. . . . Sapte views the situation entirely now from the mining point of view, and in this he says he is in agreement with the majority of the Uitlanders, whose present aim is to make money in peace. Mr Rudd [chairman of Consolidated Goldfields] . . . evidently takes the same view, and last Sunday spoke to me with horror of the possibility of any war which would further depreciate property. Sapte tells me that the Transvaal Government will probably desire soon to raise a considerable loan . . . and they are therefore now honestly anxious to encourage the gold industry, and so improve their national credit.[4]

George Farrar was another magnate who had been working for better relations between the government and the mining industry. Shortly after Chamberlain spoke in the house of commons he telegraphed to London as follows: 'Chamberlain's speech bad, most disturbing effect created. Increased unrest. Distrust among Boers who greatly resent it. There is no chance country will settle down. Friendly negotiations now almost impossible. My line [of] policy permanently injured.'[5] To Altham, the assistant military secretary already cited, Farrar said: 'If it [Chamberlain's speech] was not meant as the expression of a policy which will be firmly pressed and

[1] Hely-Hutchinson to Chamberlain, 7 Dec. 1896. Chamberlain papers, H.

[2] After the raid Rhodes, though he continued to attack the Kruger government from the outside (so to speak), refrained from active interference with regard to the internal administration of the republic. See Williams, 299.

[3] The recently passed Sunday labour law permitted the mining companies to use not more than 5 per cent. of their staff to keep their machinery going on Sundays. African (South), 516, p. 422. What action the government took with regard to the mining titles question I do not know.

[4] Altham to Northcott, 24 Dec. 1896. C.O. 537/133.

[5] George Farrar to Sydney Farrar, 15 or 16 Feb. 1897. Chamberlain papers, A.

steadily pursued, it will do much mischief, as it makes for the moment the position of the Uitlanders difficult and throws back their chances of conciliating the Boers.'[1] Altham was also told by a certain Glyn, who knew all the leading Uitlanders, that 'before Mr Chamberlain's speech . . . there was a prospect of confidence in the mining industry reviving and the capitalists were preparing to put in more money. The speech, however, has destroyed this hope of returning prosperity. . . .'[2]

The judgement delivered by chief justice Kotze in the case *Brown* v. *Leyds* threatened to undermine confidence still further. Kotze had sat on the Transvaal bench since 1877. Like his 'brother' at the Cape, chief justice de Villiers, he hankered after a political career. He had stood as a candidate in the presidential election of 1893 without resigning from the bench.[3] Fairfield of the colonial office wrote of him as 'an ambitious, intriguing man who wants to be President, or a K.C.M.G., or both'.[4] He did not see eye to eye with Kruger's Hollander officials, and was in favour of large concessions to the Uitlanders. He had on various occasions since 1881 been called to their counsels by the Boer authorities, the last such occasion being the raid crisis. At that time—Leyds being away in Europe—he had rendered the government yeoman service, and his influence had been considerable.[5] But after Leyds's return from Europe in April 1896 Kotze's influence seems to have waned. Early in 1897, a few days before he gave his judgement in the *Brown* case, he had his first of many interviews with Greene, the new British agent in Pretoria. He told the latter that 'he was not consulted in framing of recent laws [presumably the expulsion, immigration, and press laws], holds strong views respecting their legality and would be only too glad of an opportunity of having their validity tested before him in the High Court'.[6] According to Greene the 'progressives' in the republic were doing their utmost to secure Kotze's election as state secretary in the place of Leyds, when the latter's term of office expired in May.[7] Commenting on the crisis precipitated by the *Brown* judgement,

---

[1] Altham to Northcott, 8 Feb. 1897, in director of military intelligence to colonial office, 2 Mar. 1897. C.O. 537/133.

[2] Altham to Northcott, 27 Feb. 1897, in director of military intelligence to colonial office, 24 Mar. 1897. C.O. 537/133.

[3] Van Oordt, 571–2.

[4] Minute, 11 Feb. 1896. C.O. 417/152.

[5] Kotze, ii. 27–29, 33–36, 56–57, 68–71, 215–16, 231–64; Garrett, 175–6, 217–18; Botha, 499–500.

[6] Rosmead to Chamberlain, 18 Jan. 1897. C.O. 537/131.

[7] Greene to high commissioner, 21 Jan. 1897. African (South), 532, pp. 19–21.

judge Buchanan[1] of the Cape declared that it was an incident in the contest between Kotze and Leyds for the state secretaryship.[2]

The case *Brown* v. *Leyds* was tried by the high court in November, 1895. The government did not dispute the facts laid before the court on behalf of the plaintiff. On 19 June 1895 a presidential proclamation had appeared in the *Staatscourant* declaring part of a certain farm to be a public digging as from 19 July. 'One speculator, Brown, had engaged a number of men to peg [claims] for him; others did the like.' The police reported that most of these men were armed, whereupon the executive council, 'alarmed at the prospect of a collision between the charging platoons, withdrew the proclamation . . . '.[3] But the announcement withdrawing the proclamation only appeared in the *Staatscourant* on 20 July, the day after Brown had pegged 1,200 claims. Two days later he served a summons on the state secretary calling on him either to issue a prospecting licence for his claims or to pay damages to the amount of £372,400. The executive council thereupon induced the volksraad to pass a resolution legalizing its action.[4]

There seems to be no doubt that the authorities had acted in good faith to meet the kind of emergency that might suddenly face a weak government in the unprecedented conditions existing in the South African Republic. Yet the fact remains that the volksraad had passed an *ex post facto* law and interfered in a case in which legal proceedings had already begun.[5] Moreover, in this very year another attempt was made to interfere legislatively in an action pending before the court. The action had been brought by the chamber of mines against the company which owned the Macarthur–Forrest cyanide patent.[6] A committee of the second volksraad proposed certain amendments to the patent law, one of which, suggested by Kruger himself, would have had the effect of stopping the chamber's suit. The second volksraad decided, however, by the casting vote of its chairman not to proceed with the amendments until the people had been consulted.[7]

The *Brown* case was tried by three judges—Kotze, Ameshoff, and Morice. Judgement was delivered after a delay of fourteen months on

---

[1] It is not clear whether the judge referred to is James or E. J. Buchanan. Both of them knew Kotze.
[2] Altham to Northcott, 27 Feb. 1897. African (South), 532, p. 46.
[3] The quotations are from Walker (*a*), 289.
[4] Green book no. 1, 1898, pp. 9–10.
[5] Ibid., pp. 9, 27–28.
[6] See above, p. 20.
[7] *Notulen*, Tweede Volksraad, 1895, pp. 651–2, 668; Etheredge, 92–93.

22 January 1897. Morice found for the plaintiff on the ground that according to the constitution of the republic the legislature and the judiciary were separate and independent authorities acting each within its own sphere. To interfere in cases already before the court, as the volksraad had done, no doubt inadvertently, was to go counter to the spirit of the constitution. It could not be presumed that the volksraad intended to do this, unless such intention was explicitly stated.[1] Kotze, with the concurrence of Ameshoff, took higher ground, and their majority judgement became the judgement of the court.

Kotze's judgement raised the vital issue of the validity of volksraad legislation. The constitution provided that three months' notice of proposed laws had to be given before their introduction into the volksraad 'except in the case of laws which can brook no delay'.[2] Laws passed after due notice to the public came to be known as *wetten*; those passed without such notice as *besluiten* (resolutions). A great deal of the legislation of the republic was in the form of *besluiten*. In two judgements delivered in 1884 and 1887 Kotze had held that the legality of *besluiten* could not be questioned by the courts. But not long before the raid he decided that something should be done to check hasty legislation in order, he wrote later, to protect the minority in the state against the majority 'especially at a time when political feeling runs high'.[3] In May 1895, giving judgement in the case *Hess* v. *the State*, he pronounced an *obiter dictum* foreshadowing his judgement in the *Brown* case.[4]

In the latter judgement Kotze decided in favour of the plaintiff[5] on the grounds first, that the court was obliged to 'test' every volksraad *wet* by the touchstone of the constitution and that a *wet* which was in conflict with the constitution was null and void; and second, that a volksraad *besluit* was not a law at all and was therefore not binding on the courts.[6] But the so-called constitution, which had

---

[1] Green book no. 1, 1898, pp. 24–28.
[2] Arts. 12, 47, 66, and 67 of the constitution: Eybers, 365, 373, 377–8.
[3] Walker (a), 288–9; green book no. 1, 1898, pp. 1–8, 19.
[4] Webber and Kotze, ii. 114–21.
[5] The court also decided that the amount of damages to which the plaintiff was entitled would have to be determined later—after evidence and argument. Shortly after Kotze's dismissal in Feb. 1898 the court decided that the whole case would have to be argued from the beginning. This Brown refused to do, and he appealed instead to the 'Suzerain power'. The colonial office advised him in Dec. 1898 'as an American citizen . . . to bring the matter, in the first place, fully to the notice of the government of the United States'. African (South), 543, pp. 197, 230, 609–13, 669.
[6] Green book no. 1, 1898, pp. 15–16.

been drawn up between 1855 and 1858 by men with little or no legal training, contained 'much miscellaneous material alien to a fundamental law'.[1] If it was intended to be a fundamental law, its framers had shown a signal lack of foresight in omitting to make provision for its amendment. It is no exaggeration to say that Kotze's judgement was revolutionary in its implications. It rendered a great deal, perhaps most, of the republic's legislation potentially inoperative and threatened many established rights.[2]

It is hard to believe that Kotze intended to produce the chaos which would have resulted from the application of his doctrine by the courts. It seems more probable that he wanted to induce the government to devise safeguards against hasty legislation and to turn to him for assistance. Indeed, shortly after the *Brown* judgement he and his brother judges offered their help in the solution of the difficulties caused by that judgement.[3] But the government had already taken the grave decision that no judge accepting Kotze's doctrine—described as that of the 'testing right'—could remain on the bench. (Greene explained later that Kruger was very suspicious of the motives of Kotze, 'who was a rival at the time of Dr Leyds for the post of State Secretary'.[4] And Kruger did, in fact, express himself in strong terms about Kotze's lack of loyalty and patriotism.[5]) The government's decision was embodied in law 1 of 1897, which was passed by the volksraad on 26 February 1897 and empowered the president to dismiss any judge who persisted in claiming the testing right. Kotze's four colleagues resolved to stand by him in defence of 'the independence of the High Court', though two of them did not claim the testing right. When the judges were formally asked to state their attitude to Kotze's doctrine not later than 17 March they replied by refusing to go on circuit.[6]

This clash between the government and the judiciary coming as it did on top of the economic difficulties in the republic and its unresolved disputes with the British government, produced an atmosphere of crisis. The judges had appealed to the people. A resolution supporting them had been adopted by many advocates and solicitors in Johannesburg, and a protest against law 1 of 1897 obtained 13,000

[1] The quotation is from *C.H.B.E.* viii. 389.
[2] Green book no. 1, 1898, p. 72; van Oordt, 783.
[3] Green book no. 1, 1898, p. 44.
[4] Greene to High Commissioner, 20 Mar. 1897. African (South), 536, pp. 15–16.
[5] Fitzpatrick to Beit, 22 Mar. 1897 (C.O. 537/133); Sir H. de Villiers's notes of his interview with Kruger published in the *Cape Times*, 12 Feb. 1898.
[6] Green book no. 1, 1898, pp. 44, 79.

signatures.[1] 'Naturally', writes Walker, 'the Uitlander Press and its allies in the [Cape] Colony made the most of their opportunity.'[2] It was under these circumstances that chief justice de Villiers, with the concurrence of Kotze, decided to mediate between the judges and their government. De Villiers disagreed with Kotze's judgement in the *Brown* case. He said later that he 'felt constrained by an imperative sense of duty to go to Pretoria'.[3] The situation was indeed serious; and the Transvaal's internal difficulties were not the only factor that made it so. De Villiers had been deeply angered by the raid and by Rhodes's part in it.[4] Now Rhodes, after his triumphal tour of the Cape Colony,[5] was being leniently treated by the committee of inquiry in London,[6] while the government members of the committee, including the colonial secretary, were encouraging him to enlarge upon the iniquities of the republican government, which, suggested the colonial secretary, was 'a source of danger to the peace of South Africa'.[7] Rhodes's examination by the committee had been preceded by Chamberlain's speech in the house of commons,[8] in which he had expressed 'considerable anxiety' with regard to 'the situation in South Africa' and had referred to certain recent legislation of the republic as an infringement of the London convention. De Villiers had long been an ardent supporter of a union of the South African colonies and republics under the British flag. But he wished for a 'peaceful union', not one imposed by force and bought at the price of chaos in the Transvaal.[9]

De Villiers reached Pretoria on 15 March and within four days, after interviews with the judges and the president, he had negotiated an agreement between the contending parties, much to the annoyance of the British-Uitlander press in the republic and like-minded newspapers in other parts of South Africa.[10] The agreement was in the following terms:

... The Judges will ... not test the existing and future laws and Volksraad resolutions by reference to the Grondwet. The judges declare this on the understanding that your Honour [the president] will, as soon as practicable [zoo spoedig doenlijk] submit a Bill to the ... Volksraad whereby the Constitution or Grondwet (guaranteeing *inter alia* the independence

---

[1] Kotze (*a*), 10–11, 13; African (South), 536, p. 16.
[2] Walker (*a*), 291.   [3] Ibid. 300.
[4] Ibid. 273, 286, 300.   [5] See above, p. 138 n. 2.
[6] His examination started on 16 Feb. and ended on 5 Mar. The proceedings were reported in the press.
[7] Van der Poel (*b*), 202, 207.   [8] See above, p. 138.
[9] Walker (*a*), 300, 313; Headlam, i. 79–80.   [10] Walker (*a*), 292–7.

of the High Court) will be placed on a firm basis, so that no alterations can be made therein except only by special legislation. In the drafting of such a Bill the Judges are prepared to give the Government . . . all possible help.[1]

'The anti-Government . . . papers', reported Greene, 'are in a frenzy of rage. . . . The Johannesburg *Star* is especially indignant. . . . It was confidently expected at Johannesburg . . . that the crisis' would result 'in the intervention of Her Majesty's Government, and it is the disappointment felt by the British community at being baulked of this expectation that is the cause of all their heartburning'.[2]

The colonial office followed the constitutional crisis with lively interest. From the start Kotze had kept in touch with Greene. Before 10 February he told the latter about the projected law 1.[3] On 20 February Greene telegraphed his knowledge of what happened in the secret session in which the volksraad discussed the law. Chamberlain's laconic comment was *quos Deus*, which means, the missing words being supplied: 'Whom God wishes to destroy, he first makes mad.'[4] Then came the news that Kotze had spoken to Greene about law 1 as a breach of the Pretoria and London conventions.[5] About the same time Greene telegraphed: 'I learn that Commandant-General [Joubert] went . . . on Saturday night to the President and warned him . . . to refer question at issue to the decision of the people. . . .' Having read Greene's telegram, the permanent under-secretary minuted: '. . . Kruger has put his foot into it this time.' To which Chamberlain replied: 'Brer Fox he lay low—but he grin.'[6]

Brer Fox grinned too soon, as we have seen. Towards the end of March Alfred Beit delivered at the colonial office a telegram he had received, apparently from J. P. Fitzpatrick. It was dated 19 March and read as follows:

Chief Justice of Cape Colony at present in Pretoria; have every reason to believe wants make fresh ministry with J. W. Sauer, Merriman, J. H. Hofmeyr, W. P. Schreiner with Chief Justice Cape Colony Premier of

---

[1] Green book no. 1, 1898, p. 80.
[2] Greene to high commissioner, 20 Mar. 1897. African (South), 536, pp. 15–16.
[3] Greene to Rosmead, 10 Feb. 1897 in Rosmead to Chamberlain, 16 Feb. 1897. C.O. 537/131.
[4] Rosmead to Chamberlain, 20 Feb. 1897 and Chamberlain's minute, 22 Feb. C.O. 417/215.
[5] Rosmead to Chamberlain, 2 Mar. 1897. C.O. 417/215.
[6] Rosmead to Chamberlain, 2 Mar. 1897, and minutes by Wingfield and Chamberlain, 3 Mar. C.O. 537/131.

Cape Colony. Object visit obtain assistance from Paul Kruger with Cape Colony Boers, so work against C. J. Rhodes.[1]

In connexion with this telegram the following exchanges took place in the colonial office:

G. V. FIDDES: [The telegram] goes a long way to explain Schreiner's curious attitude before the Committee [of inquiry].[2] . . . I strongly hope that a letter will appear in the Times . . . which after calling attention to the puzzle of the Chief Justice's unauthorised visit to the S.A.R. will point out that the clue to the mystery is . . . in this telegram.

CHAMBERLAIN: If publicity is to be given to these suspicions I think Miss Shaw[3] should be seen. Possibly the Times would write an article.

F. GRAHAM: I saw Miss S. . . . She told me that they had received the information as to De V's scheme. I asked whether it was likely to become publicly known. She said that they did not propose to publish it at present as it was only a rumour which might be strenuously denied. But no doubt the Times would publish it if pressed to do so.

F. GRAHAM (ten days later): . . . An article dealing with the question has appeared in the Times.[4]

It would appear, therefore, that *The Times* acted, somewhat reluctantly, on a hint or under pressure from the colonial office. Its article appeared on 5 April, two days after Rhodes's departure for South Africa.

De Villiers [writes his biographer] was preparing, *The Times* declared, to fight Rhodes for the premiership in a trial of strength between Dutch and English. His visit to Pretoria was connected in . . . 'the public mind' with the formation of an 'anti-Rhodes coalition with President Kruger as an outside member'. The coming general elections, in short, would perhaps involve the issue of British supremacy in South Africa. At first de Villiers could hardly believe his eyes but at last he saw the wild accusation was serious.[5]

Chamberlain did not at once give up the hope of gaining some advantage from the constitutional crisis in the republic. He obtained

---

[1] C.O. 537/133. A similar allegation, though in more general terms, was made by Kotze, who ought to have known better, in a confidential conversation with Greene. Milner to Chamberlain, 6 May 1897. C.O. 537/132.

[2] W. P. Schreiner had been a member of Rhodes's second Cape ministry (1893–6). For Chamberlain's questioning of him see Walker (c), 91–94. He repeatedly, but in vain, tried to get Schreiner to admit the gravity of the Uitlanders' grievances. Chamberlain seemed to be convinced, writes Walker, that 'Rhodes was still the coming man in Southern Africa'.

[3] See above, p. 75.

[4] Minutes, 24 Mar. to 5 Apr. 1897. C.O. 537/133.   [5] Walker (a), 299.

an opinion from the law officers that he would be within his rights to protest against law 1 if it had been passed without the formalities laid down by the constitution. This opinion appeared to him 'very important. . . . I understand that at the present time there are Resolutions of the Volksraad which the Government enforces as laws. It matters nothing to us that the High Court will now recognise them as laws. They are not laws to us and we may remonstrate against their enforcement'. He was warned, however, by a member of his staff, that 'if we dispute the validity of such legislation we may possibly do great injury to the interests of British subjects'. This argument apparently convinced Chamberlain, since no further action was taken in the matter.[1]

In the midst of the constitutional crisis Kruger led a delegation to the Orange Free State in order to discuss the conclusion of a new alliance between the two republics. President Steyn agreed with Kruger that their states must stand or fall together. At the same time there was a great deal in his neighbour's administration of which he did not approve.[2] On 17 March a treaty was signed to take the place of the treaty of alliance concluded eight years before. The nature of the treaty of 1897 seems to have been generally misunderstood. The most important clause—binding the two republics to assist each other 'when the independence of one of the two States may be threatened or attacked, unless the State which should render the assistance can show the injustice of the cause of the other State'—was taken *verbatim* from the earlier treaty.[3] It constituted therefore, in itself,[4] no new 'threat' to British interests. A new clause was the one which provided for consultation between the two governments. Steyn declared later that this clause was inserted at his request: he wished to have the right to object to any 'steps' of his ally that might be 'dangerous'.[5] The treaty also proclaimed the ideal of a federal union between the two republics and provided for the establishment of

---

[1] Law officers to Chamberlain, 2 Apr. 1897 and minutes by Chamberlain, 10 Apr. and F. Graham, 18 Apr. C.O. 417/226.

[2] Walker (*a*), 291, 303; van der Merwe, i. 143, 158. Pp. 116–229 of volume I of van der Merwe's life of Steyn contain the latter's account of events in which he took part. It was dictated to his wife, apparently shortly before 1912, and was not intended for publication as it stood. Van der Merwe, i, preface.

[3] Except for the omission of the words 'from outside' after 'threatened or attacked'. Yet Walker, though he calls the alliance of 1889 'defensive', describes that of 1897 as 'offensive and defensive'. Walker (*b*), 409, 464. See also Cd. 1789, p. 177.

[4] For a discussion of the Transvaal's armaments, which are, of course, relevant in this connexion, see below, pp. 157–8.

[5] Van der Merwe, i. 138.

a permanent advisory council to make recommendations for the purpose of paving the way to union.[1]

Greene kept on warning the colonial office that he had secret and reliable information[2] that as a result of the alliance of 1897 the government of the South African Republic proposed 'to benefit by any treaties its ally chose to make [with foreign powers] without let or hindrance of the Queen'.[3] It should be noted, however, first, that the republic obtained an opinion from Rivier, the author of the *Principes du droit des Gens*, that article IV of the London convention forbade either of the allies to make treaties detrimental to the interests of Britain,[4] and second, that the Orange Free State did not, in fact, act in the sense suggested by Greene. I am unable to say whether Chamberlain took Greene's warnings seriously at the outset; but early in 1898 the colonial office wrote to the foreign office: 'Mr Chamberlain does not understand how the independent position of the Orange Free State is to be utilized to advance the objects of the South African Republic.' He took the precaution, nevertheless, of asking the foreign office to keep a look-out for any treaties the former state might make.[5]

II

During the months of January and February 1897 the colonial office was giving careful consideration to two important dispatches, finally dated 6 March,[6] the one summing up the British case against

[1] Botha, 769–76.
[2] During the years 1897–9 Greene gave the colonial office a great deal of information about the proceedings of the executive council of the republic, which deliberated, of course, in secret. He knew *inter alia* the contents of many of the telegrams of the republican representatives in Europe. The main source of Greene's knowledge was a certain Baron de Matalha, *alias* Edward Cohen, in whom he had great confidence and who apparently got his information from 'some clerk within the State Secretary's office'. Minute by Fairfield, 11 Aug. 1896 (C.O. 537/130). An official in the colonial office in 1899 described Matalha as 'a previous Portuguese Consul-General in Pretoria, who went bankrupt about five years ago and is now supposed to pursue the vocation of a financier but depends to a great extent for his livelihood upon Eckstein [of the firm Wernher, Beit, and company] whom he supplies with confidential information for a salary. The information Mr Beit supplies us with comes from him. Mr Fraser [Greene's secretary] . . . was inclined to doubt the value of the Baron's information.' Minute by H. W. Just, 29 Mar. 1899 on Milner to Chamberlain, 27 Mar. 1899 (C.O. 417/133); Greene to H. F. Wilson, 22 Apr. 1897 (C.O. 537/133); also Rosmead to Chamberlain, 6 Mar. 1897 (C.O. 537/133); and Kotze, ii. 210 n. 2.
[3] *C.H.B.E.* viii. 575; Greene's dispatches during 1897, *passim*.
[4] Botha, 780–4. Rivier's opinion is dated 3 June 1897.
[5] F. Graham to foreign office, 13 Jan. 1898. C.O. 537/134.
[6] C. 8423, nos. 120 and 121.

the republic on the score of the latter's breaches of the London convention, the other demanding the immediate repeal or suspension of the immigration law.[1] The draft of the latter was 'stiffened ... a little' by Chamberlain, '. . . as it is evident from Greene's letters that we must put our foot down if we are to keep our ground [?] in this matter'.[2] Early in March, and once more early in April, Montagu White, the consul-general of the republic in London, repeated to his government the warnings he had received from certain prominent Liberals. Chamberlain's attitude towards the republic, they said, had become distinctly hostile; he was doing his best to create a public opinion in favour of war; it would, therefore, be in the interest of the republic to make concessions.[3] Sir Alfred Milner, too, who was about to take over from Robinson as high commissioner, noted that Chamberlain's speech at the farewell banquet given in his honour was 'rather bellicose'.[4] The colonial office minutes also made it clear that the secretary of state was at this time keenly alive to possible causes for complaint against the Transvaal.[5]

Yet as late as the middle of March he had not made up his mind to fight if his specific demand regarding the repeal of the immigration law was turned down. He did not believe that 'our grievances though very serious would justify this extreme step'.[6] He meant no doubt that public opinion would not support a declaration of war. A year earlier he had written that if the Boers took the offensive 'they would supply that force [of public opinion] behind Her Majesty's Government which is wanting at present and without which we cannot face the despatch of an army corps and the expenditure of millions'.[7] Now he told Greene that only if the Boers 'put themselves completely in the wrong . . . would [we] secure that popular support for our action, in South Africa as well as in this country, without which we can hardly hope to carry matters to a successful conclusion'.[8]

Chamberlain might be undecided; Selborne, his parliamentary under-secretary, was not. Milner had told Selborne that he was not in favour of demanding the repeal of the immigration law; but should

---

[1] See above, p. 127.

[2] Chamberlain's minute, 28 Feb. 1897, on Rosmead to Chamberlain, 27 Jan. 1897. C.O. 417/214.

[3] Breytenbach, 187–8, 193; Scholtz, ii. 86–87.

[4] Headlam, i. 35.

[5] C.O. 417/214 and 215.

[6] Memorandum, 16 Mar. 1897, entitled 'Where do we go from here?' Chamberlain papers, C.

[7] Minute, 27 May, on war office to colonial office, 15 May 1896. C.O. 537/130.

[8] Chamberlain to Greene, 13 Mar. 1897. C.O. 537/133.

such a demand be made, then the British government must fight if it were persistently rejected, or be 'terribly discredited'.[1] Selborne had originally approved of the dispatches of 6 March, and still did so. But he now warned his chief that unless the cabinet was prepared to go to war if the republic proved recalcitrant, the dispatches should be withdrawn.[2] Selborne's outspoken minute helped Chamberlain to clarify his mind. He decided that he would have the dispatches presented and face the consequences.

On 15 April Greene presented the dispatches to Kruger, commandant-general Joubert being present, and gave him also the following message from Chamberlain:[3] The Transvaal government had 'ignored and evaded' the convention in its immigration law as well as in its extradition treaties with Portugal and the Netherlands. 'Her Majesty's Government had been considering how it might be possible to demonstrate their determination to maintain their rights in their integrity to the Transvaal Government. They had accordingly decided that a considerable force of ships, larger than any they had ever before had in these waters, should rendezvous at Durban and then at Delagoa Bay, thereby indicating their intention to all the world of preserving the status quo at that place. . . .' 'The President', reported Greene, 'evidently was greatly startled when I came to the mention of the ships; he started up and got very excited. . . . He declared that I was holding a knife to his throat, and pressing for an answer.'[4] A few days later Greene telegraphed: 'The President is reported to be off his balance and much cut up.'[5]

Chamberlain's message to Kruger seems to give some support to Walker's suggestion that the main purpose of the dispatch of the naval squadron to Delagoa Bay was to maintain the *status quo* at that port, over which the republic was striving, with the assistance of Germany, to acquire 'some sort of control, direct or indirect'.[6] But Chamberlain himself gave a conclusive answer to this suggestion. 'I am unwilling', he wrote to Greene, 'as at present advised, to send out reinforcements of troops [to show Britain's determination to maintain her rights under the convention], because such a step might have a provocative effect. . . . Accordingly the Government have

[1] Headlam, i. 27–29.
[2] Minute, 22 Mar. 1897. Chamberlain papers, C.
[3] This message was included in Chamberlain's letter to Greene, dated 13 Mar. 1897. C.O. 537/133.
[4] Greene's report, 17 Apr. 1897, of interview with Kruger. Chamberlain papers, C.
[5] Rosmead to Chamberlain, 18 Apr. 1897. C.O. 537/131.
[6] *C.H.B.E.* viii. 572–3, 575–6.

decided *as an alternative* [my italics] ... to arrange for a considerable force of ships ... to rendezvous ... at Delagoa Bay. ...'[1] This decision having been taken, Chamberlain determined to use the opportunity to refer also to the Delagoa Bay question.

III

It is the fact that Germany gave the republic no support at Lisbon or at Lourenço Marques during the years 1896 and 1897.[2] The British foreign and colonial offices, which were extremely well informed about proceedings in respect of the Bay, must have been aware of this. On the other hand, there could of course be no certainty, at any time during 1896–7, that Germany would stick to the line of non-co-operation. From time to time information reached the colonial office about the 'intrigues' of the Transvaal to obtain a footing at Delagoa Bay and its hopes of German support. Thus Greene told his chief about the intention of the republic 'to arrange on a definite basis the understanding already arrived at [with Germany] with regard to the advancement of mutual interests on the east coast and at Delagoa Bay'.[3] Nothing seems to have come of this project. In March 1897, apparently as a result of the sudden death of Beelaerts van Blokland, the republic's diplomatic representative,[4] it was decided that Leyds should proceed to Europe. According to Greene his objects were to obtain a foothold at Delagoa Bay and to secure the co-operation of France and Germany in furtherance of the interests of the republic.[5]

The co-operation of 'France and Germany' was to be, in part at any rate, economic. It has already been pointed out that it was the policy of the republic to counter British pressure, which included economic pressure, by seeking support on the continent of Europe.[6] One of Leyds's projects was to secure the laying of a second cable along the east coast of Africa as far as Delagoa Bay to compete with

---

[1] Chamberlain to Greene, 13 Mar. 1897. C.O. 537/133.
[2] See above, p. 100; van Winter, ii. 277–81.
[3] Greene to Rosmead, 30 Jan., in Rosmead to Chamberlain, 8 Feb. 1897. C.O. 537/131.
[4] Van Winter, ii. 278.
[5] Greene to Rosmead, 26 Mar., in Rosmead to Chamberlain, 31 Mar. 1897. C.O. 537/131. The colonial office does not seem to have heard of Leyds's proposed visit before 20 Mar., when the decision to send the naval squadron to Delagoa Bay had already been taken.
[6] See above, p. 46.

the existing cable of the (British) Eastern Telegraph company, whose service was considered—not only by the republic—to be unsatisfactory.[1] The republic was prepared to subsidize the new company, and Leyds hoped to interest French capital and the French government in his project. By the beginning of 1898 the plan had advanced so far that Britain took official note of it. MacDonell, the British minister at Lisbon, warned the Portuguese foreign minister that if his government permitted a cable to be laid to Delagoa Bay, 'I anticipated that it would lead to a serious question with Her Majesty's Government, the more so as I had reason to apprehend that this proposal formed part of a wider scheme to foster French interests in Portuguese East Africa, in connivance with the Transvaal, to the detriment of those of Great Britain. . . .'[2] In the end nothing came of Leyds's cable plans.

A similar fate overtook his plan to secure a weekly Franco-German shipping service, which his government was prepared to subsidize, between Delagoa Bay and Europe. The ships of both German and French lines were already calling at Delagoa Bay, but Leyds's desire was to have a more frequent service to Europe along the east (African) coast route.[3] If this hope had been realized, Chamberlain would certainly have considered that Britain had another serious grievance against the republic. As early as July 1896 one of his officials had drawn his attention to subsidized German and (projected) French east coast lines, the latter being pledged not to call at British ports.[4] On 30 July he minuted:[5] '. . . I think we have evidence of deliberate hostility to British Trade. It may not be surprising and it is not a "casus belli" but it is useless to shut our eyes to it. . . . If the case is strong enough I am determined to publish it and let the world judge. The French and the Germans may be very pleased but I desire to know what the British public think of it.' The case was not, however, thought strong enough: at any rate it was not published.

Leyds's stay in Europe lasted from April to July 1897. One of his main objects, as Greene had reported, was to obtain a foothold in

---

[1] Botha, ch. xiv; MacDonell to Salisbury, 19 Jan., in foreign office to colonial office, 27 Jan. 1898 (C.O. 537/134).
[2] MacDonell to Salisbury, 19 Jan., in foreign office to colonial office, 27 Jan. 1898. C.O. 537/134.
[3] Scholtz, ii. 27–29.
[4] Minute by G. V. Fiddes, 20 July. C.O. 417/192.
[5] Minute on Cloete to Goodenough, 19 June, in Goodenough to Chamberlain, 27 June 1896. C.O. 417/182.

Delagoa Bay. He showed an interest in two rather nebulous schemes which would issue in the republic's getting control of the harbour of Lourenço Marques and the Portuguese end of the Delagoa Bay–Johannesburg railway. But the negotiations did not get beyond the exploratory stage.[1] (Chamberlain remarked later: 'Leyds's schemes are numerous as leaves in Vallombrosa.'[2]) A more serious project in which Leyds took an interest was the exploitation of the so-called Eiffe or Katembe grant. In 1895 certain persons obtained from the governor-general of Mozambique a concession permitting them to construct a pier on the south bank of the river Espiritu Santo opposite Lourenço Marques, as well as to store coal for ships and effect shipping repairs. The grant included an area of river frontage or foreshore. One, F. R. Eiffe, a German, acting on behalf of the republican government, bought up this concession. The government decided in March 1897 that Eiffe should form a company with a capital of £250,000 to which the republic would contribute £200,000 for the purpose of exploiting the concession. The idea was to get the grant extended so that it would include permission to construct harbour works of considerable magnitude.[3] These were sorely needed. Delagoa Bay was the best natural harbour on the South African coast; but the Portuguese government, owing to chronic lack of funds, had done little to make it attractive to commerce. The harbour services and appliances were primitive. Hence the unloading of cargo at the port of Lourenço Marques was slow and difficult. There was also insufficient storage room ashore.[4]

It was easy enough to acquire a concession from the Mozambique authorities. The difficulty was to get it ratified in Portugal. That required the consent not only of the government but also of the cortes.[5] The government was subject to pressure from powerful neighbours. Before Leyds left Europe in July[6] he must have been

---

[1] Van Winter, ii. 278–80; Scholtz, ii. 30–31.

[2] Minute, 2 Mar., on report from Wernher dated 6 Jan. 1899. C.O. 417/259.

[3] Scholtz, ii. 32–35; van Winter, ii. 249–50; Roger Casement to Salisbury, 7 Mar. 1897 (C.O. 417/228).

[4] Van Winter, ii. 223–5; van der Poel (a), 91.

[5] Anderson to Fiddes, 26 Mar. 1896 (C.O. 537/129); foreign office to colonial office, 25 Jan. 1899—enclosure (C.O. 417/271); Scholtz, i. 213.

[6] In May and June Leyds had an interview and carried on some correspondence with Chamberlain. The negotiations were broken off because the former failed to obtain from his government full powers to treat. Memorandum by Chamberlain of his interview with Leyds on 15 May 1897; Chamberlain to Leyds, 7 and 17 June; Leyds to Chamberlain, 9 and 14 June; minutes by Chamberlain, Graham, and Selborne, 6–12 June. Chamberlain papers, C. See also Headlam, i. 68–69, 71; Garvin, iii. 145–7; Scholtz, ii. 91–94.

aware that there was strong opposition to the Eiffe concession and he probably suspected from what quarter it came.

That quarter was the British government. It was Britain's policy, as Chamberlain told Kruger, to maintain the *status quo* at Delagoa Bay[1]—unless it could be altered in favour of Britain. To maintain the *status quo* meant to oppose the grant of any concessions whatever in the province of Lourenço Marques. For this purpose Britain stretched to the limit—and beyond it—her right of pre-emption over Portuguese East Africa south of the Zambesi. In an unsigned foreign office memorandum transmitted to the colonial office on 1 March 1897[2] it is stated that by virtue of the right of pre-emption

and fortified by an opinion of the law officers, we have on various occasions warned the Portuguese government that we should consider that any concessions which injure the value of the territories in question[3] would be a breach of the spirit of the Treaty and engagements[4] . . . and have received assurances that pending the Berne Award[5] the Portuguese government will entertain no offer or proposal whatever for concessions [without first communicating with the British government]. We have, however, been unable to obtain any pledges as to what may happen after that event. . . . It was Sir P. Anderson's[6] opinion, and I see no reason for differing from it, that there is nothing in the Katembe Eiffe concession which would give us the right to protest against it. The air is full of rumours of concessions of all sorts in the Portuguese territories and undoubtedly French, German and Transvaal capital is largely interested in them, and seeking further acquisitions which may give their Governments ground for intervention in the future, but unless British capital will outbid its rivals it is difficult to see what we can do so long as [Portuguese] sovereign rights are not weakened.

The attitude of the British government was, however, that it could do a great deal. Its minister at Lisbon used strong language, which the Portuguese government was unable to ignore, on the subject of

---

[1] See above, p. 150.

[2] C.O. 417/227.

[3] It should be noted that this goes well beyond an injury to rights of sovereignty.

[4] The Anglo-Portuguese treaty of 1891, and the agreement made prior to the MacMahon award of 1875.

[5] In 1889 the Portuguese government had expropriated the railway which the Delagoa Bay and East African railway company—an Anglo-American concern—was building to the Transvaal frontier. See above, p. 35. On the demand of the British and American governments Portugal agreed to refer to Swiss arbitration the amount of compensation that should be paid to the company. By 1897 it was anticipated that the award could not be much longer delayed, and that the Portuguese government would have difficulty in finding the money which it would be called upon to pay. Actually judgement was only delivered in 1900.

[6] A member of the staff of the foreign office.

concessions in East Africa.[1] With regard to the Katembe concession, the minister was instructed, at Chamberlain's request, to tell the Portuguese foreign minister that the grant of part of the foreshore at Delagoa Bay to the Katembe concessionaires 'would make it necessary to raise the whole question of the pre-emptive rights of Her Majesty's Government'.[2]

It is clear from the foregoing that the British government had taken precautions to counter any move that might be construed as altering the *status quo* at Delagoa Bay. But Chamberlain was not satisfied with the mere preservation of the *status quo*. In fact the farthest reaching moves to upset it came not from the republican but from the British side. As early as March 1896 Chamberlain had suggested that in return for certain considerations, including monetary ones, Portugal might be persuaded to 'facilitate our acquisition of the [Delagoa Bay] Railway' and to extend British preferential rights so that they would cover in future the whole of Portuguese East Africa.[3] In May there is the following minute by Fiddes: 'The fiasco in the South African Republic [i.e. the failure of the Uitlander rising] makes the Delagoa Bay question more important than ever—I believe that it is in that direction that we should endeavour to recover the ground we have lost.' Any possibility just now, he asked, of lease or purchase? To which Selborne added: 'I believe that we ought now to strain every nerve to secure the Delagoa Bay railway.'[4] Shortly afterwards Chamberlain asked Alfred de Rothschild, the financier, to put out feelers.[5] In May and June 1897 the colonial secretary proposed an arrangement to the Portuguese minister in London, according to which, in return for the considerations he had suggested a year before, Britain was to get 'practical control of the [Delagoa Bay] harbour and railway'. To this the Portuguese government would not agree, but it made the following counter-proposal: 'The Portuguese Government will accept a loan secured on the revenues of their possessions in Africa, excepting the province of Lourenço Marques . . ., and will guarantee England that the *status quo* in the province shall never be even indirectly affected.' This was, however, not satisfactory to Chamberlain, who wanted at least

---

[1] Foreign office to colonial office, 24 Mar. 1897 (C.O. 537/133); MacDonell to Salisbury, 24 and 29 Mar. 1897 (C.O. 537/134).
[2] Salisbury to MacDonell, 3 Aug. 1897 (Scholtz, ii. 34); colonial office to foreign office, 24 July 1897 (C.O. 537/132).
[3] Minute, 10 Mar. 1896. C.O. 537/129.
[4] Minutes, 1 and 4 May 1896. C.O. 537/130.
[5] Garvin, iii. 309.

a guarantee, extending apparently beyond the Berne award, that Portugal would not grant any concessions within a specified radius from Lourenço Marques, and after further fruitless exchanges the negotiations petered out.[1]

IV

The British government's original idea had been, as we have seen, to send ships and not troops to back up the dispatches of 6 March.[2] This decision was taken before, probably shortly before, 13 March. On 5 April, however, Chamberlain informed the war office that 'adequate [military] measures of precaution' had now become 'a matter of pressing importance'. Lansdowne, the secretary for war, did not agree, but the colonial secretary mustered sufficient ministerial support to overcome his opposition.[3]

It is unnecessary to spend much effort on finding an explanation for Chamberlain's apparent change of front. Ever since the raid the increase of the South African garrison had been an object dear to his heart.[4] In November 1896 he had asked the cabinet—against the high commissioner's advice and without success—that the garrison should be raised 'to at least 10,000 men, including a large proportion of cavalry and artillery'.[5] It could not have needed many arguments to persuade him to revert to the position he had held in 1896. The arguments seem to have been supplied by Selborne, Graham, and Milner. About Selborne's advice I have already written.[6] Graham was inclined to regard 'defensive preparations on a scale not hitherto attempted' as sound policy.[7] As for Milner, the new high commissioner, it was his view that the British government should not play 'these high games' without sufficient force behind it and that the inadequate reinforcements which were actually to be sent out were an 'utter futility'.[8]

At the end of April the war office informed the colonial secretary that the British garrison in South Africa would be reinforced immediately by a battalion of infantry and three batteries of field artillery. These reinforcements raised the British military strength, which had been gradually increased since the raid, from 5,400 men and 6 field

[1] *British Documents*, i. 45–46.   [2] See above, p. 150.
[3] Cd. 1789, pp. 183–4; Garvin, iii. 140–1.   [4] See above, pp. 106, 116.
[5] Garvin, iii. 139.   [6] See above, p. 150.
[7] Minute, 22 Mar. 1897. Chamberlain papers, C.
[8] Headlam, i. 40–41.

guns to over 8,000 men and 24 field guns.[1] The dispatch of the reinforcements was accompanied by considerable press publicity.[2] That
was Chamberlain's idea. Wingfield and Selborne wanted the garrison
to be increased secretly. But their chief replied: '. . . I am strongly
inclined to think that whatever is done should be done openly. . . .
[War] certainly will not come *at present* from any action of ours.'[3]
In fact he did not believe that war would come at all over the dispatches of 6 March. 'If they [the Boers] see that we are in earnest',
he wrote to the prime minister, 'I believe they will give way, as they
have always done.'[4]

There can be no doubt that the first object of the increase of the
garrison was to add force to Chamberlain's demand for the repeal or
suspension of the immigration law. But we must not ignore the fact
that a number of other considerations were urged to justify the dispatch of the troops. Chamberlain drew attention to the 'vast quantities' of munitions of war which the republic was importing:[5] during
nine months of the year 1896 it had imported, according to the
intelligence department,[6] 50 field and position guns, 26 Maxims, and
45,000 rifles.[7] What was the meaning of the Boer armaments? A
sufficient explanation might perhaps have been found in the raid and
the indications Chamberlain had already given that he was not
averse to forceful methods of obtaining what he wanted.[8] Had Kruger
decided that there was a point beyond which he would not go in
meeting Chamberlain's wishes? Looked at in this light the republican
armaments might be pronounced defensive. And defensive they were
in fact pronounced to be by the high commissioner, the commander-
in-chief of the British forces in South Africa, and (at any rate as late
as October 1896) the director of military intelligence in London.[9]

Chamberlain himself was inclined to share this view. When he
asked for reinforcements in November 1896 he told the cabinet that
he believed 'that on a balance of probabilities there is no appreciable
risk of any such [offensive] action by the Boers. . . .'[10] And four

---

[1] Cd. 1789, pp. 21, 185.
[2] Greene's report to Chamberlain on his interview with Kruger and Joubert on
29 Apr. Chamberlain papers, C.
[3] Minutes, 30 and 31 Mar., on director of military intelligence to colonial office,
27 Mar. 1897. C.O. 537/133.
[4] Garvin, iii. 141.   [5] Cd. 1789, p. 183.   [6] Garvin, iii. 139.
[7] This was an exaggeration. See Breytenbach, 274–7. For the guns and rifles in the
possession of the republic in Sept. 1899 see Cd. 1789, pp. 156–7.
[8] See above, pp. 96, 106.
[9] Garvin, iii. 139; Headlam, i. 49; Cd. 1789, pp. 11–12.
[10] Memorandum for cabinet, 10 Nov. 1896. Chamberlain papers, C.

months later, in the private letter to Greene already referred to, he wrote:

> I gather . . . that Kruger's policy is to nibble at the Convention—to provoke us in small things without actually initiating a rupture and to leave it to us to take the first open action in the way of hostilities. If he has his way, and is not driven from his policy by the Hollanders [in his administration], he would yield in small things rather than come to an actual quarrel, but he may be forced by the internal difficulties of his administration to take a more decided course.[1]

In the letter to the war office,[2] however, in which he repeated the request he had made in November, Chamberlain laid all the emphasis on the 'powerful party within the State' and 'the more reckless' of Kruger's advisers who might cause the republican government to denounce the convention or even to take the offensive.[3] Let us take the second alternative first. The colonial secretary was asking the war office to believe that there was a serious risk that the shrewd old president with his strength of character and 'great personal influence'[4] might be pushed into launching an attack on the British empire. With regard to the convention, there could have been no doubt in Kruger's mind that its denunciation would be equivalent to a declaration of war.

Let us now analyse the principal objects of the military reinforcements more closely. In November Chamberlain told the cabinet that there were 'very strong reasons, which I may call "Diplomatic reasons", for largely strengthening the Imperial forces in South Africa', and he proceeded to give them as follows:

> 1. It would be a visible demonstration of the determination of the Imperial Government to maintain the *status quo*, and to insist on the observance of the Convention.
> 2. It would strengthen the loyalty of all the English in South Africa—greatly shaken by successive defeats and humiliation—and give them confidence in the Imperial factor, which there is now too much readiness to 'eliminate' at short notice.
> 3. It would be a warning to the Boers that we are in earnest, and that they must not proceed too far in their policy of intrigue and opposition. A display of strength has always impressed them. . . .[5]

---

[1] Chamberlain to Greene, 13 Mar. 1897. C.O. 537/133.
[2] See above, p. 156.
[3] Cd. 1789, pp. 183–4. See also *C.H.B.E.* viii. 575.
[4] Chamberlain to Robinson, 26 Mar. 1896: C. 8063, p. 17; Cd. 1789, pp. 11–12.
[5] Memorandum for cabinet, 10 Nov. 1896. Chamberlain papers, C.

This was apparently still his view in April 1897. At a meeting held at his request on 8 April and attended by four of his cabinet colleagues there was a discussion on the situation in South Africa. Lansdowne came away from the meeting with the impression that Chamberlain intended the reinforcements which were about to be sent out 'as a political demonstration' in reply to Kruger's military preparations, and that the objects he had in mind were to strengthen British diplomacy in South Africa and to produce an effect on the loyal colonists.[1] The first fruits of the strengthening of British diplomacy were to be the repeal of the immigration act. On this point no more needs to be said. But it is necessary to deal at some length with the loyal colonists.

After Chamberlain wrote his memorandum for the cabinet, there took place in South Africa certain events which must have made it even more desirable in his eyes to reassure the loyal colonists with regard to British policy. The most important of these events was the treaty between the two republics.[2] Chamberlain's reaction had been prompt.

It may be true [he remarked at the farewell dinner to Milner] as we have recently had it suggested to us, that there are eminent persons in South Africa who have aspirations for an independent federation of States, in which Dutch [i.e. Afrikaner] influence would be predominant, and which would look for sympathy and support rather to the Continent of Europe than to this country. If such an aspiration exists, in my opinion it is incompatible with the highest British interests. . . .[3]

At the Cape more than a month later, the acting high commissioner, trying to find an explanation of 'the forces . . . now being directed to South Africa', came to the following conclusion:

The situation, now, in South Africa appears to be that the hand of H.M. Government has been forced by the attitude assumed by many in the old [i.e. Cape] Colony. It is notorious that a propaganda has been afoot for some time past—some months—directed to gaining over individuals or classes to the cause of a united South Africa independent of Great Britain;[4] and this propaganda has shaken the minds of many in Cape Town itself

---

[1] Garvin, iii. 140–1; Cd. 1789, p. 185; Newton, 144–6.
[2] See above, p. 147.
[3] Speech at the Café Monico, 27 Mar. 1897: *Foreign and Colonial Speeches*, 224.
[4] There is no evidence that an independent South Africa was at this time regarded as anything but a remote possibility by any considerable section at the Cape or in the republics. See, for example, Scholtz, ii. 109–25; Headlam, i. 49. What did undoubtedly exist among the Cape Afrikaners was a strong sympathy with the republics, particularly since the raid.

even, and that not only among the Dutch . . . but among the weak-kneed of [the] English. . . . The avowed sentiments of the President of the Orange Free State . . . and the deliberate endeavours of President Kruger to rally the O.F.S. to his side [prompted and helped the propagandist movement, and] must have aided in bringing home to H.M. Government the nature of the danger. How then to arrest the movement of defection and drifting away? . . . A demonstration was called for. . . .[1]

These were the circumstances under which, in the opinion of the acting high commissioner, the loyal colonists needed reassurance. Who were the loyal colonists? Chamberlain had in mind primarily the British settlers throughout South Africa, including the Uitlanders on the Witwatersrand.[2] We have noted that a year before the demonstration of April 1897 he had remarked on the necessity of paying some attention to the views of the British colonists, 'who, at all events, are well-wishers to the British rule'.[3] A few months after the demonstration he told Milner, who had recently landed in Cape Town, that he hoped the right man would be found to unite the British colonists in South Africa 'as a counterpoise to any extreme Afrikaner or Dutch party'.[4] In this connexion it should be remembered that Kruger's 'climb down'[5] in the face of the British threat did much to restore British prestige in South Africa[6] after the blow it had sustained through Jameson's fiasco. This assertion of Britain's power must have encouraged the South African league,[7] which was already at work organizing British national sentiment from the Cape to the Limpopo.[8]

Chamberlain's forceful diplomacy therefore achieved certain desirable objectives. But it did so at a cost. In one important respect the hopes of the acting high commissioner were not realized. Among the Afrikaners in the 'old Colony' the growth of sympathy with the republics, so far from being arrested, was stimulated. As for the South

---

[1] Headlam, i. 47–48.   [2] See above, p. 158.
[3] See above, p. 120.   [4] Headlam, i. 71–72.
[5] Early in May the volksraad repealed the immigration law, and in July it passed a resolution envisaging the revision of the expulsion law, so that no person should be banished until he had been found guilty of subversive conduct by the courts of the republic.
[6] Headlam, i. 68; van Winter, ii. 277–8.
[7] Compare Milner's statement that the South African British were 'somewhat comforted' by the military and naval demonstration and the 'quasi-retreat of the Transvaal'. Garvin, iii. 350.
[8] There were, nevertheless, some British colonists who objected to the April demonstration. Among them were the Natal ministry, who claimed that they expressed the wishes of the 'large majority' of the legislative assembly. Hely-Hutchinson to Chamberlain, 16 Apr. and 1 May 1897. Chamberlain papers, H.

African Republic, it went on arming, not indeed 'faster than ever', as Greene asserted, but at any rate on a fairly considerable scale.[1]

V

The political association that was largely responsible for the formation of that British party which Chamberlain hoped would become a force in South African politics was the South African league. The colonial secretary felt that the British government needed an instrument which would support its policy in South Africa and at the same time afford a justification for it. The league proved to be that instrument.

Shortly after the raid two political associations were formed on the eastern frontier of (White) settlement at the Cape, where British national sentiment had always been strong. The two associations united in March 1896 to form the loyal colonial league, which gained influential support in the press and spread rapidly among the British colonists throughout and beyond the Cape's Eastern Province. By August branches of the league had been formed on the Witwatersrand, in Pretoria, and in Natal, and its name had been changed[2] to the South African league, which by October had been organized into three autonomous 'provinces'—those of the Cape, the Transvaal, and Natal.

Taking its cue from the secretary of state,[3] the league adopted as its primary aim the maintenance of British supremacy in South Africa. That common purpose was the cement that bound the three provinces together. But the constant reiteration of the cry of British supremacy from political platforms and in the press, accompanied by the suggestion of an offensive against the Afrikaner nationality,[4] did not fall pleasantly on Afrikaner ears. 'The bettermost men in the South African league are well aware that the line they have cut out is at present racial . . .', commented the *Cape Times* in August 1896.[5] There can be no doubt that the league's propaganda, especially on the Transvaal question, which was interpreted by the Afrikaners in the light of its

---

[1] Cd. 1789, p. 193; and compare Breytenbach, 273–81. Greene's statement refers to the actual arrival of arms and to completed forts, not to the dates at which the decisions as to armaments were taken by the republican government.

[2] In May 1896.

[3] See above, pp. 105, 119.

[4] See, for example, Scholtz, ii. 109, 118.

[5] Ibid. 112 n. The *Cape Times*, the most influential newspaper in the Cape, was an ardent supporter of the league.

primary aim, did a great deal to widen the rift between the two nationalities.

The three divisions of the league, operating as they did in strikingly different environments, pursued different lines of action. The Natal province had a comparatively easy task. It is true that Natal had close commercial ties with the South African Republic and in contrast to the Cape found no reason to complain of her treatment by the republic. It is true also that her leading statesmen were convinced that it was in Natal's interests that the tension caused by the raid should relax.[1] But the colony prided herself on her loyalty to Britain: so that once it became clear to the colonists that the league's cause was also that of the imperial government, they might be expected to respond to the call of their British blood.

In the South African Republic the function of the league was to reorganize the voteless Uitlanders, especially those of British extraction, in opposition to Kruger's régime. The failure of the raid shattered the first important political movement among the Uitlanders. The mining magnates drew back into their shells and for the ensuing three years confined their activities and representations—at any rate as far as the republican government was aware—to matters relating to their own industry. Moreover a split occurred in their ranks. The firms which had stood aloof from the revolt against the government seceded from the chamber of mines. The leaders of the secession, which resulted in the establishment of the so-called association of mines, were the companies of J. B. Robinson (who hated Rhodes[2] and continued to assert that a friendly approach to Kruger would prove to be to the advantage of the industry), and those of A. Goerz and G. Albu.[3] As for the Uitlander rank and file, the failure of the rising in Johannesburg spelt the end of their national union; and the compulsory withdrawal of their leaders from politics completed their discomfiture.[4]

The league stepped into the void thus created. A number of new leaders acquired a training in politics. They were helped in their task of instilling enthusiasm into the discouraged Uitlanders by the *Star* and, in due course, *Transvaal Leader* newspapers. The republican

---

[1] See above, pp. 118 and 160 n. 8.   [2] Garrett, 126–7.

[3] Early in 1897 Selborne, commenting on 'the disunion and selfishness of the [mining] industry', remarked that 'the position of affairs in the South African Republic would have been impossible already had not the prominent Uitlanders [i.e. the mining magnates] been generally so worthless and contemptible'. Minutes by H. W. Just, 23 Mar., and Selborne, 24 Mar., on Greene to Rosmead, 18 Feb., in Rosmead to Chamberlain, 1 Mar. 1897. C.O. 537/131.   [4] See above, pp. 124–5.

government soon became aware that a new national union had risen
from the ashes of the old. There were, however, certain significant
differences between the two organizations. Unlike the national union,
the Transvaal league was part of a much wider movement. The
former had protested its loyalty to the republic, and had sought to
obtain the redress of Uitlander grievances by appealing to the republican authorities and by fostering the growth among the Boers of
a party sympathetic to the Uitlander cause. The league, on the other
hand, proclaimed its loyalty to the 'Paramount Power'. It expressed
the conviction that to appeal to the government or volksraad of the
republic would be useless,[1] and addressed its remonstrances to the
British agent. In May 1897 a league deputation told Greene

after some little hesitation . . . that, speaking for themselves, they would
certainly accept the franchise, not because they wanted to become burghers
for all time (indeed they did not admit the contention that, as subjects of
the Paramount Power, they must necessarily thereby forfeit their nationality), but because they saw that without representation in the Volksraad
they could never realize their dream of uniting the Transvaal in a federation
of the States of South Africa under the British flag. . . . I [Greene] replied
that it was not unlikely that the Transvaal Government also viewed the
situation in the same light.[2]

The league's *modus operandi* in the Transvaal was in tune with
Chamberlain's policy. He wished to be a party to any settlement of
the Uitlander question in order both to obtain a foothold in the
internal administration of the republic and to consolidate the loyalty
(to Britain) of the grateful Uitlanders.[3] He needed a British party in
the republic which could be depended upon to act, or to refrain from
acting, as best suited Britain's interests at any particular time. And
the Uitlanders needed a toughening of their fibre. '. . . Johannesburg
is a revolving light', wrote Greene in July 1897, 'and one which it is
very dangerous to steer by.' And again, a few months later: 'I have
. . . so little confidence in the "thoroughness" of Johannesburg that
I hesitate to admit that any reliance whatever can be placed on its
attitude past, present or to come.'[4] Like his chief, Greene in time

[1] African (South), 516, p. 616.
[2] Ibid. 536, no. 157 (enclosure); Scholtz, ii. 165.
[3] Breytenbach, 132; Garvin, iii. 74; Hely-Hutchinson to Chamberlain, 7 Dec. 1895
(Chamberlain papers, H); Rhodes to B.S.A. company, 31 Jan. 1896 (C.O. 537/130);
Chamberlain's memorandum of interview with Leyds, 15 May 1897 (Chamberlain
papers, C).
[4] Greene to high commissioner, 7 July and 24 Oct. 1897. African (South), 532,
no. 113, and 543, no. 34.

came to look to the league to fashion the Uitlanders into a reliable instrument of British policy. It is true that at the beginning he was taken aback by the robust sentiments of some of his compatriots, who expressed to him the league's point of view. Thus, for example, he refused to accept an address of welcome from certain British subjects 'holding extreme views as to the rights and position of British subjects' in the republic, since the address called upon him to 'maintain the supremacy of the Empire in this part of the world'. He wanted them to substitute 'prosperity' for 'supremacy', which they refused to do. When the matter was referred to Chamberlain, he stated that if the framers of the address had used the words 'paramount interests' instead of 'supremacy', 'they would have correctly expressed the facts of the case'.[1] That no doubt satisfied them, as well as conveying a clear hint to Greene. From early in 1897 the latter kept in close touch with the executive of the league, exhorting it to trust the British government and to refrain from 'open demonstration', at any rate for the time being.[2] In March 1898 he avowed his sympathy with the league, but at the same time warned it, in accordance with Chamberlain's policy at that date,[3] that the time for 'promoting a critical condition of affairs' by large-scale agitation had not come.

Your Excellency will readily understand [he wrote to Milner] that in dealing with the South African League I am placed in a very delicate position. The league is . . . the only body in Johannesburg that has a spark of real Imperial feeling, or a particle of any higher ambition than the worship of mammon. It has of late largely extended the field of its labour. . . . It therefore, in a certain sense, deserves sympathy, and looks to me for encouragement. On the other hand . . . it requires careful and constant watching. Up till now I have managed to keep some sort of control over the Executive, notwithstanding that they are, of course, being continually pressed by the mass of the League to resort to more vigorous action.[4]

It is hardly too much to say that from 1897 onward the supreme direction of the league in the republic was, unofficially of course, in the hands of Greene.

We come, finally, to the part played by the league in the 'old Colony'. Its fortunes in the most populous, the wealthiest, and the

---

[1] C. 8423, nos. 84 and 107.
[2] Greene to high commissioner, 5 Mar. and 17 May 1897. African (South), 516, no. 634 (enclosure), and 536, no. 157 (enclosure).
[3] Headlam, i. 226–7.
[4] Greene to high commissioner, 24 Mar. 1898 (African (South), 543, no. 197, enclosure); Scholtz, ii. 166.

most mature of the South African states were bound to be followed with close attention by the colonial office. It was only in the Cape that the league's support of imperial policy could take the form of an attack at the polls on Kruger's sympathizers, that is to say on the Afrikaner bond. The bond's only potential rival in the constituencies at the time of the raid was the South African political association[1] of James Rose Innes, a prominent member of the small group of liberals in parliament.[2] But Innes's association, which was described by the *Cape Times* as being 'all head' instead of 'all heart' like the league,[3] was not the body to organize British sentiment after the raid, and it lost many of its members to the league.

The league directed its attention mainly to the Transvaal issue. Its leaders followed the advice of the *Cape Times* to 'rouse and marshall . . . a body of keen and bitter feeling' against the republican government.[4] They launched a sustained attack on Kruger's 'retrograde' régime, and demanded a strong policy towards the republic backed, if necessary, by force. One of the notable exploits of the league during the first year of its life was to organize a demonstration against Schreiner's evidence[5] before the house of commons committee. The anger of the leaguers was roused particularly by his repudiation of a suggestion by Chamberlain that the majority of the English colonists at the Cape would welcome a more vigorous imperial policy with regard to the Transvaal.[6] A flood of protesting resolutions was passed at public meetings and by league branches and transmitted to Chamberlain.[7] The colonial office gave one of these resolutions to British newspapers for publication.[8] With regard to another, passed by the executive of the league, Chamberlain minuted: 'I think that in acknowledging receipt we might send a full copy of Mr Schreiner's evidence and examination. I doubt if he will be Prime Minister of an English Colony as long as he holds his present views.'[9]

[1] Formed in May 1895.
[2] The liberals were the only group in parliament genuinely solicitous for Native interests. After the raid they advocated, in addition, a reduction in the duties on foodstuffs, especially meat and grain, in the interests of the urban communities.
[3] *Cape Times*, 5 Sept. 1896.
[4] Ibid., 30 Sept. 1896.
[5] See above, p. 146 n. 2.
[6] 311, Q. 4184–90. The league also objected to Schreiner's suggestion that disputes concerning the interpretation of the London convention should be referred to arbitration. Ibid., Q. 3776, 4190–3.
[7] 311—I, pp. 577–90.
[8] Minute, 5 Apr. 1897. C.O. 417/216.
[9] Minute, 26 Mar., on South African league to Chamberlain, 26 Mar. 1897. C.O. 417/233.

While the league had no inhibitions about attacking Kruger's Uitlander policy, the bond's attitude was non-committal. It adopted as
its watchword 'non-interference in the internal affairs of the republic',[1] and declined to be drawn into public debate on Uitlander
grievances. With regard to the London convention, the league proclaimed Britain's right to interpret that instrument; while the bond
advocated the principle of arbitration.[2]

The leaders of the league felt that it needed a man of standing as
the president of its executive committee. They first approached Innes.
But the latter, though he was prepared to agree to co-operation
between his association and the league, would not accept amalgamation and turned down the offer of the league's presidency. He agreed
with the league that the Uitlanders' grievances were a matter of
legitimate concern to Cape colonists;[3] but he objected to the 'racial-
ist' tone of its propaganda[4] and to the Rhodian leanings of many of
its members. He knew that Garrett of the *Cape Times*,[5] as well as
other prominent leaguers, were preparing the way for the re-entry of
Rhodes into Cape politics. The league helped to organize demonstrations on behalf of the 'fallen Colossus' in July–August 1896; and
again in December, on the occasion of his triumphal tour through the
Colony.[6] These demonstrations were, of course, distasteful to the
bond. Some months later Chamberlain himself had revised his estimate of Rhodes as 'still the coming man in Southern Africa'.[7] By
July 1897—the month in which the house of commons committee
presented its report on the raid—he had come to the conclusion that
it was impolitic for Rhodes to assume the leadership of the British
colonists. Rhodes, he wrote to Milner,

certainly does not come out well in connection with the . . . Inquiry and
it would be most desirable that he should lie low for a time.[8] . . . It is
a great pity that the British party in South Africa has no leader except
Rhodes. If Rose Innes, or some other man who was not mixed up with
Rhodes' plans, could keep them together . . . it would be a great assistance
to the Imperial Government. Unfortunately Rhodes cannot unite the
English without giving offence and cause of suspicion to the Dutch.[9]

---

[1] See, for example, Headlam, i. 255.   [2] Hofmeyr, 516.
[3] Innes, 140, 143.
[4] *Cape Times*, 15 Aug. 1896 ('The Talk of the Day').
[5] Cook (*b*), 134–5.
[6] See above, p. 138 n. 2.
[7] See above, p. 146 n. 2.
[8] The latter part of this sentence is omitted in Headlam, i. 71.
[9] Chamberlain to Milner, 5 July 1897. Chamberlain papers, D.

But Innes persisted in his refusal to lead the league. He seems to have sensed that he would be unable to prevent it from becoming a Rhodian party. He was a man of high integrity and the raid had completed his estrangement from his former chief. 'I could not', he wrote later, 'become a Rhodes man.'[1] In due course Rhodes became both leader (in all but name) of the new progressive party and president of the league.

This progressive party during the course of 1896 and 1897 consolidated itself as the parliamentary opposition to the bond. The nucleus of the party had existed since 1890, having been formed to watch the Rhodes ministry, lest its association with the conservative bond should injure 'the progress of the country and its imperial interests'. Many of the members of the group represented English constituencies in the Eastern Province, and it did not constitute an opposition to Rhodes in the full sense of the term. The real opposition, at any rate during Rhodes's second ministry (1893–6), was formed by a small group of liberals,[2] to which Innes and J. X. Merriman belonged and which was led in parliament by J. W. Sauer.[3] Shortly after the raid Innes took Sauer's place as leader of the official opposition, while Sauer and Merriman drew closer to the bond. As for the progressives, they revealed themselves in the first days of the 1896 session as the 'British supremacy' party[4]—like their counterpart in the constituencies, the South African league—and they sat, according to Innes, 'loosely upon the Opposition benches'.[5]

Their opposition to the ministry was—like the bond's support of it—provisional, until the prime minister should have revealed where he stood with regard to the South African Republic. The ministry of five formed by J. G. Sprigg after Rhodes's resignation early in 1896 contained three bond members, but two of them were adherents of Rhodes rather than of the bond. The ministry followed for about fifteen months, however reluctantly on Sprigg's part, the lead of the bond. But the prime minister could not hold out long against the pressure of his compatriots in the Colony. As early as August 1896, at a large meeting in his own constituency of East London, the league

---

[1] Innes, 144–5, 169.
[2] See above, p. 165 n. 2.
[3] Fuller, 165; Innes, 138. Innes, Merriman, and Sauer had been members of Rhodes's first ministry.
[4] Whatever other policies they might at the same time advocate. See the 'supremacy' resolution adopted by nineteen members of the house of assembly on 7 May 1896. C. 8423, no. 25.
[5] Innes, 139.

carried a motion of no-confidence in his government.[1] That was a warning which no doubt carried weight with Sprigg. He trimmed his sails to catch the prevailing wind, which was blowing in the direction of Rhodes. The latter, having absented himself from the house of assembly in 1896, returned to his place for a few weeks during the 1897 session and sat with the progressives.[2] The bond, suspecting Rhodian proclivities in Sprigg, supported a motion of no-confidence proposed by Merriman, which was lost by the Speaker's casting vote (30 April 1897). Innes and a few of his liberals also voted in favour of Merriman's motion on the ground that 'during the gravest crisis of our history the Government had never once given the country a lead'.[3] The progressives voted for Sprigg. Innes now resigned the parliamentary leadership of 'the opposition',[4] which included both his own liberal group and, more precariously, the progressives, and took his seat, with a few followers, on the cross benches. Shortly before the debate on the motion of no-confidence, Rhodes had told him that he was willing and able to consolidate the anti-bond groups. When Innes retired to the cross benches the way was left open for Rhodes.[5]

It was at this moment that Milner landed in Cape Town. Shortly after his arrival he made the following analysis of the political situation at the Cape:

The present Ministry, a weak one . . . has hitherto leant . . . upon the Bond, though with mutual distrust. . . . *Now* there is something like an open rupture, and at the next election the Ministry will stand boldly upon the 'no more Bond dictation' platform. On that platform they will have all the English on their side, and some Dutchmen, corrupted by Rhodes. But they cannot quite afford to show their hand yet. . . . The plan is to get through the session by hook or by crook, see to registration in the recess (with a fund largely supported by Rhodes)[6] and be ready for the dissolution which must come next year. Though it is impossible to feel much respect for the present Ministry, I don't see where a better is to come from just now, and . . . I think that I ought to smooth their way as much

[1] Scholtz, ii. 116.   [2] Williams, 294; Innes, 143.

[3] Innes, 144; Hofmeyr, 516.

[4] Its real antagonist was, of course, the bond and its attitude to the ministry depended on the latter's attitude to the bond.

[5] Innes, 143–4.

[6] That is, try to get—with the help of the league's organization and Rhodes's money —as many supporters as possible on to the voters' roll. About Rhodes Milner wrote early in June, after a talk with him: '. . . he is too self-willed, too violent, too sanguine and in too great a hurry. He is just the same man as he always was, undaunted and unbroken by his former failure, but also untaught by it.' Headlam, i. 106.

as possible and try to help them through these critical weeks [until the close of the session].[1]

A little later the high commissioner wrote: '. . . My chief reason for wishing to keep him [Sprigg] in office is that I think . . . the instinct of self-preservation will now keep him straight on Imperialist lines.'[2]

While Rhodes and Sprigg were preparing to take their places at the head of the progressive-league combination, the bond had solved the problem of its parliamentary leadership. Hofmeyr, the old leader, had resigned his seat in the house of assembly some months before the raid, though he did not retire from politics and remained the most influential figure in the bond organization. His advice as to the succession in the parliamentary leadership was almost certain to be followed. From the first days of the 1896 session the signs indicated that he was trying out W. P. Schreiner, and during the next session it became clear to all that his mantle had fallen on this young man, not yet forty years of age.[3]

Schreiner, who was of German-English parentage and whose wife belonged to a 'largely Dutch' family,[4] declared in 1897: 'I am a South African first, but I think I am English after that.'[5] It was as a South African—in the name of the interests of South Africa, present and future—that he was to oppose Milner and his progressive-cum-league allies.[6] 'You must either let salvation come from inside', he warned the house of commons committee on the raid, 'or else have a condition of things in [South] Africa which there is not a man in this hall to-day would wish ever to have seen or to have had any responsibility for.'[7] But South African though he might be, he was no Afrikaner. 'I should be called by the Dutch there [in the Cape Colony] an Englishman', he told the committee.[8] That Hofmeyr's choice should fall on this man is one more proof of the veteran's sagacity. It was part of the answer to the league's charge that the bond was disloyal. For Schreiner's loyalty, at any rate, could not reasonably be questioned, though questioned it was in those bitter

[1] Milner to Chamberlain, 11 May 1897. Chamberlain papers, D. This letter is not in Headlam. See also Headlam, i. 52–53.
[2] Milner to Chamberlain, 25 May 1897. Chamberlain papers, D.
[3] Hofmeyr, 510, 515; Walker (c), 99.
[4] By 'largely Dutch' Schreiner meant largely Afrikaner. 311, Q. 4177. His wife was a sister of Francis William Reitz, president of the Orange Free State from 1889 to 1895 and state secretary of the South African Republic from 1898 to the annexation.
[5] 311, Q. 4175.
[6] Walker (c), 113.
[7] Ibid. 93–94.
[8] 311, Q. 4175.

days.[1] Nor that of Merriman and Sauer,[2] the two ablest debaters in the house of assembly, who also allied themselves with the bond. The support of these as well as other people of note among the English-speaking colonists greatly strengthened the hands of the bond against the 'British party'.

VI

In Britain the counterpart of the league was the South African association formed in May 1896, with satellite committees in Canada and Australia. The aim of the association was to educate the British public on South African affairs by means of pamphlets and public meetings. Its membership included George Wyndham, M.P., an ardent supporter of Rhodes; Rider Haggard, Shepstone's private secretary when he annexed the Transvaal in 1877; and Kipling. After the outbreak of war the association summarized its activities as follows:[3]

Year	Number of meetings	Attendance	Pamphlets distributed
1896	130	50,000	150,000
1897	140	55,000	200,000
1898	146	65,000	250,000
1899	406	248,000	500,000

Two years earlier one of its spokesmen had written to the colonial office: 'The public meetings which have been held during the past five weeks by the South African Association in Lancashire, Yorkshire, Durham, Northumberland and Scotland . . . have been large—the nine Scotch audiences, for example, totalling 6,600. . . .' The meetings showed, he added, 'that on South African politics the Radical rank and file is out of sympathy with its leaders and its Press-organs. . . . Any measure tending to Anglicise the Transvaal would be applauded by Radical and Conservative alike.'[4]

---

[1] Walker (c), 99.

[2] According to J. W. Leonard, a leading Johannesburg Uitlander and at one time attorney-general at the Cape, Sauer's loyalty was 'doubtful'. Notes of an interview with Leonard by E. A. Altham, deputy assistant adjutant-general, 28 Apr. 1897. African (South), 532, pp. 81–82.

[3] *Journal of Modern History*, June 1952, p. 112.

[4] H. M. Bourke to Selborne, 21 Dec. 1897 (enclosure). C.O. 417/223.

CHAPTER VII

SIR ALFRED MILNER

Public-spirited, upright and disinterested . . . his feeble, forceful
voice . . . rigid face and wrinkled narrow brow.
Beatrice Webb on Milner (September 1906) in Our Partnership.

An idealist with a narrow soul.   *Louis Madelin on Robespierre.*

For my part I consider that it is better to be adventurous than
cautious, because fortune is a woman, and if you wish to keep her
under it is necessary to beat and ill-use her; and it is seen that she
allows herself to be mastered by the adventurous rather than by
those who go to work more coldly. She is, therefore, always,
womanlike, a lover of young men, because they are less cautious,
more violent, and with more audacity command her.[1]

I

CHAMBERLAIN's choice of Sir Alfred Milner as his principal representative in South Africa was a decision of far-reaching importance.
Who was the new high commissioner?

After a brilliant career at Oxford Milner had taken up political
journalism and acted for two years as assistant editor of the Liberal
Imperialist *Pall Mall Gazette.* Having failed as a Liberal candidate in
the general election of 1885, he shortly afterwards followed his patron,
G. J. Goschen, into the Liberal Unionist camp, where Chamberlain
also found himself, in opposition to Gladstone's policy of Irish home
rule. Goschen's influence secured him in succession the posts of under-
secretary in the Egyptian ministry of finance (1889–92) and chairman
of the British board of inland revenue (1892–7). He commemorated
the former of these tenures by his book *England and Egypt,* which ran
into five editions within eighteen months.

In Milner the colonial secretary found a collaborator whose doctrine of empire closely resembled his own. It was, if anything, even
more outspoken, and seems to have been held with a more passionate
earnestness.[2] Years later he was to refer to the imperialist doctrine as

---

[1] Unless otherwise stated the quotations at the head of this and succeeding chapters
are from *The Prince* of Machiavelli. This was one of the books which Milner read on
board ship to South Africa. Headlam, i. 42.

[2] In the rest of this paragraph I quote three extracts from statements made by
Milner long after 1897. I have felt justified in doing this since his imperialist convictions
do not seem to have changed, in essentials, since his Oxford days. See Milner, 4.

a 'great movement of the human spirit', which had 'all the depth and comprehensiveness of a religious faith'.[1] Like Chamberlain he was an ardent advocate of imperial federation. '. . . There is one question', he told the distinguished gathering come to bid him farewell in March 1897, 'upon which I have never been able to see the other side, and that is precisely this question of closer union. My mind is not so constructed that I am capable of understanding the arguments of those who question its desirability or its possibility.'[2] The men of the Dominions on whom Britain must depend in the construction and maintenance of this closer union were, he believed, the colonists of British race.

> Throughout the foregoing statement [he wrote in 1913] I have emphasised the importance of the racial bond. From my point of view this is fundamental. It is the British race which built the Empire, and it is the undivided British race which can alone uphold it. Not that I underestimate the importance of community of material interests in binding the different parts of the Empire together. . . . But deeper, stronger, more primordial than these material ties is the bond of common blood, a common language, common history and traditions.[3]

And again

> I am a British (indeed primarily an English) Nationalist. If I am also an Imperialist, it is because the destiny of the English race, owing to its insular position and long supremacy at sea, has been to strike fresh roots in distant parts of the world. My patriotism knows no geographical but only racial limits. I am an Imperialist and not a Little Englander, because I am a British Race Patriot. . . .[4]

But Chamberlain found in Milner—or was destined to find—much more than a fervid imperialist. The new high commissioner was much better known to the British public than his two predecessors. He enjoyed the confidence of influential Liberals particularly among the 'imperialist' section of the party, a point of some importance to the colonial secretary, who intended that his South African policy should be a national rather than a party policy.[5] Milner's other assets were

---

[1] Milner, xxxii. Compare his statement in 1897: 'What we . . . ought to do is to maintain religiously the [imperial] ties which exist. . . .' Ibid. 5. Headlam (i. 35) substitutes 'justly' for 'religiously'.
[2] Milner, 5.   [3] Ibid. xxxv.
[4] From 'Credo. Key to my position'—a statement found among Milner's papers after his death and published, with Lady Milner's permission, in *The Times*, 27 July 1925.
[5] Headlam, i. 13, 32–33, 35; Garvin, iii. 144.

moral and intellectual. He displayed from the beginning of his high commissionership a youthful vigour in strong contrast to Robinson's somewhat lethargic habits. Chamberlain was to have no reason to complain of Milner as he did of his predecessor: 'I would like to infuse a little more spirit into Sir H. Robinson and I wish he would show his teeth occasionally.'[1] Milner agreed wholeheartedly with Chamberlain that the high commissioner must not allow himself to be guided, in matters of imperial concern, by the policy of his Cape ministers.[2] He did not agree quite so unreservedly that the high commissioner's policy ought to be that of the British government. He was determined to probe to the essentials of the political situation in South Africa in order to discover the policy which that situation demanded. He proved to be a clever political calculator—up to a point. He was as masterful, though not as tough, a man as Chamberlain himself,[3] a man of great moral courage and a degree of candour remarkable in a statesman. And he had this advantage over his chief that he cared nothing at all for his own career provided that the interests of the empire were furthered.[4] He was also much more rigid than Chamberlain. 'His spiritual integrity', writes one who knew him well, 'made it difficult for him, when he had studied a problem, to temporise about the solution which he thought inevitable. . . . When he had satisfied himself about a particular course—and he took long to satisfy—his mind seemed to lock down on it, and after that there was no going back.'[5]

We have been discussing Milner's assets. Inflexibility, it must be confessed, can hardly be considered an asset in a statesman. Milner's training had been in fact administrative more than political. But during the first period of his high commissionership his main problems were to lie in the realm of politics. As a statesman he had another weakness besides rigidity. Along with his 'powerful administrative intelligence'[6] there went a certain narrowness of mind. He was a lonely man, lacking in geniality, not very good 'at getting on terms with folk whose experience had been different from his own'.[7] In South Africa he was inclined to see 'wrongheadedness and even moral obliquity' in those who disagreed with his diagnosis of the political situation.[8]

When Milner was offered the high commissionership for South

[1] Garvin, 138.
[2] See above, p. 68; Innes, 177.
[3] And more authoritarian.
[4] Buchan, 102; Headlam, i. 243.
[5] Buchan, 99–102.
[6] Ibid. 98.
[7] Walker (d), 4; Buchan, 99, 102.
[8] Walker (d), 4.

Africa he knew that his opportunity of rendering a signal service to the empire had come. Years before he had decided to espouse the state.[1] Now he said in his farewell speech:

A great number of people have said to me in the last few weeks . . . 'We do not know whether we ought to congratulate you; you are going to face a very ugly business. . . .' Well, to all these cheering remarks I should like to make one answer: 'Do not congratulate me, certainly. Let congratulations wait . . . until I have done something to deserve them. But still less condole with me: for no man is to be pitied, whatever happens, who in the best years of his life is not only permitted, but is actually called upon to engage in work into which he can throw himself with his whole heart and with a single mind.' A public servant must go where he is wanted. He is singularly fortunate if he is wanted for that kind of business to which he is most willing that all his energies should be devoted. . . . I feel it is a great privilege to be allowed to fill any position in the character of what I may, perhaps, be allowed to call a civilian soldier of the Empire. To succeed in it, to render any substantial service to any part of our world-wide State, would be all that in my most audacious dreams I ever ventured to aspire to. But in a cause in which one absolutely believes, even failure— for the cause itself is not going to fail—even personal failure would be preferable to an easy life of comfortable prosperity in any other sphere.[2]

II

Before Milner left England he and Chamberlain agreed that 'the waiting game was the best for this country as time must be on our side'. Time should be given for the 'irritation' over the raid to subside and an effort made to regain the confidence of the Cape Afrikaners. Furthermore, a reforming party was bound 'in the long run' to grow up in the South African Republic (presumably among the Boers as well as the Uitlanders). It would be politic, therefore, 'to avoid if possible all causes of offence' with regard to that state, so long as British treaty rights were not 'seriously challenged'.[3] To Chamberlain's instructions Hicks Beach, the chancellor of the exchequer and a former colonial secretary, added the following piece of advice: 'I believe the great thing necessary is "patience". Impatience has been at the root of our difficulties . . .' in South Africa.[4]

Milner's initial policy has, in fact, been described as one of patience.[5] is true that for about nine months he showed a disposition

---

[1] Buchan, 98; Headlam, i. 15.   [2] Milner, 3, 5.
[3] Headlam, i. 227; Garvin, iii. 350.   [4] Headlam, i. 33.
[5] Walker (d), 11; Headlam, i, ch. ii; Garvin, iii. 358.

to avoid 'causes of offence'. He and Greene 'happily disposed of a whole lot of minor questions' by informal negotiations with the republican authorities. He tried to reduce formal demands on controversial issues to a minimum.[1] Nevertheless, though he arrived with the professed intention of exercising patience,[2] his attitude of mind with regard to the republic was that of a thoroughly impatient man. From the beginning there is a note of urgency in his letters. '. . . We can afford to be very patient. . . . But they really must begin', i.e. make an 'honest beginning' in the way of reform. The Boer government must not merely refrain from breaking the convention;[3] they must show a real disposition 'to amend in their acts'. All he was prepared to concede was the desirability of 'some delay in next move on our part' (May 1897).[4] Two months later he was still 'just now' on the 'pacific and friendly tack'. In August, when he saw signs of an effective opposition to Kruger reviving among the Boers themselves,[5] he described the situation as hopeful—'but I don't see in it *as yet* an opportunity for us to "cut in" with advantage'. And again, a little later: 'The Boer Government of the Transvaal are fast going to the devil, and may be left to go for a bit.'[6] Even so he was not prepared to reduce 'the quiet but pretty steady pressure which we are always keeping up, not only in the Transvaal but throughout South Africa. . . .' In fact 'it would be a great mistake to suppose that, because S. African politics have fortunately entered upon a calmer phase, the everlasting struggle is not going on below the surface. *I am fighting all the time.*' He went on to explain that his struggle was partly in the field of 'Cape local politics',[7] which were still 'the key of the situation'.[8]

Most of the quotations in the preceding paragraph are from Milner's letters to Chamberlain. Outspoken though these letters are, Milner did not fully reveal in them at this early stage what he had at the back of his mind. About that he was more explicit in a letter to a friend. There was no talk here of conciliating the Cape Afrikaners:

. . . People sometimes say, why should not English and Dutch get on like English and French in Canada, and the [Cape] Dutch in the one case be as loyal as the French in the other? My answer is, 'Would the French Canadians be loyal, if the United States were a *French* Republic?' There

---

[1] Headlam, i. 70, 121, 182.   [2] Ibid. 65, 73, 103, 234.
[3] A pointed reference to the understanding between him and Chamberlain.
[4] Headlam, i. 52, 65; Milner to Chamberlain, 11 May 1897 (Chamberlain papers, D).
[5] See below, pp. 191–2.   [6] Headlam, i. 78, 89.
[7] See above, p. 168.   [8] Headlam, i. 119.

you have the difficulty in a nutshell. Half the white people in this [Cape] Colony, indeed I fear more than half, while owing a formal allegiance to Britain, are at heart fellow-citizens with the Free Staters and Transvaalers. . . . Of course, the remedy may be found in time in an English party in the Transvaal getting the franchise and counterbalancing on that side the influence of the Colonial Dutch on this. *But the Boer oligarchy of the Transvaal is going to die hard.* And it is not going to precipitate its own demise by provoking us too much. . . .[1]

Milner's relations with and attitude towards certain individual Cape citizens throw further light on the state of his mind during the period of 'patience'. Let us take his attitude to chief justice Sir Henry de Villiers. The latter was an anglicized Afrikaner.[2] He was a member of the royal commission which negotiated the Pretoria convention in 1881 and he had for many years been an advocate of a South African federation under the British flag.[3] Shortly before the chief justice sailed for England to take the oath as privy councillor and attend the Queen's jubilee celebrations, Milner wrote to his chief the following appreciation of him: 'He is the ablest and most persuasive of the Dutch party, and it is hoped that if he can succeed in making people in England see through his spectacles . . . English opinion may once more be bamboozled in the Dutch interest. . . .'[4] A few months later the high commissioner declared that 'our de Villiers, though he does not hate England, has a deep if almost unconscious bias on the side of the Boer'.[5]

When he made these statements Milner had not yet met de Villiers. But he had already written him off as a collaborator, if not as an instrument.[6] And so the latter, who had often been consulted by Milner's predecessors since he became chief justice in 1873,[7] now found himself cold-shouldered. He hesitated to approach a high commissioner who never consulted him, because he never felt sure, he wrote to Milner shortly before the outbreak of war, 'that your Excellency would give me your full confidence'.[8]

Other leading Cape statesmen Milner dismissed even more summarily than de Villiers. Merriman was a 'crank', Sauer a 'beast'. On the other hand, he thought that Schreiner was 'not to be despaired of'.[9] But he does not appear to have held any significant conversation

---

[1] Milner to Dawkins, 25 Aug. 1897. Headlam, i. 87.
[2] Walker (*a*), 3, 146–7, 187.   [3] Ibid. 51 and *passim*.
[4] Milner to Chamberlain, 25 May 1897. Headlam, i. 63–64.
[5] Ibid. i. 114.   [6] Walker (*a*), 309.
[7] Ibid., *passim*.   [8] Ibid., 307, 309–10, 348–9, 358.
[9] Milner to Chamberlain, 11 May 1897. Chamberlain papers, D.

with him until late in 1898, when Schreiner had become prime minister. Another Cape statesman, Innes, recalls that it was not until June 1899 that he had his 'first interview of any importance' with Milner.[1] As for Hofmeyr, the high commissioner discussed the situation with him more than once in the months after his arrival. But Milner's brief accounts of these interviews tell us only what he told Hofmeyr: and that was what he expected the Transvaal and the bond to do or to refrain from doing.[2] He wrote to Chamberlain that he had told de Villiers, Hofmeyr, and others 'that, if they wish to prevent war it is not with Great Britain that they ought to remonstrate. The centre of disturbance in South Africa is the Transvaal. It is to the Government of the S.A.R. that pacific entreaties should be addressed.'[3] It should be remarked that Milner was aware that de Villiers had urged reforms upon Kruger during his recent visit to Pretoria.[4]

Both Merriman and Hofmeyr came away disquieted by their first interviews with Milner. Merriman was convinced that 'the new man meant trouble'.[5] Hofmeyr seems to have been even more pessimistic: according to his biographer, '. . . Mr Hofmeyr saw after a few interviews with him [Milner], that war must come'.[6]

III

In London the committee of inquiry into the raid completed its report on 13 July 1897. The report, which condemned Rhodes in strong terms and exonerated the colonial office,[7] was debated a fortnight later in the house of commons. The most sensational incident in the debate occurred near the end, when Chamberlain gave his famous 'certificate as to C. J. R[hodes]'s honour'.[8] The defence of Rhodes by the secretary of state[9] seriously weakened the effect of the report which he had himself signed and demands from the historian some explanation. Dr. van der Poel quotes strong evidence in support of her thesis that Chamberlain spoke under duress, i.e. under the threat of exposure by Rhodes's friends.[10] But it seems probable that another motive was also present to his mind. We have already seen

[1] Innes, 179.
[2] Milner to Chamberlain, 11 May 1897 (Chamberlain papers, D); Headlam, i. 90.
[3] Ibid. 64.
[4] See above, p. 144; Walker (a), 302, 304, 307.   [5] Ibid. 307.
[6] He does not give the evidence on which he bases this statement. Hofmeyr, 530.
[7] See above, pp. 71–72.
[8] The words of Hawksley, Rhodes's solicitor. Van der Poel (b), 242, 255.
[9] Cook (a), 66–68; Garvin, iii. 123–5; Innes, 152–4; van der Poel (b), 240–4, 252, 255.   [10] Ibid. 241–4.

that he needed a man in South Africa to keep the British colonists together. True, he believed that it would be a pity if no one should prove capable of doing this except Rhodes. But such an eventuality had to be faced and provided for.[1] During the course of his remarks on Rhodes he told the house of commons that the proposal to deprive him of his privy councillorship would be very unpopular in South Africa, and then proceeded to read a letter in which Sprigg, the prime minister of the Cape, declared: 'Speaking for the Cape Colony, I should say that a vast majority of the English population support him strongly, and I doubt whether more than half of even the Dutch population are really opposed to him.'[2]

Chamberlain's speech had immediate repercussions in South Africa. It pleased most of the British, but among the Afrikaners it roused strong resentment. Milner told his chief that the quotation of Sprigg's letter had been a mistake:

Sprigg's . . . assurance to you as to the feelings of the [Cape] Dutch with regard to Rhodes has done a lot of harm. . . . It is quite true that a number of the Dutch, quite a considerable proportion in the House, but not, I think, many in the country, are at heart quite ready to forgive Rhodes. The process of reconciliation, not unassisted by judicious though veiled bribery,[3] was quietly going on. But it was a great mistake for Sprigg to call such pointed attention to it, for he has excited the Bond to fury.[4]

Kruger, too, was furious about Chamberlain's speech, though he declared to J. B. Robinson, the mining magnate, that it had not come as a surprise to him. 'Do you think', Robinson reports him as saying, 'that we are so innocent as not to know that Mr Rhodes . . . held a pistol at the heads of certain men in England, and said to them, If you do not support me, I will denounce you and your complicity in the Raid?'[5]

On his arrival in South Africa Milner had noted: '. . . But the mischief is, they doubt our good faith—no wonder perhaps with the Raid still so fresh in their memories and *being kept fresh*. . . .'[6] 'They' refers to the Cape Afrikaners, but the statement, of course, also holds for the Free Staters and the Transvaalers. About a month after the publication of the committee's report and the debate in the house of commons, Milner observed that the bond were still 'flogging the dead horse of the Raid, the inquiry, the telegrams, etc., with effect'.[7] That

---

[1] See above, p. 166.   [2] *Parliamentary Debates*, 4th series, vol. li, col. 1172.
[3] The phrase about bribery has been omitted by Headlam. See also Hofmeyr, 514.
[4] Headlam, i. 89–90. See also Hofmeyr, 517.
[5] Cook (*a*), 68.   [6] Garvin, iii. 350.   [7] Headlam, i. 90.

was not surprising in view of the nature of the inquiry and its outcome. Considering all the circumstances the Afrikaners in and outside the Cape could hardly look upon 'the Raid, the inquiry, the
telegrams, etc.' as a 'dead horse'. That horse remained in fact very
much alive until the outbreak of war.

One of the results of the committee's report was the dismissal of
Sir Graham Bower from his post as high commissioner's or imperial
secretary.[1] Milner sent three telegrams strongly urging the appointment of Edmund Garrett, the editor of the *Cape Times*, to fill the
vacancy. They were read in the colonial office with surprise and
disapproval. 'A reader of the weekly edition of the *Cape Times*',
remarked Graham, 'may gather that Mr Garrett is up to the eyes in
Cape politics, that he has embarked on an anti-Boer campaign, and
latterly has taken up the cause of Mr Rhodes. . . . Mr Garrett's
appointment would . . . give grave offence to the Boers and to the
Bond. . . .'[2] Chamberlain, who no doubt remembered Garrett's indis-
cretions on the subject of his complicity in the raid plot,[3] expressed
himself with greater vehemence. '. . . I saw Garrett in London',[4] he
minuted, 'and formed a very poor opinion of his wisdom. I cannot
understand how Sir A. M. has been captured by a conceited, self-
confident partizan chatterer like Garrett. However I will not appoint
him at any price.' The man he decided to appoint was G. V. Fiddes,
a member of his staff.[5] But it is clear from Fiddes's minutes during the
years 1896 and 1897 that he was at least as 'anti-Boer' as Garrett,[6]
though his views were not, of course, known to the public. Four
months before his appointment as imperial secretary he had written,
apropos of Leyds's visit to Europe:[7] 'I see no prospect whatever of
a solution [of the Transvaal question] . . . tolerable to us, save by an
appeal to arms, and the longer it is delayed the greater the difficulties
we shall have to face ultimately.'[8]

IV

Whatever his main preoccupations might actually be, a South
African high commissioner could hardly fail to define his attitude to

[1] Van der Poel (*b*), 244–5.
[2] Minute, 16 Aug. 1897. C.O. 537/132.   [3] Van der Poel (*b*), 187–93.
[4] In Jan. 1897. Cook (*b*), 151.
[5] Minutes, 11 and 17 Aug. 1897. C.O. 537/132.
[6] Colonial office records, *passim*.   [7] See above, p. 152.
[8] Minute, 17 Apr., on high commissioner to Chamberlain, 31 Mar. 1897. C.O.
537/131.

South Africa's principal problem—the question of the relations between the White colonists and the non-Whites.

One of the first questions which Milner was directed to take up with the republican government[1] was the position of the Coloured British subjects who had emigrated to the Witwatersrand from the Cape.[2] The Cape Coloured had become assimilated to Western civilization, but they had remained, on the whole, a backward group.[3] Among those who had emigrated to the republic there were, however, a number of small building contractors and skilled artisans.[4] Yet the law made no distinction between Coloured folk and raw Natives. Thus, for example, a pass law enacted by the volksraad in 1896 primarily for the control of Native labourers on the mines (and which enjoined *inter alia* that Natives on the Rand must be in the employ of a master and wear a metal plate or 'badge' on the arm in token of such employ) was enforced also against the Coloured.[5] A number of the latter, artisans among them, were arrested under this law and fined up to £10 with the alternative of two months' imprisonment.[6] In July 1897 Milner decided to approach the republican government on this '*little* matter';[7] but not to raise 'the bigger questions of marriage,[8] trading in own name and holding [immovable] property'.[9] The matter had been getting some publicity: one, W. H. P. Linden, the secretary of the protection committee of the Coloured people in Johannesburg, was collecting sworn declarations for the South African league, and a public protest meeting of Coloured men had recently been held on the Rand. At Port Elizabeth, too, a meeting, probably organized by the league,[10] had passed resolutions protesting against the disabilities of 'the coloured Uitlanders'. Whereupon Greene pointed out to Milner that British prestige would suffer unless something was done for the Coloured in the republic.[11]

---

[1] African (South), 516, no. 683.

[2] For the number of Cape Coloured in Johannesburg in 1896, see above, p. 1. Note that the Cape Malays were usually included among the Cape Coloured.

[3] See Marais, ch. ix.   [4] African (South), 516, no. 536.

[5] Green book no. 8 of 1899, pp. 2, 4.

[6] High commissioner to Chamberlain, 29 Sept. 1896 (C.O. 417/184); African (South), 536, no. 233.

[7] Headlam, i. 182.

[8] In this same month the volksraad, apparently without pressure from Milner, passed a law making it possible for Coloured persons and for Natives to contract marriages recognized by republican law. African (South), 536, no. 234; *Notulen*, Eerste Volksraad, 1897, arts. 441–3, 447–9, 454–67, 480–504, 529–33.

[9] African (South), 536, no. 229. By 'holding' Milner meant owning.

[10] The league was no doubt aware that the Coloured vote counted for something in the Cape.

[11] Ibid., nos. 93, 111. Some appeals had also been addressed to the British government.

Milner had been told by the colonial office that owing to the attitude taken up by his predecessors, Coloured people could not claim the protection of article XIV of the London convention, which guaranteed to 'all persons other than natives' full liberty of movement and trade within the republic.[1] He accordingly instructed Greene to make a 'friendly representation' to Kruger on the subject of the application of the pass law to Coloured persons.[2] The president gave a courteous answer, and shortly afterwards persuaded the volksraad, not without difficulty, to amend the pass law.[3] There followed an exchange of notes between Greene and the republican government. The latter agreed to remit the penalties of all the Coloured convicted under the pass law, and promised special treatment in future for 'better class coloured persons':[4] instead of the 'badge' and the pass renewable monthly at a fee of 2s., Coloured persons carrying on a business or practising a skilled trade might provide themselves with a certificate on payment of £3 per annum (reduced to 10s. in the case of missionaries or teachers). Those who failed to take out the certificate would remain subject to the provisions of the pass law.[5]

The high commissioner had also to define his attitude with regard to the Asiatics in the republic. Several thousands of them,[6] mainly British Indians, had gradually infiltrated into the republic from Natal, where they 'swarmed'.[7] The immigrants were 'for the most part small store keepers, and local hawkers of fruit, vegetables and stuffs etc.'[8] 'In 1884', wrote the British vice-consul in Johannesburg, 'an agitation was set on foot by the merchants and traders in the Republic against what they described as a threatened invasion of Asiatics.' This 'trade jealously . . . combined with the antipathy of the Boers to all coloured races' led to the enactment of stringent anti-Asiatic legislation (law 3 of 1885).[9] The law infringed article XIV of the London convention, but the British government waived the right of objecting to it provided certain amendments were enacted by

---

[1] Minute by H. W. Just, 24 Nov., on Rosmead to Chamberlain, 29 Sept. 1896 (C.O. 417/184); Wingfield to Milner, 14 Apr. 1897 (African (South), 516, no. 683).
[2] Green book no. 8 of 1899, pp. 1–2.
[3] African (South), 536, no. 229; *Notulen*, Eerste Volksraad, 1897, arts. 831–43.
[4] Greene's words in African (South), 543, no. 105. This was in accordance with the recent volksraad resolution. The concession applied also to 'better class' Natives.
[5] African (South), 543, pp. 21–23; green book no. 8 of 1899, pp. 3–7.
[6] For their number in Johannesburg in 1896, see above, p. 1.
[7] Walker (b), 549.
[8] Greene to Milner, 6 Dec. 1897. African (South), 543, p. 156.
[9] Report by vice-consul Evans, 2 Mar. 1898 in African (South), 543, p. 269. See also C. 7911, p. 51, and Scholtz, ii. 103.

the volksraad. The law as amended denied 'the rights of citizenship' to Asiatics, and gave to the government 'the power for sanitary purposes of showing them fixed streets, wards and locations for habitation', outside which they might not own landed property.[1] The government interpreted the law to mean that it was entitled to confine all Asiatics to such streets or locations as it might determine, both for purposes of residence and of trade, and the high court of the republic upheld that interpretation.[2] As a result of protests by the British government the matter was ultimately referred to the arbitration of the chief justice of the Orange Free State, who in April 1895 gave his award in favour of the Transvaal government. The British government accepted the award.[3]

Thus the British authorities had given away the case of the Indians more emphatically than that of the Coloured when Milner arrived in South Africa. But the republican government had as yet made no serious attempt to enforce law 3 of 1885 (as amended). After Milner's arrival he and Greene thwarted all attempts to implement the law. At first they based their representations on the fact that Indian traders were bringing a test case before the high court. When that case had at length been decided against the Indians (August 1898), the government directed that the law be now carried out.[4] But then, as will be shown later, the British officials succeeded in obtaining a further postponement.[5]

Milner and Chamberlain handled all non-White questions in the light of their primary aim, viz. the extension and consolidation of British supremacy in South Africa. In order to achieve this aim they considered it most important to have the support of a large section of the White colonists. To take too strong a line in defence of non-White interests might easily lose them that support.[6] As a leading Uitlander put it: 'There is scarcely an Uitlander in the Transvaal who would not view with dismay[7] the raising of the big question [of Uitlander enfranchisement] upon such grounds as the treatment of the natives, the Cape boys, or the Indians. . . .'[8] As far as the Indians were concerned, Chamberlain reminded Milner that those in Natal

---

[1] C. 7911, pp. 50–57.
[2] Botha, 281–2.
[3] C. 7911, pp. 27–28, 48–49.
[4] African (South), 536, p. 3; 543, pp. 143–7, 156–7, 185, 269, 545.
[5] See below, p. 258.
[6] Chamberlain to Milner, 16 Mar. 1898. Headlam, i. 228.
[7] Most of the White colonists in South Africa would have shared this dismay.
[8] Fitzpatrick, 329. By 'Cape boys' Fitzpatrick meant the Cape Coloured.

were subjected to 'certain disabilities',[1] which made it difficult to criticize the Transvaal government in so far as the latter acted similarly.[2]

While Milner found it feasible to do something for the Cape Coloured and the Indians in the republic, he did nothing for the tribal Natives or Bantu. The reason was not that the Transvaal Natives were 'beyond his reach'.[3] The London convention, he told H. H. Asquith, gave him 'the fullest right to intervene on their behalf'.[4] There were, moreover, good grounds for intervention: for their position was far worse in the Transvaal than anywhere in British southern Africa.[5] The black man there had 'no rights whatever', and there was 'neither kindliness nor wisdom to restrain the brutality of the ruling oligarchy'. His real reasons for not intervening on behalf of the Natives, continued Milner, were, first, the certainty that such intervention would arouse intense resentment among the Transvaal Boers; second and more important, the danger lest Afrikaner and British colonists elsewhere in South Africa might support the Transvaalers.[6] Greene thought, like Milner, that the Natives were treated very badly in the republic, but he was nevertheless in full agreement with the high commissioner's policy of non-intervention.[7] And so was Chamberlain.[8]

It should now be clear why non-White issues, though they caused some trouble between the Boer and British governments, were not placed by the latter near the forefront of the case against the republic.

I have said that after the advent of Milner the British authorities did not touch the issue of Native or Bantu policy. This had not always been Chamberlain's line. During his first six months at the colonial office he came very close to intervention on behalf of the Natives in the republic. In 1894 and 1895 the Boer government ordered large-scale commando operations against tribesmen living in the lowveld of the north-eastern Transvaal immediately to the east

---

[1] The disabilities of the Indians in Natal were an annual tax of £3, exclusion from the franchise, and restrictions on trading. *C.H.B.E.* viii. 550–1; Walker (*b*), 523; Walker (*c*), 126–7.

[2] Chamberlain to Milner, 22 June 1898. African (South), 543, no. 282.

[3] See *C.H.B.E.* viii. 581.

[4] Actually the republican negotiators, in articles VIII, XVIII, and XIX of the convention, gave six specific undertakings on the subject of the treatment of Natives.

[5] In the colonial office Selborne was not so sure of that. Minute, 21 Jan. 1898, on Milner to Chamberlain, 9 Nov. 1897. C.O. 417/223.

[6] Milner to Asquith, 18 Nov. 1897. Headlam, i. 177–80.

[7] Greene to Milner, 21 Aug. 1897. African (South), 536, pp. 460–70.

[8] Minutes of Chamberlain and his staff, May 1897. C.O. 417/233.

of the Drakensberg.[1] The government had recently granted farms in this region to White men without any regard to the Natives already settled there.[2] In 1894 it decided that military action had become necessary to secure the White farmers against molestation and to subject the Natives to its authority. After the tribesmen had been subdued, they were to pay the taxes laid down by law[3] and to live in circumscribed locations.[4] During the course of the operations and thereafter, information reached the colonial office of the capture of Natives in their thousands with a view to their 'apprenticeship' to White farmers, and of the death of many captives from exposure on their march to Pretoria. The informants stated also that 'innocent' Native kraals had been looted and other 'atrocities' perpetrated.[5]

When the campaign of 1895 opened, Ripon, Chamberlain's predecessor, had instructed the high commissioner and the British agent in Pretoria to keep him informed about the operations. In August Chamberlain sent the high commissioner, Robinson, some information which he had received from non-official sources.[6] Robinson thereupon asked Kruger[7] that a public inquiry in the presence of the British agent should be held by a judge of the high court or the state attorney. When this request was refused, Chamberlain's staff gave him conflicting advice as to his next step. Fairfield took the line that the British authorities would have to undertake the inquiry, but that 'it would be better to defer writing to Sir H. Robinson for a short time until we see how other matters turn out'.[8] To which the permanent under-secretary, Meade, replied: 'An independent inquiry of our own would be difficult to carry out and would stir up much mischief. If possible it should be avoided—unless of course it is necessary to quarrel with the S.A.R.'[9] In the end Chamberlain decided to give Kruger the choice between a joint inquiry by British and republican commissioners or a purely British investigation.[10] A

---

[1] Grimsehl, 236, 239, 243–5, 250; African (South), 470, pp. 164–5.

[2] Grimsehl, 207, 209–10, 223.

[3] The taxes were a poll tax of £2 on every adult male and a hut tax of 10s. on every wife. They were higher than elsewhere in South Africa.

[4] Grimsehl, 222–35.

[5] African (South), 470, pp. 93–98, 109, 125–7, 185–92, 217–18, 224, 243–7, 250, 257–70, 283–7.

[6] Ibid., pp. 164, 185–92.　　　　　　　　　　　[7] On 11 Sept. C.O. 417/151.

[8] The 'other matters' were presumably the contemplated rising in Johannesburg supported by Jameson's force.

[9] Minutes, dated 5 and 9 Nov., on Robinson to Chamberlain, 12 Oct. 1895. C.O. 417/151.

[10] From Kruger's point of view there was not much to choose between these alternatives. Both spelt British intervention.

dispatch containing this decision was sent off towards the end of December, but cancelled shortly after the raid.[1]

V

In July 1897 Steyn wrote to Milner, in the latter's capacity as governor of the Cape Colony, to ask whether the Cape government would participate in a conference of South African states and colonies, including the province of Lourenço Marques, to discuss the practicability of uniform legislation for the control of immigration into South Africa. Steyn intended to invite only the governments directly interested in this question.[2] In other words he wished to exclude the British government. For the exclusion of the British government there was recent precedent in the railway and customs conferences held since 1888 between South African states and colonies. Milner declared that the Orange Free State was acting in concert with the South African Republic and that 'their only object is to get the latter out of the embarrassing position in which it is left by the repeal of the ... Immigration Act'.[3] That was certainly one of Steyn's objects,[4] but it seems clear that he was also anxious to promote friendly inter-state relations in South Africa. It is clear, too, that he believed the 'imperial factor' to be a stumbling-block in the way of these friendly relations. He wrote later that, if the latter were represented at the conference, 'we should have had to meet under the chairmanship of the British Government, and we could not know what rights the British Government as a result thereof might arrogate to itself over the Free State and the Transvaal'.[5]

Milner was prepared to do something to allay the suspicions of the republics. Though he insisted that the British government should be represented at the conference, he told Chamberlain that it should be there not as the paramount power (which the colonial secretary would have preferred), but in the name of Basutoland, the Bechuanaland protectorate, and Rhodesia. If the republics agreed to this, a conference would be desirable 'and form useful precedent'.[6] But this 'useful precedent' was precisely what Steyn was afraid of. He

---

[1] African (South), 470, pp. 283–4, 289.
[2] Headlam, i. 73–74; van der Merwe, i. 152.
[3] African (South), 536, p. 346. For the repeal of the immigration act see above, p. 160 n. 5.
[4] See C. 8721, p. 9; van der Merwe, i. 152.
[5] Van der Merwe, i. 147–8, 152.
[6] Headlam, i. 73–74; African (South), 536, pp. 346–7.

accordingly replied that if the British government were represented, so should be the German government in respect of South-West Africa. 'I felt', he explained later, 'that thus Great Britain would not be able to claim any rights over us as a result of this conference which she could not demand with similar justification over the German possession. . . .'[1]

This put an end to any prospect of a conference for the time being. The Sprigg ministry finally clinched the matter early in 1898 by declaring, no doubt with Milner's concurrence, that the British government had necessarily to participate *inter alia* 'because they are vitally interested, as the paramount power in South Africa, in everything that concerns its welfare'.[2]

VI

Shortly before Milner's arrival the republican government had appointed the so-called industrial commission to inquire into the depression in the mining industry.[3] The chairman of the commission was the capable and honest Schalk Burger,[4] an executive councillor of the republic. Most of the members—six in all—were government officials, and only one of them, the state mining engineer, had any knowledge of the technical and economic problems of the industry. The government therefore agreed that five advisory members, representing both the chamber and the association of mines,[5] should be added to the commission.[6]

Before we deal with the commission's recommendations, it will be useful to have before us the views about the depression expressed, generally in confidence, by persons who had inside knowledge of the mining industry. The industry was clearly suffering from growing pains. There had been over-capitalization and extravagance.[7] After 'the fever of speculation' in mining shares that 'seized the world' in 1895, a set-back was 'inevitable'.[8] Before the end of 1896 investors

---

[1] Van der Merwe, i. 153.   [2] African (South), 543, no. 113.
[3] See above, p. 136.
[4] Leyds, *Eerste Jaren*, no. 92, 27 July 1889 and footnote; *Hertzog-Annale*, July 1953, p. 75; African (South), 536, p. 289.
[5] See above, p. 162.
[6] Industrial Commission, 445; van Oordt, 776; Scholtz, ii. 156–7.
[7] Report by Samuel Evans sent to colonial office on 21 Nov. 1896 (C.O. 537/130); African (South), 516, no. 442.
[8] Speech by president of chamber of mines, 20 Jan. 1898 (C. 9345, p. 37); van Winter, ii. 30.

had come to realize that some of the mining properties could never pay, while most of the deep-level mines would take long and require much additional capital before they could come into production, and their payability was not certain.[1] About half of the forty-five producing mines were being worked at a loss.[2] There seemed to be a real danger that the new capital, which was urgently needed if the industry was not to languish, would not be forthcoming because of the investing public's loss of confidence in the future of the mines.[3] It was admitted in mining circles that more could and should be done to effect economies in the working of the mines; but it was pointed out at the same time that many of the difficulties under which the industry laboured were due to government action—or inaction. True, the direct taxation imposed on the mining industry was extremely light and profits were not taxed at all. But I have already remarked that many of the mines[4] were producing at a loss, and that many others had not yet come into production at all.[5] It was especially the owners of these mines who were discouraged by the burdens for which the industry held the government responsible. It was, in fact, the contention of the mining companies that the government did not seem to be interested in encouraging an industry which was only in its infancy and whose potentialities were enormous.

The three main burdens under which the industry laboured were, according to its spokesmen, the high rates charged by the Netherlands railway company, especially for the conveyance of coal,[6] the high cost of explosives owing to the dynamite monopoly,[7] and the scarcity and expensiveness of Native labour.[8] At the beginning of 1897 Samuel Evans, who had recently come to Johannesburg as the representative of a group of British financiers, declared that the accounts of a number of mining companies showed that their average working costs *per centum* were as follows: Native labour 30; food

[1] Report by Samuel Evans; Hely-Hutchinson to Chamberlain, 5 Dec. 1896 (Chamberlain papers, H); Industrial Commission, 446.
[2] Report by Samuel Evans; African (South), 532, pp. 13–17. The industrial commission declared that there were 79 producing mines in 1896, but that some mines had 'temporarily ceased operations'. Industrial Commission, 445–6.
[3] Report by Samuel Evans; Hely-Hutchinson to Chamberlain, 5 Dec. 1896 (Chamberlain papers, H).
[4] These were mines working ore which gave a comparatively low yield of gold. The Witwatersrand mines are largely 'low grade'.
[5] See also C. 9345, pp. 45–46.
[6] See above, pp. 34, 39–40.　　　　　　　　　　　　　　[7] See above, p. 31.
[8] African (South), 532, pp. 13–17; Hely-Hutchinson to Chamberlain, 5 Dec. 1896 (Chamberlain papers, H); Altham to Northcott, 24 Dec. 1896 (C.O. 537/133); Scholtz, ii. 156; Fitzpatrick, 63.

for Natives 5; explosives 10;[1] coal 10; European labour 20; cyanide (used in the extraction of gold from the ore) 5; other expenses 20.[2] Total 100. The companies did not consider that it would be practicable to reduce the wages of White employees unless there was a substantial decrease in the cost of living. (The government should, they thought, help to bring this about by reducing import duties, especially on foodstuffs, and railway rates.[3]) But Native wages were another matter. The mining companies declared that with government co-operation a great reduction in the cost of Native labour could be effected. The government should, for example, enforce more efficiently the liquor law of the republic and thus help to diminish the high incidence of drunkenness among Native labourers.[4] It should also encourage the flow of labour to the mines, which would render a reduction of wages possible. It is true that Native wages were reduced by the industry in October 1896 and once more in May 1897,[5] but it was held that much greater reductions were practicable. Early in 1897 a spokesman of the industry, after noting the recent reduction of the average Native wage from 66s. to 60s. per month, declared that the wage could be reduced to 30s. if the government was prepared to help.[6] The industry expected the government to play an active part in the recruitment of labour.[7] At the very least it should remove obstacles which impeded the flow of labour to the mines. Thus, for example, serious charges were made of difficulties placed in the way of would-be mine labourers by Transvaal field-cornets and farmers and of the plunder of Natives returning home with their earnings.[8]

---

[1] The percentage was higher in the case of mines which had not yet reached the producing stage. Industrial Commission, 452.

[2] African (South), 532, pp. 13–17.

[3] Hely-Hutchinson to Chamberlain, 5 Dec. 1896 (Chamberlain papers, H); African (South), 532, p. 64; Industrial Commission, 448; Scholtz, ii. 156. See above, pp. 35, 39, 102.   [4] See above, p. 27.

[5] Etheredge, 78–80. Before the end of 1897 a further reduction of 30 per cent. was agreed to by most of the mining companies. C. 9345, p. 32.

[6] African (South), 532, pp. 13–17. See also Fitzpatrick, 105. In addition to the money wage the companies supplied their Native labourers with food.

[7] African (South), 532, pp. 13–17; Fitzpatrick, 101–2; chamber of mines report for 1897, p. 66.

[8] Report by Samuel Evans; African (South), 536, pp. 460–70; van der Horst, 134–5. Towards the end of 1896 Samuel Evans blamed the government for the very small number of Transvaal Natives working on the mines at that time. On the other hand, Sapte, the manager of the Consolidated Goldfields company, believed that starvation (owing to the failure of the harvest) was to blame: 'In the Northern part of the Transvaal the Natives are dying of hunger and will not come to Johannesburg to work as it would mean leaving wives and children to starve.' Report by Samuel Evans; Altham to Northcott, 24 Dec. 1896 (C.O. 537/133). Between 1890 and 1899 the total number of Native labourers in the gold mines rose from 14,000 to 97,000. Van der Horst, 136.

Spokesmen of the mining companies expressed the conviction that the government was not merely incompetent, but deliberately hostile to the industry.[1] Greene concurred, and attributed this hostility to the fact that 'the President and the older Boers . . . see in the influx of the Uitlanders [consequent on the expansion of the mines] the ultimate absorption of their own independence. . . .'[2] In support of his view he instanced Kruger's opposition to the opening up of certain new gold-fields on the ground that 1,000 more police would be required to cope with the resulting increase of population.[3]

Since the beginning of 1897 Greene had been doing his best to get the mining capitalists to combine so that they might present a united front to the government: for the chamber and the association of mines still faced each other in apparent rivalry. The British agent considered that the two men most opposed to combined action were J. B. Robinsou and Barney Barnato, each of whom was endeavouring 'to secure his own special ends', apparently by a separate approach to the government.[4] Towards the end of April he was able to report that his efforts had been successful: 'practically all the great Companie, and [mine-]owners' had agreed to draw up a 'general petition' to the government, which the public was to be asked to sign. He believed one of the principal reasons for this change of front to be 'the nomination of the present Government Commission of Inquiry [the industrial commission]. . . . I think a wholesome dread of possible revelations at the hands of the . . . Commission . . . may have urged upon them the advisability of agreeing with their adversary quickly while they were in the way'.[5] (The mining magnates rightly believed that the government expected the commission to prove that they were alone responsible for the depression.[6])

The industrial commission, after hearing a great deal of evidence, presented its report towards the end of July 1897 in spite of a cable from Leyds asking for delay until his return from Europe.[7] The chamber of mines admitted that, contrary to the intentions of the government, the commission's advisory members—i.e. the representatives of the mining industry—'assumed . . . the same rights as those

[1] Report by Samuel Evans; C. 9345, p. 37.
[2] African (South), 532, p. 45.
[3] Greene's report of a statement by Kruger in a secret session of the two volksraads in July 1897. African (South), 536, p. 340. See also Fitzpatrick, 105.
[4] African (South), 532, pp. 17–18, 45.
[5] Ibid. 536, no. 95.
[6] C. 9345, p. 35; Fitzpatrick, 303; van Oordt, 777; *Hertzog-Annale*, July 1953, p. 83.
[7] Cd. 623, p. 83. See above, p. 151.

exercised by the ordinary members' and helped to draft the report. Greene went farther: he seems to have had no doubt that the report was the work of 'the mining industry'.[1] These admissions help to explain why the commission did not go fully into all the reasons for the public's loss of confidence in the industry.[2] On the other hand, it discussed with precision and ability the steps which the government should take to lighten the burdens on the mines: otherwise '100 mines will have to close down, [and] in that case an annual amount of £12,000,000 will be taken out of circulation, with results too disastrous to contemplate'.[3] There had, in fact, been no need for the chamber of mines to ask its president to resign from the commission because of his refusal to press for the incorporation of all its demands, unaltered, in the report.[4] Down in Cape Town Milner called the report 'a startler'. And he added: 'it shows a breadth of view, a liberality of judgment, and a force of expression, which, if of genuine Boer origin, give me quite a new idea of the *niveau intellectuel* of the Boer.'[5] Greene's opinion was not so favourable. He thought it a pity that 'the mining industry' had not 'accompanied that report by sufficient proof that if the Volksraad agree to make away with the impositions of which the companies complain, the country will in the end be the gainer and not the loser by their action'. The industry had forgotten, he added, that the Boer legislator was not an economist. 'Moreover it has been pointed out to the President' by the Hollanders in the republic and by others 'that the report . . . is extremely superficial. Thus the dearth of analytical statistics is quoted as evidence of its shallowness, in as much as there are no individual proofs offered as to drawbacks occasioned to the mining industry owing to certain impositions.'[6]

The republican government, which was even more startled by the report than Milner, decided to play for time, partly, Greene surmised, in order to have the benefit of Leyds's advice, who was due back from Europe soon. It persuaded the volksraad to appoint a committee to discuss the report with the executive council, and make

[1] Industrial Commission, preface, p. v; African (South), 536, no. 271.
[2] See above, pp. 186–7.
[3] Industrial Commission, 446.
[4] Chamber of mines report for 1897, pp. 63–73; Industrial Commission, preface, p. vi.
[5] Headlam, i. 82–83. Milner wrote this before he received Greene's letter about the authorship of the report.
[6] African (South), 536, no. 271. The Hollanders' point appears to have been that the commission had not done enough to show the specific effect on mining costs of each of the impositions complained of.

recommendations.[1] Leyds's return early in September coincided with
a great mass meeting in Johannesburg—with the English newspapers
of the Transvaal, both anti- and pro-republican, in support—'to call
attention to the terrible depression now existing on the Rand' and
to ask the government to implement the industrial commission's
report.[2]

Towards the end of August Milner received from Chamberlain
a dispatch informing the republican government that the dynamite
monopoly was a breach of the London convention. He decided not
to present it.[3] This decision was in accordance with a carefully
calculated strategy. He had been 'watching with the deepest interest
the growth of opposition to the ruling oligarchy among the Boers
themselves', and British interference just now might have the effect
of stifling this opposition. He pinned his hopes on two men as the
opposition leaders. The one was Schalk Burger, 'an out-and-out
Boer', who 'was not going to let the conclusions of [the industrial]
commission be treated with contempt by the Executive'. The other
was chief justice Kotze.[4] As early as 6 May Kotze had told Greene
that he was very dissatisfied with the compromise[5] arranged by
de Villiers between Kruger and the judges.[6] Shortly afterwards the
volksraad, at the request of the executive council, appointed a
commission to make recommendations with regard to the revision of
the constitution and other matters. This meant that the legislation
desired by Kotze would not be passed during the 1897 session of the
volksraad. The chief justice thereupon declared that Kruger had
broken the compromise. But he had now taken up weak ground
whither his brothers on the bench refused to follow him.[7] In May,
and again in August, he had several long conversations with Milner,
who was glad to hear that he meant to fight but would not 'hurry
things'.[8] (Greene told the high commissioner in July that Kotze,
who had been worsted in the contest with Leyds for the state secretaryship some months before, was now 'coveting' the presidency.[9])
Though Milner did not consider Kotze a strong man, he believed he

---

[1] *Hertzog-Annale*, July 1953, pp. 100, 104; African (South), 536, no. 271; *Notulen,*
Eerste Volksraad, 1897, art. 815 (10 Aug. 1897).
[2] Greene to high commissioner, 10 Sept. 1897. African (South), 536, no. 297.
[3] African (South), 536, nos. 219, 285.   [4] Headlam, i. 89.
[5] See above, p. 144.   [6] Milner to Chamberlain, 6 May 1897. C.O. 537/132.
[7] Walker (a), 311–12, 316–17.
[8] African (South), 532, p. 109; Headlam, i. 82–83, 89; Walker (a), 311. In May
Kotze also had a long conversation with Rhodes, who 'convinced him that he was not
so black as he had been painted'. Walker (a), 311.
[9] African (South), 536, p. 289.

could rely on his friendliness to Britain: '. . . the impression he left was that of a man who desired to see British influence maintained', and who wished for 'a firm attitude on our part'. That was also the impression he left on a member of the Wernher–Beit firm, presumably Fitzpatrick. '. . . I earnestly hope', the republican chief justice told him after his first talks with Milner, 'that the Imperial factor will prove to be the salvation of South Africa.'[1]

The volksraad committee, whose deliberations the president regularly attended, presented its report on 16 October.[2] 'The Report', declared Greene, 'has been received with . . . dismay by all sections of the . . . Uitlander community, as well as by no small fraction of the Boers themselves.'[3] The general opinion among the Uitlanders was that it amounted to a rejection of the concessions recommended by the industrial commission. The volksraad accepted, in the main, the recommendations of its committee. The principal concession to the mining industry was a reduction of railway rates (especially on the carriage of coal), which was considered by the chamber of mines to be quite inadequate but which reduced the government's share of the profits made by the Netherlands railway company.[4] Certain duties on foodstuffs were also reduced; but other duties were increased 'so that', writes Walker, 'the Treasury gained by the exchange'.[5] After a nine days' debate in the volksraad, in which the president intervened several times, the dynamite monopoly, the cancellation of which had been recommended by the industrial commission, was referred to the executive council by a majority of one vote.[6] The council was instructed to obtain legal opinion whether the dynamite company had acted in accordance with its contract 'for the purpose of finding out what steps can be taken . . . and then to act according to circumstances, with the object of providing the mines with cheaper dynamite. . . .' Finally, there was the recommendation of the industrial commission that a local board should be created consisting of representatives of the government, the mining industry, and commerce to improve the administration of the pass law (which sought to

---

[1] Garvin, iii. 356; African (South), 532, p. 109; letter dated 26 June 1897 sent on to the colonial office by Beit (C.O. 537/133).

[2] *Notulen*, Eerste Volksraad, 1897, art. 1565.

[3] African (South), 543, pp. 38–40.

[4] C. 9345, pp. 19, 34; *Notulen*, Eerste Volksraad, 1897, pp. 912, 918; van Winter, ii. 308.

[5] Walker (*b*), 469; C. 9345, pp. 16–17; *Notulen*, Eerste Volksraad, 1897, pp. 843, 851.

[6] J. H. de la Rey, the later Boer general, who made a vigorous attack on the monopoly, voted in favour of this resolution, apparently in error. *Notulen*, Eerste Volksraad, 1897, pp. 903, 905; African (South), 532, pp. 135–6.

check the desertion of Native labourers), the liquor law, and the gold thefts law. The mining industry attached a great deal of importance to this recommendation. But it was turned down by the volksraad committee and in due course by the volksraad itself on the ground that the proposed board would form 'a government within the government'.[1]

In so far as the recommendations of the industrial commission involved a reduction of state revenues, the government was placed in a difficult position. Owing to the depression its revenues had been falling since the middle of 1897.[2] But its expenditure showed signs of increasing. Besides continuing to spend money on its armament programme, it had to cope with a drought as well as a serious rinderpest epidemic, which by July 1897 had destroyed some 300,000 cattle. By that date it had already spent about £340,000 on foodstuffs to ward off starvation,[3] and had embarked on a plan of importing donkeys from South America at an estimated cost of £450,000. In September the volksraad voted another £150,000, this time for loans on mortgage to 'poor burghers'.[4]

After the publication of the volksraad committee's report the discontent within the republic increased. More mines closed down and the depression deepened.[5] In the volksraad the government had to face increasing opposition, several of its measures being rejected notwithstanding the president's advocacy.[6] Boers held public meetings to express dissatisfaction with its handling of the report of the industrial commission. 'People who know the character of the Boer better than I do', reported Greene, 'foresee the possibility of something very like a revolution taking place. . . .'[7] It would appear that Fitzpatrick was among these prophets. Early in November Fitzpatrick was asked by Greene why he 'had not been approached by the English section of the Rand community to ask Her Majesty's Government to bring pressure to bear on that of the Transvaal, as had been done by the French, German and Dutch communities', who had made representations to their respective consuls. Fitzpatrick replied that the majority of the British thought 'that the introduction of the political element into the controversy' would merely help

---

[1] C. 9345, pp. 11–12, 20, 36–43.
[2] African (South), 536, p. 297; 543, p. 83.
[3] See above, p. 188 n. 8.
[4] African (South), 536, pp. 308–9; 543, pp. 5–6; van Winter, ii. 318 n. The total revenue of the republic for 1897 amounted to £4,480,217. C. 9093, p. 40.
[5] African (South), 536, no. 323; 543, pp. 10, 95–96.
[6] Ibid. 532, pp. 132–5; 536, pp. 253–6, 276; 543, p. 36.
[7] Ibid. 536, p. 453; 543, pp. 38–40, no. 57.

Kruger 'to rally the volksraad to the old cry of foreign interference'. He (Fitzpatrick) shared this view himself: the best policy to follow was, he believed, to give the Boers enough rope to hang themselves.[1]

It was at this juncture that the *rapprochement* between the chamber and the association of mines was consummated by the amalgamation of the two bodies. Any hopes Kruger might have had of gaining advantage from the division in the ranks of the mining magnates had now to be finally abandoned. The defection of J. B. Robinson in particular, who had been the leading spirit in the association of mines and whose attitude to the president had been not unfriendly, was a serious blow. For Robinson controlled a great deal of capital. He also owned a newspaper, the *Johannesburg Times*.[2] Henceforward the Kruger government would have to face stronger opposition from the English press in the republic.[3] It would also have to face increasing popular hostility, more particularly from the British Uitlanders. The deepening depression[4] and the government's unwillingness to give heed to the advice and petitions addressed to it could hardly fail to promote the purposes of the South African league.

In the meantime Chamberlain had had to make up his mind about the dynamite dispatch. Towards the end of October he suggested to the high commissioner that Greene might perhaps privately warn Leyds that he had a communication from the British government on the dynamite monopoly but was waiting to see what the president would do.[5] After the volksraad's decision to shelve the matter, Selborne minuted: 'Now we will see whether the High Commissioner and the British Agent think it the moment to take the field.'[6] Greene and Fiddes, the new imperial secretary, both thought that the time had come to present the dispatch, and their opinion received strong support in the colonial office.[7] But Milner remained adamant. He was still convinced of 'the wisdom of allowing the bitter quarrel which is springing up among the Boers themselves . . . to develop itself and the party of progress to grow up unprejudiced by any

[1] African (South), 532, p. 129.
[2] Ibid. 532, p. 131; 536, no. 96; 543, pp. 97–98.
[3] The government was supported by the Johannesburg *Standard and Diggers' News* and the Pretoria *Press* in return for subsidies. Leyds declared that the 'support' of these two papers did the government more harm than good. *Eenige Correspondentie*, 16, 216–17.
[4] See above, p. 137.
[5] African (South), 543, pp. 24–25.
[6] Minute, 9 Nov., on Milner to Chamberlain, 5 Nov. 1897. C.O. 417/223.
[7] Headlam, i. 137–8; colonial office minutes on Milner to Chamberlain, 6 Nov. 1897 (C.O. 537/132).

visible encouragement from us'. 'I believe myself', he added, 'that the monopoly is doomed.' In the end Chamberlain came round to Milner's view.

The worst thing [he minuted] that can be done in diplomacy or politics is to 'wobble'. For good and sufficient reasons, after the fullest considera-tion, I decided that our policy for the present was to let the Boers 'stew in their own juice', fight out their internal quarrels, and not to be able to coin prejudice and confuse the issues by pointing to external interference as the danger to be feared. This decision may be right or wrong but I intend that it shall have a fair trial. I am therefore prepared to support Sir A. Milner in withholding the despatch.[1]

VII

On 6 December 1897 Greene threw a bombshell into the republican camp by the presentation of the famous dispatch claiming for Britain the suzerainty over the Transvaal.[2]

This was Chamberlain's reply to the dispatch in which the repub-lican government announced the repeal of the immigration law.[3] The missive contained a great deal more than the announcement of Kruger's 'climb-down' on this issue. It dealt exhaustively with the disputes that had arisen between the Transvaal and British govern-ments regarding the interpretation of the London convention,[4] asserted that the convention 'must be interpreted according to the generally accepted principles of the law of nations', and concluded with the request that the matters in dispute should be submitted to the arbitration of a jurist nominated by the Swiss president, who had no interests to promote in South Africa.[5]

On the strength of information from Greene, Milner described the request for arbitration as a 'try-on', which the republican government did not expect to succeed.[6] Yet Selborne had anticipated that the request would be made[7] and the republic continued to urge it

---

[1] Headlam, i. 78; Milner to Chamberlain, 6 Nov. 1897 (African (South), 543, pp. 79–81) and Chamberlain's minute, 18 Dec. (C.O. 537/132).
[2] African (South), 532, p. 141; 543, p. 132.
[3] See above, p. 160 n. 5.   [4] See above, pp. 122–9.
[5] Van Boeschoten to Greene, 7 May 1897. C. 8721, pp. 6–14. Walker—(b), 474— wrongly asserts that Leyds claimed the republic's 'right to arbitration', on the analogy of 'ordinary European states'. No state—'ordinary European' or not—possessed such a right unless it had arbitration treaties.
[6] African (South), 532, pp. 90–91, 98–99, 141; Headlam, i. 68.
[7] Selborne's answer, dated 22 Mar. 1897, to Chamberlain's question 'Where do we go from here?' (16 Mar.). He had no doubt that the request should be refused. Chamberlain papers, C.

until the end. The high commissioner was dead against arbitration in any form. 'It would', he declared, 'disgust all the English [in South Africa] who have all along taken strong line against it . . . and throw away all prestige just gained.' Foreign arbitration was not desired even by the 'mass of Dutch' and there was 'no possible local arbitrator free from bias or capable of commanding general confidence'.[1] The draft reply of the colonial office to the request for arbitration contained the proposal that the questions in dispute between Britain and the republic should be submitted to the judicial committee of the privy council. But Chamberlain had it excised: 'I do not intend', he wrote, 'to make this proposal now. It will be better to keep it in hand', apparently as a 'concession' to be offered later.[2] Milner told Selborne that the republic would never accept such a proposal, but that he was not averse to its being made, since 'they would put themselves in the wrong by refusing'. He indicated that there was one *ad hoc* South African member of the judicial committee to whom he would have no objection—chief justice Kotze.[3] These references to the kind of court that Milner and Chamberlain would be prepared to accept suggest that it was not impartial arbitration that they were after. And this impression is confirmed by a passage in one of Milner's letters: 'The [London] Convention', he wrote to his chief, 'is *such a wretched instrument, that even an impartial Court would be likely to give such an interpretation to it as would render it perfectly worthless to us.' Chamberlain's comment at the foot of this letter was: 'This is a useful letter. I agree with every word of it.'[4]

The draft of the suzerainty dispatch was sent to the law officers for their comments and approval with the remark that it had been 'amended at the Foreign Office and Colonial Office'.[5] The latter had in its possession high commissioner Loch's statement that there could be no doubt 'that the Government of the South African Republic were under the impression that the suzerainty had been abolished [by the London convention], and that impression has been very generally held throughout South Africa. . . . To allude in any way to the question of suzerainty would be to excite anger and suspicion in the South African Republic itself as well as to provoke an

---

[1] Headlam, i. 68.
[2] C.O. 417/218.
[3] Headlam, i. 114.
[4] Milner to Chamberlain, 11 May 1897. Chamberlain papers, D.
[5] African (South), 536, No. 293.

accusation that the representatives of the South African Republic
had been misled.'[1] It also had the opinion given by the law officers
of the Liberal government in 1894 that '. . . on the whole, having
regard to the negotiations which preceded the London Convention
of 1884, the construction of that document itself and the subsequent
attitude of Her Majesty's Government towards the Republic, we are of
opinion that the suzerainty has been abandoned'.[2] The Unionist law
officers were not requested to comment specifically on the suzerainty,
though they *were* asked for their comments on another section of
the dispatch. It seems likely, therefore, that they got the impression
that the suzerainty claim was a settled point of policy and that their
only role with regard to it was to decide whether the arguments
employed in its support could pass muster. Their verdict was favourable,[3] but they subsequently warned Chamberlain that he could not
quote Lord Derby, the colonial secretary at the time of the signing
of the London Convention, in support of the suzerainty (as he
proposed to do). 'Whatever suzerainty meant in the Convention of
Pretoria' (1881), Derby said in the house of lords on 17 March 1884,
'the condition of things which it implied still remains; although the
word is not actually employed [in the London Convention] we have
kept the substance.[4] We have abstained from using the word because
it was not capable of legal definition, and because it seemed to be a
word which was likely to lead to misconception and misunderstanding.' These words, the law officers told Chamberlain, 'favour the
view that the assertion of suzerainty *eo nomine* was given up . . . .'[5]

In the dispatch as finally presented to the republican government
Chamberlain rejected its claim that the London convention 'must be
interpreted according to the generally accepted principles of the law
of nations'. Stripped of verbiage his contention was simply that in
the case of conflicting interpretations of the convention, the British
government's view must prevail. The convention was, after all,
merely a declaration or grant by the Crown.[6] But it was surely
something else besides that. It is true that, according to the preamble,
the Queen had been pleased to direct the substitution of one document
for another, but the preamble then goes on to say that the document

---

[1] Loch to Ripon, 2 July 1894. African (South), 470, p. 33.
[2] Scholtz, ii. 78–79.
[3] Law officers to Chamberlain, 30 Sept. 1897. African (South), 536, no. 293.
[4] Whether or not the 'substance' of suzerainty was retained in the London convention depends on the meaning given to the word suzerainty.
[5] African (South), 543, no. 394.
[6] See above, p. 126.

to be so substituted is a convention—the London convention—
signed by so-and-so on behalf of Her Majesty and by so-and-so on
behalf of the Transvaal state, which would be known in future as the
South African Republic. Having asserted that the London convention
was a unilateral declaration by the British government, Chamberlain
went on to reject the republic's request for arbitration as improper,
since it would be 'incompatible' with Britain's position as the
suzerain power 'to submit to arbitration the construction of the
conditions on which she accorded self-government to the Republic'.
Britain had in fact possessed the suzerainty over the Transvaal under
the Pretoria convention of 1881, which terminated the rising of the
Boers against the British annexation of the republic four years
earlier. Chamberlain based his claim that the suzerainty still existed
on the argument that the London convention of 1884 merely substituted new articles for those of the Pretoria convention, leaving
intact its preamble, wherein the suzerainty was asserted. But the
London convention had its own preamble. It was, in fact, as that
preamble stated, a new convention, which must be presumed to have
replaced the previous agreement, including its preamble.[1]

The first object of the suzerainty claim was clearly to supply an
argument for the rejection of arbitration. But this was not its only
object. 'The Suzerain despatch', wrote Selborne, '. . . will be of great
value as asserting our position before all the world.'[2] What did
Chamberlain wish that position to be? It seems as if he was inclined
to draw an analogy between the republic and an Indian state under
the Queen's suzerainty.

Our statesmen [wrote Westlake[3] in March 1900] are in such a matter [as
the status of the Boer republics] under the peculiar liability of being misled
by our Indian experience. For reasons of policy . . . we have built up in
the peninsula a system of our own, of which the result is that the relations
between the United Kingdom and the native states cannot be expressed
without contradiction in the terms of European international law.[4] That
does not matter, for there is no neighbour to take advantage of the circum-
stance, and it has been officially notified in the Indian Government *Gazette*
of August 21, 1891, that 'the principles of international law have no bearing
upon the relations between . . . the Queen Empress on the one hand, and

---

[1] For the Pretoria and London conventions see Eybers, pp. 455–63 and 469–74;
Chamberlain's suzerainty dispatch is in C. 8721, pp. 18–22.
[2] Headlam, i. 123.
[3] See above, p. 126 n. 5.
[4] The Indian states might not, of course, have any diplomatic relations with foreign
powers.

the native States under the suzerainty of Her Majesty on the other'. But in South Africa we dare not follow such precedents.[1]

The term 'British paramountcy in South Africa', like Chamberlain's interpretation of suzerainty, seems to have been derived from Indian precedents.[2] But from the assertion of paramountcy no rights could be deduced. It was in fact a political and not a legal concept. In other words it depended for its validity on Britain's resoluteness and the other side's acquiescence.

The suzerainty dispatch could not but be regarded by Kruger's government as an attack on the status of the republic. In due course Leyds repudiated the suzerainty in a long and weighty reply, approved by the volksraad in secret session.[3] On the receipt of Leyds's dispatch Chamberlain minuted: 'We certainly should not withdraw [the] claim to Suzerainty. . . .'[4] And he never did. He took 'the high hand'[5] in his rejoinder to Leyds, simply reasserting his claim without attempting to answer the latter's arguments. But he made one new point. If the preamble of the Pretoria convention has ceased to have legal validity, he argued, then not only has the suzerainty ceased to exist but also the republic's internal independence; for both suzerainty and independence owed their existence to that preamble.[6] The argument was a mere debating point, since the London convention clearly had reference to a self-governing republic, which was bound to observe certain stipulations inserted therein, but whose legal competence was otherwise unlimited.[7]

Milner would apparently have been content if Chamberlain had rejected the republic's request for arbitration on the simple ground of policy.[8] His attitude had at any rate the merit of straightforwardness. Some six weeks before the colonial secretary sent off the suzerainty dispatch the high commissioner had sounded the following note of warning:

The mention of the word 'suzerainty' or 'paramountcy' exercises a curiously [sic] maddening effect upon the Boers. I don't suppose the word

---

[1] Quoted in Cook (a), 323.   [2] Seeley, 353.
[3] C. 9507, pp. 7–27; Milner to Chamberlain, 12 Mar. 1898 (C.O. 537/134).
[4] Minute, dated 25 June, on Leyds to Milner, 16 Apr. 1898. C.O. 417/244.
[5] Words used by E. Wingfield, permanent under-secretary, in a minute, dated 28 Aug., on Leyds's dispatch. C.O. 417/244.   [6] C. 9507, p. 28.
[7] Milner, who was in England when Chamberlain's reply to the Leyds dispatch was sent off, wrote: '. . . I . . . am at present engaged in still further emasculating the already flabby suzerainty draft. I want it to be a mere shrug of the shoulders.' Headlam, i. 299. The republican government did not take this view of the reply when it arrived in Pretoria. See Walker (c), 132–3.
[8] See above, p. 196; C. 9507, p. 7.

matters much to us, so long as we have got the substance, and that the President apparently does not deny, inasmuch as he acknowledges more explicitly than I expected the restriction upon his treaty-making power. This is, since the unfortunate substitution of the 1884 for the 1881 Convention, the strongest hold we have upon the Transvaal, and inadequate as it is, there is no doubt of its importance, and more than that, there is now no longer any doubt in the minds of the Boers that we mean to hold on to it.

Chamberlain had thus had due notice of the effect which the claim to suzerainty might be expected to have on the Boers. As for Selborne, he knew that the suzerainty dispatch would 'give the old man a fit at Pretoria'. Milner's own reaction to the dispatch when it arrived was: 'an exceedingly good despatch, which I hope will be published some day, for it defines our position in a way that will always be useful.' It was only after Leyds's reply had come into his hands that he reverted to his original position.[1]

VIII

A few weeks before the suzerainty dispatch was delivered at Pretoria, the campaign preceding the presidential election had opened. Three candidates presented themselves to the burghers: Kruger, commandant-general Joubert, and Schalk Burger. In his address to the electors Kruger made no promises; but he reminded them that he had proved his trustworthiness in the matter of the country's independence.[2] The Uitlanders believed that they had little to hope for from him, but they differed in their attitude towards his opponents and, more particularly, towards Burger. 'Slim Piet' Joubert seems to have been regarded as unreliable, especially by the mining magnates, who took a greater interest in the election than the rest of the Uitlanders. But the influence which the magnates could expect to have on the result was limited. There were comparatively few Uitlander voters, and it was difficult to reach the Boers, *inter alia* because the law forbade 'canvassing, election committees and wire-pulling generally'.[3] The principal magnates decided to use their influence, such as it was, in the interests of Burger. This line of action was strongly recommended by J. B. Robinson, and the Johannesburg representatives of the Wernher–Beit firm agreed to follow suit,

---

[1] Headlam, i. 88, 123, 139; C. 9507, pp. 6–7.
[2] African (South), 543, pp. 99–105.
[3] Greene to High Commissioner, 18 Nov. 1897. Ibid., pp. 99–100.

though one of them, J. P. Fitzpatrick, thought that it was 'quite useless, of course, but perhaps a few hundred pounds spent this way[1] will not be wasted if the result should be a cemented fusion of the industry. . . . You cannot trust one of them [the Boers].'[2] Fruitless attempts were made to induce Joubert to retire in Burger's favour by the offer of a *solatium*.[3] But though the magnates gave Burger their support, they did not wish to see him win the election. They believed that as president he would be able to accomplish little in the teeth of obstruction from Kruger; but if he were defeated by a narrow majority—which was what they desired—he might lead an opposition in the volksraad strong enough to force Kruger to agree to reforms. So much for the magnates. As I have said, other Uitlanders, members of or sympathizers with the South African league, took a different line. They had no confidence in Burger either as head of the government or as leader of the opposition. Their man was Kruger, 'first' wrote Greene, 'because Mr Burger has never disguised his pro-Boer and anti-English sympathies; and secondly, because they hope that Mr Kruger, if re-elected and elated by success, will be encouraged to persevere in his present policy, and thus precipitate a crisis, which [by bringing about British intervention] might . . . make an end of the present unsatisfactory condition of affairs'.[4] Finally, the Johannesburg *Star*, like the magnates, supported Burger's cause. But its advocacy was probably an embarrassment to him. For while soliciting the votes of the intelligent members of the Boer 'species' in Johannesburg, it dwelt contemptuously on the backwardness of 'the hinterland Boer, the benighted denizen of Darkest Transvaal'.[5]

The main plank in Burger's platform was the implementation of the industrial commission's report. He also declared himself convinced that the constitution should be remodelled 'to make it compatible with the demands of the times, so as to avoid the making of changes therein each year'; that the independence of the high court should be secured; and that there should be a very guarded extension of the franchise.[6]

[1] The *Volksstem*, which supported Kruger, declared that the magnates had put up £50,000 to secure Burger's election. African (South), 532, pp. 135–6.

[2] Letter from Johannesburg, dated 8 Nov. 1897 but unsigned, to the Wernher–Beit firm. Ibid. I judge the author of this letter to be Fitzpatrick from internal evidence, mainly that of style. Fitzpatrick's colleague Rouliot, the president of the chamber of mines, did not agree with him: he thought Robinson's plan might be worth trying. Ibid.

[3] African (South), 532, pp. 135–6, 139–41; 543, no. 34, p. 119.

[4] Greene to high commissioner, 10 Dec. 1897. African (South), 543, pp. 121–2.

[5] The *Star*, 5 Jan. 1898.

[6] African (South), 543, pp. 99–105, 121–2; the *Star*, 1 Dec. 1897, 11 Jan. 1898.

Early in January the newspapers of the republic announced the arrival of the suzerainty dispatch. The *Star* predicted that the government would knuckle under, since it knew 'the exact length of John Bull's foot'. The *Volksstem* for its part expressed gratitude to Chamberlain for dealing Kruger a trump card in his contest against the 'progressive liberal party', and then proceeded to remind Burger how he had repeatedly stated during his recent election tour 'that the people of the South African Republic could rely with confidence on the British Government's respect for the prescriptions of the law of nations'. Stung by the attack, Burger protested that he had been misreported: 'He had never trusted England, nor did he now (*loud cheers*). This he had proved as a son of the soil, by his actions on the battlefield.'[1] (It was apparently this utterance that Milner had in mind when he referred shortly after the election to Burger's 'Chauvinist speech of some weeks back'.[2])

The campaign proceeded quietly to its climax.[3] Those who had anticipated a repetition of the violent party strife of the previous (1892–3) election were disappointed. The candidates seem to have realized that the times were too dangerous for the whipping up of partisan passions among the electors. To the very end Greene kept on reporting that Burger's prospects were 'promising', especially if Joubert could be induced to withdraw.[4] But the result belied these prognostications. For Kruger obtained 12,764 votes as against Burger's 3,716 and Joubert's 1,943. The president did very well in Pretoria, and even Johannesburg, where the 'progressives' had hoped to score a resounding success, gave him a 2 to 1 majority over Burger. Wise after the event, Greene explained that Kruger's victory was due to his 'impressive', in fact one might say his 'immense' personality; to his 'extravagant protestations' about the independence of the country; and to the fact that the voters had scant sympathy with Burger's reforming policy and looked upon him as 'somewhat weak, and as too young and inexperienced'.[5] The electorate had evidently been unwilling to change horses in midstream.

---

[1] *Star*, 7 and 11 Jan. 1898; *Volksstem*, 5 Jan. 1898; African (South), 543, pp. 150–1.
[2] Headlam, i. 214.
[3] African (South), 543, pp. 167–8, 191–2.
[4] African (South), 543, no. 34, pp. 119, 121–2, 184. Greene's reports were by no means irresponsible: Middelberg, who was close to the Boer government, did not dare to predict a Kruger victory. Middelberg letters (*Hertzog-Annale*, July 1953, pp. 114, 122).
[5] African (South), 543, pp. 155, 191–2.

CHAPTER VIII

'THE GREAT DAY OF RECKONING'

And it is as if the day of judgment is at hand.
> G. A. A. Middelberg, 12 September, 1897.
> Hertzog-Annale, July 1953, p. 105.

A prince is also respected when he is either a true friend or a down-right enemy, that is to say, when, without any reservation, he declares himself in favour of one party against the other. . . .

I

ON 5 February 1898, five days before the announcement of Kruger's re-election, chief justice Kotze wrote to the president that since the draft of the promised new constitution had not yet been published,[1] he now desired to withdraw his provisional pledge not to exercise the testing right; and he sent the letter to the newspapers for immediate publication. Kruger replied by dismissing him under law 1 of 1897.[2] Judge Gregorowski, whom Greene had described in 1897 as the ablest member of the republican bench after Kotze, was appointed to succeed him.[3] By his precipitate action Kotze had placed himself in the wrong, as was duly noted in the colonial office,[4] and the government made full use of its opportunity. At the same time there can be

---

[1] The constitutional commission, whose meetings Kruger frequently attended, completed the draft in Oct. 1898, and the volksraad passed it with a few alterations in July and Aug. 1899. The constitution as finally adopted did not enhance the independence of the high court (see above, p. 144), notwithstanding a plea by the chief justice of the Orange Free State. He also pleaded in vain that law 1 of 1897 should be repealed or amended. The new constitution required a majority of votes in two successive volksraad sessions for its amendment, but it expressly debarred the high court from pronouncing any duly published enactment of the volksraad to be unconstitutional. There was, furthermore, no provision against hasty legislation (see above, p. 142) which did not amend the constitution. On the other hand, the constitution as finally passed did provide that disputed volksraad elections should be dealt with no longer by the legislature but by the high court. In Aug. 1899 Kruger himself proposed a new clause providing for the abolition of the religious tests which had hitherto debarred Catholics and Jews from membership of the volksraad and (in theory) also from appointment as state officials. But the volksraad decided to postpone consideration of the clause until the people had expressed their views on it. *Notulen*, Eerste Volksraad, 25 July–29 Aug. 1899 *passim*; African (South), 543, p. 536; 571, p. 240; 572, pp. 165–8; 600, pp. 431–4, 475–7, 519–22, 657–8; Leyds, *Eerste Jaren*, no. 45; L. M. Thompson in *Butterworths S.A. Law Review* (1954), p. 71; Saron and Hotz, 186, 199.

[2] See above, p. 143.

[3] Greene to high commissioner, 2 July 1897. African (South), 532.

[4] Colonial office minutes on Greene to Milner, 9 Feb., in Milner to Chamberlain, 15 Feb. 1898. C.O. 537/134.

no doubt that the bench, at no time a strong one, was weakened by his dismissal. True, he had dabbled in politics; but he was regarded as an excellent lawyer and an incorruptible judge.[1] On the other hand, to declare as Milner did, that the dismissal of Kotze meant 'the destruction of the independence of the Bench'[2] and its subjection 'to the caprices of the Executive', was to overshoot the mark.[3] It should have been clear that Kotze had been dismissed because he had reasserted a new and far-reaching doctrine of judicial competence.

Kotze's defiance of Kruger did not produce the effect anticipated by Milner. 'The immediate effect of [Kotze's] resignation', he wrote to Greene, 'has been disappointing. I thought it would have attracted more attention and excited more indignation throughout South Africa. There are people who say that the storm is coming yet, but I feel no assurance of it.'[4] This must not be taken to imply that the incident passed unnoticed. There was some agitation in the press.[5] In the Cape the South African league showed its teeth,[6] and its counterpart in the republic, assembled in congress, called upon the British government to intervene in order to protect the menaced liberty and property of the Uitlanders. As for the legal profession in the Transvaal, Greene reported two days after the publication of the Kotze letter that their feelings were 'somewhat mixed, some holding that the Chief Justice's action is inopportune, and others that it is uncalled-for and due to personal motives'. After his dismissal, however, members of the Johannesburg bar and side bar did protest.[7] But the agitation soon died down throughout South Africa, and Kotze's declaration that he was appealing to 'the Suzerain Power' failed to sustain it,[8] though there were indications for a short time that it might.[9]

The re-election of Kruger and the Kotze fiasco led Milner to reveal his mind more fully than he had yet done in his official and semi-official correspondence. He had looked to Kotze and Burger to provide the rallying points of a 'strongish opposition' which would lean upon the support of Uitlanders and sooner or later achieve the

---

[1] Headlam, i. 82; African (South), 532, p. 109.
[2] Walker repeats this statement in somewhat milder language. *C.H.B.E.* viii. 582.
[3] Headlam, i. 216, 218, 219, 233, 235.
[4] Ibid. 216.
[5] Walker (*a*), 321.
[6] In reply to the press and league agitation a motion approving Kotze's dismissal was drafted at a congress of the Afrikaner bond. But it was not put. African (South), 543, pp. 247–8.
[7] Walker (*a*), 319; African (South), 543, pp. 188 and 557, p. 11.
[8] Headlam, i. 225–6.
[9] See below, p. 209.

enfranchisement of some of them. But Kotze had just been eliminated with surprising ease and Burger had proved 'a broken reed'.[1] 'Like everybody else', the high commissioner told Greene, 'I thought Kruger would get in again, but I took it implicitly from all the best-informed people—yourself, Kotze, Fitzpatrick, etc.—that he would have a close shave.'[2] He declared now that his policy during the latter part of 1897 had been misconceived. He had in fact miscalculated the political effects of the depression and the strength of the Boer opposition to Kruger's government. So far from 'going to the devil' that government had emerged from the recent election stronger than before. Having been given rope the Boers had not hanged themselves in accordance with Fitzpatrick's prophecy. There was no longer any sign of the 'revolution', which Greene had foreshadowed and which 'might have justified, or indeed necessitated, British interference'.[3]

Milner's mood changed now—unalterably—from over-optimism to extreme pessimism. He was willing to wait no longer. He had given the republic nine months to produce something substantial in the way of reform. Time was slipping by, and the outlook had darkened. He would hold out no hope that the prospects might yet improve. 'There is no way out of the political troubles of S. Africa', he told Chamberlain, 'except reform in the Transvaal or war. And at present the chances of reform in the Transvaal are worse than ever. The Boers quarrel bitterly among themselves, but it is about jobs and contracts, not politics!' And to Selborne ten weeks later:

The whole political power in the Transvaal is in the hands of the Boer oligarchy—armed to the teeth. And there is no *reform party* among that oligarchy. The delusion, under which most of us, including myself, laboured on that point, has been finally dispelled by the [presidential] election and by the desertion of Kotze by even the most progressive of his fellow-burghers. . . . Two wholly antagonistic systems—a medieval race oligarchy, and a modern industrial state, recognizing no difference of status between various white races cannot permanently live side by side in what is after all *one country*. The race oligarchy has got to go, and I see no signs of its removing itself. To hope that we shall ever have the sympathy of any considerable number of our [Cape] Dutch subjects in removing it—a Dutch monopoly—by force, seems to me to be idle . . . . In the fight for [the] establishment [of the principle of equality], if it comes to a fight, we shall have to rely on British forces alone. And whether we shall have the whole of

[1] Headlam, i. 89, 221, 226.　　　[2] Ibid. 214.
[3] Ibid. 79–80, 234; and above, pp. 175, 193–4.

British South Africa enthusiastically on our side, depends . . . on letting everybody understand that, whatever the immediate occasion of the quarrel, our real cause is . . . the establishment of a good system of government —pure justice and equal citizenship—in the Transvaal.[1]

So Milner had made up his mind that the time had come for the use of force. If the British government gave him his head, 'the great day of reckoning' was at hand.[2] In preparation for 'the day' of military intervention or the threat thereof, he now began to assemble his civilian forces in South Africa with greater determination than before. The Afrikaners might be written off except for some stragglers.[3] And the British had to be stimulated to greater unity and zeal. Chamberlain evidently believed that 'a very large section of the English party' in the Cape was still opposed to 'Imperial interference'.[4] The Cape's prime minister was among the waverers. Possibly with his eye on Milner as much as on Chamberlain, he repeated to the latter the warning he had uttered a year before. Having asserted that the Cape had many 'staunch friends' in the Orange Free State who had no sympathy with the policy of the Transvaal government, he continued: 'My counsel and my practice has always been Patience. That alone is the virtue by which Dutch doggedness can be successfully overcome. Nothing has ever been done well in South Africa in a hurry. And I feel sure, notwithstanding everything said to the contrary, that there is no desire on your part to force the pace.'[5] And then there was Henry Binns, the new prime minister of Natal. In order to promote the colony's commercial interests, he had actually caused Kruger to be informed that he had always been one of his admirers, and that he 'need not have any anxiety about the Natal Ministry on account of Bale and Hime being in it, as both these gentlemen intended leaving the South African League'. The presidential election took place shortly after this, and Binns sent Kruger a telegram of congratulation. This was too much for Milner. Binns's attitude, he told the Natal governor, was disloyal. And he added: 'There has got to be a separation of the sheep from the goats in this sub-continent. . . .'[6]

To separate the sheep from the goats, i.e. the 'loyal' from the

[1] Headlam, i. 221, 234–5.   [2] Ibid 215.
[3] See above, pp. 175–6.
[4] Chamberlain to Milner, 16 Mar. 1898. Headlam, i. 228.
[5] Sprigg to Chamberlain, 8 Apr. 1898. Chamberlain papers, J.
[6] Hely-Hutchinson to Chamberlain, 16 Dec. 1897 (Chamberlain papers, H); Headlam, i. 215–16.

'disloyal', appears to have been the main object of the famous speech which Milner delivered at Graaff-Reinet on 3 March 1898.[1] Since the re-election of Kruger and the dismissal of Kotze he had been waiting for an opportunity to make a public pronouncement on the question of loyalty in relation to the Transvaal problem.[2] It was given him by an address in which the local branch of the Afrikaner bond complained about the aspersions cast upon their loyalty by the league. In his reply Milner said: ' . . . Of course you are loyal. It would be monstrous if you were not.' He then proceeded to indicate that the Afrikaners belonging to the bond had only themselves to blame if they were accused of disloyalty. They were, in fact, partisans of Kruger. If they wished peace to be preserved in South Africa, let them use all their influence—apparently by way of public protest—to induce the Transvaal to reform. The Graaff-Reinet speech could hardly have been intended to 'win over'[3] an appreciable number of those to whom it was ostensibly addressed. The speech was, in fact, a challenge to all South Africans to choose their side. The response was immediate. Milner informed Chamberlain, who expressed entire approval of the speech,[4] that the English press in South Africa was 'wild with delight'. He told his chief also, perhaps to remove any misgivings the latter may have felt, that several (unnamed) 'leading Dutchmen and Bondsmen' had thanked him for the speech.[5] Up in Pretoria the old president told his executive council that Milner's attitude reminded him of his equally masterful predecessor, Sir Bartle Frere. Kruger is said to have declared that he did not trust the high commissioner: 'Sir B. Frere . . . had taken up a similar line and what had been the result?'[6] He meant that the result had been the Anglo-Boer war of 1880–1. More than a year later Hicks Beach, who was colonial secretary at the time of Frere's high commissionership in South Africa, also drew a parallel between him and Milner.[7]

The Graaff-Reinet speech, writes Walker, was delivered 'in the midst of a fierce general election [campaign] for the Cape Upper House' or legislative council, which the progressives ultimately won with little to spare.[8] On 12 March Rhodes 'underlined Milner's main

---

[1] Ibid. 243–6.   [2] African (South), 543, pp. 247–8.
[3] Walker in *C.H.B.E.* viii. 583. Walker adds that 'by clearing the air' the speech 'helped to bring about better relations between Great Britain and Germany in Southern Africa'. I doubt this. The German government already understood the British position with regard to southern Africa. See above, pp. 99–100.
[4] African (South), 543, p. 328.
[5] Ibid., pp. 247–8.
[6] Report by Greene. Ibid. 557, p. 36.   [7] Gardiner, ii. 498.
[8] *C.H.B.E.* viii. 583; Headlam, i. 254.

theme'[1] in a speech in which he expounded to the voters the policy of the progressive party. Milner's utterance combined with the emergence of Rhodes as the potential leader of the progressives intensified the 'turmoil'—the political passions—in South Africa, for which Milner threw all the responsibility on the republican government.[2] From this time he was regarded as the commander-in-chief of the 'British party'—the Cape's progressive party and the South African league—with Rhodes as his principal lieutenant.

A fortnight after the Graaff-Reinet speech Milner received a telegram from his chief which pulled him up sharply in his tracks. It read as follows: 'The principal object of H.M. Government in S. Africa at present is peace. Nothing but a most flagrant offence would justify the use of force. . . .'[3] The telegram was followed by a letter in which Chamberlain reiterated the policy agreed upon between himself and Milner at the time of the latter's departure for South Africa—the policy of patience and restoration of confidence.[4] He warned Milner that his war policy would not be supported by public opinion in Britain and concluded:

I have hitherto spoken of the position entirely without regard to the general Imperial outlook, but I need hardly add that this affords a very strong addition to the arguments in favour of a policy of reserve and delay. We have on hand difficulties of the most serious character with France, Russia, and Germany. We are engaged in an important expedition in the Sudan. . . . We may emerge from all these troubles without a war, but I cannot conceal from myself that the prospect is more gloomy than it has ever been in my recollection. . . . Accordingly I wish to emphasize the fact that for the present at any rate our greatest interest in South Africa is peace, and that all our policy must be directed to this object.[5]

On the receipt of Chamberlain's telegram Milner wired to Greene: 'I have reason to believe that H.M.'s Government are not at all anxious to bring matters to a head. We must keep up our wickets but not attempt to force the game.'[6] The warning was necessary, for Greene had been doing his bit to forward the high commissioner's policy. Early in March he reported that, according to *The Times*'s

---

[1] Walker (c), 105. The speech is in Vindex, 529–35.
[2] Headlam, i. 64, 215, 253–4.
[3] Chamberlain to Milner, 19 Mar. 1898. Ibid. 226.   [4] See above, p. 174.
[5] Headlam, i. 228–9. Chamberlain would not allow the publication of a dispatch which Milner intended to be his first move in 'working up to a crisis', on the ground that it 'would only stir up Jingo feeling here at a time when we want to keep things quiet'. Minute on Milner to Chamberlain, 23 Feb. 1898 (C.O. 417/242); Headlam, i. 218–23.   [6] Ibid. 226–7.

correspondent in Johannesburg, there was dissatisfaction among people of all nationalities owing to the depression, while the *Star* was 'meditating an energetic propaganda against the government and an appeal to British sentiment as strong as they dare to make it'. Next day Greene wrote that the *Star* had opened its campaign with an editorial, which had been written as a feeler to try the Uitlanders' temper and 'sails very near the wind as regards the attitude to be recommended to the Uitlanders. . . . The people are very generally clamouring, as openly as they dare, for interference by Her Majesty's Government. There is more, I take it, now in this [imperial] sentiment than at any previous time. . . .' The Uitlanders wanted a wholesome rule, 'if need be under the British flag, established in the place'.[1] This was the state of affairs in Johannesburg when Milner's warning arrived. Greene understood at once that the public clamour would have to be postponed to a more convenient time. He took steps accordingly to curb the exuberance of the South African league,[2] which had, as he put it, 'of late largely extended the field of its labour and is now opening branches all along the line of the Witwatersrand reef. . . .' A deputation of the league wanted to know from him whether a great public meeting to call upon Britain to intervene in the Kotze issue would strengthen the hands of the British government. In reply Greene told them, after drawing their attention to Britain's 'delicate' situation in West Africa, China, Egypt, and India, that 'it would . . . be more in harmony with the spirit of true patriotism not to force matters in this part of the world at the present time, but to place full confidence in Her Majesty's Government'.[3]

The rest of the year 1898 was for Milner a period of irksome waiting.

The only thing to do [he told Greene] is quietly and in a scientific spirit to knock on the head, whenever opportunity offers, the illusions on which the policy of 'laisser aller' is based. It is quite natural that, not knowing the real facts, they [the colonial office] should believe that 'time fights on our side'. The thing is steadily, uncontentiously, to make them realise the facts. They will draw the conclusion for themselves sooner or later. The only thing we must never do is to give them any encouragement in cherishing the 'couleur de rose' view of the South African future, if left to itself.[4]

Chamberlain would have to realize, for example, that the Afrikaners in the Cape, not to speak of those in the Orange Free State,

[1] African (South), 557, pp. 31–34.   [2] Ibid. 543, pp. 303, 333.
[3] Ibid., pp. 333–4; Headlam, i. 227. See also above, p. 164.   [4] Headlam, i. 237.
6371   P

were 'our irreconcilable enemies'.[1] And there was another thing, in
Milner's view, that Chamberlain would have to realize, namely, that
the British treaties with the South African Republic, i.e. the London
convention and the Swaziland convention of 1894, would prove of
little assistance to them in their aim of securing British supremacy
throughout South Africa,[2] even if the republic could be made to
accept the British government's interpretation of them. If she persisted in rejecting a British demand based upon 'these wretched
Treaties',[3] such action would no doubt constitute a *casus belli*. But
the trouble was that

the points which arise under the Conventions are very apt to be thin and
technical . . . some trumpery thing which nobody cares about, and which
would excite absolutely no sympathy either in S. Africa or elsewhere. . . .
Therefore, in our dealings with the S.A.R. I say let us look to the big facts,
all of them internal Transvaal questions, with which *in theory* [i.e. legally]
we have nothing to do and not think that we can disregard them because
they may not be 'breaches of the Convention'.[4]

II

In his pleas for a 'show-down' with the republic Milner laid some
emphasis on her armaments.[5] At the same time Greene reported that
further supplies of arms were to be acquired. He stated (correctly)
that the government had recently ordered an additional 8,000 rifles.
Furthermore, he had been told that more rifles, 'quick-firing guns',
and field artillery were to be purchased. He then proceeded to discuss
the amount of war material already in the possession of the republic.
Arms and ammunition to the value of £121,396 and £256,291 had
been imported in 1896 and 1897 respectively. (The bulk of these
supplies had been ordered during the six months succeeding the raid.)
In addition forts had been constructed at Pretoria and Johannesburg
at a cost of over £1½ million.[6]

What significance did the British authorities attach to these preparations? Though Chamberlain toyed with the idea of a possible
attack on the British empire, the only kind of overt republican
aggression he and Selborne appear to have entertained seriously was
the denunciation of the London convention. And then only if Britain
was involved in a war with one or more of the great powers of Europe:

[1] Headlam, i. 187, 267–8.   [2] Ibid. 267–8.
[3] See above, p. 196.   [4] Headlam, i. 223, 232–3, 398.
[5] Garvin, iii. 370; Headlam, i. 234. See also above, p. 157.
[6] Cd. 1789, pp. 192–3; Breytenbach, 274–7.

'in which case', declared Chamberlain, 'Her Majesty's Government could consider the situation at leisure.'[1] Milner took a similar line. It is true that on one occasion he used language which on the face of it contradicts the colonial office view. 'If they thought our hands were *quite full*', he wrote to Chamberlain in March 1898, 'they would be down on us [fly at our throats][2] at once for a certainty, for they are armed to the teeth and their heart is black.'[3] This outburst may, however, reflect Milner's chagrin at the peace telegram which he had received from Chamberlain a few days before rather than his considered judgement.[4] This was that he did not 'in the least' anticipate 'physical aggression . . . for which [i.e. to resist which] an army of 8 to 10,000 men [such as Britain actually had on the spot] should just suffice. . . .'[5]

The British authorities, therefore, do not appear to have feared physical aggression. What they did fear was that the Boer armaments would encourage the government and volksraad to resist reform indefinitely, unless they were confronted with the threat of war, and to behave in a manner calculated to undermine British paramountcy. About seventeen months after the time here dealt with Milner told Chamberlain:

> The question of armaments is of supreme importance to future position. Already, in spite of permanent garrison of 9,000, we are so weak, as compared with Republics, that for effective pressure in support of any demand on S.A.R. we have to bring out an army from home. If present crisis results in leaving S.A.R. still stronger as military power or free to become so, we cannot expect S.A.R. to pay slightest regard to our representations hereafter. The sacrifice necessary to enforce them would be too great. . . .

In the colonial office Graham commented:

> . . . The Boers are gradually forming themselves into a military power out of all proportion to the strength of our garrison in South Africa. We cannot complain of it, as it is said to be for purposes of defence against the large military force we could throw into the country in a short time. But the fact remains that it will give them an immense advantage in political negotiations in future, and must have a certain effect on the native mind.

Chamberlain agreed with Milner and Graham.[6]

---

[1] Cd. 1789, p. 191; Headlam, i. 230. [2] Milner, some lines further down.
[3] Garvin, iii. 370. [4] Contrast Walker (*d*), 12.
[5] Headlam, i. 223. See also ibid. 232, 352–3, 477. Professor Walker, writing with the advantage of hindsight, does not agree with Milner. See *C.H.B.E.* viii. 584–5.
[6] Headlam, i. 511; Graham's minute (18 July) on Milner's telegram dated 16 July 1899 (C.O. 417/263); Garvin, iii. 468.

Milner did what he could to place impediments in the way of the further arming of the republic. On the strength of information received from R. K. Loveday, the only English-speaking member of the volksraad, to the effect that the republican government was negotiating a loan of £2½ million,[1] he asked Chamberlain in March 1898 whether something could not be done 'through international influence of big financial houses in London, to make difficulties for the Transvaal Government in borrowing money. It only goes in strengthening their armaments, making ultimate struggle more severe, and in prolonging present system, which costs the finances millions a year in excessive taxation and bribes. If only supplies could be cut off the Transvaal might be brought to reason without a catastrophe.'[2] Chamberlain allowed Selborne to find out what could be done: 'but after all', he added, 'the Transvaal will go its own way and in the end it will not matter whether it has built one fort or four or whether it has one million or two million [sic] rifles.' Having consulted Bertie of the foreign office—who 'has had much experience of cosmopolitan financiers'—as well as Lord Rothschild and Beit, Selborne reported: 'The conclusion is that any loan can be stopped, and would be, in London, and probably in Paris, but that we cannot influence the market in Holland or Germany.'[3] As will be seen later, the republic did, in fact, experience considerable difficulty in raising her loan.

III

In April 1898 Leyds resigned the state secretaryship of the republic in order to take up the post of envoy extraordinary and minister plenipotentiary in Europe, which had been vacant since the death of Beelaerts van Blokland a year before. He left South Africa worn out and with his health impaired.[4] His departure had been delayed by the refusal of the volksraad to sanction the expenditure that the new appointment was expected to entail. In March the raad at length agreed to vote £7,200 for the envoy and his staff, but cut down the £6,225 proposed by the government for 'allowances' to £3,725.[5]

Shortly after Leyds's embarkation for Europe the colonial and

---

[1] On the Transvaal loan see below, p. 229.
[2] Milner to Chamberlain, 9 Mar. 1898 (C.O. 537/134); African (South), 557, p. 34.
[3] Minutes of Chamberlain and Selborne on Milner to Chamberlain, 9 Mar. 1898, and on director of military intelligence to colonial office, 23 Feb. 1898. C.O. 537/134.
[4] *Hertzog-Annale*, July 1953, p. 142.
[5] African (South), 532, pp. 132–5; 543, pp. 288–9.

foreign offices consulted together about the recognition of his status by the British government. It is clear that Chamberlain wished the question of the republic's diplomatic representation to be reconsidered in the light of Britain's claim to suzerainty. He suggested to the foreign office that the governments of the Netherlands, Belgium, and Portugal, where Britain had representatives equal in rank to Leyds, should be told that 'whatever rank those Governments may, as a matter of courtesy, grant to Dr Leyds, Her Majesty's Government could not consent that he should be placed upon a footing of equality with the Queen's representatives, and still less that he should ever have precedence over them'. The foreign office refused to take this step on the ground that it would be irregular and might lead the powers concerned formally to question the suzerainty. But it agreed that its representatives abroad should be told to stay away from 'any function, official or social' at which they might meet a republican representative claiming to take precedence of them. It took the further step of instructing British diplomats to inform Leyds that they did not recognize his diplomatic status with regard to themselves.[1]

These European developments had a sequel in South Africa some months afterwards. The republic established the post of consul-general in Cape Town, and approached Milner in order to obtain the British government's *exequatur* for its nominee. A similar procedure had been followed five years previously, when the republic appointed its first consul in Natal. But on this occasion Milner wanted to know why the post had been created. The state secretary replied, in diplomatic language, of course, that this was none of his business, which, indeed, according to international usage, it was not. Milner's attitude, nevertheless, made it impossible for the post to be filled. He explained to Chamberlain that the state secretary wished to appoint in Cape Town a representative with the 'high-sounding' title of consul-general, merely 'to magnify the importance of the South African Republic', and to get rid of 'any semblance of [British] Suzerainty or Superiority'. 'The Consul-General . . .', he added, 'will of course claim precedence of mere Consuls. . . . In conceivable circumstances he might become the *doyen* of the whole Consular body.'[2]

---

[1] Ibid. 543, pp. 434–5, 463–4; 557, p. 75 and *passim*; Leyds, *Tweede Verzameling*, part II, pp. 15–18, 22–23, 27–28; Scholtz, ii. 57–59.

[2] African (South), 571, pp. 170, 324–5; green book no. 3 of 1899 *passim*; Leyds, *Eenige Correspondentie*, pp. 93, 100–2, 238; Botha, ch. 37; Scholtz, ii. 59–61.

When Leyds arrived in Europe towards the end of June 1898 there had been set in motion a train of developments which were to be fatal for the success of his mission. But before we deal with the negotiations which culminated in the treaty between Britain and Germany with regard to the Portuguese colonies, it will be necessary to take a glance at the Anglo-Boer rivalry at Delagoa Bay and its neighbourhood during the year preceding Leyds's arrival in Europe. The British minister at Lisbon continued to keep an eagle eye on every transaction or proposal affecting the bay during the term of office of major (later Sir) J. Mousinho d'Albuquerque as royal commissioner in Portuguese East Africa (1896–8). Mousinho believed that 'the position of Portugal, its existence as a colonial Power, render more necessary to it than to any other Power the good offices of Britain'. But he was also convinced that 'we cannot retain the most important points on the East African coast and continue to play the part of [mere] Custom-house officials, hampering the exploitation of these districts and placing every obstacle in the way of the mercantile and industrial development of the adjacent countries'. He declared that at Lourenço Marques in particular the position was serious owing to the totally inadequate harbour works.[1] Unfortunately the mother country was powerless to take ameliorative action, since the British colonial and foreign offices looked askance at any proposal to issue debentures which might fall into the hands of the Transvaal or another foreign government. As one of Chamberlain's officials remarked, the colonial office was pursuing 'a dog in the manger policy' with regard to Delagoa Bay.[2] As long as the South African Republic remained an independent state and continued to pursue an 'isolationist' policy, it suited the colonial office very well that the harbour of Lourenço Marques should remain unimproved. The inadequacy of the harbour would seriously hamper the competitive effectiveness of the Delagoa Bay–Johannesburg railway as against the British colonial lines. Yet the Delagoa Bay line made steady progress, and by the end of 1898 it was carrying a heavier tonnage to the Rand than either the Cape or Natal lines.[3]

In May 1898 the Anglo-Portuguese negotiations with regard to

---

[1] Foreign office to colonial office, 7 July 1899, enclosing précis of a book by Mousinho on his administration of Portuguese East Africa. C.O. 417/272.

[2] Colonial office to foreign office, 4 Dec. 1897; Salisbury to MacDonell, 21 Dec. 1897 (C.O. 417/230); MacDonell to Salisbury, 1 Feb. 1898 (C.O. 537/134); minute by H. Lambert on foreign office to colonial office, 31 Oct. 1898 (C.O. 417/251).

[3] See above, p. 39.

Delagoa Bay, broken off a year before, were resumed. On being informed by Chamberlain of the possibility that Britain might acquire control over the bay and its railway, Milner expressed great satisfaction. 'I look on possession of Delagoa Bay', he wrote, 'as the best chance we have of winning the great game between ourselves and the Transvaal for the mastery in South Africa without a war.' To the governor of Natal he said a little later that he thought the British government would use the bay as its 'trump card in the game for uniting S. Africa as a British State'. But he was afraid, he added, that 'we are all a little previous in supposing' that Britain had got hold of the bay.[1] Milner was right. For after more than two years of quiescence, Germany had intervened and stopped the British game. As early as April 1897 the German ambassador in London had advised his government that if Germany played her cards well she might acquire part of the Portuguese empire in Africa. Now—in June 1898—the ambassador was instructed to tell Salisbury that there could be no change in the *status quo* at Delagoa Bay without the concurrence of Germany. It soon became clear that the attitude of the German government had changed since the years 1894–6. So far from desiring to maintain the *status quo*, it was now ready to abandon all Portuguese East Africa south of the Zambesi to Britain, provided Germany received suitable compensation. With this territory were to go the Boers. It was well understood that if an agreement could be reached satisfactory to Germany, she was willing to abandon the South African Republic to its fate. On this basis Salisbury and Chamberlain were prepared to do business, and an Anglo-German convention, accompanied by two secret instruments, was signed on 30 August. These agreements provided for simultaneous British and German loans to Portugal on the security of the Portuguese possessions in Africa and on the island of Timor. If Portugal were to default, they envisaged the division of these colonies among the two contracting powers. The agreements remained a dead letter, since Portugal obtained in Paris the money she desperately needed. Britain, nevertheless, derived the important advantage from them that Germany was eliminated as a factor to be reckoned with in her dealings with the republic. Towards the end of 1898 Milner wrote from England after several visits to the colonial office: '. . . I am now *sure* that the Anglo-German agreement . . . does formally and forever eliminate Germany as a *political* influence in the Transvaal and the

[1] Headlam, i. 267–8.

countries immediately surrounding it.'[1] Germany did in fact honour the agreement, though it soon became apparent that the prospect of obtaining any advantage therefrom was remote. After its conclusion she gave the republic even less encouragement (if that were possible) than in the years immediately preceding, and the British government was aware of this. Now Germany had been the republic's main prop in Europe. When she agreed to stand aside, it was most unlikely that France and Russia would take any action with regard to the republic that would offend Britain.[2]

While in the act of finally withdrawing her support, Germany rendered one service to the republic. In one of the secret clauses of the Anglo-German agreement Britain promised that she would no longer oppose the confirmation of the Eiffe or Katembe concession by the Portuguese government.[3] Henceforward, as a counterpoise to the German concession, the foreign office pushed the claims of an English company, which had been formed to exploit a concession at Delagoa Bay—the so-called Lingham grant—rather similar in character to the Katembe concession. Chamberlain wished the foreign office to continue to place difficulties in the way of the ratification of the latter concession. But it was hardly practicable to support Lingham and persist in the opposition to Eiffe. In the end the foreign office agreed to the confirmation of the Katembe concession on condition that the company exploiting the concession was to be and remain a Portuguese company and that it should be prohibited from transferring any of its rights without the consent of the Portuguese government. In the opinion of the colonial office these safeguards were illusory. But even if they had been real, their practical importance would have been slight. For by the time the British government withdrew its objections to the Katembe concession the Anglo-Boer war was only seven months off.[4]

[1] Headlam, i. 299.
[2] On the Anglo-German agreement and its implications for the republic see *British Documents*, i. 71–75; Garvin, iii. 313, 315, 317–20, 333; Langer, 529, 618–19, 652–3; van Winter, ii. 282–94. Early in 1899 there arose a sharp dispute between Britain and Germany over their respective interests in Samoa. The dispute was not settled until November. The German government, nevertheless, continued to advise the Boers against taking the risk of war, and in August the German ambassador in London informed the British foreign office that Kruger had been told of Germany's final determination not to interfere. At the same time the German negotiators warned the British government that with war in South Africa on their hands, it was in the interests of Britain to settle the Samoan question. Garvin, iii, ch. lxii.
[3] See above, pp. 153–5.
[4] Foreign office to colonial office, 31 Oct. 1898, and minutes by Chamberlain and his staff; colonial office to foreign office, 30 Nov. 1898 (all in C.O. 417/251); foreign

In the face of the attitude which Germany had agreed to adopt towards the republic, Leyds's efforts to obtain official support on the Continent were bound to fail. Thus, for example, he found it impossible to persuade the French and Russian governments to back his plan for neutralizing Delagoa Bay. The most he could do was to encourage the French government—it was the time of the Fashoda crisis—in its desire to obtain money for Portugal which might forestall the implementation of the Anglo-German treaty, and to assist in mobilizing Portuguese public opinion against the dismemberment of the empire. He had informed his government as early as 11 September 1898 that he believed Britain and Germany had reached an agreement and that Delagoa Bay was included in it.[1]

IV

After the resignation of Leyds as state secretary and the new appointments which followed in its wake, the barometer appeared to be set fair for reform and improved relations with Britain. The election as Leyds's successor of A. Fischer, a member of the Free State government, was a good omen, for that government was more than ever convinced that reform was necessary in the Transvaal and liked to regard itself as a mediator or 'bridge' between its ally and the British colonies. But Fischer declined the appointment, notwithstanding a personal appeal from Kruger. The volksraad thereupon elected F. W. Reitz, a Cape colonist by birth, an English barrister by training, and a former president of the Free State. Piet Grobler, a young grandson of Kruger, who had been educated for a time in England and was said to have 'somewhat progressive ideas', succeeded the Hollander van Boeschoten as under-secretary of state. About the same time J. C. Smuts, then twenty-eight years old, was appointed state attorney. Like Reitz, Smuts was by origin a Cape colonist. After a brilliant career at Cambridge he had returned to the Cape in 1895 to practise at the bar and enter politics. A few months before the raid he began his long political career with a public speech in support of Rhodes. After the raid he denounced Rhodes, emigrated to the Transvaal, and gave up his British nationality. Greene learned

office to colonial office, 16 Jan. 1899, with enclosure; foreign office to colonial office, 8 Feb. 1899; colonial office to foreign office, 17 Feb. 1899; foreign office to colonial office, 8 Mar. 1899, and minutes by Wingfield, Graham, and Lambert (all in C.O. 417/271).
[1] Botha, 243–8, 668–9; van Winter, ii. 288–90; Scholtz, ii. 42–45.

that his selection as state attorney was due to the 'strong stand' he took in support of the dismissal of Kotze.[1]

Greene described Reitz as 'conciliatory' but 'very weak' and Milner was inclined to accept that estimate.[2] Reitz's attitude certainly formed a contrast to the rigidity of Leyds, and paved the way for the friendly settlement of what might have been a troublesome controversy over Swaziland.[3] He even suggested that Milner should come to Pretoria so that he and Kruger might talk over their differences.[4] As for Smuts, no one ever accused *him* of weakness. In his memoirs dictated some years later Kruger singled out Smuts as 'the man of iron will . . .'.[5] Coming from Kruger, that description is significant indeed. From the beginning Reitz and Smuts indicated that they intended their accession to the government to make a difference. Milner ascertained that there was a great deal in the administration of which Reitz disapproved and that he wished to see the Uitlanders gradually enfranchised.[6] Both Reitz and Smuts tried to establish relations of mutual confidence with Edmund Fraser, who deputized for Greene during the latter's absence on leave. They spoke to him with surprising frankness about the inner workings and the failings of the government, and they told him of important improvements which they proposed to make in the administration of laws like the liquor law, the Native pass law, and the gold thefts law affecting the interests of the mining industry.[7] All this Fraser reported to Milner with the comment that Smuts was 'certainly a man of much greater energy of character than his predecessors'.[8] The new state attorney soon gave a practical demonstration of his energy. He obtained the dismissal of the chief of the detective force, one Ferguson, for his failure to curb the illicit sale of liquor to Native mine-workers, after 'a very violent struggle in the Executive Council which lasted until late in the evening'.[9] A motion was thereupon

---

[1] African (South), 543, pp. 435–7, 479, 533; Millin, i. 52–59.

[2] African (South), 543, pp. 246, 473; Headlam, i. 189.

[3] See below, p. 221.   [4] Headlam, i. 189.

[5] Kruger added: '. . . If Smuts is spared, he will one day still play a great role in the history of South Africa.' *Gedenkschriften*, 170. Milner's view in Mar. 1899 was: 'I am inclined to think him high-minded, as he is certainly able, but whether he has real staying power and real political insight I have no idea.' Headlam, i. 336.

[6] Headlam, i. 190–1; see also Walker (*a*), 338.

[7] Headlam (i. 344) has a fantastic story that 'part of the [republic's] Secret Service fund was obtained by employing agents to purchase on its behalf gold and amalgam stolen from the mines'. For the probable origin of this story see African (South), 543, pp. 519–20; Leyds, *Eenige Correspondentie*, 240–5.

[8] African (South), 543, pp. 557–9; 557, pp. 85, 90.

[9] Ibid. 571, p. 4.

introduced in the volksraad instructing the government to transfer the control of the detective force from the chief of police to the attorney-general. The motion had the support of Reitz, but after a long debate it was lost by the casting vote of the chairman.[1] There was accordingly little improvement in the administration of the liquor and gold thefts laws. Smuts persevered, however, until he achieved his purpose. On 13 June 1899 the volksraad at length vested the control of the detective department in him, and he immediately embarked on a thorough cleansing of the Augean stables.[2]

Milner appreciated Reitz's conciliatory attitude. It would make his relations with the republicans easier until the time came 'to "round" upon them'.[3] Beyond that the entry of the new men into the government made no difference to him. He was still as determined as ever that there must be a 'show-down' as soon as possible. 'There is just one chance in a hundred', he wrote, 'that their attitude both towards us and the Uitlanders may undergo a change—a permanent change I mean in the Reitz Direction. In that case the ultimate fight might yet be averted. . . .' And again: '. . . I frankly confess that if I thought Reitz—either the man or the attitude—were going to be any more than an interlude, my opinion of the whole situation would be wholly altered. But I do not think anything of the kind.'[4] He continued, in fact, to base his policy on the assumption that there would be no serious reforms in the republic without at least the threat of force.

V

The departure of Leyds meant a considerable weakening of that Hollander influence in the republic which was so displeasing not only to the British throughout South Africa, but to many Afrikaans-speaking people as well. Leyds left the republic with the foreboding that 'the night was coming' for the Kruger régime as he had known it, 'and the judgment'.[5] Later he wrote: 'Since I left, young [South] Africa is beginning to govern and the Hollanders are beginning to feel insecure.'[6] Another Hollander, Middelberg, declared in September 1898: 'That game in South Africa is played out. . . . The

[1] *Notulen*, Eerste Volksraad, 1898, pp. 1134, 1198–1207.
[2] African (South), 571, pp. 477–8; 600, pp. 137, 222; reports of mine managers, Sept. 1899 (Smuts papers, Pretoria archives); Hobson, 81.
[3] Milner's words in a letter to Chamberlain. Garvin, iii. 370.
[4] Headlam, i. 191, 237–8.
[5] Middelberg's letters. *Hertzog-Annale*, July 1953, p. 109.
[6] Ploeger, 235.

Hollanders as leaders here are on the decline, the Afrikaners on the upgrade.'[1]

One of the fields in which the growing Afrikaner opposition to Hollander influence made itself felt was that of education. Both Mansvelt and his principal assistant, de Jonge—the secretary of the education department—felt that their position had become weaker since Leyds's departure.[2] The Jameson raid had silenced the anti-Hollander party for a while.[3] Utilizing the respite thus obtained Mansvelt had secured the passage of law 14 of 1896 empowering him to defray the travelling costs of teachers coming from abroad. In this way he was able to speed up the importation of Hollander teachers.[4] But the respite did not last long. Soon the demand for more English instruction began to be voiced again, more insistently than ever, by republican Boers as well as Cape-educated Afrikaners. At the same time the attack on the Hollander domination of the schools was intensified.[5] Towards the end of 1897 the synod of the *Nederduitsch Hervormde of Gereformeerde Kerk* or Dutch Reformed Church (D.R.C.) passed a number of resolutions which requested *inter alia* the appointment of more Afrikaner teachers and inspectors[6] and greater use of English in the schools for Afrikaans-speaking children. Early in 1899 this influential church decided to sponsor an education congress. The congress met at Germiston in March and was attended by members of school committees and other persons interested in education. It demanded the resignation of de Jonge, who had attacked Mansvelt's opponents among the D.R.C. clergy as politically untrustworthy, and of Mansvelt himself. The demand was supported by the D.R.C. *kerkeraden* (consistories) of Pretoria, Heidelberg, and Klerksdorp. A few months later a counter congress at Pretoria, sponsored by the education department and its supporters, passed a motion of confidence in the superintendent and his assistant. The opposition persisted, however, and in September it carried the struggle for the secretary's dismissal to the floor of the volksraad. Notwithstanding a half-hearted attempt by Kruger to save him, the raad resolved to dismiss de Jonge by 13 votes to 12.[7]

[1] *Hertzog-Annale*, July 1953, pp. 146, 159–60.
[2] Ploeger, 266, 278.   [3] See above, p. 55.
[4] Ploeger, 178–9, 181–2; Lugtenburg, 200–1; Basson, 104; Malherbe, 273.
[5] Ploeger, 236–43, 261; Basson, 127; Lugtenburg, 205–6; Malherbe, 273–4.
[6] In 1897 five of the six inspectors of schools were Hollanders. Lugtenburg, 205; Ploeger, 260.
[7] Ploeger, 243–4, 264–5, 269, 272–8, 285–8, 290–4; Basson, 129–35; Lugtenburg, 212–16.

In 1899 Mansvelt's system also came under severe fire from the Uitlander camp. In March, not long after the chamber of mines had decided to collaborate with the British government,[1] a number of mining magnates led by the Wernher–Beit firm bethought themselves of the educational needs of the Uitlander children and agreed to contribute munificently to the depleted funds of the Witwatersrand council of education.[2] There is some evidence that this new threat to his system spurred Mansvelt to take counter measures. In July one, H. J. Evans, who taught in one of the state schools for English-speaking children, declared in a letter to Milner that in these schools English was used as the sole medium of instruction in all classes. Milner doubted whether Evans's statements were true. If they were true, he added, Mansvelt's volte-face should probably be ascribed to the espousal of the Uitlander cause by the British government[3] or to the resources recently acquired by the council of education.[4]

I conclude that by the time war broke out Mansvelt's system appeared to be tottering.

VI

Towards the middle of 1898 trouble broke out in Swaziland. It has already been pointed out how Chamberlain kept his weather eye open for republican breaches of the London convention. He kept a close watch also on the Swaziland convention.[5] The colonial office and Milner between them accumulated a formidable list of alleged breaches of the letter or 'spirit' of this convention, and in February 1898, when Milner asked for permission to 'work up to a crisis', he proposed to lay great stress on these infringements. But he soon came to realize that, even if the British case proved to be altogether sound, which he knew it was not, it was too thin to excite public sympathy.[6] On the other hand, he was in complete accord with his chief that the republic must on no account be allowed to 'incorporate' Swaziland. On that point Chamberlain made his position quite clear in a discussion with his staff on the future of Swaziland. One of them had

[1] See below, pp. 244–5.
[2] C. 9345, pp. 76–79, 184; Ploeger, 206–10.
[3] See below, p. 276.
[4] African (South), 600, pp. 341–2, 383–4. See also Hobson, 38–39, quoting a letter by Evans to the *Transvaal Leader*.
[5] For the Swaziland convention of 1894, see above, p. 52.
[6] African (South), 499, pp. 288–9, 316–17, 407–9; 553, pp. 349–51, 417–18, 468–70; Headlam, i. 218–20, 223, 232–3.

remarked that the 1894 convention was 'impracticable' and that sooner or later Swaziland 'must become "incorporated" with the South African Republic'. To which Chamberlain replied: 'I do not see the necessity. If it is meant "into the South African system" I agree but it may be some time yet.'[1] In other words he looked upon Swaziland as a useful card 'in the game for uniting S. Africa as a British State'.[2]

The 'crisis' that arose in Swaziland towards the middle of 1898 raised an issue which in Milner's view was by no means 'thin' or 'trumpery'.[3] The convention of 1894 envisaged that the courts established in Swaziland to deal with European or 'mixed' cases would be authorized by the republican volksraad to take cognizance also of serious crimes committed by Natives against one another. But the volksraad neglected to pass the necessary legislation. In 1896 the high commissioner's law adviser suggested that the attention of the republican government should be drawn to this omission, especially since certain Native criminal cases had already been dealt with by the Swaziland courts and a technical breach of the convention had therefore taken place. But Chamberlain decided that nothing need be done in the matter.[4] In April 1898, however, an incident occurred which brought this question of jurisdiction prominently to the fore. Mbaba, the chief *induna* (councillor) of the Swazi paramount chief, Bunu, was murdered under circumstances which pointed to the implication of the latter. The government of the republic decided to bring Bunu to trial before a Swaziland court. Whereupon Milner reacted in a manner that alarmed the colonial office. He telegraphed on 25 May that Bunu was not likely to appear in court and that a conflict between the Swazis and the republic was 'increasingly probable'. If Chamberlain attached any importance to the 'semi-independence' of the Swazis, now was the time to act. The colonial office replied that it did not want war with the republic over the Swazis unless there was a clear breach of the 1894 convention.[5] Though Milner protested that he had been misunderstood and 'never at this stage contemplated any suggestion to the Transvaal Government which would, if rejected, involve forcible intervention', he

---

[1] Minutes by Graham, Wingfield, and Chamberlain on Milner to Chamberlain, 25 May 1898. C.O. 417/244.
[2] See above, p. 215.
[3] His description of many conventional issues. See above, p. 210.
[4] African (South), 499, pp. 160–5.
[5] Headlam, i. 185; African (South), 557, pp. 53–54.

nevertheless took Chamberlain's warning to heart. For he telegraphed to the British agent in Pretoria: 'Have heard from Secretary of State who is determined not to commit Her Majesty's Government,[1] but willing to allow me to discuss matters in a tentative way with Government of South African Republic. Please see State Secretary and talk it over in not too anxious and quite unmenacing way.'[2]

Approached in this spirit Reitz and Smuts, though they argued at considerable length, were willing to meet Milner half-way. They accepted his suggestion that Bunu should be dealt with administratively, i.e. by a fine imposed by the republican government after consultation with the high commissioner, while he agreed in his turn to induce Bunu—that 'wretched creature', who had fled to Natal instead of offering armed resistance as Milner originally anticipated —to appear before the *landdrost's* court in Swaziland 'in order that the facts of the charge against him may be investigated'.[3] When this matter had been settled, a protocol supplementing the 1894 convention was negotiated by Smuts and Fraser, the acting British agent, in accordance with which serious crimes committed by Natives against one another would be tried in future by the Swaziland courts, following a procedure intended to secure fair play. On the whole the agreement reached about this Swazi question was 'another backdown' for the republic, as Smuts told Fraser. It was part of the price Reitz and Smuts were prepared to pay for better relations with the British government.[4]

VII

At the Cape the Sprigg ministry met parliament in May 1898 with defeat staring it in the face. During the recess the ministry had prepared a measure designed to give more seats in the house of assembly to the towns, which were admittedly under-represented. The measure was known as the 'redistribution' bill. Since it would

---

[1] A month later Chamberlain once more refused to commit the British government on another issue. The volksraad had just re-enacted the aliens expulsion law, which had been suspended in July 1897. Milner wished to be allowed to intervene at once, if the republican government in the execution of this law committed 'some arbitrary act, which is the subject of general public interest and excitement'. Chamberlain refused to permit this on the ground that for the present 'we must keep our hands free'. Actually, perhaps as the result of a warning from Milner, the government of the republic expelled only one Uitlander under this law. He had shot another Uitlander dead and had been acquitted by a jury. Milner to Chamberlain, 29 June 1898, and minute by Chamberlain (C.O. 417/245). See also African (South), 571, pp. 488, 529–30, 551.   [2] Headlam, i. 185–7; African (South), 557, pp. 61–62.
[3] C. 9206, pp. 30, 67–70; Headlam, i. 188–9.
[4] C. 9206, pp. 122–4; Headlam, i. 192.

undoubtedly improve the prospects of the progressive party, the
bond decided to fight it tooth and nail and, as a necessary corollary,
to turn out the ministry. On 20 June the assembly passed the second
reading of the redistribution bill. But two days later, owing to a
split in ranks of Innes's small liberal group, which had voted solidly
for redistribution, the government was defeated on a motion of no-
confidence introduced by Schreiner. Milner consented to the dissolution of the assembly, and Sprigg appealed to the constituencies.[1]

The election campaign that followed was the bitterest in the history
of the Cape Colony. The dominant issue was the Transvaal question,
since the progressives and the high commissioner wanted it so. In
April Rhodes had told the shareholders of the British South Africa
company that 'one section of the people wants to make a Republic in
South Africa, and another section wants to make a united South
Africa under our flag. . . . Those are the politics of South Africa. . . '.[2]
During the course of his election speeches he said: 'There is one
great question before the country. The whole basis of one side in this
election is to make the Transvaal paramount, however much the
Transvaal may insult Her Majesty.' He then went on to stress that
in fighting the bond he was attacking 'Krugerism'.[3] The opposition
to Rhodes and Sprigg, under the leadership of Schreiner, denied that
they were a republican or a Krugerite party. The name Schreiner
gave to his party, which included men who, like himself, were not
members of the bond, was the South African party. He based his
platform on 'true Imperialism and true Colonialism' and advocated
friendly relations with the colony's neighbours, including the South
African Republic.[4] After his victory at the polls he spoke to his
electors about 'the noble Empire which is yours and to which you
belong'. Milner admitted Schreiner's 'moderation', which, he said,
had 'taken many people by surprise'. But he pointed out to Chamberlain that Schreiner's moderation was not shared by the majority
of his followers, however often the bond organ, *Ons Land*, might
repeat '*ad nauseam* . . . that the new [Schreiner] administration is not
hostile to British interests, or to the Imperial Government, but only
to the personal domination of Mr Rhodes, to "the Chartered clique"
and their corrupt methods of government, "the influence of Mammon
in politics"'. Yet the fact remained that whatever the rank and
file might feel about his moderation, Schreiner 'being a man of

[1] Headlam, i. 258; Innes, 166–9.   [2] Vindex, 685.
[3] Ibid. 553–4, 558, 604, 606, 627.   [4] Walker (c), 112–13.

independent opinion and strong will is apparently determined to be really their leader and not their instrument'. It remained to be seen, concluded Milner, 'whether he is strong enough, and has time enough allowed to him, to "educate" his party'.[1]

'The influence of Mammon in politics.' The elections were fought, writes Schreiner's biographer, with an 'expenditure of money unexampled in the sober annals of the Cape Colony'. On the side of the progressives, most of the money came from Rhodes, who made no secret of the fact.[2] They enjoyed the additional advantage of the patronage at the disposal of ministers. British officials stated that one of the latter, Sir James Sivewright, who had brought about the disruption of Rhodes's first ministry by giving an important contract to a personal friend without asking for tenders, was at his old tricks again, this time for politics' sake. The same sources reported Sivewright's wife as saying: 'It is too bad that people should take Jimmy's money for their votes and then not vote for his measures!'[3] The South African party, on the other hand, 'was sorely hampered by lack of funds',[4] though it was accused of having at its disposal large sums of Transvaal secret service money. Evidence about the employment of secret funds is, in the nature of the case, not easy to find. Rhodes publicly accused his opponent at Barkly West of having received money from the Pretoria government. An action was brought for libel, and one of Rhodes's prominent supporters admitted that 'the evidence at present to hand is distinctly weak'.[5] The strongest evidence comes from the acting British agent in Pretoria, who wrote: 'I am informed that the Transvaal Government have received advices from Cape Colony that more funds are urgently required to assist Mr Hofmeyr's party. The Executive Council consider that in spite of the sums already sent . . . they must needs comply', though Kruger would have to be consulted first.[6] According to a report received in the colonial office, Sauer was the distributing agent of the Transvaal secret service funds 'and not J. H. Hofmeyr . . . as was supposed'.[7]

Independent candidates received short shrift in this election.

---

[1] Headlam, i. 262, 277, 282.
[2] Walker (c), 113; Williams, 294; Innes, 170.
[3] Assistant military secretary of G.O.C. (S. Africa) to Henderson, 12 July 1898. African (South), 557, p. 82.   [4] Walker (c), 113.
[5] African (South), 557, p. 103. Rhodes lost the case.
[6] Fraser to Milner, 24 June 1898. Ibid. 67–68. Compare Headlam, i. 264 n. 3.
[7] Information from 'Tame Spy'. Major H. J. du Cane to E. A. Altham, director of military intelligence, 30 Aug. 1898. C.O. 417/252.

Rhodes remarked: 'I can respect your Bondmen, and I can fight your Bondmen. . . . But these Independents! I cannot stand them.'[1] The South African league was of the same opinion. The league in the Transvaal sent help to the Cape brethren—canvassers, for example, to help 'catch the coloured vote'. The league helped to bring about the defeat of Jagger, the Innesite candidate for Cape Town, but its leaders admitted that many progressives in that city refused to join.[2] The leaguers were, of course, exceptionally strong on the question of 'the Flag'. 'There is too much flag-wagging going on', lamented Innes, 'one would think the British Empire is in danger here.' He continued: Cape Town is not 'going wrong . . . but no more is the rest of the country on that point'. It was of no avail. Innes himself was indeed returned unopposed, but his followers in the assembly were practically annihilated.[3]

The final returns were announced on 15 September 1898. The South African party had scraped home by the narrowest possible margin, 40 seats to 39, Innes being counted among the progressives. When the new session opened Schreiner increased his majority to two by securing the election of a progressive to the Speaker's chair. But before the assembly could get to work it had been necessary for the governor[4] to deal sharply with Rhodes and Sprigg, however much the progressive cause might be his own also—indeed, for that very reason. Just before its dissolution the assembly had granted the Sprigg ministry £1 million on account, on the definite understanding that parliament should assemble as soon as possible after the election.[5] By the time the election was over, the vote on account had been exhausted. Rhodes and Sprigg wished to postpone the meeting of parliament as long as possible, hoping in that way to avert the defeat of the ministry in the new assembly; for they wanted to test the validity of some of the election results in the courts. (So, for that matter, did the South African party.) But Milner would not have this, and in his own words 'practically forced Sprigg to summon Parliament for the 7th of October'.[6] Then the progressive leaders tried another dodge. When parliament met Sprigg indicated to Milner that he hoped to be able to cling to office notwithstanding the motion of no-confidence which Schreiner would certainly move. The governor

---

[1] Vindex, 607.
[2] African (South), 557, pp. 95–99.
[3] Ibid. 82; Innes, 170.
[4] Milner was, of course, governor of the Cape Colony as well as high commissioner for South Africa.
[5] Headlam, i. 273.
[6] Ibid. 274.

replied that in such a case he would dismiss the ministry.[1] The prime minister had come to the end of his tether. Schreiner's motion was carried, and the governor asked him to form a new ministry.

Milner had undoubtedly acted with constitutional propriety. There was, he wrote, 'a moral side to such matters', which Rhodes and his friends 'steadily refuse to see'. And there were important tactical considerations also. It might well happen, for example, that 'a man like Innes, and perhaps some others' might be disgusted by 'too unscrupulous tactics' and withdraw their support from the progressive party. 'But such a split among the "Progressives" might disorganize and seriously weaken the party for some time to come', which would be a pity from the point of view of British interests.[2]

Schreiner's ministry consisted of Merriman, Sauer, Richard Solomon, A. J. Herholdt, and T. te Water. Of these only te Water and Herholdt were members of the bond. The latter was described by Milner as 'extremely moderate' and 'friendly with the English'. Solomon had been a member of Innes's liberal group in the previous parliament. It was 'the evident intention of Mr Schreiner', wrote Milner, 'to make his government one of compromise and concilia-tion, or, perhaps it would be more true to say, of comprehension'. He noted two additional facts about the ministry: first, 'the high average of capacity and character in its individual members'; and second, its practical immunity from attack on the score of being 'reactionary or anti-British'. Schreiner himself regarded his ministry as 'truly South African'.[3] From the standpoint of Milner's Transvaal policy it was the most dangerous kind of ministry that could have come into power in the Cape. For though by no means anti-British, it was resolutely anti-war, and its views might well carry weight with Chamberlain or with British public opinion.

The defection of one of its supporters forced the new government to agree to a redistribution measure which created eighteen new seats in the assembly, and according to Innes, who helped to draft the measure, markedly favoured the opposition. Nevertheless, writes Walker, in the 'semi-general election' that followed during the recess, the ministry did so well, both in the newly created constituencies and in those vacated 'either on petition or by the prudent resignation

[1] Ibid. 279.
[2] Letters from Milner to Chamberlain and Selborne. Ibid. 273–4, 277. See also ibid. 286–7.
[3] Ibid. 280–2; Walker (c), 126.

of one or two Progressive members', that its position was henceforward secure—at any rate until the outbreak of war.[1]

VIII

Since the opening up of the Witwatersrand gold-fields the republic had covered the expenditure of the state entirely out of current revenue. But during the course of the year 1897 the government began to feel the need of borrowing money abroad. Its revenues were shrinking without a corresponding decrease in its expenditure.[2] In April 1898 the *Star* informed the public that the 'bankruptcy [of the State] is at last within quite measurable distance'.[3] But that was wishful thinking so long as the production of gold within the republic continued to expand. In November 1898 the government at length decided to impose a tax of 5 per cent. on mining profits, partly on the ground that the industry was opposing its efforts to raise a state loan.[4] The volksraad had requested the government to frame a law on mining taxation to be dealt with in its next session. But the latter declared that the law was a matter of urgency and rushed it through the raad within twenty-four hours. The chamber of mines immediately, and with practical unanimity, issued a strong protest.[5] Yet despite the united front that the magnates had been presenting to Kruger since the end of 1897,[6] there were those among them who had by no means given up his government as hopeless. Thus, for example, shortly before the tax was sanctioned, George Albu stated in public that '. . . this Government, though we are labouring under certain grievances, is not so black as it is painted. . . .' Goerz's company also showed itself to be relatively well-disposed towards the government.[7] And so did the Consolidated Goldfields company. Its chairman, Lord Harris, told Chamberlain: 'I may say that we are by no means ill disposed towards Kruger. We wish he could establish an honest executive, and then try [to] secure the observance of the provisions of the drink laws: but we don't think the principle of taxing declared nett profits of mining Co[s] unfair, or that we are working under a crushing tyranny.'[8]

[1] Walker (c), 149; Innes, 174.   [2] See above, p. 193.
[3] *Star*, 19 Apr. 1898.
[4] C. 9345, p. 47; see also African (South), 557, p. 79.
[5] *Notulen*, Eerste Volksraad, 1898, arts. 1609–10, 1771, 1781–2; C. 9345, pp. 44–48.
[6] See above, p. 194.
[7] African (South), 543, p. 648; van Winter, ii. 312.
[8] Harris to Chamberlain, 20 Nov. 1898. Chamberlain papers, A.

To return to the state loan. Kruger first referred publicly to his project of raising a loan in May 1897.[1] Almost a year later he asked the volksraad's permission to raise up to £6 million for the financing of railways and public works of a civil nature, but his attempt to justify the expenditure of such a large sum was so unconvincing that the raad shelved his request.[2] The project encountered opposition from other quarters as well. Several of Kruger's most trusted counsellors, including Leyds, advised against it, at any rate in 1897. They were aware of the danger of placing large additional funds at the disposal of a government whose financial administration was poor.[3] They anticipated also that the financiers would refuse to lend unless the report of the industrial commission was implemented.[4] This anticipation was soon to be verified. By July 1898 the government had been informed (presumably by Leyds, who had recently arrived in Europe) about 'the exceedingly hostile attitude of nearly every financial house in Europe', which was said to be 'entirely due to . . . a conspiracy . . . arranged by the Johannesburg capitalists'.[5] (Leyds could not know about the hint which Rothschild and Beit had received from the colonial office.[6]) Some continental newspapers also did their bit to spoil Kruger's pitch. Thus the *Journal des Débats* of Paris declared that it was 'absurd' to lend money to the republic; while the *Kölnische Zeitung*, speaking perhaps for the German government but more obviously for German mining interests, told its readers about the 'deep feeling of dissatisfaction' among the Uitlanders.[7] In London the colonial office, which was kept fully informed about Kruger's loan plans by the British agent, continued to obstruct them. Towards the end of 1898 both Harris and Rothschild asked Chamberlain for his views. Harris's company was prepared to lend the republic £2 million, 'but would not proceed if it were contrary to the policy of the [British] Government'. Harris had already seen the prime minister, who told him 'that . . . if there were people in this country willing to lend money to Pres[t]. Kruger he (Lord S.) did not consider that it was his business to interfere'.[8]

---

[1] *Notulen*, Eerste Volksraad, 1897, p. 100.
[2] Ibid. 1898, buitengewone zitting, arts. 337–9.
[3] Van Winter, ii. 318–19; also Smuts in a conversation with Fraser in Dec. 1898 (African (South), 572, p. 2).   [4] Van Winter, ii. 318–19.
[5] Report by Fraser in African (South), 557, p. 79. Also ibid., p. 85.
[6] See above, p. 212.
[7] Foreign office to colonial office, 1 July 1898, and minutes by Graham, Just, and Lambert (C.O. 417/250); African (South), 543, pp. 340–2, 428–9; van Winter, ii. 310–12; Cook (a), 81–82.
[8] Minute by Chamberlain, 29 Nov. 1898. Chamberlain papers, A.

Chamberlain did not agree. 'My opinion distinctly is', he wrote to Rothschild, 'that your friends should not advance a sixpence to the Transvaal Government without satisfactory guarantees of some effective reform in the administration. . . . I may add that Lord Harris consulted me . . . on a similar question and I gave him the same reply. . . .'[1]

In the meantime Kruger had been having a great deal of difficulty with the volksraad. The latter did not like the idea of burdening the state with a national debt.[2] It was not until 1 September 1898, six months after the president had first approached the raad and after several secret sessions, that this body agreed to the principle of a loan.[3] But it rejected, in secret sessions, various offers which were accompanied by onerous conditions.[4] On 23 November the government was at length authorized to go ahead with the negotiation of a loan of not more than £2½ million 'on the most advantageous terms for the State'.[5] It succeeded in obtaining £2 million in March 1899 through the good offices of the Netherlands railway company.[6]

[1] Chamberlain to Rothschild, 30 Nov. 1898. Ibid. See also E. Drus in *Bulletin* (1954), pp. 171–2.
[2] African (South), 557, p. 91.
[3] *Notulen*, Eerste Volksraad, 1898, arts. 1043–52; African (South), 557, pp. 85, 91.
[4] African (South), 557, pp. 85, 93–94, 100, 107–8.
[5] *Notulen*, Eerste Volksraad, art. 1814.
[6] African (South), 571, p. 300; van Winter, ii. 322–4.

CHAPTER IX

THE BEGINNING OF THE END

> If, therefore, all the steps taken by the duke [Caesar Borgia] be
> considered, it will be seen that he laid solid foundations for his
> future power; and I do not consider it superfluous to discuss them,
> because I do not know what better precepts to give a new prince
> than the example of his actions; and if his dispositions were of no
> avail, this was not his fault, but the extraordinary and extreme
> malignity of fortune.

I

EARLY in November 1898 Milner sailed for England in order to
confer with the colonial office. To a friend he had written three
months before:

> I want to come home to refresh myself for a harder struggle, a struggle
> in which humanly speaking, I am going to win. You may say 'humanly
> speaking' is a big *if*. And so it is. The Higher Powers seem twice in the
> past to have wrought a miracle for the Afrikanders. Why not a third time?
> It is small wonder that the pious parsons of the Dutch Reformed Church
> really believe that the Lord of Hosts is always on the look-out and will get
> them out of any tight place. But I have my private heresy and doubt
> whether He will *always* do it.[1]

After all, the situation had changed, and this time 'He' would have
to reckon with the high commissioner.

Part of the two months that Milner spent in England was taken
up in discussions with Chamberlain, Selborne ('my great stand-by'),
and senior men in the colonial office, especially Graham, and in
dealing with the South African dispatches. But most of the time he
was busy seeing people not connected with the colonial office in order
to prepare them for the impending struggle. He wanted to interview
'*all* the leading politicians and pressmen . . . and to stamp on rose-
coloured illusions about S. Africa. . . '.[2]

It so happened that 'the lull in our eternal fight with the Transvaal', which Milner expected just about to outlast his stay in England,[3]
was illusory. Who were the men called upon to deal with the situation
that arose during his own absence and that of the British agent?

---

[1] Headlam, i. 286. [2] Ibid. 298–301. [3] Ibid. 287–8.

The man on the spot in Johannesburg was J. E. Evans, the British vice-consul since the end of 1896. Before his appointment to this newly created post he had been an employee of the Standard bank, having been successively a bank inspector in the Transvaal and branch manager at Durban. He was recommended to the high commissioner by Lewis Michell, the manager of the Standard bank and a personal friend of Rhodes. A few months before his appointment he told a British intelligence officer that he considered war with the republic to be inevitable, and two years later he talked as if no reasonable person could doubt the necessity of a British occupation of the republic or at any rate of her administration coming under British control.[1] In Pretoria the acting British agent was Edmund Fraser, who had been transferred from the Brussels legation during the course of 1897 to become Greene's secretary. He was described by Milner as 'able' and 'clever', but the latter added in January 1899 that he had 'latterly shown signs of "swelled head"'. Fiddes, Milner's secretary, thought him 'as a rule very smart'.[2] Like Evans and Greene, Fraser expressed his lack of faith in the prospects of reform in the republic; and he was aware of Milner's attitude towards the Boer government. In his official references to republican officials he sometimes used language that displeased the acting high commissioner, lieutenant-general Sir William Butler, the newly appointed commander-in-chief of the British troops in South Africa.[3]

Milner had wished this post to be filled by 'special selection'. He told Chamberlain that he wanted a man 'of energy and resource and of some political sense', not 'some worn-out Lt.-General', though (he added prophetically) 'even that is not the worst that might befall us'. But before this letter reached London, Butler had already been appointed.[4] The appointment was probably not 'the ordinary departmental routine', as Milner had feared. But as it turned out, the war office could hardly have chosen a better man to thwart Milner's policy. The choice of Butler was presumably due to the fact that he had some experience of South Africa, having served there in 1875 and again in 1879. Since then, he tells us in his *Autobiography*,

[1] Altham to Northcott, 20 July 1896 (C.O. 537/130); Rosmead to Chamberlain, 14 Nov. 1896 (C.O. 417/185); Evans to Greene, 16 Oct. 1898 (African (South), 557, pp. 101–2).

[2] Milner to Chamberlain, 18 Jan. 1898 (Chamberlain papers, D); Milner's minute on Butler to Chamberlain, 18 Jan. 1899 (C.O. 417/259); Fiddes to Graham, 7 Sept. 1898 (C.O. 417/245); Headlam, i. 188.

[3] Butler, 390–1; Butler to Chamberlain, 28 Dec. 1898 (African (South), 571, p. 99).

[4] Headlam, i. 288–9.

he had kept up his interest in South African affairs, though his knowledge of the state of affairs in the Transvaal in recent years was no doubt superficial. He had also studied South African history, having just completed his *Life of Sir George Pomeroy Colley*, a British officer who had served on the Cape's eastern frontier in the fifties and sixties and had been high commissioner for South-East Africa, including the Transvaal, in 1880–1.[1] He described later how he loathed the religion of 'the top Dog and the under Dog' preached 'first at Kimberley and later in the other mining centres'.[2] He was, in fact, almost the perfect foil to Milner—an Irish Catholic, a man of the world largely self-taught, pacific at the age of sixty, and convinced that South Africa did not need 'a surgical operation'.[3] In him Schreiner and his ministry had, for two and a half months, a high commissioner after their own heart. He was prepared to listen sympathetically to them and to accept their estimate of Rhodes as the chief menace to the peace of South Africa as well as their low opinion of the Uitlanders of Johannesburg.[4]

To the latter—in so far as they were represented by the Transvaal province of the South African league—we must now turn. Since March 1898 the league had kept comparatively quiet. Its leaders were content to perfect its organization and to stimulate the loyalty of the British Uitlanders by means of patriotic speeches.[5] In September and October the two principal officers of the league wrote to Greene, who had apparently retained its complete confidence, describing the situation in Johannesburg and the league's plans for the future. They were not at all pleased with the attitude of the mining magnates, who were, according to them, engaged in an 'active intrigue' with Kruger's government. The magnates, they declared, were very bitter at Rhodes's re-entry into politics, and were showing a tendency to thwart his unification policy and the British imperial idea. As for themselves, they accepted Rhodes's leadership. On the subject of their plans, they wrote: 'The . . . municipal elections [in Johannesburg] are on, and the League organization is proving itself an unexpectedly—to the public as well as to our own little Tammany—respectable power in the community. There is every prospect of the whole face of municipal life experiencing a sudden change through

---

[1] Butler, 380–5.
[2] Ibid. 184. See, for example, Scholtz, ii. 176 n., quoting the *Star* of 21 Jan. 1899.
[3] Butler, 398.
[4] Ibid. 396, 400, 402, 405, 409–10, 414–15; Walker (c), 124, 139.
[5] Scholtz, ii. 167–8.

our entrance into the field.' They also made certain remarks about the
field-cornet of Johannesburg, which may be significant in view of
later developments. 'You may have noticed', one of them wrote,
'that the Veld Kornet here (one Lombaard) has got into dire trouble
[with the government].[1] . . . He has already been to us in secret to
know by what act of treachery to the Krügerite gang he can make
friends with the mammon of our unrighteousness, and we look to
make use of him as a very valuable weapon.'[2]

When the republican government decided to tax mining profits,[3]
the leaders of the league must have experienced a sense of relief.
The tax was certainly looked upon as a serious grievance by at any
rate some of the magnates.[4] According to Fraser it was generally
regarded as 'a serious step towards the political suicide of the
Republic', and league spokesmen seized the opportunity to present
the magnates as 'martyrs of patriotism'.[5]

Towards the end of 1898 the league was once more ready for action.
It may be asked why the leaders decided to act in the absence of the
high commissioner and the British agent. The answer appears to be
that they did not regard this as being necessarily a disadvantage,
since these two officials would surely support the league's case at the
centre of authority.

II

The final crisis of the republic opened with an attack by the league
on the police or 'Zarps' as they were called. In two successive
petitions to the Queen drawn up by the league's executive in the early
months of 1899 it was stated that 'for years past your subjects have . . .
had constantly to complain of innumerable acts of petty tyranny at
the hands of the police'; and that 'the constitution and *personnel* of
the police force is one of the standing menaces to the peace of
Johannesburg'. Chamberlain took up this complaint in his indictment
of the republic dated 10 May 1899, when he enlarged upon 'the
arbitrary and illegal action of officials, especially of the police',

---

[1] See above, p. 134.
[2] Letters to Greene from T. R. Dodd and P. A. Ogilvie. African (South), 557,
pp. 95–104.
[3] See above, p. 228.
[4] See the strong public statement by the president of the chamber of mines in
C. 9345, pp. 46–47.
[5] African (South), 543, p. 660; minute by Chamberlain on Cox to Chamberlain,
19 Nov. 1898 (C.O. 417/247).

which contributed its quota to the 'continual menace to the security of the lives and property of the Uitlander population'.[1]

Who were these Zarps that were said to 'bully' the Uitlanders?[2] They were the 600 foot and mounted police of Johannesburg,[3] armed with batons and revolvers, the latter being considered necessary in view of the heterogeneous population among whom order had to be kept.[4] This is what a British officer writing from Johannesburg had to say about the Zarps in 1896:

The police are *not* mainly Germans as the papers say [they knew better by 1898] and do not behave in the way they are said to do. They are bad because they are chiefly raw [Boer] boys and do not know their work,[5] and are corrupt because their discipline is bad and corruption is rampant in every department of the Government.[6] They reserve their extortions and bullyings chiefly for the natives, and do not trouble the Europeans so far as I can learn to any serious extent.[7]

There is no reason to believe that this state of affairs had changed appreciably since 1896. With all their faults the police managed to keep order in Johannesburg, and the lives and property of the White Uitlanders were reasonably secure.[8]

The first action taken by the league's executive was over certain alleged outrages perpetrated by the police on Cape Coloured people in Johannesburg during the night of 29 October 1898. It appeared subsequently that one of the pass officials called in the assistance of the police under the field-cornet, Lombaard, in order to deal with non-Whites who had transgressed the pass law.[9] The police thereupon raided a Coloured quarter of Johannesburg at night, entered a number of houses without a warrant, and arrested about forty persons.[10] The league obtained affidavits from four of these alleging brutal treatment by the police, and some of the allegations were subsequently supported by other Coloured eye-witnesses in evidence before

---

[1] C. 9345, pp. 115, 187, 228–9.   [2] Walker (c), 139.
[3] This was the number in 1896.
[4] See, for example, C. 9345, p. 114.
[5] For a similar criticism see the *Volksstem* of 12 June 1897.
[6] On governmental corruption see above, chs. i and ii.
[7] Capt. C. M. Radcliffe to 'My dear Colonel', 4 May 1896. C.O. 537/130.
[8] See, for example, Hobson, 52–55.
[9] Fraser declared, apparently with some justification, that the raid took place in retaliation for the refusal of Coloured men, claiming exemption as British subjects, to be commandeered for an expedition against a Native tribe. C. 9345, pp. 84, 95–96; green book no. 8 of 1899, p. 20.
[10] Report of government commission of inquiry, green book no. 8 of 1899, p. 15; C. 9345, p. 83.

a government commission of inquiry.[1] Lombaard (who had been suspended by the government), the pass official, and the police denied the allegations. The commission, two of whose three members had been approved by Fraser, produced a somewhat perfunctory report, which failed to examine the evidence and without making an explicit statement to that effect, gave the impression that the charges of brutality were groundless. It did admit, however, that certain 'irregularities' had been committed by the police.[2] The government, which had told Fraser that any officials found guilty of the charges against them would be dismissed, now reinstated Lombaard. In explanation of this action Fraser remarked that '. . . mere harsh treatment of coloured people is not, as a rule, in most parts of South Africa, thought a sufficient reason for punishing officials, unless an actual crime is committed'. He added that 'any punitive action by this Government would have had the appearance of deferring to the opinion of the League', which had 'raised so much resentment among the burghers' by its first petition to the Queen.[3] As for Butler, he had already decided that the whole question had better be dropped. Having at his elbow the Cape ministry, which detested the league, and drawing his own conclusions from a private letter he had received from Fraser, he expressed to Chamberlain the conviction that a large part of the case against the republican officials was not genuine.[4]

It will be remembered that in August 1897 Greene had made an 'arrangement' with the republican government regarding the 'better class' of Coloured persons: they might take out a certificate costing £3 per annum and thus escape the obligation of carrying a pass and wearing the 'badge'. Fraser reported that very few had acquired the certificate because it was so expensive.[5] It would appear that Greene had informed Fraser and vice-consul Evans, who passed on the information to the league and the Coloured people, that the arrangement of 1897 had abolished the badge. The people had therefore ceased to wear it, and this was the reason for some of the arrests that

[1] Further arrests took place about 20 Dec., and a few of the affidavits regarding these were also laid before, and their authors examined by, the commission of inquiry. The affidavits were all published in the British grievances blue book, C. 9345, pp. 88–92.

[2] Green book no. 8 of 1899, pp. 15–23; C. 9345, pp. 83–103. The report was not published by the government until some months after it had been submitted.

[3] African (South), 571, pp. 94, 200–1; C. 9345, p. 99. Fraser's sentence about 'mere harsh treatment of coloured people' is omitted from the version of this dispatch published by the colonial office.

[4] Butler, 399–400; C. 9345, pp. 91–92.

[5] See above, p. 181; C. 9345, p. 83.

had taken place. (In other cases passes could not be produced.) The badge was not actually abolished until February 1899.[1]

Whatever may have been the motives of the league, the Coloured people clearly derived some benefit from its intervention, accompanied as this was by considerable publicity in the press.[2] The government was constrained to recognize that there was room for improvement in the behaviour of the police and minor officials towards Coloured people,[3] and there was reason to believe that lesser officialdom would in future watch its step more carefully. Such being the position, it seems necessary to ask why Milner re-opened the whole question after his return from London. The ostensible reason for the acrimonious dispatch he sent to Reitz on the subject was the reinstatement of Lombaard on 25 January 1899.[4] But he used the occasion to make a lengthy analysis of the evidence in the case and to bring the unwarranted charge that the arrangement of 1897 had not been 'honourably observed' by the republic. Reitz replied in kind, and made it clear that his government resented Milner's 'style of correspondence'.[5] The latter told Chamberlain that he hoped his dispatch would have 'some practical effect'—presumably on the treatment of Coloured people.[6] But his main purpose appears to have been to make a contribution to the case against the republic which the colonial office published a few months later.[7] For he had returned to South Africa with the full intention of 'working up to a crisis'.

III

Whatever effect the league's championship of Coloured people might have on public opinion in Britain, the response in South Africa was bound to be somewhat cool. But the next incident in which the Zarps were concerned, involving as it did the life of a White man in Johannesburg, was more serious in its consequences. On 18 December 1898 an Uitlander called Edgar, returning home after midnight, heard a remark by another Uitlander which he considered insulting, and knocked him down unconscious. Under the impression that the man was dead, one of his friends called the police. Four policemen arrived on the scene and followed the alleged murderer to his house.

[1] African (South), 543, no. 240, and 571, pp. 521–2; C. 9345, pp. 83, 92, 97, 128.
[2] Butler, 399.   [3] C. 9345, p. 107.
[4] Milner to Chamberlain, 14 Mar. 1899. Ibid., pp. 99–100.
[5] Ibid., pp. 99–107.   [6] Ibid., p. 104.
[7] In the blue book marked C. 9345. See in this connexion Headlam, i. 348.

When he failed to open the door, one of the policemen, a man named Bart Stephanus Jones, forced an entrance. Edgar hit the policeman on the side of the head with an iron-tipped stick, and the latter thereupon shot him dead. Jones was arrested on a charge of murder, but the public prosecutor soon afterwards reduced the charge to culpable homicide and let the accused out on bail of £200. At the request of Fraser, the state attorney (Smuts) ordered the re-arrest of the policeman. The charge brought by the state at the preliminary examination on 29 December was murder, but thereafter this was once more altered to culpable homicide. When the case came on for trial towards the end of February Jones, who was defended by ex-chief justice Kotze, was found not guilty by the jury, and the judge—a young man of twenty-five—remarked in discharging the accused that he agreed with the verdict and hoped that the police, under difficult circumstances, would always know how to do their duty.[1]

The Edgar case was made a political issue from the beginning. Immediately after the shooting an Edgar committee was formed consisting mainly of office-bearers and prominent members of the league in Johannesburg. When Jones was released on bail, there was set on foot an agitation, which soon became, in the words of vice-consul Evans, 'a huge thing'. The Edgar committee obtained affidavits describing the shooting, which were sworn before Evans and published in the *Star*. At the same time leaflets were distributed and notices published in the newspapers calling on British subjects to assemble in large numbers for the purpose of making a representation to the vice-consul. But Fraser had already intervened on 22 December and obtained the re-arrest of the policeman Jones. He had, moreover, caused the Edgar committee to be informed of his action. Early on 24 December he once more telegraphed Evans as follows:

. . . British subjects . . . should avoid anything in the shape of a public meeting outside the Consulate, especially as this seems unnecessary for the purpose of making representations to you, either on the Edgar case, in which first satisfaction has already been given . . . or in the cases of persecution of coloured British subjects by local officials,[2] in which I have already obtained the suspension of the Field-cornet (pending an official Commission of Enquiry). . . . Please show this telegram to the Edgar committee.[3]

The meeting nevertheless took place on the afternoon of 24 December,

---

[1] C. 9345, pp. 108–39, 147–59.
[2] See above, p. 235.
[3] C. 9345, pp. 108–10, 113, 116–17; African (South), 571, p. 217.

since the organizers regarded the Edgar incident as only one symptom 'of the intolerable state of affairs existing here'. A crowd of between four and five thousand persons assembled at the Market Square in Johannesburg, and marched in procession to the consulate singing British patriotic songs like *Rally round the Flag, Boys*. Their spokesmen appeared on the balcony of the consulate, and in the presence of the vice-consul one of the league's officers read out to the crowd a petition addressed to the Queen. Whereupon Evans declared that he would be glad to send it on to the proper quarter.[1]

The first attempt by the league to secure the intervention of the British government ended in a fiasco. This was due to the attitude of the acting high commissioner, aided and abetted by the Cape ministry. Fraser had wanted to send on the petition after it had been purged of 'exaggerated passages', on the ground that its rejection would be 'a sensational step'. But Butler told him that he would refuse to transmit the petition in any form because it had been published in the *Cape Times* before being presented to the vice-consul. As for the league, so far from allowing them to force his hands by newspaper publicity, he would 'see them all damned first'. On 4 January Fraser accordingly wrote to Evans that he could not send on the petition.[2]

The petition had a sequel—in fact more than one sequel. Reitz demanded the dismissal of Evans since he had broken the law by taking part in an unauthorized open-air meeting. Fraser managed to smooth this matter over, but he was instructed by Butler to 'caution Vice-Consul against mixing himself up with political and financial agitators, which he appears to be disposed to do'. On 5 January the government ordered the arrest of two officers of the league for their part in the proceedings of 24 December. They were released on bail of £500 each, and Fraser was given to understand 'that the charge against them will not be pressed very far,[3] and that in any case it is unlikely to go farther than the Landdrost's Court, who has . . . only a right to inflict fines in such cases up to £25. . . '.[4] All three 'provinces' of the league were immediately up in arms. Thus, for example, a crowded public meeting called by the league at Port Elizabeth agreed:

That this meeting respectfully calls the attention of the Imperial Government to the condition and status of British subjects in the South African

---

[1] C. 9345, pp. 113–16, 133; African (South), 571, p. 217.
[2] African (South), 571, pp. 133, 135; C. 9345, p. 130.
[3] They were acquitted in April. African (South), 571, pp. 472–3.
[4] Ibid., pp. 217–21; 572, pp. 4–5; C. 9345, pp. 130–1.

Republic, and to the recent outrages which have been perpetrated on British subjects by officers of the said Republic contrary to the principles of freedom and liberty, and in defiance of the usage and custom of all civilised countries.

That further toleration of this condition of affairs on the part of the Imperial Government must affect the peace of the country and lead to the contempt and degradation of every British subject throughout South Africa unless remedied by Imperial intervention.

At the same time the Central committee of the league in the Cape protested

in the strongest manner possible against the entirely unjustifiable arrest of league officers in Johannesburg for their part in forwarding the petition setting forth the disabilities Her Majesty's loyal subjects suffer under in one of her Suzerain States. . . .

The Schreiner ministry, disturbed by these portents of another South African storm, now sent a long minute to Chamberlain which stated *inter alia*:

In the opinion of Ministers, the persistent action, both beyond and within this Colony, of the political body styling itself the South African League, in endeavouring to foment and excite, not to soothe and allay, ill-will between the two principal European races inhabiting South Africa, is well illustrated by these resolutions, the exaggerated and aggravating terms of which disclose the spirit which informs and inspires them.[1]

In Johannesburg the protest meeting of the league took place on 14 January in a large hall known as the amphitheatre. It ended in uproar. Before the meeting it was known that one of the objects of the organizers was to 'endorse' the petition of 24 December.[2] The league's evident purpose of procuring intervention from outside roused intense resentment among the burghers,[3] and a hostile crowd broke up the meeting. The league obtained evidence alleging that government officials had organized the disturbance in the hall, and that the police remained inactive though a number of persons were injured.[4] Fraser, relying mainly on information received from the league but also on reports in the press, including the pro-government press, gave the government the names of officials and others involved in the disturbance. But the government did nothing.[5] On the other

[1] C. 9415, pp. 59–74.
[2] C. 9345, pp. 144–7.
[3] Ibid., p. 99.
[4] Ibid., p. 159.
[5] Ibid., pp. 136–43.

hand, the league's handling of the affair was not helpful. It had accumulated twenty-eight affidavits relating to the disturbance, but sat on them for more than two months. It took no action in the republican courts on the ground that it could not hope to obtain justice there, though early in March it had expressed the intention of proceeding against one of the government's officials.[1] After Greene's return to Pretoria the president of the league gave him copies of the affidavits and Milner sent them on to the colonial office. Chamberlain thereupon expressed his regret that the league had not prosecuted the 'ringleaders of the riot' and—four months after the event—ordered the affidavits to be communicated to the republican government. In June 1899 he published them in the British grievances blue book (though their value had not been tested in the courts or elsewhere), having already summed them up in his indictment of the republic, which was published at the same time.[2]

IV

In England Milner was perturbed and annoyed by the attitude which Butler was taking up towards the South African league and the Edgar case. On 30 December, immediately after the preliminary examination of the case, the acting high commissioner telegraphed: 'Edgar shooting affair originated in a drunken brawl, in which Edgar grossly assaulted another man, whom he left, it was thought, dead. Police were then called in, Edgar resisted, struck policeman, who fired fatal shot. S.A. League adopted case, hence excitement.'[3] This was followed in due course by an explanatory dispatch, which elicited the following comment from Wingfield, the permanent under-secretary: 'I think that Sir W. Butler to some extent justifies his telegram of 30 December. . . . He had some reason for seeking to correct the impressions which might be derived here from the public telegrams which represented the action of the police as a wanton attack upon Edgar.'[4] Milner had been taking a different line. Writing before a full account of the case had reached the colonial office he commented:

Edgar etc. Butler is superb. He starts right away with a complete theory and if the facts do not fit the theory, so much the worse for the facts. I think

---

[1] African (South), 571, pp. 26–27.
[2] C. 9345, pp. 143–4, 159–75, 177, 229.   [3] African (South), 571, p. 38.
[4] Minute, 14 Feb., on Butler to Chamberlain, 25 Jan. 1899 (C.O. 417/259); Cd. 1789, pp. 204–5.

his famous telegram of December 30th, blowing away the Edgar case, was *seriously misleading*. Anyone would think from reading it that it was a thoroughly rotten case and the excitement quite artificial. It turns out to be a strong *prima facie* case such as would have excited strong public feeling anywhere, let alone in Johannesburg. Of course the League took it up—small blame to them. (I may observe that the discovery that the League are a lot of reckless fire-eaters is quite contrary to my experience, and, I believe, to Greene's). . . . So much for Edgar himself. Unless subsequent despatches throw a quite different light on it, I feel that we have not been fully or impartially informed, and I regret more than ever that the petition was sat upon. . . . I am going to pay dearly, dearly for this holiday.[1]

After Jones's acquittal Milner, back in South Africa, reviewed the Edgar case in a dispatch. His conclusion was that the trial justified Uitlander feeling that the courts would not dispense justice when Boer interests and sympathies clashed with those of the Uitlanders. The verdict of the jury and its endorsement by the judge created, he thought, an alarming situation.[2] On this dispatch Wingfield remarked: 'I do not take so strong a view of the case as Sir A. Milner. I see no reason to doubt the evidence of the police that they believed Forster[3] to have been killed. The real point of the case is that there was no justification for the shooting—but even for that there is something to be said when a man is struck on the head with a stick with an iron end.' Chamberlain supported Milner's view: 'The case is a bad example of the treatment British subjects are liable to in this semi-barbarous community. If we publish a despatch on the whole question of our relations with the Transvaal, this incident will help to open people's eyes in this country.'[4] The colonial office decided not to publish Milner's dispatch, but Chamberlain dealt sharply with the case in his indictment of the republic, and later claimed £4,000 compensation for Edgar's widow on the ground that there appeared to have been 'a clear miscarriage of justice on the criminal trial'.[5]

It has been noted that Milner regretted that the first petition to the Queen had been 'sat upon' by Butler. Yet by this action the latter had gained for the colonial office time to think. Two days after Milner's departure for South Africa H. W. Just, who now occupied

---

[1] Milner to Graham, 19 Jan. 1899. C.O. 419/259. Henceforward Butler was, in Milner's eyes, a 'Krugerite'. Headlam, i. 301, 303, 473.

[2] Ibid. 313.

[3] Forster was the man who was knocked down by Edgar.

[4] Minutes by Wingfield (4 Apr.) and Chamberlain (9 Apr.) on Milner to Chamberlain, 8 Mar. 1899. C.O. 417/259.

[5] C. 9345, p. 229; Headlam, i. 314.

Fiddes's place in the colonial office, minuted:

The acceptance of this petition would . . . have constituted a new departure of a serious kind. . . . So long as the policy of simply keeping the S.A.R. to the Convention is pursued, petitions of this character can do no good and will only demonstrate the impotence of Her Majesty's Government. If friction is to be avoided, it would seem good policy to prevent further petitions, and Mr Greene will be able to manage this no doubt, as he has found the S.Af. League in the past very willing to defer to his advice on such matters.[1]

Just's superiors made no comment on this suggestion, nor did they send any instructions to Greene. For the situation had changed inasmuch as Britain's international position was in process of decisive improvement.

Milner left England towards the end of January, 'well pleased' with the result of his visit. Chamberlain had not been able, of course, to commit the British government to a policy which might lead to war with the republic, since the South African question had not seriously engaged the attention of the cabinet for almost a year. But Milner was satisfied that if he could get things 'forrarder' in South Africa by his own actions he would 'have support when the time comes'.[2]

V

While Milner was still in England there was set in motion a series of events which had a decisive influence on Britain's relations with the republic. On 12 December 1898 the colonial office learned that the Boer government had proposed to the volksraad the prolongation of the dynamite monopoly, which still had ten years to run, for a further fifteen years. It is true that the volksraad postponed consideration of the proposal until February, but Fraser expressed the belief that it would then be agreed to.[3] On receiving this news Milner wrote to Graham:

I have hoped against hope that we should be able to keep out of this business. *I hate it.* But I really cannot see how some action on the part of Her Majesty's Government can *now* be avoided. . . . But we want—or rather we should be better for—some recent peg to hang our remonstrance on. I think we should try to stir up the Roburite Company. . . .[4] I think

---

[1] Minute, 30 Jan., on Butler to Chamberlain, 11 Jan. 1899. C.O. 417/259.
[2] Headlam, i. 301–2.
[3] African (South), 543, p. 668.
[4] This company had protested against the monopoly in 1897 and earlier.

too that, if we decide to take the matter up, Fraser should be warned by telegraph, and asked about the attitude of the mining magnates [who had voiced no protest].[1] Personally I should be inclined to give him a hint to pull their tails. But I learn the Secretary of State would hardly agree to go so far as that. . . .[2]

Three weeks later Milner told Graham 'that if Krüger's [concessions] policy continues, the day will come when the administration of the Transvaal will have to be undertaken by us burdened with innumerable monstrous concessions and monopolies.[3] We shall in fact get the shell of the nut, the kernel having gone into the pockets of Krüger and his accomplices.' Chamberlain was sufficiently impressed by Milner's statement to inquire of his officials whether something could not be done 'to anticipate this situation' by a statement of policy regarding republican concessions.[4]

With regard to the dynamite question, Chamberlain instructed Fraser to ascertain whether the mining industry was likely to take 'strong or concerted action' against the proposed extension of the monopoly.[5] Fraser consulted the president and prominent members of the chamber of mines, who told him that 'no further protest was in contemplation until Raad take action. . . . No open and direct appeal has been made to Her Majesty's Government, nor can such an appeal be expected so long as such action is regarded by Transvaal Government' as 'treason and we [mining magnates] are without any assurance or evidence of intention on the part of Her Majesty's Government to protect us. We ask for the cancellation of the monopoly and a free market in explosives. . . .'[6] Milner now recommended that Fraser suggest to the chamber of mines that it should make as soon as possible a 'strong but temperate protest' against the monopoly, and that the protest should be made public. With the words 'I am willing to take the risk of this course', Chamberlain allowed a telegram to go to Fraser in the sense recommended by Milner.[7]

This decision had momentous consequences. Chamberlain entered into an understanding with the mining magnates. Henceforward their

---

[1] See Headlam, i. 300.

[2] Milner to Graham, 18 Dec. 1898. C.O. 417/247. There is no question of Milner's agreeing reluctantly (see *C.H.B.E.* viii. 589) to Chamberlain's sending off the dynamite dispatch. This time it was he who recommended it.

[3] See above, ch. II.

[4] Minutes by Graham and Chamberlain, 7 and 8 Jan. 1899. C.O. 417/247.

[5] African (South), 571, p. 68.

[6] Butler to Chamberlain, 17 Jan. 1899 (C.O. 417/259); African (South), 571, pp. 104–5.

[7] Minutes by Milner and Chamberlain, 19 Jan. 1899; Chamberlain to Butler, 22 Jan. 1899 (C.O. 417/259); African (South), 572, p. 6.

leading spirits acted in close concert with him and his representatives in South Africa. Milner and Greene were thus able to reconstitute the reform movement of pre-raid days on the Rand with some of the magnates taking a share in public.[1] Chamberlain had, in fact, stepped out along the road that led to vigorous intervention within the republic. His first attempt at intervention had been spoilt by the raid. This time he was to be more successful.

On 28 January Fraser telegraphed:

I have arranged that President of Chamber of Mines shall comment on prolongation proposal in his annual speech public meeting tomorrow and that Chamber will summon another meeting before the Raad meets and publicly pass Resolution offering Government [a] loan of 600,000 [pounds][2] for purpose of compensating the monopoly for their expenditure on factories in event of cancellation. This loan already guaranteed and Government informed today by delegates from Chamber. . . . They [the Chamber] consider protest H.M.G.[3] opportune . . . to probably prevent prolongation but believe that fear of revelations are [sic] so great as to make cancellation impossible without an ultimatum, which however they do not at all expect, being satisfied for the present that the President [of the republic] should thus be placed absolutely in the wrong and unable to complain again that the capitalists here refuse to assist him. . . .[4] The comments of the colonial office on this telegram were:—GRAHAM, 'The offer of £600,000 . . . seems to leave the Government without a leg to stand upon . . .'; WINGFIELD, 'I dont expect that this will draw Kruger—but it is a good move'; CHAMBERLAIN, 'Satisfactory'.[5]

Fraser presented Chamberlain's dynamite dispatch on or about 11 February. It protested against the dynamite monopoly on the ground that, being intended to benefit the monopolists rather than 'the State generally', it constituted an infringement of article XIV of the London convention.[6] A member of the staff of the colonial office had warned Chamberlain that Kruger's reply would be 'that the monopoly *is* maintained by the Government of the Republic "acting in good faith and for the purpose of carrying out a national object"'.[7]

[1] Ibid., pp. 31–34. See also above, p. 221.
[2] Or more if necessary, the service of the loan being met by a special tax of 10s. on every case of dynamite. C. 9317, p. 9.
[3] Chamberlain's dynamite dispatch.
[4] Butler to Chamberlain, 28 Jan. 1899 (C.O. 417/259); African (South), 572, pp. 6–7.
[5] C.O. 417/259.
[6] This was in accordance with an opinion by the law officers. African (South), 516, no. 682. On the other hand, the opinion of English counsel consulted by the mining industry was 'not very decided'. African (South), 571, pp. 187–9.
[7] Minute by H. W. Just, 5 Jan., on Butler to Chamberlain, 12 Dec. 1898. C.O. 417/247.

The state secretary did, in fact, reply more or less in these terms. Having consulted three authorities on international law he protested his inability to see the relevance of Chamberlain's argument to article XIV of the convention, but insisted that, even if the argument was relevant, it was for the republic alone to decide what was best for itself. He accordingly rejected Chamberlain's protest in the name of his government.[1]

That government also rejected the proposal of the chamber of mines to buy out the dynamite company.[2] In March 1899 it laid before the volksraad a proposal by the company which, if accepted, would have condoned the breach of the regulations of September 1893.[3] (Max Philipp had written to his son[4] in Pretoria in October 1898: '. . . Before we know where we are there will be war between England and the Transvaal, and then—I would not like to fall into the hands of the English before our concession has been recognised by the Volksraad, and we get either a simple discharge from our liabilities or else an extension of the concession.'[5]) The volksraad was aware that the government had consulted four lawyers, three of whom had declared that there had been a breach of the regulations, while the fourth, Smuts, had given a contrary opinion. It resolved by 15 votes to 13 to reject the company's proposal and to instruct the government to act strictly in accordance with the resolution of 4 November 1897.[6] Towards the end of July the government tried again. It first summoned the volksraad to a secret session. A few days later a resolution was passed in open session to appoint a committee which, in consultation with the government, was to 'submit a proposal which will lead to the final settlement of the dynamite question'. The majority report of the committee was adopted by the raad on 25 August by 18 votes to 9. By this decision it agreed at long last to the continuation of the monopoly in return for a decrease in the price of dynamite to 65s. per case.[7]

How far bribery of honourable members contributed to this decision it is impossible to say, though we know that on 26 August Vorstman drew £18,267 in notes and gold from a special account in his bank at Pretoria.[8] But we also know that the government was

[1] C. 9317, pp. 3–7, 14–16; Botha, 726–37.
[2] See below, p. 247.   [3] See above, p. 30.
[4] For Philipp *père* and *fils* see above, p. 31.
[5] Cd. 625, p. 179.
[6] See above, p. 192; C. 9317, pp. 10–14, 16.
[7] Cd. 625, pp. 199, 201–2; African (South), 600, p. 456.
[8] Cd. 623, pp. 92–93. For Vorstman see above, pp. 28, 30.

just as interested in the maintenance of the monopoly as the dynamite company. The allegation has never been made that the government resorted to bribery. It had, however, as we have seen, several reasons to give members to justify its support of the monopoly.[1] These reasons no doubt influenced some of them in the perilous days of August.[2]

VI

Kruger and his advisers must have noted that the £600,000 offer by the chamber of mines appeared to be timed to coincide with the British government's protest against the dynamite monopoly. Under the circumstances some action other than a mere rejection of the protest was obviously called for. It seems to have become clear to the president that if he wanted to retain his cherished monopoly, he would have to pay a price in the shape of concessions to the mining industry. And while he was about this, he might as well do something for the rest of the Uitlanders too,[3] and thus cut the ground from under the feet of the South African league, who were the enemies of the republic's independence[4] and were doing their best to bring about British intervention in her affairs.[5] But the first step was obviously to make an approach to the leaders of the mining industry. Other Uitlanders could be brought into the discussions later.

Among the Smuts papers in the Pretoria archives there is a memorandum of a conversation that took place between him and Fraser on 22 December 1898. The latter, remembering perhaps a letter Milner had written him in August,[6] spoke as follows: Both before and after the battle of Majuba (1881) the Boers had had a vague aspiration towards 'a great Republic over the whole of South Africa'. It was not the intention of the South African Republic 'to play a humble role' like the Orange Free State. She 'would not have anything to do with the paramount influence of England, but has always tried to play a part among the nations, and has therefore always coquetted with the European powers'. In his (Fraser's) opinion the time had

[1] See above, pp. 32–33.
[2] For the position of the republic in August, see below, ch. XI.
[3] See Headlam, i. 321–2, 325–6, 331, and some further evidence quoted below.
[4] Ibid. 310 (Reitz's remarks on the league).
[5] 'Fraser says that Milner's visit to England has made the Government nervous...'. Cox (acting high commissioner) to Chamberlain, 29 Nov. 1898. African (South), 557, p. 111.
[6] Headlam, i. 191.

come to 'strike a blow' and 'make an end to all this by showing the Boers that England was master in South Africa'. Smuts asked Fraser what reasons the British government would give for taking action against the republic. His reply was that it would act on the score of her maladministration and especially the maltreatment of British subjects. The memorandum closes with this comment by Smuts: 'I see a connection between these things [i.e. Fraser's statement] and the rumours in the newspapers that England is strengthening her [military] power in South Africa and that she is going to make serious representations to this Government.'

Besides Reitz and Smuts, Leyds also had a share in the so-called 'capitalist negotiations'. Indeed, Milner 'incline[d] to believe' that Leyds was the 'real inspirer' of the negotiations. That seems to have been true in the sense that it was he who first suggested the idea.[1] On the other hand, Smuts had had discussions with Fitzpatrick before Leyds's brief visit to Pretoria, and Smuts took from the beginning a prominent share in the talks with the capitalists.[2] As for Leyds, he had arrived in Pretoria towards the end of January to explain the failure of his diplomatic mission. Shortly before the opening of the capitalist negotiations Fraser reported that Leyds was having frequent discussions with the executive council about foreign affairs.

He sees, however [continued Fraser], much less of the new State Secretary and State Attorney than of the President, and the two former officials [Reitz and Smuts] have even expressed to myself the awkwardness of his presence here, and their unwelcome necessity for great caution in their utterances while Dr Leyds is here. I regret, and the State Attorney has spoken to me in the same sense, that Dr Leyds should be in Pretoria while the Executive is discussing the different possibilities of the dynamite question. . . .[3]

On 27 February E. Lippert, one of the principal beneficiaries of the dynamite monopoly, approached three Johannesburg firms— H. Eckstein and company (a subsidiary of the Wernher–Beit firm), the Consolidated Goldfields of South Africa, and A. Goerz and company —with a proposal to discuss terms on which 'peace' could be made between the government and 'the whole Uitlander population'. It was suggested that the capitalists should acquiesce in the dynamite monopoly, support if necessary the efforts of the government to

[1] Headlam, i. 321, 327; Leyds, *Eenige Correspondentie*, 1, 201–3.
[2] Fitzpatrick (*a*), 164–5; Headlam, i. 321–2.
[3] African (South), 572, p. 16.

obtain a loan,[1] help it in the Indian and Cape Coloured questions,[2] discourage press agitation against the republic in South Africa and overseas,[3] and dissociate themselves from the South African league. In return the government was prepared to settle the *bewaarplaatsen* question[4] on terms favourable to the mining companies, to appoint a qualified financial adviser without whose consent no new taxes would be imposed, and to recommend to the volksraad[5] that the Uitlanders should be enfranchised after five years.[6]

Fitzpatrick immediately communicated these 'startling' proposals to Greene[7] (who had returned to his post in Pretoria on the same ship as Milner) and Milner telegraphed them to the colonial office.[8] At the same time Fitzpatrick, whom I take to be the author of the Michaelis telegram, informed his principals, the Wernher–Beit firm in London: 'Believe Transvaal Government must be hard pressed to make such overtures. Try and ascertain Chamberlain's views.'[9] Milner agreed that the republicans were 'frightened', especially in face of the league's proceedings. He thought the government's offer a good one 'on the face of it', though it looked suspicious that enfranchisement was put off for five years: 'gradual enfranchisement beginning now' would be better than 'wholesale enfranchisement' five years hence.[10]

'What I fear', Milner told Greene, 'is that the C[olonial] O[ffice] may take the non-committal line, and tell the big houses . . . to take their own course. My view, as you know, is to keep in the closest possible touch with the Uitlanders.' He need not have worried.[11] It is

---

[1] See above, pp. 229–30.   [2] See below, pp. 258–61.

[3] On 11 Mar. Milner referred to the Uitlanders' 'local agitation and the working of the Press in Europe'. Headlam, i. 325.

[4] See above, p. 20.

[5] It was known to the capitalist negotiators from the beginning that Kruger had still to be persuaded to accept five years. He wanted nine years' residence for newcomers, and seven for those who had resided in the republic two years or more. Fitzpatrick (?) to Michaelis, 3 Mar. 1899. C.O. 417/259.

[6] Milner to Chamberlain, 4 Mar. 1899, and Fitzpatrick (?) to Michaelis, 3 Mar. 1899 (C.O. 417/259); C. 9345, pp. 222–3.

[7] 'Startling' is Milner's word. Headlam, i. 322.

[8] Walker (in *C.H.B.E.* viii. 589) makes the curious statement that the capitalists were permitted by the republican government to cable its proposals to their principals in London *and to the secretary of state*; whereas its whole purpose was to forestall imperial interference.

[9] Fitzpatrick (?) to Michaelis, 3 Mar. 1899. C.O. 417/259.

[10] Milner to Chamberlain, 4 Mar. 1899. C.O. 417/259.

[11] Headlam, i. 322. Walker (in *C.H.B.E.* viii. 589–90) is apparently unaware of the important part played in the capitalist negotiations by the colonial office and its representatives in South Africa. It is also incorrect to say, as Walker does, that, presumably in order to give the negotiators a clear field, 'Chamberlain shelved the plea that the dynamite monopoly was a breach of the Convention'. He reiterated the plea.

true that Chamberlain's staff counselled him against giving the capitalists any advice. But Selborne, and Chamberlain himself, thought otherwise. The latter minuted:

> Whether this offer is genuine or not I regard it as the most important move made since the Raid. It should certainly be treated as serious. . . . My own opinion is that the government of the S.A.R. are anxious to settle. Their financial difficulties, the strength of the South African league, their position with regard to the Dynamite Monopoly, the loss of support from Germany, the altered position of England since Fashoda—all make in favour of a settlement—of course on their own terms. The terms offered will not do.

After which he proceeded to instruct Selborne as to the line he should take at his interview the following day, 9 March, with Julius Wernher, one of the principals of the Wernher–Beit firm.[1]

At the beginning of the interview Wernher handed over to Selborne the telegrams he had received regarding the republican proposals. He then went on to explain the reasons for the overtures.[2] They were due, he said, first, to the desire for a settlement on the part of Reitz and Smuts, who had been adopting 'a new and friendly attitude to the Uitlander leaders now for some time past'; second, to the failure of Leyds, who 'has met with rebuffs everywhere on the Continent. He has everywhere, in France, in Germany, in Holland, been met with the criticism, "Why don't you settle with these people?".' Wernher thought the negotiations would fail owing to the intractability of Kruger and the fact that no final settlement seemed possible so long as the volksraad could alter the constitution of the republic by a bare majority. What puzzled him, concluded Wernher, 'was the fact that this overture came at the very moment when the Transvaal had actually obtained their loan of two millions sterling through the Netherlands railway company'.[3] Selborne now gave him Chamberlain's message, which was that the capitalists should tell the republican negotiators that the agitation against their government could be effectively countered only by a reform of the administration.

> Mr Wernher asked me what I meant by a reform of the administration. I replied that the most obvious necessity and a reform which Kruger could grant with the utmost ease was the concession of a bona fide municipality

---

[1] Minutes by Just, Graham, Wingfield, Selborne, and Chamberlain, 6–8 Mar., on Milner to Chamberlain, 4 Mar. 1899. C.O. 417/259.

[2] What follows is Selborne's account of the interview.

[3] See above, p. 230.

to Johannesburg. . . . Mr Wernher said, 'but what about the franchise?' I replied that that was going at once to the point of most resistance. . . . They might well refrain from putting that question in the forefront of the negotiations without any prejudice to their future attitude.

Selborne also impressed on his interlocutor the importance of obtaining the fullest details in writing of the proposals of the republican government.[1]

The 'bona fide municipality' referred to in the previous paragraph was a solution tenaciously advocated by Chamberlain. As explained by Selborne it was essentially the same plan of 'home rule' or 'limited autonomy' for the Rand as his chief had put forward in February 1896.[2] Why did the home rule plan appear so attractive to Chamberlain? Partly, no doubt, because he agreed with Milner that enfranchisement delayed for five years would be of little value,[3] and believed that it would be difficult to obtain an acceptable franchise from Kruger. But partly also because under his 'home rule' scheme the Uitlanders would not need to renounce their British citizenship and could continue to look to the British government for support. In other words he would feel more at ease about the loyalty of the British Uitlanders if they remained 'Outlanders' instead of becoming citizens of the republic. 'I have never . . . concealed my opinion', he had written in June, 1896, 'that whatever defects may exist in the present form of government in the Transvaal, the substitution of an entirely independent Republic governed by, or for, the [cosmopolitan] capitalists of the Rand would be very much worse both for British interests in the Transvaal itself and for British influence in South Africa'.[4] Milner, though paying lip-service to the virtues of the home-rule plan, was in fact strongly opposed to it. He had more confidence than Chamberlain in the loyalty of the British Uitlanders even if they became citizens of the republic. He declared also that 'a genuine municipality' would be harder to obtain than an acceptable

---

[1] Minutes by Selborne and Chamberlain, 8 and 9 Mar. 1899. C.O. 417/259.
[2] See above, p. 112.
[3] Chamberlain to Milner, 9 Mar. 1899. African (South), 572, p. 13.
[4] Garvin, iii. 74; see also Breytenbach, 132. 'What I have always feared is the establishment of a real live Republic on the ruins of the sham Republic that now exists—a Republic that may tend to form the nucleus of the independent United States of South Africa. I know that there are not wanting people in Johannesburg and Pretoria, strongly opposed to the existing system, who look forward to this.' (Hely-Hutchinson, governor of Natal, to Chamberlain, 7 Dec. 1895. Chamberlain papers, H.) 'The franchise is a sore subject to the South African Republic, and it is doubtful whether it would be in our own interests to create a British Republic by claiming it for the Uitlanders.' (Minute by F. Graham, 11 June 1897. Ibid., C.)

franchise, which would prove, moreover, the more stirring 'battle-cry'. The home-rule plan accordingly played no part in the capitalist negotiations.[1]

Chamberlain did what he could to secure a united capitalist front. We have seen that Lord Harris and his Goldfields company were inclined to be friendly to Kruger.[2] On 14 March Harris told Chamberlain that his company was prepared to accept the republican terms unless he objected. The latter thereupon gave it to Harris straight from the shoulder: 'I said that Her Majesty's Government would not interfere but that public opinion would probably say that the Financiers had sold their cause and their compatriots—and sold them cheap and would not in the long run get even the price they had accepted. It was however their business not ours. . . .'[3]

It was a cardinal point in the policy of Chamberlain and Milner that any settlement of the Uitlander question must be made by themselves as the representatives of the paramount power, rather than by those whose interests were most directly involved. Fitzpatrick, who was the principal negotiator on the side of the capitalists,[4] was in full agreement with this attitude. Between him and Milner there existed a thorough sympathy and understanding.[5] The latter believed that the negotiations would fail, but that they might serve a good purpose, apparently from the point of view of his own future action.[6] As for Fitzpatrick, he never took them seriously. What he did take seriously was Chamberlain's message about obtaining details of the republic's proposals in writing.

Generally [i.e. in general] he says [Greene telegraphed Milner on 13 March] attitude of Rand[7] representatives will be firm but reasonable, their object being to go on with the negotiations no matter how sceptical, in order to secure for future use a number of witnesses and plenty of evidence to demonstrate that the Govt. admit impossibility of position and propose radical change. You will notice that F. takes a very unfavourable

---

[1] African (South), 572, p. 14; Milner to Chamberlain, 4 Apr. 1899 (C.O. 417/260 and African (South), 572, pp. 40–42); Headlam, i. 359.

[2] See above, pp. 228–30.

[3] Minute by Chamberlain, 14 Mar., on Milner to Chamberlain, 11 Mar. 1899. C.O. 417/259.

[4] At about this time 'a British subject holding an important position in one of the Large Houses in Johannesburg' told Milner that Fitzpatrick was 'the soundest statesman we have on the Rand'; and Milner himself declared that he had the makings of a political leader. African (South), 572, pp. 29–30, 42–43.

[5] Ibid., pp. 42–43; Fitzpatrick (a), 167, 173, and (b), 10.

[6] Headlam, i. 325.

[7] Not 'Raad' as in Headlam. See enclosure A in Milner to Chamberlain 22 Mar. 1899. C.O. 417/259.

view of the whole Govt. attitude, which he considers to be a plant and anticipates a certain breakdown of the negotiations, but I think that, having regard to the attitude of the State Secretary and State Attorney, there is some ground for doubting whether his view is justifiable.

To this Milner replied that the 'attitude of Rand representatives . . . as described by Fitzpatrick seems thoroughly statesmanlike' and suggested that the latter be informed of the 'increasingly defiant attitude of S.A.R. Govt. to H.M. Govt'.[1]

The day after he received this reply, Greene telegraphed again to tell Milner of a dinner which had just been held at the Rand club in Johannesburg. The dinner was attended by twenty-four 'leading English' including the presidents of the chamber of mines[2] and the chamber of commerce, and the president and secretary of the South African league. Fitzpatrick addressed the gathering and described the 'whole course of negotiations' up to the moment. Those present expressed approval of 'continuation of negotiations with the Government emissaries in the friendliest and most reasonable spirit in order to induce Government to show their hand. . . . The general conclusion of all . . . was that the whole affair was a mere "spoof" on the part of Govt. with the view of frustrating the aims of H.M. Govt., sowing dissension among Uitlanders, and stopping agitation pending solution of dynamite question. . . .'[3]

On 16 March the London firms interested in the mining industry communicated their views to their representatives in the republic and Chamberlain cabled Milner the gist of the recommendations. They concluded with the suggestion that Leyds, who was on the point of leaving for Europe, should negotiate a 'comprehensive' settlement in London. But Kruger, Milner, and Fitzpatrick were all opposed to this.[4] The negotiations, therefore, continued in the republic a little longer.

The day after the dispatch of the London capitalists' message Kruger addressed his burghers at Heidelberg. The objects of the speech were no doubt to prepare the burghers for the concessions that would have to be made to the Uitlanders and to damp down the continuing agitation among the latter. The reforms he foreshadowed cannot be taken as the limit of the concessions which he might be

---

[1] Headlam, i. 326–7.

[2] Actually a Frenchman named Rouliot—a member of Fitzpatrick's firm.

[3] Greene to Milner, 15 Mar. 1899 (enclosure D in Milner to Chamberlain, 22 Mar. 1899—C.O. 417/259); Headlam, i. 327–8.

[4] African (South), 572, pp. 20, 27; C. 9345, pp. 215, 221; Greene to Milner, 17 Mar. 1899 (enclosure E in Milner to Chamberlain, 22 Mar. 1899—C.O. 417/259).

induced to make in the negotiations with the capitalists.[1] In his speech he defended the dynamite monopoly, but promised the appointment of a competent state financier,[2] a fair settlement of the *bewaar-plaatsen* question and a reduction of the qualifications for the franchise. His proposal was that the Uitlanders should be able to acquire the franchise after nine years instead of the actual fourteen. But he added that he 'was in favour of the State President and Commander-in-Chief [Commandant-General] being elected from the old burghers of the country'.[3] Three days later Chamberlain said in the house of commons with regard to this speech: '. . . after reading the telegram which professes to give an account of what President Kruger has lately promised, I confess that, so far as I can see these promises are entirely illusory. I do not think that what he suggests as to the franchise is of the slightest advantage.' He also said that Kruger 'had kept no promise with regard to the Uitlanders and redressed no grievance'.[4] These statements were much resented by the republican government, which believed that they revealed Chamberlain's intention of wrecking the negotiations with the capitalists.[5]

Milner agreed with Fitzpatrick that Reitz and Smuts were (unlike Kruger, Leyds, and Lippert) 'quite genuine'.[6] Leyds left the republic for the last time on 24 March, and Lippert went with him.[7] Four days later the capitalist negotiators' reply to the government's proposals was handed to Reitz. According to Milner, the reply was 'not . . . agreed to without some difficulty, and the discussion which led up to it manifested . . . a considerable divergence of view as to the extent of the demands which should be put forward. . . . The result was a compromise . . . in which the advocates of a firm attitude, especially

---

[1] See, for example, Walker (*c*), 143.
[2] See also Leyds, *Eenige Correspondentie*, 10–11.   [3] C. 9345, pp. 193–5.
[4] *Parliamentary Debates*, 4th series, vol. lxviii, col. 1377.
[5] African (South), 572, pp. 20–21, 34–35; C. 9345, p. 199; Walker (*c*), 143; Leyds, *Eenige Correspondentie*, 18; Butler, 428.
[6] Headlam, i. 325–7, 331. With regard to Smuts, Fitzpatrick added: 'he aims at a Republican South Africa.' Ibid. 322.
[7] Leyds, *Eenige Correspondentie*, 2–4. Walker writes (*C.H.B.E.* viii. 591–2) that Leyds was in the republic once more in May 1899. He is mistaken. He continues: 'Worst of all, Leyds's final departure for Europe [in May] reawakened the British Government's fears of foreign complications, and left the conduct of the Transvaal's diplomacy in the inexperienced and downright hands of the patriotic Reitz.' I have no quarrel with the second part of this sentence. As for the first part, it is not clear what is meant by 'foreign complications'. All that the colonial and foreign offices appear to have been worried about were alleged 'intrigues' by Leyds in Lisbon to acquire rights at Delagoa Bay or over its railway. But with these the British government could easily deal, especially since Germany's withdrawal from the scene. There is some correspondence about Leyds's 'intrigues' in Lisbon in C.O. 417/259, 260, and 271 (27 Mar. to 8 May 1899). See also Headlam, i. 327.

on the franchise, got decidedly the best of it.'[1] The reply did, in fact, state that the franchise was 'a vital point upon which a permanent . . . settlement must hinge'; and it contained as an annexure a memorandum on the franchise drawn up by Fitzpatrick and said to represent 'the views of a very large and influential section of the [Uitlander] community'. The memorandum proposed in effect a five years' retrospective franchise for the Uitlanders and the redistribution of seats in the volksraad. But it put forward this 'suggestion' as a basis of negotiation, not as 'an unalterable proposal foredoomed to failure'.[2]

The position was now that the government had stated its proposals and the capitalists had replied stating theirs. In other words, the time had arrived at which the two sides would have to come to grips with each other. Smuts had already indicated that the government's first words with regard to reform were not necessarily its last.[3] At this moment Milner received from Fiddes, whom he had sent to take soundings in Johannesburg, a letter hinting at a speedy end to the negotiations. He did not like this news at all. Though he held that the negotiations would—and should—break down, he was sure that the time for this had not yet arrived. 'It is too soon yet in my opinion to break the crockery', he told Fiddes. 'People generally would not understand why. They would say "why just now, when Kruger is on the road to amendment". Before breaking the crockery, it must be evident that the amendment is a sham. . . .'[4] But Fitzpatrick had either taken already, or was on the point of taking, the fatal step. He was evidently afraid that once the negotiators came to grips the apparently united Uitlander front might split.[5] In any case he now had the government's proposals in writing in accordance with Chamberlain's wishes. He thought that his part of the job was done, and that the time had come for Milner and Chamberlain to take over.

Fitzpatrick has told us himself how he broke up the negotiations. He says that he gave the correspondent of *The Times* the money required to obtain by bribery the capitalists' reply, which he had just delivered to the state secretary and whose opening paragraphs gave an account of the course of the negotiations up to the moment of writing.[6] Whether the document came to be published in the precise manner related by Fitzpatrick does not matter. What does matter is that the responsibility is almost certainly his. Reitz, suspecting foul

[1] African (South), 572, pp. 42–43.
[2] African (South), 572, pp. 42–43; C. 9345, pp. 216–18.
[3] Headlam, i. 321, 331.
[4] Ibid. 331.
[5] Ibid. 328, 346.
[6] Fitzpatrick (a), 175–9.

play, issued a denial of some of the statements in the capitalists' letter. Whereupon the latter, with the professed object of substantiating their assertions, forthwith published the secret correspondence between themselves and the government.[1]

Thus ended the government's attempt to make peace with 'the whole Uitlander population'. Writing to Leyds shortly after the breakdown Smuts remarked bitterly that 'our earnest attempt to promote a lasting reconciliation has been a disastrous failure. Conditions are worse here today than they have been for fifteen years—thanks to our efforts'.[2] The failure of the capitalist negotiations left the road clear for the intervention of the British government in the internal affairs of the republic. In other words, a new and more dangerous phase in Anglo-Boer relations was about to open.

At this point it should be noted that the depression within the republic passed away during the first quarter of 1899. By February the share market was booming. The restoration of confidence was no doubt partly due to the £5 million paid out in dividends by the mining companies in 1898 (as compared with under £3 million in 1897), which in its turn was due mainly to a number of deep-level mines coming into production.[3] Politically also there were some encouraging developments. One half of the seats in the volksraad had to be filled by an election held in February. Some of the successful candidates, reported Fraser, 'though not so entirely progressive as Mr. Loveday . . .',[4] were yet men 'from whom support is hoped by the, at present, very small progressive party, at least against acts of retrogression'. Loveday himself thought that there might be a progressive majority in the volksraad when the ordinary session opened in May. This expectation was so far fulfilled that the raad did actually elect two progressives, Lucas Meyer and W. H. van Niekerk, as chairman and vice-chairman. At the same time Loveday also sounded a note of warning. 'Altogether', reported Greene, 'he viewed the situation, unless it should be complicated by outside interference, as more hopeful in respect of internal reform, at the present moment [10 March 1899] than at any time since the tendency in that direction which had . . . first manifested itself just prior to . . . the Jameson raid.'[5]

[1] C. 9345, pp. 218–23.   [2] Leyds, *Eenige Correspondentie*, 17.
[3] African (South), 571, pp. 187, 273, 520–1; Garvin, iii. 392; Scholtz, ii. 160.
[4] The raad's English-speaking member.
[5] African (South), 571, pp. 242, 520–1; 572, p. 24; *Notulen*, Eerste Volksraad, 1899, arts. 6 and 7. See also Ploeger, 266, and Walker (c), 143.

VII

Towards the end of March Milner received from one of the capitalist negotiators an account of the progress of the negotiations. It concluded as follows: 'We consider it necessary to get our full reply in before the public get to know about the Petition to the Queen.'[1] This was the second petition sponsored by the Transvaal province of the South African league which had obtained signatures in support of it 'secretly and noiselessly'.[2] The capitalists' reply to the government bears the date of 27 March. On the same day the *Star* published a statement that the Uitlanders were going to present the petition which had in fact been transmitted to Milner three days previously.

I have not been able to find much evidence as to the genesis of the second petition, which was a more comprehensive indictment of the republican government than its predecessor. It is thus not possible to determine to what extent Milner and Greene influenced its contents and the manner of its handling in Johannesburg. What we do know is that Milner had returned from England determined to get things 'forrarder' in South Africa and that Greene knew Milner's mind.[3] 'I talk very freely to them [the Uitlanders]', he told Greene in April, 'and often say "If it was my game, I should do so and so".'[4] While the petition was being prepared he promised the Transvaal leaders of the league to forward it to London; and on 7 March Greene informed him officially that the petition 'would . . . be shortly presented to me [Greene] in whatever form I thought most desirable', since the league was anxious to act in accordance with official etiquette.[5]

In order to obtain signatures to the petition the league's executive employed canvassers, who were 'paid the wages of a superior working man'.[6] In this way, according to the president of the league, the signatures of over 21,000 British subjects had been obtained when the petition was handed to Greene. Kruger's reply was a counter-petition, which deprecated foreign intervention and was said to have been signed by 23,000 Uitlanders by the end of May. But Greene informed Milner that the counter-petition need not be taken seriously, 'as it is openly stated that signatures have been obtained through the

[1] African (South), 572, pp. 29–30.
[2] Milner to Chamberlain, 29 Mar. 1899. Ibid., pp. 31–34.
[3] Headlam, i. 301–2, 322, 325.   [4] Ibid. 332.
[5] Headlam, i. 340; African (South), 572, pp. 26–27.   [6] C. 9404, p. 61.

instrumentality of Government officials and railway servants, who
. . . have no right to take the lead' on behalf of the Uitlander community.[1]

VIII

The second petition contained no direct reference to the grievances
of the Queen's Coloured and Indian subjects. Yet their interests
continued to engage the attention of Her Majesty's representatives in
South Africa. Towards the end of 1898, at the time of the police
action against Coloured persons in Johannesburg,[2] Chamberlain had
authorized Fraser to invoke article XIV[3] of the London convention
for the protection of the Coloured people. This was a new departure[4]
which the law officers had recently sanctioned. Fraser determined to
reach a settlement of both the Coloured and the Indian questions by
making appropriate use of Chamberlain's authorization. It will be
remembered that when the Indians lost their test case the republican
government decided to carry out the segregation law of 1885.[5] Fraser
obtained a postponement of this move by engaging the government
in a comprehensive negotiation. 'I am using a threat', he told the
acting high commissioner in December 1898, 'to declare Cape
[Coloured] people entitled to full privileges of other British subjects
. . . as a lever to extract concessions for Asiatics.' He discussed with
Smuts the draft of an agreement which was to regulate the position
of all Coloured persons of whatever origin 'other than the Aboriginal
Natives'. The agreement provided that Coloured persons and
Asiatics (as well as their Coloured employees) at present living or
trading in towns might stay where they were, provided that 'on the
cessation of the existing business, from death or otherwise, no transfer shall be permitted to others than white successors'. Coloured and
Asiatic town-dwellers would be required to take out a half-yearly
pass, to be issued gratis, and their employees had to provide themselves with 'a supplementary employment pass' likewise issued gratis.
All new-comers would have to reside in locations, 'but hawking may
continue as at present both in towns and country'. The fee payable by
Asiatics on entering the republic was to be raised from £3 to £25.[6]

---

[1] C. 9345, pp. 185, 237–8.   [2] See above, p. 235.   [3] See above, p. 125.
[4] See above, p. 181.   [5] See above, p. 182.
[6] Fraser considered the increased fee to be not unreasonable owing to the increasing
number of 'coolies' entering the republic from Natal. 'Moreover', he added, 'Indian
merchants tell me that most of such coolies' could easily obtain the extra £22, 'so that

The acting high commissioner sent these proposals to the colonial office, which instructed Milner and Greene to deal with them on their return to South Africa. But before the two officials could take any further steps, an outbreak of bubonic plague was reported from Madagascar, and two cases occurred within the republic. This was early in February 1899. The republican government immediately convened a conference of medical men from all the South African states, which was to make recommendations to the various governments. Among the delegates present was one from the province of Lourenço Marques, whose railway gave access to the republic from the east, but the high commissioner was not invited to send a representative. Acting on a resolution passed at the conference by 4 votes to 3, the government of the republic prohibited temporarily the entry across the eastern frontier of all Asiatics as well as of Coloured persons from Madagascar and Mauritius. In addition, Indians and other Asiatics were for the time being forbidden to travel within the republic without a permit from the state secretary.[1]

As soon as he heard of this 'extravagant' proclamation, Milner instructed Greene to inform the state secretary that it was a breach of the London convention, but that he would refrain from entering a formal protest for the present. He realized full well that Britain's interests in South Africa, as he and his chief understood them, demanded great caution in the handling of the Indian question. Only two years before there had been a violent agitation in Natal against the further entry of unindentured Indians; and the colonial office had judged it politic to assent to an act framed with the object of excluding them. At this very moment angry anti-Indian sentiments were being expressed from Port Elizabeth in the south to Bulawayo and Umtali in the Rhodesian north. Greene transmitted to the colonial office a leader in the pro-Milner *Star* of Johannesburg, which maintained the right of the republic to defend itself against the incursion of Indians, since 'the Asiatic is . . . a menace to the European's life'. To Milner it appeared obvious that '*we shall have to bend to the blast, if it is not to break us*'. He was aware that the anti-Asiatic movement was, 'undoubtedly, due in the first instance to jealousy' on the part of white traders, almost all of them British. It would be a pity to antagonize British settlers and run the risk of their making common

the restriction would not be so great as is believed by this Government'. African (South), 543, pp. 518–19; 571, pp. 55, 62–64.
[1] Ibid. 571, pp. 238, 257–8, 266; Headlam, i. 305.

cause with the Afrikaners, the majority of whom 'habitually take sides against coloured people'.[1]

Milner's policy held two *desiderata* in view: first, not to estrange an influential section of the British colonists by opposing the exclusion of Indians from the Cape (as they had already been excluded from Natal) and by pressing the republic too hard on the score of its Indian legislation; second, to prevent a common South African approach to the Indian problem. Not long after he became prime minister at the Cape, Schreiner proposed a conference of the states of South Africa in order to discuss immigration, especially that of Asiatics. But Milner—in England at the time—persuaded Chamberlain 'to put a spoke in the wheel of the Conference through Natal', whose ministry were convinced by the argument that they had already achieved their aim with regard to Indian immigration. 'The whole thing is simply an anti-British Boer intrigue', the high commissioner told the governor of Natal. '. . . Do not let us have a General South African Conference passing anti-Asiatic resolutions in the most offensive possible form by a large majority. . . . It would be four to two for a certainty, if not worse, in favour of anything that was most outrageous, most opposed to British sentiment and most embarrassing to Chamberlain.'[2]

In the face of the attitude of the high commissioner and the Natal ministry it was impossible to hold a conference on the Indian question. But it might still be possible to confer on other questions of common interest. In January 1899 Merriman, a member of the Cape ministry, was accordingly authorized by Schreiner to put out feelers. It was Merriman's idea that by conferring and acting together the South African states could show that they were capable of solving their problems without the intervention of the imperial factor. If more co-operative relations could be established among the different states, the existing tension in South Africa would surely relax. The proposed conference was to explore the practicability of 'a joint board of health, free interchange of South African products, a South African appeal court, mint and university, common legislation covering joint-stock companies, banks, insurance, and extradition, and a common method of settling riverine rights'.[3] Milner was not in favour of a South African conference even with the Indian item

---

[1] Hely-Hutchinson to Chamberlain, 6 Feb. 1897 and J. Robinson to Chamberlain, Feb. and Mar. 1897 (Chamberlain papers, H and J); African (South), 543, pp. 156–7; 571, pp. 267, 307–9; 572, pp. 16–17; Headlam, i. 304–5.

[2] Headlam, i. 304–5.   [3] Walker (*c*), 132.

excluded from the agenda. But if it was to take place he declared that he must be represented on it, mainly so that his delegates might speak on behalf of Rhodesia. This proviso, which was accepted by Schreiner, wrecked the prospects of a conference. If the republics had refused to accept the proviso in 1897,[1] they were not likely to agree to it now, in the face of Chamberlain's claim, recently reiterated, to the suzerainty. The conference was accordingly abandoned (April 1899).[2]

Meanwhile Milner and Greene had resumed the negotiations with regard to Indians and Coloured persons in the republic, and the republican government had repealed its bubonic plague proclamation. But the negotiations broke down early in April because the high commissioner wanted to deal separately with the Indian and Coloured questions instead of discussing an arrangement which included both groups on the lines agreed upon between Fraser and Smuts.[3] The government now prepared—once again—to enforce the segregation law against all Indians, except for a few traders with long-standing vested interests. The Indians were ordered to move before 1 July into the locations set aside for them; and hawking was to cease in the towns within a short time. Milner instructed Greene to tell the Indians that they should obey the order but report cases of harsh treatment to him. At about the same time Chamberlain told the India office about 'the extreme improbability of strong representations, in favour of the Indians generally, having any good result . . . and the certainty that such representations would be highly unpopular all over South Africa. . . '.[4] But the segregation order was not enforced. In August, when Milner and Chamberlain had got British opinion in South Africa enthusiastically behind them against Kruger, it became practicable to take a stand on behalf of the Indians which they had not ventured to attempt before. Greene had just been informed about the intention of the government to remove the Indians of Johannesburg to a new location nearly five miles from the centre of the town. Chamberlain thereupon agreed that the republic should be officially notified that 'we . . . claim strict compliance with the sanitary reasons for applying the [segregation] law of 1885, so as to

---

[1] See above, pp. 185-6.
[2] Headlam, i. 305-6, 363-5; Walker (c), 127-9, 131-3, 135, 137.
[3] African (South), 571, pp. 309-10; 572, p. 22; Headlam, i. 312-13.
[4] African (South), 571, pp. 371, 539-40; 600, pp. 41-44, 225. In the blue book (C. 9345) stating the British case against the republic there was no reference to the Queen's Indian subjects. The blue book was published in June 1899.

exempt Indians who can produce a medical certificate that their premises are not insanitary. . . '.[1] This amounted to a repudiation of the arbitration award of 1895.[2] Greene recommended that the presentation of the note should be deferred, since it had become very uncertain whether the government was going to move the Indians after all. But Milner ordered him to deliver the note forthwith.[3] It may be added here that one of the seven demands eventually made in the British ultimatum read as follows: 'The concession of most-favoured-nation rights to Great Britain . . . in all matters affecting British interests or the position of British subjects, whether white or coloured.'[4] This meant in effect a demand that non-White British subjects in the republic should have the same civil rights—not the same political privileges—as the Whites.[5] But the ultimatum was not intended to form the basis for a settlement, since the British government knew that it meant war.

One more word in conclusion. After the war the Coloured people in the Transvaal were treated better than in the days of the republic, though they did not obtain the same civil rights as the Whites. As for the Indians, their position became in actual practice worse. The London convention secured them an almost unimpeded entry into the republic, and the latter had not enforced its segregation law against the immigrants. But within a year after the peace of Vereeniging, Milner, as governor of the Transvaal colony, was foreshadowing legislation which would exclude Indians from the colony. At the same time he sanctioned the enforcement of the segregation law of the late republic, while declaring his intention 'not to disturb Asiatics who had established themselves in business before the war' and to exempt those who could prove to the government that they were 'a superior class' from all special legislation.[6]

---

[1] African (South), 600, pp. 331, 369.
[2] See above, p. 182, and Wingfield's minute, 25 June, on Milner to Chamberlain, 26 Apr. 1899 (C.O. 417/260).
[3] African (South), 600, pp. 483–4, 485–6.
[4] For the British ultimatum, see below, p. 322.
[5] Garvin, iii. 464; African (South), 600, pp. 293, 295.
[6] Cd. 1684, pp. 3–7. On the position of the Indians after the British annexation of the republic, see C.H.B.E. viii. 625–6; Walker (b), 523–4, 550; Hancock, i. 193–9.

CHAPTER X

THE BLOEMFONTEIN CONFERENCE

When the evils that arise have been foreseen (which is only given to a wise man to see), they can be quickly redressed, but when, through not having been foreseen, they have been permitted to grow in a way that everyone can see them, there is no longer a remedy. Therefore, the Romans, foreseeing troubles, dealt with them at once, and, even to avoid a war, would not let them come to a head, for they knew that war is not to be avoided, but is only put off to the advantage of others.

. . . If . . . there was a fight, it would be better to fight now than 5 or 10 years hence, when the Transvaal . . . will be stronger and more hostile than ever. Bold words these, you will say.

Milner to Selborne, 17 May 1899. Headlam, i. 385.

I

WITH the transmission of the second petition to the Queen at the end of March 1899, there began for Milner a period of intense activity. He had taken over from Greene the direction of the activities of the South African league in the Transvaal and worked mainly through Greene and Fitzpatrick. He told the former early in April: 'The game has been admirably played so far, but it cannot be won by one or two moves. It requires, above all things, steady persistence. British Govt. is slow to move. . . . What the Uitlanders have to do is to keep on pegging away.' In reply both Greene and Fiddes warned him that the pro-British Uitlanders would not hold together and incur the risks of 'an open policy of "unrest"', unless it became clear within two or three months that the British government had decided to intervene on their behalf.[1] In the meantime how were the Uitlanders 'to keep on pegging away'? Milner's advice to Greene was that, since the government would not permit open-air mass meetings, the Uitlanders should be induced 'to express in any way they can—by a series of smaller meetings along the Rand,[2] if they can be organised—their approval of the scheme of reforms *outlined in the memorandum*.[3] This would have a double effect. It

---

[1] Headlam, i. 345–7.
[2] Fitzpatrick declares that the idea originated with Reitz, but his evidence appears to be unsupported. Fitzpatrick, 360, 364; Headlam, i. 333, 343 n.
[3] See above, p. 255.

would, so to speak, *canonize* that scheme as the Uitlanders' recognized programme, their Petition of Right ... and it would keep up English interest and *rub the real issue well into the public mind.*[1] It would appear that the organization of the meetings recommended by Milner was entrusted to the league. They were 'working men's meetings' held at a number of mines on the Witwatersrand,[2] and after listening to speeches—some of them strongly anti-Boer—they passed identical resolutions in the sense indicated by Milner. They also elected delegates who, as Greene confided to Milner, might be regarded as the nucleus of 'a new representative body, recruited from all professions, formed to act as a sort of Uitlander Parliament...'. Milner telegraphed brief reports of these meetings to the colonial office, which duly published them in the British grievances blue book (June 1899).[3]

The policy of unrest soon evoked a response from the Boer side. April was not yet out when a certain Danie Theron, a young Krugersdorp lawyer, who had first drawn public attention to himself by his heckling of Kruger at an election meeting fifteen months before and was later to become a commandant in the Boer forces, entered the offices of the *Star* and assaulted the editor, newly arrived from England. He gave as his reason a recent editorial disparaging the status of the republic.[4] Milner agreed that the article was 'rather irritating certainly in its language', but added that there was 'strong writing' on the Boer side too. In the colonial office Chamberlain's staff used this opportunity to make some comments on the *Star*. Graham, the expert on South Africa, hoped that the Boer government would suppress the paper, adding that this would not be an infringement of the London convention. Another official remarked: '*The Rand Post* on the other side has been a worse offender.'[5] Now the colonial office had recently received from Milner two newspaper extracts 'as indicating views which I find are being expressed, more or less openly, in a certain section of the Press ... in this [Cape] Colony and in the Transvaal'. They were later published in the British grievances blue book, accompanied by Milner's comment. Both expressed strong anti-British sentiments, the second talking

---

[1] Headlam, i. 332.
[2] They were held late in April and early in May. But Walker's reference to 'the cyclone on the Rand' is unwarranted. *C.H.B.E.* viii. 591.
[3] C. 9345, pp. 203–4, 236; African (South), 571, pp. 548–9.
[4] *Star*, 21 and 25 Apr. 1899. Theron was fined £20.
[5] African (South), 572, pp. 47–48; minutes by Graham and Just, 2 May, on Milner to Chamberlain, 26 Apr 1899 (C.O. 417/260).

about war between Britain and the republic as inevitable. The first consisted of a letter published in an obscure paper called the *Stella-lander*. The other was an editorial in the *Rand Post*.[1] The colonial office had probably never heard of the *Stellalander*, but it knew something about the *Rand Post*. At the time of the Edgar agitation the acting British agent had written about this paper as follows:

> Two very inflammatory leading articles have appeared in a little known and less read paper called the *Rand Post*. . . . No importance is attached to these effusions here, but through translations in the English press on the Rand and in Pretoria, these articles have become widely known, and have, so the cablegrams state, been communicated in part to the English press at home. . . . The President himself, in an [published] interview enclosed herewith, has seen fit to condemn the articles as trash, and to use language the reverse of complimentary to the courage of their authors.[2]

At the same time as he was 'getting things "forrarder" locally', Milner sent Chamberlain a series of outspoken dispatches with the apparent intention of strengthening his hands with the cabinet. Three of them were in fact used by Chamberlain for that purpose. The dispatches became progressively stronger in language. In the third of the series Milner wrote that 'as regards the answer to the petition, the tone of it will no doubt depend . . . on what we may yet learn as to the degree of public feeling behind the petition', but that the movement on the Rand would probably persist if the British government declared that they had a moral right to intervene on behalf of their subjects in the republic. South Africa, he continued, was one country 'geographically, morally and socially', and the 'disease' of the Transvaal—the 'most important' of the South African states—'keeps the whole body in a fever'. In dispatch no. 4 he asked Chamberlain to demand the franchise for the Uitlanders. This would rouse much more sympathy throughout the empire than any attempt to remedy the grievances of individuals or small groups like 'Indian traders, Swaziland concessionaires and Cape Boy cab-drivers'.[3] He insisted that nothing would 'come right' by mere waiting, and showed some anxiety about the attitude of James Bryce, the author and Liberal statesman, who had published a book called

---

[1] C. 9345, pp. 182–3.
[2] African (South), 571, p. 121. The colonial office was also informed—by the assistant adjutant general in South Africa—that the *Rand Post* was supported to some extent by the republican government, 'having the advertising for the Education Department'. Ibid., pp. 310–11.
[3] Cape Boys were Cape Coloured persons.

Impressions of South Africa in 1897 and had recently made 'the astounding assertion that "the position of the Uitlanders is no worse than in 1895"'. The dispatch concluded:

. . . Persistent oppression must ultimately weaken the spirit of the oppressed. Some will go over with might and main to the winning side. . . . I fail to see, so far as the local situation is concerned, what is ever going to make it easier for us than it is to-day to tell the Transvaal Government that it *must* reform, and to offer to act as mediators between it and its discontented subjects, with the full determination not to allow such proferred mediation to be refused.

In the next dispatch he warned Chamberlain that to offer intervention meant to take the risk of war. 'The Boers will yield to nothing less than the fear of war, perhaps not even to that. But then this is a risk which, with the present rotten government in the Transvaal, we are running all the time. . . . If we succeed we shall get rid of this nightmare for ever.' The last dispatch of the series had as its theme the impending struggle for 'the complete vindication of British supremacy'.[1]

Though most of the series were marked 'secret', Milner would have liked to see some of their 'vitriol' in the blue book on British grievances which he urged Chamberlain to issue—not that the latter needed any urging at this stage.[2] He asked in particular for the publication of the 'nightmare' dispatch. But this the colonial office would not permit. One of the officials minuted that Milner 'could not remain in South Africa, if the Cape Ministry asked for his recall'; and Chamberlain added: 'I am astonished that Sir A. Milner should wish—or allow—this to be published. . . . The latest telegram giving his opinions will render its publication quite unnecessary for the purpose of representing Sir A. M.'s views.'[3]

This was Milner's lengthy 'helot' telegram. This famous document was written in response to a telegram from Selborne asking him to send a full statement of his views on the petition, in a form suitable for publication. Selborne's telegram included suggestions as to the lines on which the high commissioner should construct his exposition as well as a summary of the main points in Chamberlain's indictment of the republic, which had been prepared for the consideration of the

[1] The series was written between 15 Mar. and 26 Apr. and is in African (South), 571, pp. 489–90; 572, pp. 25–26, 31–34, 40–42, 42–43, 52–53; ibid. Headlam i. 328–9.
[2] Ibid. 348.
[3] Minutes by Just and Chamberlain, 8 May, on Milner to Chamberlain, 19 Apr. 1899. C.O. 417/260.

cabinet.[1] Milner's statement was to a considerable extent influenced by the suggestions and the information in Selborne's telegram. But the style of the crucial passages was entirely his own. He wrote *inter alia*:

South Africa can prosper under two, three or six Governments, but not under two absolutely conflicting social and political systems, perfect equality for Dutch and British in the British Colonies side by side with permanent subjection of British to Dutch in one of the Republics. . . . The case for intervention is overwhelming. . . . The spectacle of thousands of British subjects kept permanently in the position of helots . . . calling vainly to Her Majesty's Government for redress, does steadily undermine the influence and reputation of Great Britain and the respect for the British Government within the Queen's dominions. A certain section of the press,[2] not in the Transvaal only, preaches openly and constantly the doctrine of a Republic embracing all South Africa, and supports it by menacing references to the armaments of the Transvaal, its alliance with the Orange Free State, and the active sympathy which in case of war it would receive from a section of Her Majesty's subjects. I regret to say that this doctrine, supported as it is by a ceaseless stream of malignant lies about the intentions of the British Government, is producing a great effect upon a large number of our Dutch fellow colonists. . . . I can see nothing which will put a stop to this mischievous propaganda but some striking proof of the intention of Her Majesty's Government not to be ousted from its position in South Africa. And the best proof alike of its power and its justice would be to obtain for the Uitlanders in the Transvaal a fair share in the Government of the country which owes everything to their exertions.[3]

If and when the British government allowed this telegram to be published, it was bound to make a difference. Chamberlain's comment was: 'This is tremendously stiff, and if it is published it will make either an ultimatum *or* Sir A. Milner's recall necessary. . . .'[4] As for Milner, he had written to Greene in August 1898: 'If we know what we are driving at, then I don't the least mind public attention being directed elsewhere during the slow operations of the siege. We can easily make noise enough when the time has come to storm.'[5] Here was a loud bang indeed, which could not but powerfully affect the British public. It is said that H. H. Asquith counted the adjectives.[6] Cook, the editor of the Liberal *Daily News*, wrote to Milner in

---

[1] Selborne to Milner, 28 Apr. 1899. African (South), 572, p. 48.
[2] It is not clear what newspapers Milner had in mind. Maybe the *Rand Post* and the *Stellalander*. See Scholtz, ii. 217–18.
[3] The quotation is from the telegram as published in C. 9345, pp. 209–12.
[4] Wilde, 102.   [5] Headlam, i. 237.   [6] Garvin, iii. 395.

July: 'The British Public has worked itself up finally at "helots".'[1] But surely not at 'helots' alone. For alongside the helots, Milner had conjured up the spectre of a republic of South Africa. He had also made not merely the helotry of the Uitlanders, but the very existence of an armed Transvaal with a will of her own, into a challenge to the prestige and power of Great Britain. Before the publication of the helot dispatch the people of Britain—and of other states—might not have appreciated the adverse effect on British prestige of the non-coercion of a small power like the South African Republic. But once the British government had publicly adopted the argument of prestige it was committed to a policy of coercion. All that remained to be seen was how far the argument and the policy would take it.[2] By mid-July Chamberlain and Milner were saying to each other, the former that 'to some extent we have been able to show that the question at issue is greater than any particular grievance' and involved 'the maintenance of our position in South Africa . . .'; the latter that 'franchise and every other question have merged in one big issue; is British paramountcy to be vindicated or let slide?'[3] By early September Chamberlain could go farther. 'It is a great thing to say', he informed Milner, 'that the majority of the people have, as I believe, recognized that there is a greater issue than the franchise or the grievances of the Uitlanders at stake, and that our supremacy in S. Africa and our existence as a great Power in the world are involved in the result of our present controversy.'[4]

The acquisition of the franchise for the Uitlanders would not only be a 'striking proof' of Britain's supremacy in South Africa, but would also strengthen the British position in a more tangible manner. Milner told the public in the helot telegram that the franchise would be 'the true remedy' for the Uitlanders' grievances. But privately he explained that it would serve an even more important purpose than that.

Personally I am not afraid [he wrote to the governor of Natal early in May] that if the Uitlanders are admitted to political power by our aid— and it is *de toute evidence* that they would never have got it otherwise— they will turn and rend us. Possibly the Transvaal may never become part of our S. African Empire, though I think, with statesmanship on our side,

[1] Headlam, i. 355.

[2] For the opinion of Sir Edward Grey, the Liberal 'imperialist', about the helot telegram, see Headlam, i. 560–1.

[3] Actually he wrote this to Selborne.

[4] Garvin, iii. 410; Headlam, i. 457, 526.

it must come in time. But in any case I cannot see, how a Transvaal which is either Anglicized, or like the Cape Colony, neutralized by an Anglo-Dutch fight *on equal lines*, can be the danger to us and the focus of dis-affection in all our possessions which the Transvaal is to-day.[1]

In the meantime, during the month preceding the dispatch of the helot telegram, the colonial office had been drafting the comprehensive indictment of the republic, which was finally dated 10 May 1899. The draft, which Chamberlain described as 'a protest and still more ... an appeal to public opinion', was circulated to the cabinet and discussed at its meeting of 2 May. Ministers realized that they were being asked to take a decisive step, from which there could be no retreat; several of them felt 'uncomfortable', as Chamberlain's bio-grapher puts it. 'Arthur Balfour', he writes, 'on behalf of those, no doubt including Salisbury himself, whom we may call the uncom-fortable Ministers, was the most acute critic of the Milner position.'[2] And, it may be added, of the Chamberlain position as well. On 1 May Balfour wrote a long memorandum for the cabinet in which he remarked:

No doubt the Boers are engaged in fighting a hopeless cause. The South African Republic may last for ever, but it cannot for very long be a Boer Republic. In the nature of things, Boer supremacy means a condition of political equilibrium, which gets day by day more unstable. But I do not think we can complain of the Boers not taking this view, nor (if they do take it) of their struggling to the last in favour of a lost cause. Were I a Boer, brought up in Boer traditions, nothing but necessity would induce me to adopt a constitution which would turn my country into an English Republic, or a system of education which would reduce my language to the *patois* of a small and helpless minority. We have, of course, a *right* to ask for these and for other like concessions, but I do not think the practice of international law would justify us in doing more than ask for them, and, in existing circumstances, a request not accompanied by a menace is quite certain to be disregarded.

After the adjournment of the cabinet meeting Balfour returned to the charge:

... Are there then [he wrote to Chamberlain] any peculiarities in our relation to the Transvaal which would justify us in submitting it to more summary treatment than any ordinary Foreign State? I do not think that any such peculiarity arises out of the [London] Convention except in regard to matters in which the Convention itself has been broken. Such peculiarity,

---

[1] Headlam, i. 359. [2] Garvin, iii. 393.

if it exists . . . can only be found in the fact that Englishmen are not merely a majority in one town, but are a majority of the whole population of the Republic.[1] This state of things, without parallel in history, may perhaps be a sufficient ground for exceptional measures. But this point would have to be worked out much more carefully than the Cabinet seemed disposed to work it out last Tuesday. It cannot be dismissed as 'Metaphysics'. . . .[2]

When Milner learnt that the meeting of 2 May had been inconclusive he telegraphed his chief: 'I think it much better to delay answer [to petition] than send an equivocal one. The enemy, simply because they are frightened, are wavering all along the line. . . . But we shall get nothing at all if Transvaal Government has the least suspicion that we are half-hearted.'[3]

In preparation for the adjourned meeting of the cabinet Chamberlain circulated the helot telegram, which had arrived on 5 May.[4] The next day he circulated a revised version of his dispatch embodying some of the suggestions made by his colleagues. 'The general effect of the changes made', he wrote, 'is to lessen the emphasis put on financial grievances and to lay more stress on the personal disabilities of the Uitlanders and the inequality of their treatment as compared with the Boers. I have endeavoured to show that this is inconsistent with the spirit of the Convention.'[5] He could not, of course, satisfy Balfour and the other 'uncomfortable' ministers, including Hicks Beach and perhaps Lansdowne in addition to the prime minister. But at the crucial meeting of 9 May Balfour presumably did not press his objections,[6] and Chamberlain won the day.

The cabinet had crossed its Rubicon. A few days earlier Chamberlain telegraphed Milner: 'Proposed despatch will not be in the form of definite ultimatum, but it will be a very strong one. You will consider it quite firm enough I think.'[7]

II

Towards the end of April statesmen of the Cape Colony began to intensify their efforts to ward off the war that seemed to be threatening South Africa. A month earlier Merriman had written to his

[1] That was not so, even if 'Englishmen' are taken to include all English-speaking British subjects. See above, pp. 1–3.

[2] *Bulletin* (1954), pp. 173–5.   [3] African (South), 572, pp. 50–51.

[4] Garvin, iii. 396.   [5] Chamberlain papers, B.

[6] *Bulletin* (1954), p. 175.

[7] African (South), 572, p. 51. Chamberlain's dispatch is in C. 9345, pp. 226–31; Reitz's delayed reply in Cd. 43, pp. 74–82.

chief, Schreiner, who was away in the eastern Cape, about an interview he had just had with the high commissioner: 'Milner is bitterly hostile and unsympathetic to the Transvaal. He is prepared to take the first opportunity to show his teeth in that quarter. . . . Recollect that to keep the peace in South Africa is the main object of our Government though we cannot say so. . . .' Shortly after receiving this news, Schreiner asked chief justice de Villiers to go north late in April in order both to persuade the Pretoria government to grant reforms and to broach the subject of a conference between the unsuspecting high commissioner and the presidents of the two republics.[1] While de Villiers was in Pretoria Schreiner had several long talks with Milner. It is clear from the account of the interviews which Milner telegraphed to Chamberlain that the two men found themselves at cross-purposes. Schreiner said that he was willing to assist in solving the Transvaal problem if the high commissioner would tell him what the British authorities 'really wanted'. This Milner would not do, though he spoke in general terms about the 'radical reforms' which were required. He answered Schreiner that he was prepared 'to consider carefully the possibility of co-operation', provided Schreiner and his friends were willing to follow his advice. Milner then proceeded to comment on the interviews as follows:

His [Schreiner's] move is, of course, a feeler to find out what is the least that we will take, but at the same time I consider him to be acting honestly. . . . Whether Schreiner and Hofmeyr, who is certainly behind him in this action, can shake obstinacy of Transvaal I greatly doubt, but if we could commit them to advocate substantial reforms it would be a point gained, and I believe they could be pushed into advocating something really radical in the way of enfranchisement if convinced of the determination of Her Majesty's Government.[2]

To the governor of Natal Milner gave a frank explanation of the tactics he was henceforward to pursue in order to bring South African pressure to bear on the republican government.

The great thing now [he wrote] in this intervening breathing space before the bomb bursts, is for us to stiffen the wobblers. I know perfectly well that as soon as it becomes . . . evident that H.M.G. mean business, we shall have the usual outcry (à la Sivewright)[3] that there is nothing to

[1] Walker (c), 133–4. [2] African (South), 572, pp. 49–50.
[3] Sivewright, ex-minister and now a member of the progressive party, had recently been unseated at Stellenbosch by Schreiner's South African party, and was at this time in England confusing people, as Milner had it, by '"time and patience" twaddle'. Ibid. 572, pp. 63–64.

fight about, that a race-war would be something too awful, etc. It is under cover of these bogeys that Kruger and Co. have kept up their game so long. *Once you convince the wobblers*—and you have yours as I have mine, both plenty of them—that the British government is *resolute*, the whole force of the peace-at-any-price party will be directed to getting the Transvaal to give in. Sir H. de Villiers is decidedly on that tack already, and with a little more pushing, Schreiner will follow suit. I can picture to myself Binns[1] very much on the Sivewright line, but I believe that he and every other mugwump if he knows that Great Britain means to have her way this time, will be very careful how he does anything which by any possibility could have the effect of making Kruger more obdurate and thus making war a certainty.

Milner's idea clearly was to utilize the horror of war, which was bound to take on the character of civil war as far as South Africans were concerned, to compel South African statesmen to get to work on the republican government without prejudice to his own and Chamberlain's subsequent action.[2]

Immediately after his interviews with the high commissioner Schreiner wrote to Smuts to urge that Kruger should better the francise reforms he had so far announced. 'It is only a deep sense of urgency', he concluded, 'that makes me speak to another brother in the filial duty we owe to our own Mother Country.' Smuts, in reply, held out some hopes of an improvement of Kruger's offer, and Schreiner closed the correspondence with the remark that, if reasonable reform were conceded, '*there might be a good chance now of gaining . . . a recognition of the big principle, for which I would think that much indeed might be yielded, of arbitration in Convention matters.* I mean . . . arbitration not by Powers but by jurists—impartial and learned—not necessarily South African. . . .'[3]

De Villiers returned from Pretoria on 4 May and reported to Schreiner that Reitz, Smuts, and Schalk Burger had agreed 'to work for a liberal franchise and an inquiry into the dynamite monopoly. But on one condition. All the British demands must be presented fully and finally, once for all. . . . For the rest they believed that good might come of a conference between the High Commissioner and the

---

[1] The prime minister of Natal.

[2] Headlam, i. 359. The following passage, written to the governor of Natal about this time, is in the authentic Machiavellian tradition: 'A strong line . . . might lead to a great fluttering of the dovecots in the first instance but like every strong line it would presently attract support and put heart into our own people.' Ibid. 398.

[3] Schreiner to Smuts, 1 and 19 May 1899 (Smuts's private papers, vol. i); Smuts's letter is in Walker (c), 143–4.

two Presidents.'[1] But Milner had his own ideas about a conference. On 8 May he telegraphed Chamberlain urging him to conclude the dispatch indicting the republic with the suggestion of a conference in order to arrive at 'such a programme of reforms as the Uitlanders could be advised by Her Majesty's Government to accept'. The telegram continued:

I believe the Government of S.A.R. are in such a tight place that they would concede a great deal if assured that such concession would buy off our hostility. If we merely threaten . . . but do not indicate any way out, they may make reforms which look well but are quite hollow and then . . . say . . . that we have no right to complain of their plan of dealing with the needs of the case when we suggested none of our own. On the other hand if we can only get into negotiations with them we can compel them either to adopt specific reforms, or else, by refusing them, to show their invincible obstinacy and justify us in taking stronger measures. And I think if we propose negotiations I can put the screw on their Cape friends to urge them to accept it, and failing such acceptance to wash their hands of them.[2]

The cabinet accepted Milner's advice and a few paragraphs added to Chamberlain's dispatch accordingly suggested a conference at Pretoria between Kruger and the high commissioner, for the purpose of settling not only the Uitlander question but all matters at issue between Britain and the republic.[3]

The Milner–Chamberlain plan was to hold the conference after they had published their indictments of the republic supported by a blue book on Uitlander grievances, and if Kruger refused the concessions they considered necessary, to proceed at once to 'stronger measures'. But at this point the leaders of the South African party at the Cape unexpectedly intervened and upset the time-table. On 4 May Chamberlain had an interview with Sivewright which produced a result the former had not anticipated. Sivewright cabled to Hofmeyr urging that Milner and Kruger should meet without delay. Whereupon Schreiner, Sauer (a member of his ministry), and Hofmeyr agreed that president Steyn should be asked to invite the high commissioner and the president of the South African Republic to confer together at Bloemfontein, on the ground that the atmosphere would be calmer there than at Pretoria. Hofmeyr cabled this news to Sivewright, who conveyed it to Chamberlain. On 9 May the proposal was laid before Milner.[4] Chamberlain and Milner both realized that

---

[1] Ibid. 141.   [2] C.O. 417/261; African (South), 572, p. 54.
[3] C. 9345, p. 231.   [4] African (South), 572, p. 55; Headlam, i. 360, 371.

to reject it would be impolitic, and that its acceptance would mean the postponement of the publication of their case. Otherwise they would be accused of spoiling the atmosphere for the 'friendly' discussion that was envisaged.[1] But neither Chamberlain nor Milner nor the British Uitlanders on the Rand liked the idea of this conference. Milner wrote: 'The funk here on the part of the Afrikander party. . . has been something terrific. . . . Conference . . . is a very clever move and has already produced one effect, viz. that of mollifying the British press a bit and relaxing for the moment, unfortunately as I think, the screw upon the enemy.' And again: 'That [conference] really *is* a good stroke of business on the part of the enemy, as it hangs up the despatch and spoils, or at least delays, a great stroke on our part.' As for the British Uitlanders—or the leaguers among them—Greene expressed their view as follows: 'What they do not wish is that the High Commissioner should . . . come down from his pedestal for anything less than the final crisis, as his acceptance of the invitation, if the Conference were to prove abortive, would be explained by the official gang here as having been a concession to the pressure of inter-State and South African sentiment, and would make it more difficult for his resumption of his position as the dominant factor.'[2]

Kruger accepted Steyn's invitation to come to Bloemfontein, provided that the independence of his state was not touched. On this proviso Milner commented to Chamberlain: 'As regards his reservation about independence, I see no harm in passing it over in silence. I shall at present stage certainly not propose anything which could be reasonably alleged to impair whatever measure of independence he at present possesses.' He likewise agreed to the conference with the proviso on his side that he could not consent to Steyn's participation as an intermediary between Kruger and himself.[3]

III

While the preparations for the conference were going forward there occurred two incidents which did not help to improve the relations between the British authorities and the republic. The first was the discovery by the latter's detective department of a so-called

[1] African (South), 572, p. 57; Garvin, iii. 401.
[2] Headlam, i. 378–9, 384.
[3] Milner to Chamberlain, 16 May 1899 (C.O. 417/261); Headlam, i. 374.

conspiracy against the state. Since 1897 the British officials in the republic had been aware of organizations of one kind or another in Johannesburg planning violent action, but they had received strict instructions from the colonial office to have nothing to do with them. If the detective department had been competently run it might have succeeded in uncovering a real, even if innocuous, conspiracy.[1] As it was, the elaborate edifice of affidavits and evidence constructed by the acting chief detective, Richard Beatty, crumbled when the case came on for trial after the Bloemfontein conference. But when the news of the conspiracy was first published in the press, it caused a great deal of excitement. It was alleged that the conspirators, among whom there were said to be five ex-officers of the British army, had plotted to seize the fort overlooking Johannesburg and to hold the town pending the arrival of British troops from Natal. The detective department tried to implicate not only the South African league but also the British war office in the conspiracy.[2] It seems clear that the men mainly responsible for this disgraceful affair were Schutte, the chief of police, and his subordinate, Beatty.[3] At the conclusion of the preliminary trial of the 'conspirators' Milner telegraphed Chamberlain: 'Whole case seems intimately connected with struggle between State Attorney and Schutte for control of detective force.' According to this theory Schutte and Beatty invented the conspiracy in order to prove their zeal in the service of the state and retain their offices and emoluments.[4] Why the state attorney (Smuts) allowed the accused men to be arrested on the unsatisfactory evidence placed before him by Beatty is no doubt an intriguing question. But it takes us into the realm of speculation. What is certain is that the case further damaged the reputation of a state already seriously compromised. Smuts no doubt bore this affair in mind—along with much else—when he dismissed Beatty and many of the men under him immediately after assuming control of the detective force.[5]

The second incident to which reference must be made was the reply of Reitz to Chamberlain's claim that the republic's right to self-government depended on the preamble of the Pretoria convention.[6] There had been several indications during the last few months

[1] Bitensky, 14–20; African (South), 572, pp. 78–79.
[2] C. 9521, pp. 1–4, 17–18.
[3] Walker's attribution of the prime responsibility to Smuts is, I think, mistaken. See *C.H.B.E.* viii. 592 and Walker (*c*), 146.
[4] African (South), 600, p. 29; C. 9521, p. 18.
[5] African (South), 600, p. 222, and above, p. 219.
[6] See above, p. 199.

that the state secretary was not bearing up very well under the strain of the deepening crisis. He now played into Chamberlain's hands[1] with the retort that 'the now existing right of absolute self-government of this Republic is not derived from either the Convention of 1881 or that of 1884, but simply and solely follows from the inherent right of this Republic as a sovereign international State'. The colonial office grasped, and held on to, the advantage which 'this terrible faux pas of Reitz' gave them.[2] It fitted in very well with their claim that the republic was challenging the British position in South Africa. Though Reitz did his best to retire, with some measure of dignity, from his untenable position, Chamberlain continued to the end to rub it in that the republic was not a sovereign international state.[3]

IV

During the second half of May the Cape statesmen continued working on Kruger and his advisers. Their combined and urgent representations at this moment were due undoubtedly to the realization that Milner 'meant business'. Both they and prominent Free Staters like Steyn and Fischer[4] had long been aware—quite apart from any 'persuasion' by Milner—of the need for reform in the republic, and had said so to members of the Transvaal government, including Kruger. But they were aware also, through their correspondence with Transvaal leaders, that Milner's policy of imperial intervention might easily end in war. They disliked Milner's attitude to the republic. But they disliked war even more, and they therefore urged Kruger's government to promise at Bloemfontein reforms sufficiently generous to cut the ground from under the feet of the republic's enemies.[5]

While the Cape statesmen were bringing their influence to bear on Kruger, Milner asked Chamberlain to allow him to inform the signatories of the petition to the Queen 'that H.M. Government . . . cannot but express their general sympathy with the view of the memorialists. . . . That at this moment they refrain from any further

---

[1] Reitz admitted in August: 'I know I am no diplomat, and never shall be because I am apt to get indignant (and show it) at what appears to me as rascally and bullying conduct. . . .' Walker (a), 348; see also ibid. 339. Leyds declared later that Smuts and Grobler composed Reitz's dispatch. *Vierde Verzameling*, Deel II, 21.

[2] Selborne's minute, 21 May, on Milner to Chamberlain, 20 May 1899. C.O. 417/261.

[3] C. 9507, pp. 32–33; C. 9521, pp. 53, 64; C. 9530, pp. 12, 16; Leyds, *Eenige Correspondentie*, pp. 203–14.

[4] See above, p. 217.

[5] Headlam, i. 393–6; Walker (a), 336–9, and (c), 132–3, 143–4, 146.

reply to the memorialists is due to the fact that a meeting between the High Commissioner and the President of the South African Republic has been arranged. . . .' Milner's cable concluded: 'I think something of this kind becoming public just now very important to keep up courage of our friends. If the President S.A.R. were to take offence at it and break off meeting he would put himself in the wrong. . . .' In the colonial office they hesitated. Selborne supported Milner, as he almost always did. Wingfield was dubious. He thought that the action suggested by Milner 'can hardly fail to exasperate the S.A.R. Govt. but Kruger may think it better policy to pocket the affront, and attend the meeting'. On 23 May Chamberlain authorized Milner to publish an interim reply to the petitioners on the lines he had recommended and the South African league, taking the hint, published the petition *in extenso* in the Johannesburg press.[1]

Chamberlain had no sooner granted Milner's request with regard to the interim reply, than the latter cabled again to ask his chief to give Sivewright,[2] who was still in England talking 'time and patience', a hint strong enough to induce him to 'hold his tongue'. 'Besides,' he added, 'it would be certain to get back to Hofmeyr and to increase the very salutary alarm of that gentleman, who is pressing Kruger to give in and will certainly do so just as long as and no longer than he thinks that we mean business.' In spite of the warnings of his staff Chamberlain decided to follow Milner's advice and drafted a letter to Sivewright 'which may induce him to frighten Mr Hofmeyer' (*sic*). Chamberlain wrote: 'I have read the report of the meeting of the Volksraad with feelings akin to dismay. . . .[3] [The] situation [is] . . . even more grave than I had originally supposed. I most earnestly desire a peaceful settlement—not because I fear the result of hostile operations. . . .' If the Bloemfontein conference were to end in failure 'we shall have exhausted conciliatory methods and the crisis . . . will be upon us'. Now is the time, he concluded, to bring to bear moderating influences on the Transvaal.[4]

The letter was not sent. While it was still under consideration a telegraphic correspondence was taking place between Milner and

---

[1] Minutes by Wingfield, 19 May, and Selborne, 20 May, on Milner to Chamberlain, 18 May 1899 (C.O. 417/261); Headlam, i. 377; African (South), 572, p. 61; ibid. 600, p. 38.

[2] See above, p. 271 n. 3

[3] The volksraad had 'quietly shelved' the franchise question 'for a year by referring it to the people'. Reitz to de Villiers, 26 May 1899. Walker (*a*), 338.

[4] Milner to Chamberlain, 25 May 1899, and Chamberlain to Sivewright (draft), 27 May 1899 (C.O. 417/261); African (South), 572, pp. 63–64.

Chamberlain on the subject of Schreiner's presence at Bloemfontein while the conference was on. (The high commissioner had already refused to have Hofmeyr there.[1]) Schreiner strongly urged on Milner his claim to be present so that he might be consulted 'if wanted', on the ground that 'the interest of the [Cape] Colony in a peaceable settlement was so enormous that he felt in a painful position in not being able to contribute to it'. In reporting to Chamberlain his refusal of this request Milner remarked: '. . . It is no use yielding any more to Schreiner, as, if we mean to take a decided line about the Transvaal, split with[2] present Ministry is bound to come sooner or later and anything that weakens my hands at Bloemfontein will only make critical situation more probable.'[3] Chamberlain's reply showed that his hand had lost none of its cunning.

If I were in your place [he cabled] I should let Mr Schreiner come. He wants peace and will try for a settlement. No doubt he will press both sides to yield but if he finds you firm I think he will be driven to take your side rather than Kruger's—because South African feeling generally is in favour of reasonable reforms. In this way he might, in the event of a failure of Conference, be committed a long way in support of our views. If he is not allowed to go and the Conference breaks down, he is pretty sure to think and to say he could have saved the situation and he will attribute failure to your and my obstinacy. Suppose that you and Kruger are at first far apart. It is inconceivable that Schreiner should support Kruger in his extreme views. If he supports you we have gained enormously. He will probably try for a compromise. If we can accept this we shall have reached at any rate a temporary settlement. Probably it [the compromise] will be unsatisfactory to both sides. Then we must work to let refusal come from Kruger and in this case again Schreiner will be on our side and his opposition to strong measures will be very much weakened. The only danger is that Kruger should accept Schreiner's proposals and that you should decline. No doubt this would throw him into Kruger's arms but how are we worse off then than if Conference breaks down in his absence and he is able to say that fault lies with our unreasonable attitude? In my opinion there is therefore nothing to lose in taking Schreiner and a good probability of something to gain. But having expressed my own views I am ready to leave decision with you as you are on the spot. . . .

Milner replied somewhat curtly that these arguments had been fully present to his mind and that he remained of his original opinion.[4]

---

[1] Hofmeyr, 536; Walker (c), 146–7.
[2] Not 'split in' as Walker suggests in (c), 148 n.   [3] Headlam, i. 391–2.
[4] Chamberlain to Milner, 26 May 1899, and Milner to Chamberlain, 27 May 1899 (C.O. 417–261); African (South), 572, pp. 65–66.

The officials now returned to the attack on the letter to Sivewright. They asked Chamberlain whether he was prepared to commit the government to a policy of coercion if Milner failed at Bloemfontein. Would public opinion support the government in such a policy? Chamberlain admitted that he could not be certain about public opinion, and regretted once more that he had been obliged to put off publishing his case, since 'its reception would probably have enlightened us'. In further explanation of his decision not to send the letter he minuted:

I do not like the tone of Sir A. Milner's last telegram.[1] It seems to betray the existence of somewhat strained feelings[2]—whereas coolness and sweet reasonableness are more than ever necessary at the present stage. I am afraid of doing anything which can add fuel to the fire. Otherwise I should still incline to frighten . . . Hofmeyer. But if Sir A. Milner is to keep in close sympathy with H.M.G., I think that he requires to be restrained rather than encouraged at this moment.[3]

So much for Chamberlain's attitude on the eve of the conference. As for Milner, he went to Bloemfontein expecting that the conference would fail.[4] There was good reason for this pessimism. It was not only, as a member of Schreiner's ministry put it, that 'two hard stones will grind with difficulty'.[5] It was also that the form taken by the conference made success much harder to achieve. It had been the idea of the Cape statesmen who first suggested the meeting at Bloemfontein that the proceedings would be private and informal.[6] The public might then have been informed of the results achieved by a *communiqué* issued at the conclusion of the negotiations. This would have been in conformity with the usual practice in inter-state discussions. As it turned out, the discussions at Bloemfontein were private only in the sense that the public was not admitted while they were actually taking place. How did this come about? Shortly after the breakdown of the capitalist negotiations, Milner had told Greene: 'The great point seems to be . . . to keep the course of future negotiations public. . . .'[7] Three weeks later, after Hofmeyr had telegraphed the

---

[1] The telegram in which he reiterated his decision with regard to Schreiner.
[2] Milner did, in fact, complain of strain and fatigue about this time. Headlam, i. 354, 361, 378, 391.
[3] Minutes of Chamberlain and officials on Milner's telegrams dated 22 and 27 May 1899. C.O. 417/261.
[4] Headlam, i. 384, 400, 405, 423.   [5] Ibid. 393.
[6] Hofmeyr to Sivewright, 8 May, enclosed in Sivewright to Chamberlain, 8 May 1899 (C.O. 417/282); African (South), 572, p. 55; van der Merwe, i. 164.
[7] Headlam, i. 332.

Cape suggestion of a private conference, one of Chamberlain's officials minuted: 'If it is made clear to President Kruger that the proceedings of the meeting will have to be made public, he will in all probability decline the meeting.'[1] The official appears to have been mistaken,[2] but the whole character of the conference was altered by the decision to publish a verbatim account of the discussions. It followed that each of the two protagonists, while ostensibly talking to the other, was actually addressing the public, both in South Africa and overseas. For the purpose of this public debate the accomplished Englishman had the advantage of the untutored old Boer. It was to be expected that he would argue more cogently and persuasively than his antagonist and that his argument, when published, would contribute to that rousing of the British public on which so much depended. But appeals to public opinion, whether by Milner or Kruger, were on a different level of discourse from genuine negotiations.

V

The conference opened on 31 May. Milner's tactics were to confine the discussion to the single point of the franchise. Only if he obtained satisfaction on that point would he attempt a settlement of other issues. It is true that in the afternoon of the second day he raised the question of the dynamite monopoly, but the ensuing discussion was purely exploratory and no attempt was made to reach a settlement. Thereafter he would not bring up any other points though invited by Kruger to do so. This gave the latter his opportunity. He wanted to know from Milner what he was prepared to give in return for his wishes on the franchise being wholly or partially met. It would be easier, he said, to carry his volksraad and burghers with him if he could show them some *quid pro quo*: 'I must tell them that something has been given in to me, if I give in to something.' The high commissioner replied that he did not intend to make the franchise the subject of a 'sort of Kaffir bargain': for the Uitlanders' request for the franchise was reasonable and just and it was in the republic's own interests to grant it. But Kruger was, of course, aware that Milner was pressing for the franchise in the political interests of Britain. So

---

[1] Minute by H. W. Just, 11 May, on Milner to Chamberlain, 10 May 1899. C.O. 417/261.

[2] I have not been able to discover at what stage Kruger was told that the conference proceedings would be published in full.

he stuck to his point about a *quid pro quo* and obtained at any rate some sort of an answer to his proposals. What about the complete incorporation of Swaziland in the South African Republic,[1] he asked. Was Milner prepared to discuss the indemnity payable for the Jameson raid? Would he agree to the settlement of differences between the British and republican governments by arbitration?[2] On the first question—Swaziland—Milner knew his own mind and Chamberlain's: they were both opposed to incorporation. He replied therefore that 'the very last thing to do is to bring up Swaziland at this moment'. On the other two questions he was unable to say anything definite. But that was not his fault. Two months before the conference he had urged Chamberlain not to delay any longer in settling the 'admitted but unsatisfied claim' of the republic to an indemnity for the raid. Its extravagant demand, he wrote, need not be met, but a 'reasonably liberal offer . . . not glaringly dispropor-tionate to the very serious injury inflicted' should now be made.[3] This Chamberlain would not do but sent instead a temporizing dispatch, the gist of which was telegraphed to Milner shortly before the conference.[4] On the question of arbitration Milner had once more to temporize, since Chamberlain had requested him to avoid that 'delicate subject' without further instructions.[5] It is not surprising, therefore, that Kruger found Milner's reaction to his proposals unsatisfactory. 'I consider', he concluded, 'I am beaten out of the field. The Swaziland point has only been touched, the indemnity matter is still on the water, and on the other point His Excellency has not said anything I can take hold of.'[6]

Milner now brought the discussion back to the point from which it had started—the franchise. In the morning of the second day he had proposed that the franchise should be given at once to Uit-landers who had lived in the republic for five years, and that a number of new volksraad constituencies should be created on the Rand in order that the Uitlander representatives might not be 'in a con-temptible minority'. He had already explained to Chamberlain, in a telegram which was published immediately after the conference, that what he had in mind was at least seven new seats for the Rand which would give the Uitlanders nine representatives in a house of

---

[1] See above, p. 221.
[2] C. 9404, pp. 25, 28–37.
[3] African (South), 572, pp. 31–34.
[4] C. 9343, *passim*; Van der Poel (*b*), 248–9. No indemnity was in fact paid.
[5] Garvin, iii. 403; African (South), 572, p. 73.
[6] C. 9404, p. 37.

thirty-five. Kruger replied, in effect, that he was not prepared to hand over his country to foreigners.[1] Milner pressed him to say what sort of a franchise he was prepared to concede. This led him to consult the three advisers he had brought with him from Pretoria,[2] as well as the Free Staters Steyn and Fischer. Steyn declared later that he urged Kruger to accept advice, recently received from de Villiers, which involved the acceptance of Milner's scheme with one important modification: for de Villiers advocated the adoption of the British naturalization law, which authorized the secretary of state, at his discretion, to grant the full privileges of British citizenship to foreigners who had resided in the country for five years. The discretion allowed the president by such a law, wrote de Villiers, would enable him to 'prevent any undesirable or disloyal persons from obtaining the franchise'.[3] It seems certain that Milner, who did not trust the president, would never have agreed to a provision of this nature. But the five years' retrospective franchise, if accepted in principle by Kruger, would at least have provided that basis of discussion which Milner did not find in the president's actual proposal. Steyn's advocacy was strongly supported by Fischer and Smuts, but he got no help from Kruger's executive councillors, the 'progressive' Schalk Burger and the 'conservative' A. D. Wolmarans. These two might, he thought, have been influenced by a numerously signed petition brought to Bloemfontein during the course of the conference, which begged Kruger not to give way on the franchise.[4] So much for Steyn's testimony. Among Smuts's papers there is a letter he wrote to his wife on the second day of the conference. Though he does not refer explicitly to the franchise, his letter deserves notice if only because of his account of the impression made on him by the high commissioner. 'Milner', wrote Smuts, 'is as sweet as honey, but there is something in his very intelligent eyes that tells me that he is a very dangerous man. Although it is a great humiliation for us to confer on our own affairs with Her Majesty's representative, it . . . remains my earnest wish that all may come right. The present . . . tension is having a very harmful effect on the spirit of our people and is retarding the development of the country.'

Kruger produced his franchise scheme in the afternoon of the third day. Taken together with a few additions made the day after, it

[1] C. 9404, pp. 25, 41–42, 54; C. 9345, p. 242.
[2] Smuts, Schalk Burger, and A. D. Wolmarans.
[3] Van der Merwe, i. 179–80, 188–9; Cd. 369, p. 2.
[4] Van der Merwe, i. 188–9.

provided for a sliding scale varying from two to seven years for the attainment of the full franchise, including the presidential vote.[1] Uitlanders who had settled in the republic before 1890 could get the franchise after two years; settlers of two or more years standing, after five; the rest, after seven years. Aliens on becoming naturalized were no longer to be asked, in so many words, to renounce their former citizenship. Kruger was wise enough not to attempt to assume the discretionary powers of the British secretary of state (except in so far as his government was to be authorized to dispense at its discretion with the proposed property qualifications). In his scheme he proposed instead to admit every Uitlander who, in addition to satisfying the residence and property qualifications, had not had a 'dishonouring sentence' imposed on him, and could prove that he had obeyed the laws, had been guilty of no act 'against Government or independence', and had enjoyed 'franchise or title thereto in former country'. The Uitlanders were to be represented in the volks-raad by five members.[2]

Milner admitted that the scheme was 'a great advance' on the existing position. But he nevertheless had many objections against it. He strongly criticized the dispensing power given to the government. He objected also to the disloyalty clause, which would permit the exclusion of the reform committee of Jameson raid days. The scheme as a whole he thought too complicated: it contained too many 'pit-falls' and seemed to take away with the one hand what it gave with the other.[3] But these 'pit-falls' were details which could have been dealt with at the conference table. His reasons for rejecting Kruger's scheme in principle were first, that under it no Uitlanders at all would be enfranchised immediately and relatively few after two years; and second, that Uitlanders who had settled in the republic after 1890 would have to become naturalized, i.e. lose their former citizenship, five years before they could obtain the full republican franchise, a proviso which most Uitlanders would find unacceptable.[4] From his point of view the immediate enfranchisement of a large body of Uitlanders was vital. This would be achieved, he reckoned, by the five years retrospective qualification, since his information indicated that the main Uitlander immigration had taken place before 1895.[5]

---

[1] Contrast Walker in *C.H.B.E.* viii. 592, and see C. 9404, pp. 42, 52; green book no. 4 of 1899, pp. 30–31, 37.
[2] C. 9404, pp. 51–52, 54.
[3] African (South), 572, p. 83; C. 9404, pp. 53, 56–58.
[4] C. 9404, pp. 53, 56–58.   [5] African (South), 600, pp. 132–3.

It was his intention that this franchise question should be settled once for all during his own and Chamberlain's term of office, and the enrolment of the Uitlanders as voters would give him the data he required for his next step. For no one knew, though many were prepared to guess,[1] how many foreigners had actually immigrated into the republic before or after 1895. As soon as he knew the number of Uitlander voters he meant to demand for them something approaching equal volksraad representation with the old burghers, i.e. something approaching 'one vote, one value',[2] notwithstanding the indications he gave at Bloemfontein that he would be satisfied with a limited representation, and that he would leave the Uitlanders to fend for themselves once it had been attained.[3]

On Sunday, 4 June, Milner telegraphed: 'Conference seems likely to fail. I have been studiously conciliatory. . . . My view is that a big concession on the franchise would be such a score that we could afford a compromise on other controversies or let them quietly drop into the background. . . .'[4] Chamberlain replied the next day: 'I hope you will not break off hastily. Boers do not understand quick decisions but prefer to waste a long time over a bargain without coming to terms. I am by no means convinced that the President . . . has made his last offer, and you should be very patient and admit a good deal of haggling before you finally abandon the game. It is of the utmost importance to put the President . . . clearly in the wrong.' He went on to authorize Milner to humour Kruger by discussing arbitration and Swaziland.[5] But before his telegram reached the high commissioner, the latter had already terminated the proceedings with the words: 'This Conference is absolutely at an end, and there is no obligation on either side arising out of it.'[6]

---

[1] See above, pp. 1–2.
[2] African (South), 600, pp. 226–8.
[3] C. 9404, pp. 27, 51, 53, 57–58; C. 9415, p. 46.
[4] C.O. 417/262; African (South), 572, pp. 83–84.
[5] Garvin, iii. 408; African (South), 572, p. 84.
[6] In the post mortem on the conference held in the colonial office one of the officials remarked that Milner adopted a threatening tone notwithstanding his disclaimers. The official agreed that under Milner's franchise proposals the new burghers would not swamp the old in volksraad elections; but what, he asked, about presidential elections? 'The proceedings of the conference', he continued, 'show that President Kruger was prepared to go on with the discussion, if Sir Alfred Milner had not pinned him down to deal with and settle the franchise question first. The President could not bring himself to give way on the franchise without having any concession to show his burghers as a make-weight, especially in regard to arbitration, so as to be able to assure them that a way was provided for preventing future intervention in internal matters.' H. W. Just, 4 July, on Milner to Chamberlain, 14 June 1899. C.O. 417/262.

CHAPTER XI

BRITISH SUPREMACY

With us there is great justice, because that war is just which is necessary, and arms are hallowed when there is no other hope but in them.

I

THE failure of the Bloemfontein conference ushered in the last stage of the South African crisis. That this stage took four months to live through was not the fault of the high commissioner. For he had already begun to advocate a military solution of the Transvaal problem. A fortnight before the conference he wrote to Selborne:

> . . . The Boers and their sympathizers have never been in such a funk for many years. . . . Therefore my advice to you is, if I fail with Kruger, to assume at once the diplomatic offensive and to back it with a strong show of material force. . . . My view is, (1) that absolute downright determination plus a large temporary increase of force will ensure a climb down. It is 20 to 1. And (2) that, if it didn't and there was a fight, it would be better to fight now than 5 or 10 years hence, when the Transvaal, unless the Uitlanders can be taken in, in considerable numbers, will be stronger and more hostile than ever.[1]

It could not have been difficult to persuade Chamberlain, to whom Selborne showed this letter (like the rest of Milner's correspondence with him), that the high commissioner's view was correct.[2] A week later Milner explained in more detail what he had in mind. He wanted an '*overwhelming*' force—'it may be 10,000 men'[3]—to be sent out at once to Natal, and Laing's Nek on the republican frontier to be occupied. 'This forward position once assured', he wrote, '. . . we should have a means of pressure which would be irresistible.'[4] Walker appears to hold that the British government should have followed Milner's advice.[5] Yet it can hardly be doubted that the dispatch of

---

[1] Milner to Selborne, 17 May 1899. Headlam, i. 385.
[2] See Garvin, iii. 141, 410, 470–1.
[3] i.e. 10,000 at most rather than '10,000 at least' as Walker has it in *C.H.B.E.* viii. 593.
[4] Headlam, i. 401.　　　　　　　　　　　　　[5] *C.H.B.E.* viii. 593.

10,000 troops to South Africa would have precipitated the outbreak of hostilities. As will be seen later, the republican government conceded a great deal to 'moral' pressure. But when Britain decided to send out 10,000 men, it made up its mind that the time had come to fight. In his correspondence during May and June Milner indicated that this might conceivably happen. He did not consider it likely, but if it did happen, so much the better. For the Boers could then be said to be the aggressors. The war would be almost a walk-over, a matter of a few months though its beginning would be '*very unpleasant*', and at the end of it British supremacy could be decisively secured in South Africa. But if the Boers did not attack, then perhaps the next best thing would be for Kruger to refuse to yield and for 'the smash' to come in that way (though he did not think 'we ought to aim at that'). If war came it would mean the end of the republic. '*Thousands* of people would at once swarm into the Transvaal, and the balance of political power which even now would be clearly ours in South Africa as a whole under a system of equal rights, would be rapidly and decisively turned against the Boer for ever.'[1]

Milner's letter advocating forceful determination arrived on 2 June, and a few days later came the news of the breakdown at Bloemfontein. Chamberlain now decided to recommend the dispatch of an ultimatum accompanied by troops. The cabinet with considerable misgivings agreed to follow his lead. He accordingly telegraphed Milner: 'What should H.M.G. ask for if they decide to send an ultimatum? . . . I suggest "the repeal of all legislation since the Convention of 1884 restrictive of the rights and privileges enjoyed by aliens when the convention was arranged". What do you think of it?' But this was going too fast even for Milner and he replied: '. . . Ultimatum now would be premature. . . .' The high commissioner's reply decided the issue, for the cabinet had already begun to feel, as Selborne put it, 'that they could not send an ultimatum yet, but that another stage or stages must intervene before public opinion would permit it'.[2]

The first of these stages was the publication in the middle of June of the blue book detailing in its 243 pages 'the complaints of British subjects in the South African Republic'. The blue book consisted mainly of dispatches from Milner, Butler, Greene, and Fraser,

---

[1] Headlam, i. 359, 400–2, 425. 'The Boer' in this context meant the Afrikaner.
[2] African (South), 572, pp. 85–86; Garvin, iii. 411, 527; Headlam, i. 430–1, 446; *Letters of Queen Victoria*, 3rd series, iii. 382–3.

carefully selected and edited by the colonial office. It contained in addition Milner's helot telegram and Chamberlain's indictment of the republic.[1]

In South Africa the reaction was immediate and strong. The leaders in both republics were confirmed in their worst fears. Writing to Merriman about the helot telegram Smuts declared: '. . . The situation is being forced from the outside in order by an armed conflict to forestall or defeat the work of time. . . . I have great hope that within a few years all just causes of complaint will have disappeared altogether and it fills me with a savage indignation to think that the work of those who are spending their . . . lifeblood for South Africa is to be undone in a moment by academic nobodies who fancy themselves great imperial statesmen.'[2] On the other hand, Milner gained some additional supporters from among those whom he described as the 'wobblers' or 'mugwumps'. The most notable of these was James Rose Innes. In his *Autobiography* Innes describes his interview with Milner which took place shortly after the latter's return from Bloemfontein. He had refused to take part in a deputation organized by Edmund Garrett—editor of the *Cape Times*,[3] progressive member of parliament, vice-president[4] of the South African league in the Cape, and a close collaborator of Milner's[5]—to congratulate the high commissioner on his firmness, explaining that he was opposed to 'any demonstration calculated to excite public feeling'. Milner thereupon summoned him to his presence and convinced him, though he no doubt continued to object to public demonstrations.[6] But these were part of Milner's technique. He had just told Chamberlain that if the Cape and Natal governments would not support him when called upon, crowded meetings could be held in all the considerable towns at a moment's notice.[7] The eventuality he had in mind did not arise, but crowded meetings did take place in June and July. The news of their holding was officially telegraphed to Chamberlain, who published it in a blue book issued in July. The first of the series took place in Johannesburg. This time the republican government, acting perhaps on a warning it had received from Cape

[1] C. 9345, *passim*.
[2] Smuts to Merriman, 16 June 1899. Smuts's private papers.
[3] Towards the end of June the *Cape Times* wrote: 'We have come to the point when the gun must be loaded and the aggressive combination calling itself the Afrikander nation must be made to believe it is loaded even by its discharge, if no other way succeeds.' C.O. 417/262.   [4] The president was Rhodes.
[5] See above, p. 179, and Headlam, ii. 113.
[6] Innes, 178–9; Cook (*a*), 136.   [7] African (South), 572, p. 94.

friends,[1] took steps to ensure that the meeting was not interfered with. The meeting endorsed the formation of an Uitlander Council,[2] which included prominent office-bearers of the league in the Transvaal. It also acclaimed Milner's policy.[3] This refrain was taken up at a large number of meetings in the Cape and Natal.[4] Schreiner's South African party kept quiet, though its leaders had been urged by members of both republican governments to speak out in favour of Kruger's Bloemfontein proposals.[5] They tried instead to secure an improvement of them.

While they were trying, Milner continued urging the dispatch of troops to prove that the British government was in earnest,[6] and Greene supported him to the best of his ability. Milner telegraphed information sent by Greene that the volksraad had decided in secret session to grant a seven years' retrospective franchise but only if the demand for it was accompanied 'by strong and unmistakable pressure of force', and that chief justice Gregorowski had actually advocated a display of force. Both stories seem unlikely. Greene added that it was the 'general conviction here' that troops would have to be sent.[7] But Chamberlain knew that the cabinet would not agree to this. Between mid-June and mid-July, as the Boers continued to yield, its warlike ardour cooled off. On 11 July Salisbury told the Queen that he 'was much impressed with the more pacific tone of the cabinet. Some members were averse to any such abatement of their indignation of [with?] the Transvaal. But the majority . . . were impressed with the want of support such a war would seem likely to command with public opinion in this country; and were in favour of very circumspect action.' A week later he declared that 'this country, as well as the cabinet, excepting perhaps Mr Chamberlain, were against a war'.[8] The colonial secretary found it necessary therefore to warn the high commissioner as early as 16 June that 'it is clear that we must be able to show, before we take more active measures, that every form of diplomatic pressure and every suggestion for arrangement has been exhausted'; and (on 21 June) that large reinforcements

[1] Smuts's private papers; van der Merwe, i. 206.
[2] See above, p. 264.
[3] It was attended by over 5,000 persons. A few days later another crowded meeting held in the same hall expressed confidence in the republican government. C. 9415, p. 41.
[4] Ibid. 6, 8, 22, 24–28, 30, 36–38, 46–47.
[5] Ibid. 29; Hofmeyr, 538–9; Walker (c), 153–4.
[6] African (South), 572, pp. 95, 102–3, 106–7; Headlam, i. 507.
[7] African (South), 572, pp. 104, 106.
[8] *Letters of Queen Victoria*, 3rd series, iii. 382–4; Salisbury to the Queen, 11 July 1899 (Royal Archives, A75/73). See also Headlam, i. 445, and Garvin, iii. 410–11.

were for the present out of the question.[1] But if the republic would not grant a satisfactory franchise, he asked Milner, what then? Why then, replied the latter, an ultimatum and troops. The most probable result, he reiterated, would be 'a complete climb down' or 'surrender'. If not that, then war, which ought to be over before summer started in November. And war, though 'deplorable' in itself, 'would at least enable us to put things on a sound basis for the future better than even the best-devised Convention can'.[2] This telegram—and a few others sent by the high commissioner at this time—alarmed Graham in the colonial office. Milner's telegram and the press reports[3] from South Africa, he minuted, 'make me very anxious. . . .I begin to think that there is something excitable in the South African air which prevents men taking a cool and dispassionate view. . . .'[4]

Chamberlain was inclined to agree, for there now arrived a telegram from Milner demanding the recall of the commander of the British troops in South Africa, general Butler. When Milner got to know Butler better after his return to South Africa in February, he admitted the general's ability with his usual candour. But he also recognized that if his policy was to be carried out Butler would have to go. For the latter made no secret of his view that peace should be maintained.[5] He impressed this view on the war office (though Milner was not aware of the fact till late in June), and he even sent on to Salisbury, for the information of the Queen, a letter from Schreiner containing an implied censure of Milner's policy. In his *Autobiography* he explained his attitude as follows: 'As commander of the troops in the Cape Colony and Natal, I held the balance. There would be no war while I was there.' When Milner told him in May that he thought the Boers would not fight, he replied that 'they would fight for their independence but not on lesser matters'; he said also that to bring military pressure to bear on the republics would require 40,000 men, but decided later that this figure was very much too low. (Milner declared afterwards, 'His merit was that he knew the size of the job'.)[6] On 22 June Butler received a message from the war

---

[1] African (South), 572, pp. 103, 107. According to Garvin, iii. 454, Chamberlain wanted to send 10,000 men to South Africa about the middle of July but the cabinet would not agree.   [2] Headlam, i. 444; see also ibid. 400.

[3] Referring to an exodus of women and children from Johannesburg and a standstill of business. Milner also referred to a business standstill, which Graham very much doubted, thinking that the object of the report might be to 'force the situation'.

[4] Minute, 24 June, on Milner to Chamberlain, 22 June 1899. C.O. 417/262.

[5] Headlam, i. 403, 425–6. Milner declared towards the end of May that Butler regarded him as 'a brawler'. African (South), 572, p. 270.

[6] Butler, 414, 425–8, 432–6, 439–40, 445–8; Garvin, iii. 453.

office ordering the purchase of wagons and transport mules, foreshadowing further purchases, and asking for his observations. His
reply was: 'You ask my observations. Present condition of opinion
here is highly excited and doubts the news of preparations referred to
in your telegram. If it transpires, will add largely to the ferment which
am endeavouring to reduce by every means. Persistent efforts of a
party to produce war form . . . gravest element in the situation here.
I believe war would be the greatest calamity that ever occurred in
South Africa.' It was these observations, which he showed to Milner,
that decided the latter to ask for his recall.[1] The request annoyed
Chamberlain. 'Milner', he minuted, 'is really rather trying. Think
of our difficulties and how they would be enhanced by recalling
Butler at this juncture. In my opinion such a course would strengthen
the hands of the opposition immensely. . . . I shall do my best for
Milner and for the policy which is mine as well as his, tomorrow[2]—
but he is overstrained.[3] I wish he would remember the advice to the
lady whose clothes caught fire, "to keep as cool as possible".' He
accordingly asked Milner 'to bear with him [Butler] a little longer
till present crisis changes its character'.[4] Shortly afterwards Butler
received a private letter from the war office advising him to resign if
certain reports about his political opinions current in London were
true. He denied that they were, but went at once to see Milner. On
being told by the latter that he had been a hindrance to him, he wrote
to place his resignation in the hands of the war office. It was accepted
by telegram on 8 August.[5]

II

In the middle of June the Cape friends of the republic, who now
knew the franchise that Milner wanted, embarked on their supreme
effort to obtain as near an approximation to it as was possible. It
was arranged, in consultation with Steyn, that Fischer should come
to Cape Town and then proceed to Pretoria. In Cape Town he had
discussions with the Schreiner ministry and Hofmeyr, and a franchise
scheme was agreed upon which he was to recommend to the republican

---

[1] Milner to Chamberlain, 24 June 1899. C.O. 417/262.
[2] The reference is to a speech he was about to make at Birmingham.
[3] He was, in fact, beginning to suffer from sleeplessness. Headlam, i. 510.
[4] Minute (for Selborne), 26 June 1899 (Chamberlain papers, C.); Chamberlain to
Milner, 26 June 1899 (C.O. 417/262).
[5] Butler, 450–3.

government.[1] Fischer also saw Milner and informed him of the plan confidentially. The latter agreed that it was a considerable advance on Kruger's Bloemfontein proposals. But he then went on to say that the government of the republic should officially submit any new franchise scheme to the British government before laying it before the volksraad. This was a further step along the road of intervention, for the discussions at Bloemfontein had been conducted on the understanding that Milner was merely making suggestions for the consideration of the Boer government. It was to be expected that the republic would resist this step as in fact it did.[2] As for Chamberlain, he was not yet able to support the high commissioner's move.[3] But the latter was already contemplating another. Fischer had hardly left Pretoria and Hofmeyr was already on his way thither to apply further pressure, when he telegraphed his chief that the time had come to face the Boer authorities with what was, in effect, a penultimatum, to which an early answer should be requested. They were to submit the details of any new franchise measure to the British government. If an understanding was reached, 'the [franchise] rights to be conferred on the Uitlanders should be secured by an agreement between the two Governments'. After which it would be necessary to regulate a number of 'particular' and 'serious' subjects of dispute. 'If on the other hand, agreement as to franchise were to prove impossible, Her Majesty's Government must proceed to press for the redress of most serious grievances enumerated in the despatch of June 10th[4] on authoritative lines, as well as for the settlement of other outstanding questions. . . .'[5] But Chamberlain refused to allow this message to be delivered, on the ground that public opinion was not yet ready for such a step, and warned Milner to hold himself in check. The government, he declared, was anxious to accept a compromise on the franchise issue without insisting on guarantees.

The newspaper telegrams all appear to indicate further concessions on the President's part. If these are really substantial, it will be practically impossible for us to find a *casus belli* in minor differences. I am sure in this case our policy is to accept them for what they pretend to be, and if they fail of their object or prove subsequently to have been made in bad faith our case will be stronger than it has ever been. . . .[6]

[1] Van der Merwe, i. 207; Hofmeyr, 539; Walker (c), 157.
[2] Headlam, i. 447–8; C. 9404, pp. 15–16.
[3] Headlam, i. 450; African (South), 572, pp. 117–18.
[4] Chamberlain's indictment.
[5] Milner to Chamberlain, 1 July 1899 (C.O. 417/263); African (South), 572 pp. 117–18.   [6] Ibid., pp. 119, 122–3; Garvin, iii. 411.

Fischer had meanwhile completed his mission to Pretoria. While he was negotiating with the republican government, there arrived cable reports that Chamberlain had concluded a speech at Birmingham with the words '. . . Having undertaken this business we will see it through. We have tried waiting, patience and trusting to promises which were never kept. We can wait no more. . . . I believe that we have reached a critical, and a turning, point in the history of the Empire. . . .' His main purpose was, as he told Selborne, 'to get the water into good condition' in England.[1] But the speech was bound to have repercussions in South Africa. Schreiner's comment was: 'Can it be that no such settlement [no peaceful settlement?] is desired? . . . The fundamental error which may yet embroil this subcontinent is the belief that when sufficient pressure is used Kruger will yield *everything*.'[2] Fischer telegraphed Hofmeyr that the speech had hindered him in his negotiations. To Greene he said that it 'had knocked the bottom out of his mission, that the Transvaal might be coaxed into making concessions, but never could be forced by threats'. Milner was quick to point out that this assertion was contradicted by the fact that 'the remodelling of Kruger's scheme is going on still'.[3] But there was, nevertheless, in Fischer's statement an undercurrent of truth, which came to the surface in due course. Meanwhile he had obtained much more from Kruger and his government than he let on to Greene, in spite of opposition from executive councillors Burger, Wolmarans, and Kock. But the Cape friends reckoned that he had not obtained enough to satisfy Milner.[4]

Whatever the effect on the Boer government of Chamberlain's speech, Milner and the Uitlander council-cum-league section on the Rand were jubilant. Greene, still doing his best for Milner's policy of firm determination, reported that the speech 'has filled the Uitlander community with unbounded satisfaction. . . . The suspense of the last few weeks . . .' had 'greatly affected' the Uitlanders. 'Depression was universal in all branches of trade and business; thousands of persons, chiefly women and children, had left Johannesburg . . . generally producing a feeling of uncertainty and unrest throughout the country. This feeling has now been greatly allayed and public confidence strengthened. . . .' Some thought, he continued, that the speech would cause the Boers to climb down, 'a result which not a

---

[1] Garvin, iii. 415–16; Headlam, i. 448. [2] Walker (c), 162.
[3] Van der Merwe, i. 219; African (South), 572, pp. 112–13.
[4] Van der Merwe, i. 217–19. Walker has got the sequence of events wrong in *C.H.B.E.* viii. 594, para. 1.

few, I am afraid, of the Uitlanders hope may not be verified, fearing as they do that if by this means a temporary settlement is arrived at now, in the course of a year or two there will be a repetition of the present condition of things'. He concluded by supporting in tough language, apparently with Milner's approval, the demand of the Uitlander council for the dismantling of the republic's forts and the disarming of the Boers.[1] The disaffected section among the Uitlanders were in fact taking the bit between their teeth: five days after the Birmingham speech the Uitlander council published a manifesto requesting the British government to obtain for them immediately, not only the franchise and the automatic redistribution of volksraad seats, but a far-reaching reorganization of the republic.[2]

III

During the six weeks following the Bloemfontein conference the attitude of the Natal ministry caused Milner and governor Hely-Hutchinson some anxiety. The Binns ministry[3] was succeeded early in June by one led by colonel Hime, and two of its six members, F. R. Moor and C. J. Smythe, advocated a policy of 'patience and conciliation'. Their views had the support of Harry Escombe, who was the ablest man in Natal politics and had a strong following in the house of assembly. Perhaps the only statesman of Natal who dared to speak his mind to Kruger, he believed that the problems of South Africa should be left to the South Africans to solve. Confident of the assembly's support, Moor and Smythe compelled the ministry to subscribe to a minute (17 June) stating that

. . . South Africa ought not to be exposed to war, by any act of Her Majesty's Government, without their opinions having been heard. They ask that before a final step is taken, before a position be adopted by Her Majesty's Government which is likely to lead to war, their views may be considered by Her Majesty's Government. . . . Ministers will be glad to co-operate in conjunction with the other Governments of South Africa in any steps which might tend to bring about a peaceful solution of the present difficulties.

To Milner the prospect of the Cape, Natal, and the Orange Free State co-operating in order to bring pressure to bear not only on Kruger

---

[1] African (South), 600, pp. 58, 230–1. [2] C. 9518, pp. 17–21.
[3] See above, p. 206.

but on himself was intolerable. '. . . I feel', he cabled Chamberlain, 'that idea of allowing Colonial governments to interfere with action of H.M. Government in protecting rights of its subjects in Transvaal is inadmissible and would ruin the whole game. . . .' But despite all the efforts of Hely-Hutchinson, who was in full sympathy with Milner, Moor and Smythe continued on their course. 'Ministers agree', reported the governor, 'that if the High Commissioner's reply is not . . . satisfactory, they will, before the House rises this Session, introduce and support a Resolution in similar terms to those of the Minute to the High Commissioner.' It was Hime's opinion, he added, that if Escombe were to propose such a resolution, 'not more than nine members [in a House of thirty-seven] . . . could . . . be relied on to vote against it'. On 22 June the ministry was compelled to go farther. It now requested Milner to communicate the minute of the 17th to the Cape ministry. According to Hely-Hutchinson, Hime only endorsed this request 'to avoid breaking up the Ministry. . . . The result would have been a ministry led by Escombe and Moor, and probably greater complications.' Milner agreed to show the Cape prime minister both the Natal minute and his reply. The reply made it quite clear that if the Natal ministers were prepared to work on Kruger, well and good; but that as far as he was concerned, he would not take advice from them. With this reply the ministry declared itself satisfied. 'Moor consented to keep quiet', Hely-Hutchinson told Milner, 'though objecting that you had put into their mouths approval of [the] measures urged by Her Majesty's Government.'[1]

The opportunity of gaining the support of the assembly for a policy of patience and conciliation was rapidly passing. On 10 June the governor had told Milner that the Natal press 'is sound and I will try to keep it right'. Chamberlain's speech at Birmingham and the publication of the helot telegram and the Uitlander grievances blue book no doubt made it sounder still. Early in July mass meetings at Durban and Pietermaritzburg and a petition signed by over half the adult male colonists of Natal expressed 'profound confidence' in Milner's policy. According to the governor, Hime declared on the 11th 'that there is no chance now that a Resolution contrary to the policy of H.M.G. would pass the Natal legislature and . . . if it did pass he would . . . advise dissolution, and . . . is confident of a large

---

[1] Laurence, 164–5; Headlam, i. 57–58; Cd. 44, pp. 2–3, 5; Milner to Chamberlain, 10 and 14 June 1899, with enclosures (C.O. 417/262); African (South), 572, pp. 108–9, 120, 123.

majority in the event of a general election on that issue'. But he had
not done yet with the two dissentients in his ministry. In mid-July
they had their last tilt against him, strongly opposing his proposal
to ask the British government for additional troops. But he won them
over by producing a minute from the military commander in Natal.
Milner seized this opportunity to again urge Chamberlain to send out
'as quietly as possible' a force large enough to occupy Laing's Nek.
'Hitherto', he telegraphed, 'every Natal Ministry has been opposed
to our placing troops on border for fear of irritating S.A.R. Now
Government Natal is virtually asking us to take this course. It is an
opportunity which may never recur.' But the British government
decided to send for the present only about 2,000 men and to announce
their dispatch to the public.[1]

While Moor and Smythe were still hesitating over the question of
reinforcements, the assembly, by a unanimous vote, committed itself
to the support of the imperial policy. 'Natal Assembly did splendidly',
Milner wired to the governor. 'Warmest thanks to you and Hime.
. . .' Hely-Hutchinson's comment to Chamberlain was:

. . . The present Transvaal oligarchy, if it be left, after this crisis, with
power to injure, will . . . revenge itself on Natal . . . for the attitude of
uncompromising support of Her Majesty's Government which it has
publicly adopted. Loyal and patriotic feeling has, at length, overcome the
considerations of commercial prudence which have for so many years
enabled the Transvaal to play Natal off against the Cape. Up to within
the last six weeks these considerations turned the balance in the minds of
many. . . . But if expectations which have been formed be disappointed . . .
it may even be too little to say that serious and almost universal resentment
will be aroused.[2]

IV

A few days after Fischer's departure from Pretoria Hofmeyr went
north accompanied by Herholdt, a member of Schreiner's ministry.
At Bloemfontein they had long discussions with Smuts, Grobler,[3]
Steyn, and Fischer. Thereupon the two Transvaalers and Fischer
left for Pretoria, where the latter with the powerful support of Smuts,

---

[1] Hely-Hutchinson to Milner, 10 June 1899 (C.O. 417/262); C. 9415, pp. 27–28, 47;
Milner to Chamberlain, 11 July 1899 (C.O. 417/263); African (South), 572, pp. 130, 136;
Headlam, i. 511–12; Cd. 44, pp. 3–7.
[2] C. 9415, pp. 52–53; Headlam, i. 462; African (South), 572, p. 214.
[3] Under-secretary for foreign affairs of the South African Republic.

succeeded in persuading Kruger and his executive council that further concessions would have to be made. Kruger agreed also to invite Hofmeyr and Herholdt to come to Pretoria.[1] While the two Cape delegates were at Bloemfontein, the volksraad, by 14 votes to 13 and in the teeth of a protest from Kruger, passed a resolution instructing the government to frame a redistribution scheme giving fifteen new seats to the rural constituencies and Pretoria. The scheme was to be submitted the following year, and the new representatives were clearly intended to swamp those that might by then have been granted to the gold-fields. On their return to Cape Town the Cape delegates told the press that

the case is . . . temporarily disposed of, and cannot come up again before next year. But should it then crop up . . . not only Messrs. Hofmeyr and Herholdt, but also Mr Fischer, have the assurance of almost all the members of the Executive that the subject of redistribution or the increase of the Volksraad will be treated as a general one and the mining centres will have due consideration, especially in the light gained from the working of the present reformed scheme.[2]

'The present reformed scheme' embodied the further concessions which the Cape delegates had recommended at Pretoria. They had first met the executive council,[3] and then both volksraads in secret session. Hofmeyr was the principal speaker at the joint session and, according to his biographer, the proposals he had come to make were agreed to by an almost unanimous vote.[4] Schreiner's ministry, which, like the Afrikaner bond, had hitherto refused to commit itself in public on the subject of Kruger's Uitlander policy, now stated publicly that 'this government regards these proposals as adequate, satisfactory and such as should procure a peaceful settlement'. Resolutions to the same effect were passed at bond meetings throughout the Cape Colony.[5]

Both Schreiner and Hofmeyr discussed with Milner the concessions made by Pretoria. Soon afterwards the high commissioner told them

[1] Van der Merwe, i. 219–24.

[2] *Notulen*, Eerste Volksraad, 1899, arts. 380–2; C. 9518, pp. 18–19, 27. On 12 July Smuts informed Greene that 'the redistribution scheme recently passed by the Volksraad will be dropped'. Greene confirmed this on 27 July. C. 9518, pp. 7, 37.

[3] Hofmeyr's biographer writes: 'Mr Hofmeyr himself, believing that British diplomacy was tending inevitably towards war, went so far as to advise the President, that . . . he should express his willingness to allow his State to be incorporated with the British Empire, with the prospect of Union with the rest of South Africa—on certain definite conditions. . . .' Hofmeyr, 544.

[4] Ibid. 543–4.

[5] Walker (c), 166; C. 9518, p. 31.

that he had been authorized by the British government to 'request that full particulars of the new scheme may be furnished . . . officially'. This request was rejected by the republican government on the ground that Milner had refused at Bloemfontein to deal with the franchise as an integral part of a comprehensive settlement. The Cape friends failed to persuade Kruger and his advisers to change their mind on this point; but they succeeded in obtaining an improvement of the 'reformed scheme'.[1]

Between 7 and 18 July—the dates on which the 'reformed scheme' and the 'improved reformed scheme' were announced—Milner poured a constant stream of telegrams into the colonial office. He warned Chamberlain and the cabinet not to be 'jockeyed' by the 'Afrikander coalition' into accepting a sham franchise intended to 'bamboozle' the British public. The cabinet should realize that the republic's refusal to submit its franchise reforms to the British government was a challenge to British supremacy. That would certainly be the view taken by the British colonists throughout South Africa.

It makes all the difference both to the security of the Uitlanders and to our position in South Africa whether measure is shaped and secured by H.M. Government. . . . To assert our power and retain confidence of loyalists are after all two main objects to keep in view. [A little later he telegraphed:] It is practical assertion of British Supremacy in forcing S.A.R. to move in direction of equal rights and genuine self-government which is the real issue.[2]

One of Milner's telegrams produced a sharp reaction in the colonial office. He transmitted a statement from Greene purporting to describe public feeling in Johannesburg:

Suspense is demoralising Johannesburg and it will not be possible to hold Uitlanders together more than three weeks longer, as they are beginning to starve and will certainly abandon us if no sign is given by H.M.G. . . . It is proposed to hold another great Uitlander meeting next Saturday when . . . franchise proposals of government S.A.R. will be condemned. This . . . is the last shot in the Uitlanders' locker and if it produces no response the game will be lost.

The statement infuriated Chamberlain.

This telegram [he minuted] need not go to Cabinet or Queen. It ought

---

[1] Headlam, i. 456; C. 9415, pp. 45–46; Walker (c), 166–9.
[2] African (South), 572, p. 134; Headlam, i. 456–7, 465–6.

never to have been sent and the leading Uitlander[1] should have been told at once that he was an ass. I am sorry that Milner and Greene should forward such rubbish. If the Uitlanders are really prepared to make terms with Kruger—and can do so—unless H.M.G. secures redress of all their grievances in 24 hours—they had much better go to Kruger and relieve us of their complaints. But of course it is all nonsense of a most pestilential kind. I should like a hint given that I want no more.[2]

On 18 July Smuts informed Schreiner that the volksraad had agreed to a seven years' retrospective franchise 'with a simplification of procedure', and Chamberlain told *The Times* that if the newspaper reports to this effect were correct, the crisis was at an end.[3] Selborne thought that his chief, when he made this 'impulsive' statement, assumed 'that we had now secured all we wanted'. Yet Chamberlain's next dispatch, which was lying all but ready in the colonial office, does not indicate any such assumption.[4] It is possible that Milner was nearer the mark when he told the Uitlander council, which had just implored Chamberlain not to depart from the five years' 'compromise' accepted by the Uitlanders 'with great reluctance', that 'British Government could not afford not to admit largeness of advance made by President without alienating reasonable public opinion in England'. At the same time he warned the council that 'moderation of tone [is] desirable. There is danger of Uitlanders adopting a too uncompromising attitude and being thought to be for "War at any price"'. Yet though he tried to cheer up 'our friends' in Johannesburg, he was himself in the grip of an extreme depression which persisted throughout the latter half of July. 'Very great feeling of depression . . .', he wrote in his diary on 23 July, 'British public opinion is going to be befooled. . . .' But whatever he might think of public opinion in Britain or of the 'mugwumps' in the cabinet, it never occurred to him to doubt Chamberlain, who had been supporting him 'magnificently' and whom he did not fail to remind that 'opinion growing that Government S.A.R. and its sympathisers are

---

[1] Greene had got his information from a 'leading and trustworthy Uitlander'—not Fitzpatrick but, as the colonial office minutes indicate, another member of the Wernher-Beit firm. Fitzpatrick had gone to England, where he stayed till some time after the outbreak of war. He took with him a note from Milner introducing him to Selborne, to whom he remarked that Kruger would not yield an effective franchise until he 'looked down the cannon's mouth'. Selborne's memorandum of his interview with Fitzpatrick, 3 July 1899 (Chamberlain papers, C); Headlam, i. 437.

[2] Milner to Chamberlain, 14 July 1899, and minutes by Wingfield, Selborne, and Chamberlain (C.O. 417/263); African (South), 572, pp. 133–4.

[3] Walker (c), 169; Garvin, iii. 419.

[4] C. 9518, pp. 10–11, and below, p. 303.

still bluffing and will yield further if pressure kept up'. The British colonists in South Africa were magnificent too. As reports of resolutions and petitions supporting his policy kept pouring in, Milner (notwithstanding his dejection) exulted: 'Loyal British South Africa has risen from its long degradation and stands behind me to a man with an enthusiasm which has not been known since before Majuba. It is a great thing to be, even for a few brief days and weeks, *the leader of a people*, possessing their unbounded confidence. . . . I have absolutely rallied all our forces on the spot.'[1]

V

The volksraad completed its consideration of the franchise bill on 19 July. With regard to redistribution, Milner had an assurance from Smuts that the Witwatersrand would be represented in the volksraad by four additional members, which would give the Uitlanders a total of six members in a house of thirty-two[2]—three fewer than the number suggested by the high commissioner just before the Bloemfontein conference. For the moment, however, he devoted his attention mainly to the newly passed franchise law. He could not reject it in principle, because the republican authorities had met his two main objections against their Bloemfontein proposals by conceding a seven years' retrospective franchise and enabling the Uitlander to retain his former citizenship until he should acquire the full franchise. He now concentrated his attack on the other conditions which had to be fulfilled by the Uitlander seeking the franchise. These had also been made easier since the government first formulated its proposals at and immediately after the conference.[3] But Milner declared that the law was still too complicated and that it still contained many 'traps'; while de Villiers expressed the view that the law stood condemned because the state attorney had thought it necessary to issue an explanatory memorandum[4] which could bind neither the government nor the courts.[5]

It cannot be denied that the law wore a complicated look. This was to some extent inevitable, as Milner admitted two months later.[6]

---

[1] Headlam, i. 356, 468–74; C. 9415, pp. 47, 52; C. 9518, pp. 6, 15, 31 (colonial office note).
[2] C. 9518, pp. 14, 37; Hugo, 45.
[3] Headlam, i. 459–60.
[4] He wrote this before he had seen the memorandum.
[5] C. 9518, pp. 45–47, 51–53; Cd. 369, p. 3. See also Walker in *C.H.B.E.* viii. 594–5.
[6] Headlam, i. 530.

Let us examine the reasons for the form assumed by the law. First, provision had to be made for at least four classes of Uitlander: those —not many—already naturalized without the full franchise; those— again not many—who might wish to become naturalized after two years and acquire the franchise five years thereafter; those already domiciled who wished to achieve the franchise (plus naturalization) as soon as the seven years' 'probationary' period had elapsed; future immigrants. Second, more effective provision than had been the case in the past had to be made for ascertaining the period of residence of future immigrants who intended to apply for the franchise.[1] It was therefore laid down that every such alien should give notice to his field-cornet of his intention to seek the franchise and that the field-cornet—'under pain of a fine of £10 in each case of neglect'—should transmit this notice to the state secretary for publication in the *Staatscourant*. Third, provision had to be made to determine past residence. The difficulty here was twofold: many aliens had disregarded the registration law which enjoined periodical registration in the field-cornet's book; and in some cases field-cornets' books had been lost or destroyed. The provision made to establish a man's residence in such cases was the same as that made to establish his character as a law-abiding person, with which I shall deal under point number five. Fourth, the government wanted to know in advance how many aliens already resident in the republic intended to apply for the franchise.[2] It was accordingly provided that any resident alien who did not within six months give notice of such intention would lose the benefit of his previous residence. Fifth, it was judged necessary that the applicant for the franchise should produce evidence that he had 'obeyed the laws of the land and committed no crime against the independence of the South African Republic'. (The explanatory memorandum stated that crime against the independence of the state meant high treason and that 'by obedience to the laws . . . is meant that the applicant has not purposely set himself against the laws. . . . It does not mean that he has in all cases strictly abided by the laws.') If the applicant's field-cornet and *landdrost* were not able to vouch for him, the required evidence had to take the form of an affidavit sworn by 'two well-known fully-enfranchised burghers' of his district. (The legitimate criticism of this provision was that it might be difficult for the Uitlander to find two such burghers to vouch for him.) Sixth, the applicant for the franchise had to produce

[1] C. 9518, p. 36. See also Hugo, 50–51, 172.   [2] C. 9518, p. 36.

a sworn declaration made by himself that he had not been convicted of 'high treason, murder, rape, theft, fraud, perjury or forgery', and he had to produce 'further proof of good behaviour'. (The explanatory memorandum stated that this proof should consist of 'certificates of ministers or any other respectable persons'.) Seventh, there was to be a property qualification. The applicant for the franchise had to possess unmortgaged fixed property to the value of £150, or pay rent of £50 per annum, or draw a fixed salary or wage of £100 per annum. (The explanatory memorandum stated that 'A person has unmortgaged fixed property to the value of £150 so long as the value of the property exceeds the bond thereon by £150 or more. The salary or wage need not be fixed for a whole year. A monthly salary that shall total £100 per annum is sufficient.'[1])

Several of the provisions just outlined were inserted in order to limit as far as possible the government's discretionary power in respect of the grant or refusal of the franchise.[2] The government was nevertheless authorized to dispense at its discretion with the franchise qualifications laid down in the law in the case of persons 'who take up a position in the service of the country, or have rendered services to the country, or who have in any other respect rendered themselves of service to the country'. Milner pointed out at once to his chief that this clause gave the government too wide a discretion.[3]

We come to de Villiers's point about the explanatory memorandum. The memorandum was intended to assist both subordinate officials and Uitlanders by explaining as simply as possible the procedure that had to be followed by applicants for the franchise, and by giving the government's (not merely the state attorney's) interpretation of certain expressions used in the law. The memorandum was signed by the state secretary and published in the *Staatscourant* as an annexure to the law.[4] The government could, therefore, justly be held to be bound by the memorandum, and it was open to the high commissioner to ascertain what it proposed to do if the courts should disagree with its explanations.

It was similarly open to the high commissioner, after seeking the permission of the secretary of state, to instruct the British agent to discuss the law with the republican government with a view to obtaining amendments of unreasonable or obscure details. While the bill was passing through the volksraad Smuts, acting on behalf of

[1] Ibid., pp. 64–70.   [2] See above, pp. 282–3.
[3] C. 9518, p. 53; Headlam, i. 460.   [4] C. 9518, pp. 62, 64, 68.

the government, had shown himself very willing to discuss it with Greene and to answer the high commissioner's questions. He had told Greene also that it was proposed to alter the registration (of voters) law of the republic as well as the method of electing the president and the commandant-general.[1] These matters might also have been discussed with the government. With regard to the franchise law, Reitz wrote to Greene on 13 July that his government would 'always be ready to take into serious consideration any friendly counsels from Her Majesty's Government'.[2]

Throughout the discussions that took place in July it was evident that the republic was anxious to avoid a formal submission to British intervention in a purely internal matter like the franchise. As late as 7 July Chamberlain had been willing to accept this situation, declaring that, if the republic played false, there would then be solid ground for intervention.[3] In the absence of a formal Anglo-Transvaal agreement, which the republic indicated that it meant to resist, the guarantee of its good faith would lie not so much in the word of the Boer statesmen as in the fact that the franchise reforms had been granted, and would have to be worked, under the eyes of many vigilant men both in South Africa and in Britain. Under the influence of Milner, the British government decided that such guarantees were not enough.[4] How it committed itself to formal intervention will be the theme of the next section of this chapter.

VI

On 18 July Chamberlain telegraphed Milner informing him of the cabinet's decision that another conference between him and Kruger should take place, this time at Cape Town, 'to arrange details so as to secure *bona fide* representation [of the Uitlanders] . . . and to discuss all remaining points of difference between two governments'. It is clear that this conference was to be of a more formal nature than its predecessor, since the negotiators were to agree upon certain protocols. The telegram continued: 'Protocols of conference are better security than new convention which would stereotype terms obtained, whereas we consider them as part of gradual advance

---

[1] C. 9518, pp. 36–39, 43–44.   [2] Ibid., pp. 40–41; C. 9521, p. 46.
[3] African (South), 572, pp. 122–3; Garvin, iii. 411.
[4] Headlam, i. 356.

towards equality promised in 1881.'[1] Milner replied that it would be useless to discuss 'multitude of complicated details' with Kruger, and suggested instead a joint inquiry by British and republican commissioners. On this suggestion the colonial office commented as follows:

JUST: . . . But it would be possible to unite a discussion of details by a joint commission[2] with a meeting of the President and of the High Commissioner. . . . A Conference between President Kruger and Sir Alfred Milner would strike the public eye and imagination and imply a climbdown on President Kruger's part from his attitude of *noli me tangere* on internal affairs. . . .

WINGFIELD: The combination of a Conference between Sir Alfred Milner and Kruger and a subsidiary discussion of details by their respective officers would perhaps be the best solution.

CHAMBERLAIN: I think despatch[3] will have to be altered as to meeting between Kruger and Milner and the combination above may be suggested. The moral effect of a new conference would be as Mr Just suggests. But I will settle this after the cabinet to-morrow.

JUST (*a day later*): New paragraphs have now been added to the despatch.[4]

This dispatch, ultimately dated 27 July, was the next long communication addressed to the republican government since the indictment of 10 May. It accused that government of bad faith, discussed its franchise law and its recent arbitration proposal,[5] and then went on to propose a joint inquiry into the franchise law to be followed by a conference between Milner and Kruger.[6] Six successive drafts of the dispatch had been printed for the cabinet, and on circulating among members the penultimate draft, dated 20 July, Chamberlain asked for their written agreement or objections. The most serious criticism came once more from Balfour. He laid his finger on two points, on which Chamberlain could not have met him without sacrificing the whole character and intention of the dispatch:

(i) Is it sound policy to introduce controversial matter respecting the past—which may possibly be irritating and is at best superfluous—into a Despatch written primarily for the purpose of expressing general assent to

---

[1] African (South), 572, p. 143; Headlam, i. 468. For the equality allegedly promised in 1881, see Chamberlain's long dispatch of 27 July 1899 (C. 9518, pp. 8–9) and Wilde, 122.

[2] For Chamberlain's adoption of this device just before the Jameson raid, see above, p. 184.

[3] The dispatch dated 27 July, which will be dealt with below.

[4] Milner to Chamberlain, 21 July 1899, and colonial office minutes, 22–24 July. Milner's telegram is also in African (South), 572, pp. 146–7.

[5] See below, p. 307.   [6] C. 9518, pp. 7–12.

what we believe to be Kruger's latest proposals? I allude to some of the matter contained upon pages 2, 3, 4, 5 and 6. [The despatch as printed for the cabinet was eight pages in length.] (ii) Is it prudent to commit ourselves to the proposal of a second Conference between Kruger and Milner? If Kruger refused on the ground that while he was anxious to do full justice to the Uitlanders, he was of opinion that this was a matter of internal administration with which we had nothing to do, we should have received a diplomatic rebuff which would probably do us harm in South Africa. Would it not be enough . . . to use a form of words which would indicate no preference for a meeting between the President and the High Commissioner over any other method of settling satisfactorily the points of detail to which we attach importance?[1]

As has been seen the cabinet, so far from paying heed to Balfour, decided to sanction formal intervention in two stages, first the joint inquiry and then the conference.[2]

Immediately after the cabinet had approved the dispatch of 27 July in its final form, the principal debate of the session on the South African situation took place in both houses of parliament. In the commons Chamberlain endorsed, on behalf of the British government, the 'prestige' and 'supremacy' arguments of Milner's helot telegram. He claimed for Britain the right 'to interfere in what are admitted to be the internal affairs of the Transvaal', partly on the ground that she was 'the suzerain power'. He claimed also that 'the foreign relations'—not just the treaty-making power—of the republic were 'under the control of the British government', and he appeared to include the foreign relations of the Orange Free State in this claim.[3] 'We want', he said, 'to see it [the Transvaal] continuing in existence on similar lines to the Orange Free State, protected as to its outside relations and independent as to its internal affairs.'[4] The speech, consisting for the greater part of a bitter attack on Kruger's republic,[5] achieved its main purpose of further rousing public opinion. The day before Chamberlain spoke, Selborne wrote to Milner as if the hesitation which had been apparent in the country and in the cabinet in June and part of July was passing, or had passed, away:

Parliament has been much less favourable to your views and mine than the Press; London than the Provinces; the 'governing classes' than οἱ

---

[1] Balfour to Chamberlain, 21 July 1899. Chamberlain papers, B.
[2] C. 9518, pp. 11–12, 29.   [3] Fischer took note of this. Hofmeyr, 548.
[4] *Parliamentary Debates*, 4th series, vol. lxxv, cols. 697–716.
[5] Contrast Walker (c), 170. Goschen wrote to Milner about this speech: '. . . You will, I think, be perfectly satisfied with its tone.' Headlam, i. 472.

πολλοί. The idea of war has been very unpopular among our own party in both Houses; this gave rise to much difficulty. But the position now stands thus. Public opinion insists on our using great patience and endeavouring to avert war. It will acquiesce in war if it is convinced that without war we cannot secure effective practical (as distinct from pedantic) compliance with your Bloemfontein demands. It would fiercely resent any backing out on the part of the Government. . . . The Cabinet is all right.

That the cabinet was now 'all right' was confirmed by one of its members, Goschen, writing to Milner at the same time as Selborne.[1]

Chamberlain delivered his speech on 28 July. A few days later Milner asked Kruger to appoint delegates to take part in the joint inquiry and informed him also of the conference which it was proposed to hold.[2] (The dispatch of 27 July was not delivered until almost a month afterwards.) From many quarters—Cape friends, Liberal statesmen in England, ministers of state in the Netherlands— there came advice that the republican government should not reject the joint inquiry.[3] As far as the Cape friends were concerned, their advice was dictated by the desire to prevent war at all costs, as Milner had prophesied that it would be.[4] Hofmeyr was for outright acceptance of the British demand. Schreiner, writes his biographer, 'begged the Transvaalers not to let a mere matter of form spoil a good settlement'. But he agreed that the republic should seek an official assurance 'that acceptance [of] Joint Commission will not now or in future be construed by Imperial Government as admission either of its right to interfere in internal affairs of republic or of sacrifice of any part of existing Transvaal rights'. De Villiers admitted that the acceptance of Chamberlain's 'olive branch' might be regarded as 'a *partial* surrender of independence'; but, he added, 'would that not be better than a possible *total* loss of independence?'[5] The republican government decided, however, to take a stand on principle, as the British government, on Milner's advice, had already done.[6] Kruger expressed his attitude in these words:[7] 'They [British Uitlanders] do not want any franchise under a republic'; and added, 'It is our interest to keep the peace, but if our independence is to go it must be taken from us by force.' To Steyn he telegraphed: 'The government S.A.R. deem

---

[1] Ibid. 472–4.   [2] C. 9518, pp. 29–30.
[3] Scholtz, ii. 257–8.   [4] See above, p. 272.
[5] Hofmeyr, 546, 548–9; Walker (c), 171–2; Cd. 369, p. 3.
[6] '. . . If they kick at our demands [to shape the republican franchise] we shall have a principle to contend for and not mere details.' Milner to Chamberlain, 17 July 1899. Headlam, i. 466.
[7] In a letter to de Villiers.

a compliance with this request [for a joint inquiry] impossible, as it would be equivalent to a destruction of our independence.' The Free State leaders concurred.[1]

While the republican government was considering how to reject the British demand without eliciting an ultimatum, Milner and Chamberlain kept in close touch with each other. They began by agreeing that if the Boers rejected the inquiry the next step should be an ultimatum.[2] Then they proceeded to discuss the manner in which the president and the commandant-general of the republic should be elected in future. According to information given to Greene by Smuts on 12 July, it was proposed either 'that candidates should be nominated by the Volksraad itself; or . . . that selection should be made by electoral district. . . .' (Smuts added that the president was opposed to any change.) A fortnight later Greene reported: 'I am told latest scheme as to election President S.A.R. and Commandant-General is, while leaving the election open to all enfranchised persons . . . to restrict candidates to sons of soil or burghers who have been enfranchised for considerable number of years.'[3] With this information before him Chamberlain telegraphed Milner:

> It would be impossible, consistently with our avowal that our present proposals were not intended to swamp the old Burgher vote, to object to a modification of present system of voting for President and Commandant-General. . . . I suggest that we offer to accept the exclusion of the vote for president and commandant-general from the votes of enfranchised aliens, on condition that they shall not be subject to the liability of bearing arms against the Paramount Power. . . . There would thus be removed a strong objection to naturalization which British subjects must entertain.

But Milner would not hear of any such exclusion, and Chamberlain decided that the high commissioner's view should for the present be accepted as conclusive.[4] This matter having been settled to Milner's satisfaction and the republic continuing to preserve silence on the demand for the joint inquiry, Chamberlain instructed Milner, if the Boers rejected a joint commission, to appoint his own, and suggested Innes or, even better, de Villiers as a member, since he wished to have 'one independent Afrikander' on it. But Milner demurred, trying to

---

[1] Walker (*a*), 347; Headlam, i. 483; van der Merwe, i. 232; Hofmeyr, 548–9.
[2] African (South), 572, pp. 166–8.
[3] C. 9518, p. 37; Milner to Chamberlain, 25 July 1899 (C.O. 417/264). See also Leyds, *Eenige Correspondentie*, 127, where Reitz indicates that this was still the plan on 28 Aug.
[4] African (South), 572, pp. 175, 179.

hold Chamberlain to his promise of an ultimatum if the joint inquiry were rejected. Chamberlain reassured him with the words: 'We shall base our ultimatum on their report,[1] although, if we think well, we may add something to it.' But he added, 'I much regret that you cannot find an Afrikander of influence who could be trusted to make one of three in such a Commission—the presence of such a man would enormously add to weight of report.'[2] It proved unnecessary, however, to appoint the commission, for at this point the republic replied to the original proposal of the British government with one of its own. But before we consider this proposal, it is necessary to retrace our steps and deal with the question of arbitration, which was an integral part of the project for a settlement now put forward by the republic.

VII

We have seen that the British authorities had rejected arbitration in 1897 and that Milner had been instructed not to commit himself on the subject at the Bloemfontein conference.[3] Shortly after the conference the republican government submitted a detailed scheme which provided for the submission of disputes about the London convention to a tribunal consisting of a nominee of each of the two parties with an independent, i.e. a foreign, president acceptable to both.[4] Apropos of this proposal Milner wrote to Chamberlain:

I have always found here that even with our friends it is felt to be a weak point that we claim to interpret the Convention authoritatively for both sides. . . . For the settlement of such [Conventional] disputes I think a purely South African court would be both sufficient and popular. Let either party select say two S. African judges from any country outside the Transvaal—and let these four then choose between themselves a fifth S. African judge. . . . If a wide range of choice were allowed over all *S. African Benches* outside the S.A.R., we should choose 2 British minded judges . . . they would choose say the 2 de Villierses[5] and these 4 between them would agree on some Mugwump.

This, declared Milner, would be 'a perfectly good court'. As for the actual republican proposal, which was 'a mere ruse', it should be rejected outright for three reasons: it was premature, since the

---

[1] i.e. the report of the British-appointed commission.
[2] African (South), 572, pp. 180–201.
[3] See above, pp. 195–8, 281.   [4] C. 9518, pp. 3–4.
[5] Chief justices of the Cape and the Orange Free State.

Uitlander question must be settled first; it did not exclude 'foreign interference'; and lastly, it was too vague.[1]

But the colonial office decided against outright rejection. Immediately before the Bloemfontein conference one of the officials had pointed out that it would be impossible any longer to reject the principle of arbitration, since the British government had just proposed a permanent arbitration court at the first peace conference at The Hague. When the republican proposal arrived in Downing Street the same official minuted: 'This proposal wears a reasonable look. . . . The selection of a President [of the arbitration tribunal] would bring in the foreigner, but not a foreign government.' But Chamberlain would not have a foreigner of any description.[2] To Milner he replied:

> . . . We may agree in principle to the idea of a judicial decision. The tribunal might be the Judicial Committee of the Privy Council, or perhaps a more plausible scheme would be a Court consisting of two members nominated by the Judicial Committee and one by the Boers. I doubt, however, whether we shall come to an agreement, although we must not meet Kruger's proposal with a flat negative. I do not see easily how we can submit to a purely South African court. The choice is so limited except among those who have Africander prejudices. I should not like to submit any question of British rights to Sir H. de Villiers, for instance.

In the end Milner was instructed to inform Kruger that he would be 'ready . . . to discuss . . . arbitration . . . without . . . foreign element' at the conference which it was proposed to hold after the termination of the joint inquiry.[3]

VIII

On Saturday, 12 August, J. W. Wessels, a prominent Johannesburg lawyer and an ardent supporter of the Uitlander cause, came to see Greene. He had been sent by Smuts to ask the British agent whether his government would waive its demand for a joint inquiry if the franchise law was further simplified and a further increase of seats in the volksraad was granted to the gold-fields. Smuts and Greene now came together, and the former, after consulting his government,

---

[1] Headlam, i. 424–5, 434–6.
[2] Minutes by H. W. Just on Milner to Chamberlain, 27 May 1899 (C.O. 417/261), and 11 June 1899 (C.O. 417/262), and Chamberlain's minute on the latter telegram (C.O. 417/262).
[3] Chamberlain to Milner, 7 July 1899 (Chamberlain papers, D); C. 9518, p. 29.

offered a project for a settlement which Greene promised to recommend to the British government. Commenting to Milner on this scheme Greene remarked:

> They are . . . horribly frightened at our evident intention to settle trouble by force if need be. . . . Generally I consider that though the whole scheme may not satisfy all the aspirations of Johannesburg still it is a huge surrender[1] and worthy of serious consideration by H.M.G. The attitude of government of S.A.R. is that they are open to discussion of anything through the ordinary diplomatic channel, but they cannot face what they call the humiliation of the joint inquiry and will I am assured [by Wessels *inter alios*] resist it if cornered.[2]

The republican offer implied on the face of it the acceptance of Milner's Bloemfontein demands regarding the franchise and the number of Uitlander seats in the volksraad.[3] But three conditions were attached to this 'surrender', in the following terms:

> The Government of the South African Republic, in putting forward the above proposals, will assume that Her Majesty's Government will agree that a precedent shall not be formed by their present intervention for similar action in the future, and that no future interference in the internal affairs of the Republic will take place contrary to the Convention. Further, that Her Majesty's Government will not insist further upon the assertion of suzerainty, the controversy on this subject being tacitly allowed to drop. Lastly, . . . arbitration, from which the foreign element is excluded, to be conceded.[4]

As a recent writer has remarked, the Boer government considered these conditions to be 'vital to the preservation of the republic, in view of the political power to be given to the Uitlanders'.[5]

Greene dispatched two telegrams dealing with the negotiations. The first contained the offer of the republican government and concluded with the words: 'The formal note which embodies these proposals was drafted to-day and will be submitted to me beforehand for approval, as soon as I am informed whether Her Majesty's

---

[1] Greene told Smuts at the outset that the only chance for the republic was 'an immediate surrender to the Bloemfontein minimum'.

[2] Milner to Chamberlain, 15 Aug. 1899 (C.O. 417/264); African (South), 572, pp. 202–4. The published blue book (C. 9521, pp. 44–45) omits parts of Greene's account of the negotiations.

[3] In addition to the ten seats offered the Uitlanders, there was a chance that in at least six other constituencies, three of them returning two members each, the Uitlander vote would secure the return of 'moderate and comparatively Progressive Boers'— to use Milner's words—at the next election. C. 9518, p. 27; Headlam, i. 478.

[4] C. 9521, p. 44.

[5] Ethel Drus in *Bulletin* (1954), p. 177; C. 9530, pp. 11–13.

Government will consent to my [continuing the] negotiations on [the] lines specified above.'[1] The second telegram was of a very different type. It purported to be 'explanatory' of the first, and contained a somewhat incoherent account of what had been said by Greene himself, Wessels, and Smuts. Included in it were certain further concessions which the republic was prepared to grant—or so Smuts, as reported by Greene, had said. It seems clear that the whole offer which the republic was officially prepared to make at this stage was contained in the first telegram, though other points—like the use of English in the volksraad and the manner of election of the president and the commandant-general[2]—might have been raised in the subsequent negotiations.[3]

Milner was annoyed at the 'extraordinary conduct of Greene'. He wanted Chamberlain to insist on a reply to the demand for a joint inquiry, in other words he wished the republic's offer to be rejected out of hand. Their offer, he told Chamberlain, '. . . shows their absolute determination not to admit our claim to have a voice in their [internal] affairs as the Paramount Power in South Africa'. (This is what 'paramountcy' had come to mean to Milner and Chamberlain.) There followed the usual refrain: 'I think the result all depends on staying power. They will collapse if we don't weaken, or rather if we go on steadily turning the screw.'[4] But Chamberlain decided that the republic's offer ought not to be immediately rejected, and he telegraphed Milner in this sense. To Salisbury he wrote: 'I think . . . that he must understand my telegram and see how important I consider it to be that the Boers should not be snubbed at this stage but rather encouraged to put their concessions on record. . . .'[5] Milner understood, and proceeded to ask the republican government for a formal statement of its proposals, which, he added, would be considered on their merits.[6]

The formal statement, though it omitted a few words and phrases from the original statement telegraphed by Greene, does not appear

---

[1] That is to say, on the new franchise proposals (after acceptance of the conditions attached thereto).

[2] Mentioned by Greene in his references to further concessions.

[3] C. 9521, p. 48. Letters by Greene on the negotiations are in C. 9530, pp. 21–24, and Cd. 43, pp. 48–50. Smuts's accounts are in green book no. 10 of 1899, no. 3, C. 9530, p. 24, and Cd. 43, pp. 50–53.

[4] African (South), 572, p. 204; Milner to Chamberlain, 16 Aug. 1899 (Chamberlain papers, D); Headlam, i. 516.

[5] Garvin, iii. 435–6. Compare his attitude at the time of the capitalist negotiations, pp. 250–1 above.

[6] C. 9521, p. 46.

to have been intended to alter the latter materially.[1] But Chamberlain, reading together the two telegrams sent by Greene just after his talks with Smuts, asked the Boer government formally to state that it adhered also to the concessions mentioned in the second telegram. This it refused to do.[2] Reporting this refusal Milner telegraphed: 'It is impossible to fix the responsibility for a private conversation between the State Attorney and the British Agent upon the Government of S.A.R., especially if the accuracy of the British Agent's version of it is denied by the State Attorney.'[3] In the colonial office Graham minuted: 'From this telegram it seems clear that Greene has been a little too previous and too eager to score a diplomatic triumph. We must consider the new proposals of the S.A.R. as if the conversation between Greene and Smuts had never taken place. We cannot even allude to it in our formal reply. . . .' Though Chamberlain demurred strongly to these remarks, he allowed himself to be overruled by the officials.[4]

Two days after forwarding the formal statement Reitz asked Greene to telegraph an amendment thereof.[5] The concessions which the Boer government had offered were now stated to be expressly conditional[6] on the guarantees it had asked for. In other words it wished the British government clearly to understand that the guarantees were an integral part of its offer, which would have to be accepted or rejected as a whole. Walker writes that after the receipt of Reitz's amending telegram there was an immediate stiffening on the British side.[7] This assertion is not supported by the evidence. It is true that Milner telegraphed: '. . . letter of State Secretary [i.e. the amending telegram] appears to me to stiffen appreciably the terms of the note [i.e. the formal statement] and make it more difficult for H.M.G. to agree to it without the strongest reservations.' But the colonial office was not influenced by this telegram. Graham minuted: 'This does

---

[1] Ibid., pp. 46–47.
[2] The refusal was received in the colonial office on 26 Aug.
[3] African (South), 572, pp. 225–6. The rest of the telegram is in C. 9521, p. 49.
[4] Minutes by Graham, Wingfield, and Chamberlain on Milner to Chamberlain, 26 Aug. 1899. C.O. 417/265. From these minutes it would appear that the colonial office may genuinely have believed that Greene had been authorized by Smuts to transmit the concessions mentioned in his second telegram. On the other hand, Milner, commenting on 20 Aug. on the republic's formal statement, made no reference to any discrepancy between it and Greene's telegrams reporting the negotiations with Smuts. As for Greene, he had been instructed by Milner not to comment on the formal statement. African (South), 572, p. 216; C. 9530, p. 22.
[5] C. 9521, p. 47.
[6] For the original wording see above, p. 309.
[7] C.H.B.E. viii. 596.

not affect the question of the reply. It merely emphasizes Milner's telegram of 20th August, no. 2 on which we are acting.' (This latter telegram, sent before the receipt of Reitz's amendment, outlined the reply Milner wished to be sent to the republic's offer.[1]) Chamberlain had in fact made up his mind as early as 16 August on his reply to the republican conditions. On that day, in a telegram to Milner, he foreshadowed a reply substantially the same as that ultimately sent.[2]

On 24 August Chamberlain wrote the following minute:

> ... It is clear that we cannot go on negotiating for ever and we must try to bring matters to a head. The next step in military preparations is so important and so costly that I hesitate to incur the expense ... so long as there seems a fair chance of a satisfactory settlement. But I dread above all the continual whittling away of differences until we have no *casus belli* left,[3] although the Boers may claim a partial diplomatic victory and be as disagreeable and intractable in the future as in the past.[4]

Two days later he tried for the last time the effect on the Boers of threats unaccompanied by force. He said in a public speech at Birmingham:

> Mr Kruger procrastinates in his replies. He dribbles out reforms like water from a squeezed sponge and he either accompanies his offers with conditions which he knows to be impossible or he refuses[5] to allow us to make a satisfactory investigation of the nature and the character of those reforms. . . . The issues of peace and war are in the hands of President Kruger. . . . Will he speak the necessary words? The sands are running down in the glass. . . . If we are forced to make further preparations we shall not hold ourselves limited by what we have already offered,

but go on to secure conditions 'which once for all shall establish which is the Paramount Power in South Africa'.[6]

Shortly before replying to the republic's offer Chamberlain ordered the dispatch of 27 July[7] to be handed to the Boer authorities preparatory to its immediate publication. It no doubt helped to prepare the latter for the British reply, on one issue at any rate. For it uncompromisingly reasserted the suzerainty in these words:[8] . . . 'there

---

[1] African (South), 572, p. 216; Milner to Chamberlain, 22 Aug. 1899, and minute by Graham (C.O. 417/265).
[2] African (South), 572, p. 209. The telegram is summarized in Headlam, i. 489–90.
[3] Compare this with the passage quoted on p. 291 above.
[4] Minute on Milner to Chamberlain, 20 Aug. 1899, no. 1. C.O. 417/265.
[5] A reference apparently to the refusal of the joint inquiry.
[6] Garvin, iii. 438–9; Headlam, i. 493.
[7] See above, p. 303.
[8] Contrast *C.H.B.E.* viii. 597 and Walker (*b*), 483.

can be no question of the interpretation [by an arbitration tribunal] of the preamble of the Convention of 1881 which governs the Articles substituted in the Convention of 1884. . . .'[1] The British reply was telegraphed to Milner on 28 August.[2] It accepted the republic's concessions with the proviso that the British agent should investigate whether they conferred 'immediate and substantial representation' on the Uitlanders. With regard to the republican conditions, it accepted arbitration in principle.[3] But it dealt with the other two conditions in equivocal language, which amounted in fact to rejection. On the suzerainty issue, it referred the republic to a previous dispatch. That brief reference read in conjunction with the passage I have quoted from the dispatch of 27 July, meant a refusal to give the undertaking asked for by the republic. On the vital issue of intervention it stated: 'Her Majesty's Government hope that the fulfilment of the promises made and the just treatment of the Uitlanders in future will render unnecessary any further intervention on their behalf, but Her Majesty's Government cannot of course debar themselves from their rights under the Conventions [sic] nor divest themselves of the ordinary rights of a civilized Power to protect its subjects in a foreign country from injustice.' The second half of this statement was superfluous, since the republic did not question the validity of the London convention[4] nor Britain's right to protect her subjects in accordance with international law. But the first half implied a rejection of the request concerning intervention. For the republic had not inquired what the hopes of the British government were, but what it was prepared to undertake. Now it was the view both of Chamberlain (who with his staff was responsible for the phrasing of the British reply) and of Milner that the franchise and representation offer of the republic was not yet satisfactory, though Chamberlain was prepared to accept it for the time being. He and Milner intended to demand better representation for the Uitlanders in due course.[5] Hence their unwillingness to tie the hands of the British government.

The British note concluded with the statement that a conference between Milner and Kruger would have to take place in Cape Town in order to settle certain unspecified 'matters of difference' which

---

[1] C. 9518, p. 11.   [2] C. 9531, pp. 49–50.
[3] But see above, pp. 307–8.
[4] The preamble of the Pretoria convention of 1881, which was still valid according to the British government, conferred no rights on the Uitlanders.
[5] See above, pp. 284, 302–3; African (South), 572, p. 216; C. 9521, p. 62; Headlam, i. 527.

were not suitable for arbitration. The note was accompanied by the following instruction from Chamberlain:

British Agent may inform State Secretary as his own opinion based on Lord Salisbury's reference to Sibylline Books[1] and speech of Secretary of State at Birmingham on Saturday, that if reply to last telegram from H.M. Government is not prompt and satisfactory, and if it becomes necessary to despatch further troops, H.M. Government will feel justified in withdrawing previous suggestions for compromise and will formulate their own demands for a settlement not only of Uitlander question but also of future relations between Great Britain and the Transvaal State.[2]

The reply of the republic was delivered to Greene on 2 September: she withdrew the offer of 13 August and reverted to the previous offer of a seven years' franchise and four additional seats for the Witwatersrand.[3]

This was the end, though the protagonists continued to send each other notes for some weeks to come. The republic's attempt to reach a settlement by compromise had foundered on the rock of British supremacy.

ADDENDUM

(Note on C.H.B.E. viii. 595–7)

The pages referred to form part of professor Walker's chapter entitled 'The Struggle for Supremacy, 1896–1902'. I have repeatedly indicated my disagreement with statements made in this chapter including some of those on pp. 595–7. But since I consider these pages to be particularly misleading I wish now to devote special attention to them. Walker gives the impression (without making an unequivocal assertion) that the republican government, when it allowed Smuts to negotiate with Greene, did not seriously intend to reach a settlement but to 'play for time' and to 'stave off war till October when the grass would be grown for their [the Boers'] horses, and masses of hastily ordered munitions be safely delivered for use in a struggle'.[4] Now it is permissible to hold that Reitz and Smuts were poor diplomats, and that they ought to have known better than to expect the British government to accept their conditional offer.[5] But to hold that their offer was insincere and that their primary object was to

---

[1] See below, p. 318.
[2] Chamberlain to Milner, 28 Aug. 1899 (C.O. 417/265); African (South), 572, p. 228.
[3] C. 9521, pp. 52–54. [4] p. 595.
[5] Walker (a), 351, 354; Hofmeyr, 550.

'play for time' is not permissible, since the evidence points in the opposite direction. Greene had given them some ground for believing that their conditional offer would be acceptable to the British government.[1] In his *Lord de Villiers* Walker himself quotes a letter from Reitz which seems to establish the latter's sincerity.[2] As for Smuts, he wrote to his superiors shortly after the British rejection of the republican offer: '. . . our last proposal of a five years' franchise and one quarter representation for the gold fields[3] under conditions which would have made it an honourable solution for both parties has also been refused—notwithstanding the fact that the British government well knew that this refusal would weaken its position before the world and before its own public also.'[4] We come to Walker's second point—that the republican government was playing for time. True enough, for twelve days (1–12 August) it could not make up its mind about its answer to the proposal of a joint inquiry. But this delay was not unduly long in view of the important issues it was considering. True also that it received advice from several quarters to play for time.[5] It is possible, however, to receive advice without following it. So far, indeed, was the republican government at this juncture from wishing to spin out the negotiations, that it asked Chamberlain to 'expedite' his reply to its offer owing to 'the urgency of an early termination of the present state of affairs'.[6]

Walker lays some stress on the influence which he supposes Leyds to have exercised on the Boer government.[7] In July and August Leyds sent several cables and letters to Pretoria warning them against giving away too much and vigorously denouncing their offer of a settlement.[8] But there are good grounds for believing that Leyds's influence at Pretoria was by this time small.[9] He was kept in the dark about the views of the members of the executive council.[10] His advice

---

[1] C. 9521, p. 45; C. 9530, p. 21; Leyds, *Eenige Correspondentie*, 157.

[2] Walker (*a*), 349–50, 354.

[3] i.e. one-quarter of the number of seats in the volksraad.

[4] Smuts's memorandum for the executive council dated 4 Sept. 1899. Smuts papers (Pretoria archives).

[5] Garvin, iii. 430; Leyds, *Eenige Correspondentie*, 84–85.

[6] C. 9521, p. 47. The excitement in South Africa was mounting. See, for example, Headlam, i. 498–500; *Bulletin* (1954), p. 180.

[7] *C.H.B.E.* viii. 595–6.

[8] Leyds, *Eenige Correspondentie*, 73, 84–85, 109–12, 117–18.

[9] For the attitude to him of Reitz and Smuts in Feb. 1899, see above, p. 248.

[10] Leyds, *Eenige Correspondentie*, 111. In this letter printed on p. 111, Leyds declared: 'About the inside of the machinery I hear something occasionally from Riekert, who is in correspondence with Piet Grobler and others. To judge thereby, the President is himself the man who is driving towards the making of further concessions and who is letting the people be influenced towards that end. What has, I will not say disheartened

to play for time was ignored. He was told nothing about the Smuts–Greene negotiations (in spite of a cable asking for information) until 19 August, the date on which the formal offer was dispatched. (His own assumption that a telegram from Pretoria went astray seems to me mistaken in view of the temporizing reply sent on 15 August to his request for information.)[1]

Walker swallows (p. 597)[2] Chamberlain's statement, made after the outbreak of war, that he intended his reply to the republic's offer to be a 'qualified acceptance'. (Chamberlain borrowed the expression from Milner, who used it in a dispatch published after the war had started.)[3] Walker considers, therefore, that he must try to explain why 'the Transvaal authorities . . . read the qualified acceptance as a definite refusal'. He finds the explanation in the fact that 'the Portuguese, who had of late been holding up munitions at Delagoa Bay, had given way under German pressure[4] and let the vital consignments through at the end of August'. But before he heard this news Reitz had already indicated that Pretoria would be satisfied with nothing less than an unequivocal acceptance of their offer.[5] There is no need, however, to prolong the argument. The simple truth is that Pretoria read as a refusal what was intended to be a refusal.[6]

me, but not exactly cheered me up, is his account that in Rustenburg the people are signing petitions to the government, asking it to give way further. These petitions are being signed by the President's people, the same people who still stood so firm a few months ago, and they must have been brought to this opinion by emissaries of the president and of Schutte, the Superintendent of Police. In this way the people are being asked to sign their own downfall.'

[1] Leyds, *Eenige Correspondentie*, 105–6, 115–18, 126.
[2] See also Walker (*c*), 187.
[3] Cook (*a*), 248–9; C. 9530, p. 57.
[4] Actually it was combined German and French pressure. Foreign office to colonial office, 26 Aug. 1899, enclosing MacDonell to Salisbury, 25 Aug. 1899 (C.O. 417/272).
[5] Leyds, *Eenige Correspondentie*, 126–7.
[6] See also Wilde, 134.

CHAPTER XII

THE ULTIMATUMS

And he who becomes master of a city accustomed to freedom and
does not destroy it, may expect to be destroyed by it, for in rebellion
it has always the watchword of liberty, and its ancient privileges as
a rallying point, which neither time nor benefits will ever cause it
to forget.

IN its reply of 2 September[1] and an addition thereto a few days later,
the republican government professed its willingness to agree to the
joint inquiry. But it did so in ambiguous language. The British
rejoinder on 8 September was a refusal to go back to the seven years'
franchise, accompanied by a warning that unless the republic agreed
to an unconditional five years' franchise as well as an inquiry, whether
joint or unilateral, it must expect an ultimatum which might be far-
reaching in scope.[2]

About this time a member of each of the two governments expressed
his views on the situation. The one was Smuts. On 4 September he
sent a memorandum to his government in which he wrote:

... The relations between the South African Republic and England are
daily becoming more strained; if at Bloemfontein last June there was still
a hope of a peaceful solution, honourable to both sides, the last months
have taught that this hope is idle; that the enemy is determined that this
country shall either be conquered or be brought by diplomatic means to
the position practically of a British colony.... Every attempt at *rapprochement* from our side has been haughtily rejected. ... Our latest despatch,
in which our government accepts the idea of a joint inquiry in a tempered
(gematigden) form will likewise miss its mark. ... Humanly speaking war
between the Republics and England is certain.

Smuts then proceeded to recommend a plan of campaign. The
republics should assume the offensive from the beginning. The main
attack should be directed against Natal, with Durban as the objective.
The possibility of foreign intervention was by no means excluded,
provided the republics won the first few battles of the war. Furthermore, in the latter eventuality the British position in India and
Egypt would be shaken. The war was sure to be long, bloody, and

---

[1] See above, p. 314.   [2] C. 9521, pp. 52–54, 64–65; C. 9530, p. 1.

exhausting. 'South Africa', he concluded, 'is on the eve of a terrible blood bath, from which our people will emerge either as an exhausted remnant, wood-cutters and water-carriers for a hated race, or as victors, founders of a United South Africa, of one of the great empires of the world . . . an Afrikaner republic . . . stretching from Table Bay to the Zambesi.'[1]

The second opinion I wish to quote is that of the British prime minister. He was writing in comment on one of Milner's letters, presumably a letter to Chamberlain[2] dated 2 August 1899, in which Milner repeated his request for troops.[3] But the comment is actually on the whole Milner attitude and policy. Salisbury wrote:

Milner's letter suggests many reflections—but they may wait. His view is too heated, if you consider the intrinsic significance and importance of the things which are in controversy. But it recks little to think of that now. What he has done cannot be effaced. We have to act upon a moral field prepared for us by him and his jingo supporters. And therefore I see before us the necessity for considerable military effort—and all for people whom we despise, and for territory which will bring no profit and no power to England.[4]

A few days later, in a memorandum for the cabinet, he directed his attention to Chamberlain. He protested that he had not used the words 'Sibylline books', nor had he expressed himself in favour of raising the British demands.[5] 'I cannot conceive', he added, 'any advantage in such a course. It would give us no additional strength; and it would widely extend the impression of our bad faith, which, unfortunately, and most unjustly, prevails in many quarters abroad. . . .' He declared also, and Hicks Beach agreed with him, that Chamberlain had been wrong in 'mixing up . . . ultra-arbitration questions' with the franchise negotiations.[6] 'They can only create distrust, and they certainly are not of sufficient importance to sustain a war. They are not specified as the Boers justly complain; and they may, for aught the Boers know, include demands more important and more objectionable in their eyes than any that have yet been made. . . .' But Chamberlain asserted: 'What is now at stake is the position of Great Britain in South Africa and with it the estimate formed of our power and influence in our Colonies and throughout

---

[1] Memorandum, 4 Sept. 1899. Smuts papers (Pretoria archives).
[2] See *Bulletin* (1954), p. 179.   [3] Headlam, i. 513–15.
[4] Salisbury to Lansdowne, 30 Aug. 1899. Newton, 157.
[5] See above, p. 314.   [6] See above, p. 313.

the world . . . the necessities of the case make . . . an advance in our claims imperative if the S.A.R. still continue their recalcitrant attitude.'[1] Chamberlain's view prevailed in the cabinet and the note of 8 September[2] not only demanded a settlement of the unspecified 'ultra-arbitration questions' but foreshadowed also a raising of the British claims.

In the meantime Milner had been deluging Chamberlain with advice and appeals.

. . . Distress is now really very serious. Johannesburg is suffering most severely. Business is at a standstill. . . . British South Africa is prepared for extreme measures. . . . We have got the S.A.R. to go as far as they will go without not merely the threat but the actual application of force. I do not say war, for there is always a probability[3] that with an army actually on their borders they will submit to anything and everything including disarmament. . . . It is evident that, as someone[4] said to me long ago, Kruger will 'bluff up to the cannon's mouth'. . . . The Afrikanders both here [in the Cape] and in the Orange Free State are more frightened than ever and a tremendous screw is being put on Pretoria to give way further—a great deal further—and indeed to accept almost any demand. For it is evident that if it comes to blows, however serious the consequences to us, the consequences to the great Afrikander idea, which Hofmeyr has been nursing so patiently and skilfully for many years, will be much more serious. If the Transvaal were to disappear from the map as an independent State or if it were to become an Uitlander Republic, the 'Afrikander Nation' idea would be for ever doomed. If there is a climb down, it will almost exceed the wit of man to prevent their cheating us. The Pretoria gang will for some time to come retain the administration, and it will be very difficult —it may be impossible—to prevent the Colonial Afrikanders (once the pressure is removed) from again playing into their hands.[5]

There seems to be here quite clearly implied that Milner, as he had indicated before,[6] preferred war to a peaceful settlement.

On 4 September Milner telegraphed Chamberlain his idea of an ultimatum to the republic. 'Personally', he declared, 'I should prefer to ask directly for what we really want', viz. absolute political equality

[1] *Bulletin* (1954), pp. 178–81.   [2] See above, p. 317.
[3] 'A probability.' So Schreiner had been right in June, at any rate as far as Milner was concerned. See above, p. 292.
[4] He may have been Fitzpatrick (see above, p. 298 n. 1) or Rhodes. The latter had been telling crowded audiences in the Cape in July and August that Kruger would not fight. Walker (c), 174. See also Rhodes to Milner, 13 Sept. 1899, in Headlam, i. 536.
[5] These quotations are from letters and telegrams to Chamberlain sent between 23 Aug. and 6 Sept. Headlam, i. 499–500, 518, 531.
[6] See above, pp. 286, 289.

for all white men in the republic; recognition of British paramountcy —that is to say, control of the republic's foreign relations and the right of interference in internal affairs; and, lastly, partial disarmament.[1]

The same cabinet meeting which sanctioned the British note of 8 September also decided to send troops at once to South Africa. A contingent from India was to arrive in Natal in five weeks, the rest of the reinforcements a week later. These troops would raise the British military strength in South Africa from 12,000 to 22,000 men. (Smuts had recently calculated that the allied republics could put about 40,000 citizens into the field.) The dispatch of the reinforcements was announced in the press, as well as the full details of a 'possible expeditionary force' in the shape of an army corps.[2] According to Milner, this news caused 'intense excitement' in the republics—as well it might.[3]

For the news meant war. The Transvaal government were determined to give way no further. They knew that they must expect an ultimatum, and here were the troops coming to enforce it. It was obviously sound military strategy to strike as soon as possible. On the other hand, it was sound diplomatic tactics to wait for the British ultimatum provided there was no undue delay. If there was such delay, military considerations might be expected to prevail.

Immediately after the British government had committed itself to the dispatch of troops to South Africa, Milner's attitude on the probability of war underwent a change. He began now to warn Chamberlain that war must be expected and that, if it came, the Free State would fight side by side with the sister republic. He warned Chamberlain also that the Boers would 'most probably' strike first.[4] But governor Hely-Hutchinson, with an invasion of Natal staring him in the face, could not think that the Boers 'would be so crack-brained as to strike the first blow at us'.[5] As for Chamberlain, he remained startlingly sanguine until the end. Two days before the Boers delivered their ultimatum he wrote:

My own opinion is, as it has always been, that both Milner and the military authorities greatly exaggerate the risks and dangers of this cam-

---

[1] Headlam, i. 525. For Chamberlain's idea of an ultimatum, see ibid. 527.
[2] African (South), 572, pp. 265, 269. The mobilization of the army corps began unobtrusively on 22 Sept. Garvin, iii. 462–3.
[3] African (South), 572, p. 269.
[4] Headlam, i. 535, 538, 545–7.
[5] Hely-Hutchinson to Chamberlain, 29 Sept. 1899. Chamberlain papers, H.

paign.[1] I have never believed that the Boers would take the offensive at this stage—nor do I fear a British reverse if they do. There must be risks in all wars, but I think the risk of a successful attack on a fortified position chosen by us is a very small one. When all the reinforcements [the 10,000 men recently sent] are landed my own feeling is that we shall be quite a match for the Boers even without the army corps.[2]

Milner was right about the pressure that was being applied in Pretoria, by the Cape friends at any rate. But the republican government gave no further heed to them.[3] It did, indeed, in a note of 16 September, appear unequivocally to accept the joint inquiry. But the inquiry was to be into the seven years' franchise, which the British government had just firmly rejected. In view of this decision the Boer leaders must have expected that their offer would be unacceptable. The British reply breaking off the negotiations was telegraphed to Milner on 22 September.[4]

Immediately after the receipt of this telegram the republican government began preparing its ultimatum in consultation with the Free State leaders.[5] The preparation of the British ultimatum also got under way. On 19 September Salisbury wrote to Chamberlain: 'I want to get away from the franchise issue, which will be trouble-some in debate—and to make the break [i.e. go to war] on a proposal to revise or denounce the Convention of 1884 on the ground that it has not been carried out as we were promised. . . .'[6]

On Milner's advice the cabinet decided (22 September) to delay the presentation of the British ultimatum until the reinforcements now on their way should be in position on the frontier of the republic.[7] A few days later Milner telegraphed again to say that further consideration of the ultimatum should be dropped, since the Boers were likely to take the offensive.[8] On 29 September he added: '. . . Personally I am still of opinion not to hurry in settling ultimatum, as events of next few days may supply us with a better one than anybody can compose. Ultimatum has always been great difficulty, as unless we widen issue there is not sufficient cause for war, and if we do so, we are abused for shifting our ground and extending our demands.'[9]

---

[1] In fact they greatly underrated them.
[2] Chamberlain to Hicks Beach, 7 Oct. 1899. Chamberlain papers, C.
[3] Hofmeyr, 551–3.   [4] C. 9530, pp. 11–13, 16–17.
[5] Walker (a), 354; Headlam, i. 545.
[6] *Bulletin* (1954), p. 181.
[7] Headlam, i. 541, 545.   [8] Ibid. 545–6.
[9] Chamberlain papers, B. Published in part in *Bulletin* (1954), p. 181. Headlam (i. 552) omits the second sentence of the passage I have quoted.

But Chamberlain thought that the Boers would not attack and the preparation of the ultimatum continued.

The Boers were now beginning to mobilize. On 30 September Reitz requested that the British ultimatum might be delivered within forty-eight hours. Chamberlain replied that it would not be ready for 'some days'. Kruger was impatient to 'begin', but Steyn would not allow the Boer ultimatum to be presented. He wished to await the British terms, which would, he believed, strengthen the republican cause in the eyes of the world. It has been suggested, with apparent justification, that it was not only Steyn's attitude that delayed the dispatch of the Boer ultimatum, but defective supply arrangements for the commandos along the Natal frontier.[1]

The British ultimatum,[2] which, as was admitted by prominent members of the government including the prime minister, the Boer leaders could not have accepted,[3] was sanctioned in principle by the cabinet on 29 September.[4] Details were left for subsequent consideration. On the day of the cabinet meeting Chamberlain wrote to Hicks Beach: 'I am wondering whether after all we shall have to consider an ultimatum. Milner thinks the Boers will certainly take the offensive. If so the Lord will have delivered them into our hands—at least as far as diplomacy is concerned.'[5] The Boers, however, did not attack, and during the week 2–9 October the bulk of the reinforcements from India disembarked in Durban and went straight towards the frontier.[6] On 9 October Chamberlain wrote the following minute for the cabinet: 'I propose to telegraph this despatch [the ultimatum] . . . on Wednesday next [the 11th], in order that it may be printed in a Blue Book to be circulated on Monday [the 16th] . . . the day before the meeting of Parliament.'[7] But Kruger had at length overcome Steyn's hesitation, and on the afternoon of 9 October the Boer ultimatum was handed to the British agent in Pretoria. It was, in effect, a declaration of war.[8]

---

[1] C. 9530, p. 42; van der Merwe, i. 245–6, 249, 262–70; Amery, i. 370–2; Headlam, i. 551; *C.H.B.E.* viii. 598–9.
[2] Published in full in *Bulletin* (1954), pp. 182–6. See also Garvin, iii. 463–4.
[3] *Bulletin* (1954), pp. 181, 186–7.
[4] Garvin, iii. 463, 467.
[5] *Bulletin* (1954), p. 188.
[6] *C.H.B.E.* viii. 599; van der Merwe, i. 267; Amery, i. 372.
[7] Chamberlain papers, B.
[8] Headlam, i. 557; C. 9530, pp. 65–67.

CHAPTER XIII

CONCLUSION

I

THE advent of Joseph Chamberlain as colonial secretary marked the turning-point in Anglo-Boer relations during the last two decades of the nineteenth century. Up to that point the clash between Britain and the South African Republic had been on the outposts. The outcome of this 'battle of the outposts' was the virtual encirclement of the two Boer republics with British territory, and in particular the denial to the Transvaal of access to the sea. There remained the neutral port of Delagoa Bay, but the neutrality of the bay was precarious. When Chamberlain became colonial secretary in 1895 the struggle was transferred to the citadel itself, within which the Trojan horse in the shape of the Uitlander population had been introduced during the preceding decade. Before the end of the year there followed the Jameson raid. To Chamberlain the raid was by no means an unmitigated disaster. 'I even regard it as possible', he wrote after the fiasco, 'that it may bring matters to a head and lead to the settlement of many pending questions.'[1] The question we must try to answer in conclusion is: Which of these 'questions' were soluble without war and which insoluble; or in other words, what was the war about?

There are those who have answered the question in accordance with some doctrine of historical determinism. It has been said, for example, that the war was one between the sixteenth (or seventeenth) and the nineteenth (or twentieth) centuries with the implication that it was inevitable.[2] Sir James Rose Innes in his valuable *Autobiography* does not adopt the war-of-the-centuries view, but considers, nevertheless, that war was inevitable.[3] I do not see how the historian can adopt a determinist standpoint. The 'inevitable outcome' is, actually, descried only after it has come about. When it is descried in advance, it usually fails to take place. Determinist history implies in fact a claim to omniscience.

[1] Chamberlain to Hely-Hutchinson, 8 Feb. 1896. Chamberlain papers, H.
[2] An early exponent of this view was Theodor Mommsen. *Journal of Modern History*, June 1952, p. 122, quoting Mommsen's view.   [3] Innes, 191.

The responsibility for the war has often been laid at the door of the mining magnates. More precisely, it is alleged that they engineered the war for the sake of their dividends. But the interests of these financiers or 'capitalists' required certain well-understood reforms in the administration of the republic, not an attack on her independence. For the purpose of promoting these interests united action by the capitalists was desirable and practicable. But it became impracticable when these limits were transgressed. This was one of the lessons driven home by the fiasco of the raid. An important section among the capitalists were altogether opposed to the plan of an armed rebellion, and even among those who supported it there were misgivings about the political aims of their leader, Rhodes. This distrust of Rhodes the statesman contributed its share to the ruin of the enterprise. Yet it remains true that a powerful group of capitalists played a leading and indispensable role in the plot that led to the raid. Chamberlain kept in the background, intending to show his hand only after the capitalists had led Johannesburg into actual revolt.

In the prolonged crisis that culminated in war the roles were reversed. In 1895 Rhodes and a number of Rand capitalists took the lead, but counted on the support of the British government at the critical moment. The mess they made of the enterprise taught the capitalists their lesson. They withdrew into the shell out of which they had ventured in 1895, and left the political initiative to the British government. As the crisis deepened they emerged out of their shell once more, this time as instruments of British policy. They acted now as men under orders, relying on the superior political wisdom of the professional statesmen.

It was not until late in 1897 that the capitalist front could be effectively reconstituted with the circumscribed object of taking united action in the interests of the mining industry. But in their attitude to the republican government the capitalists continued to differ among themselves. The most important of them, the Wernher–Beit firm, remained uncompromisingly hostile. But certain other big firms did not share this hostility. In January 1899 Milner and Chamberlain took the important step of arranging joint action between themselves and the chamber of mines in opposition to the dynamite monopoly. They were making a bid for the support of the capitalists during the critical months that lay ahead. The bid was sufficiently, if not entirely, successful. The joint action against the dynamite monopoly led directly to the fateful negotiations between the republican government and the capitalists, in which the latter were guided by the advice of the senior partner, the colonial office. But even at this juncture, the capitalists were not unanimous. They could not agree on the demands to be made on Kruger. It was not only 'foreign' firms like those of Goerz and Albu that were unwilling to ask too much, but also a 'British' firm like the Consolidated Goldfields. It was partly due to his awareness of this fact that Fitzpatrick broke up the negotiations and handed over the job to the British government. When the latter took over, the capitalists retired into the background. Those of them who did not agree with the British government's policy were prepared to acquiesce under the combined pressure of the colonial office and Wernher, Beit & Company.[1]

II

A well-known historian declared recently: 'The essential British problem in South Africa was strategical and political, not economic. . . . The British needed a united white South Africa in order to have strategic security at the Cape—the lynch-pin of the British Empire. . . . The naval station at the Cape was . . . fundamental to them. . . .'[2] Though British statesmen undoubtedly attached great importance to the naval base at Simonstown, it is not clear why a united South Africa was necessary for the security of the base. The British garrison and naval squadron provided an effective enough guarantee.[3] The game that was played in South Africa in the 1890's was for other stakes than the security of Simonstown. In the eyes of British statesmen a united South Africa—like a united Canada and a united Australia—would be a source of additional strength to the British empire instead of a source of expense. It is true that Lord Salisbury appears not to have agreed with this view;[4] but Salisbury was in a minority in his cabinet.

'No one', writes professor C. W. de Kiewiet, 'who has read . . . the records of British policy since the achievement of Confederation in Canada can miss the picture of a British Government groping for

[1] See above, *passim*, and Leyds, *Eenige Correspondentie*, 11–13, 18, 30, 33–35, 49–50, 63.
[2] A. J. P. Taylor, 363–4.
[3] Milner had little doubt on this point. See Headlam, i. 87 and Milner to Chamberlain, 23 Aug. 1899. Chamberlain papers, D.
[4] See above, p. 318.

some means of ending South African disunity.'[1] So far, so good. But he then goes on to write as if he had adopted as his major premiss the theory that the political federation of South Africa was an historical necessity. It is an assumption that lies at the base of a great deal of South African historiography. Those who write history in this way naturally conclude that the opponents of federation could not but be swept aside, since they had placed themselves athwart the destiny of South Africa.[2] But I have said already that the historian cannot steer by the light of a determinist philosophy.

It was the Great Trek of the 1830's that was responsible for South African disunity. The British government was naturally reluctant to acquiesce in the birth of a second source of 'White' political power in South Africa. It took that government the best part of twenty years to make up its mind to recognize the independence of two Boer states in the interior, and then only after annexing the coastal republic of Natal and in the confident anticipation that the inland states would remain of small account, if indeed they managed to maintain themselves at all in the face of internal dissensions and Native hostility. But what if the new states survived and grew in strength? The only step taken by the British government in the early days to insure itself against such an eventuality was to veto a union between the two republics.[3] It was a significant step; but it did not go far enough since it failed to forestall an inter-republican alliance. The next step, taken much later, was to propose a South African federation under the British flag. But two successive attempts to put the plan into practice encountered armed resistance and by 1896—after the failure of the second attempt—the prospects looked particularly unpromising.

Federation was the ideal solution, but it might not be attainable. The British authorities felt therefore that they had to provide some alternative answer to the problem of the duality of political power (or will) in South Africa. They found the answer in the concept of paramountcy or supremacy. British paramountcy proved to be an elastic term, but even in its mildest interpretation it meant the denial of full republican independence. The republics, and more particularly the Orange Free State, got an unmistakable taste of paramountcy when the British, after intervening in quarrels between the latter state and independent Native chiefs north of the Orange, annexed both the territory of Basutoland and the diamond fields of Griqualand West

---

[1] De Kiewiet (c), 139.   [2] Ibid.
[3] De Kiewiet (a), 120–2, 139–40.

(1868–71).[1] The annexation of the South African Republic in 1877 was a vigorous demonstration of paramountcy, undertaken with a view to South African federation. When the republic was restored in 1884, certain limits were set to its independence particularly in regard to treaty-making power. But the claim to paramountcy, while it included and was partly expressed in these legal limitations, was not exhausted by them.

That the British authorities, speaking in the name of a powerful empire, should assert their paramountcy over two republics struggling to find their feet was natural. It was equally natural that the republics should oppose the claim. Having undertaken the responsibilities of independence, they claimed also its rights. It was not really a question of petty African communities claiming to be 'ordinary European states'.[2] It was a question rather of the meaning of political independence. (This is not to deny that it was in fact European jurists and statesmen who were the creators of modern international law—not, however, for Europe only but for the world.) As for paramountcy, the republics did not formally repudiate the claim as an abstract proposition. But they protested whenever its application affected their interests. They did not, however, carry their protests to the length of armed resistance except in the case of the annexation of the South African Republic.

III

When it had become clear by 1895 that the gold-fields of the Witwatersrand had vast potentialities, the problem of the duality of political power began, in the eyes of British statesmen, to take on a new urgency. Writing to Chamberlain late in 1896 on 'the South African question' Selborne remarked:

In a generation the S.A.R. will by its wealth and population dominate South Africa. South African politics must revolve round the Transvaal, which will be the only possible market for the agricultural produce or the manufactures of Cape Colony and Natal. The commercial attraction of the Transvaal will be so great that a Union of the South African States with it will be absolutely necessary for their prosperous existence. The only question in my opinion is whether that Union will be inside or outside the British Empire.[3]

[1] C.H.B.E. viii. 412–14, 419, 422–4, 426, 437, 439–41; de Kiewiet (a), 161–2.
[2] See Walker (b), 337, 474, and de Kiewiet (c), 122, 131.
[3] Selborne to Chamberlain, 18 Oct. 1896. Chamberlain papers, C.

About two years later Milner expressed the fear 'that the over-whelming preponderance in wealth and opportunity on the side of the Transvaal may turn the scale against us'. As for Chamberlain, he publicly warned the two republican presidents in 1897 against aspiring to an independent federation.[1]

The colonial office had in its files many warnings that Britain might lose the loyalty of the British settlers not only in the Transvaal but throughout South Africa. Rhodes had sent such a warning shortly after the raid.[2] Greene sent another early in April 1897. He was describing a dinner party given by Abe Bailey, one of Johannesburg's mining magnates. Jorissen of the republican bench urged those present 'to join him in an attempt . . . to frame a new Constitution which would give the Uitlanders all the rights they wanted', including a seven years' retrospective franchise, on condition that they 're-nounced allegiance to the land of their birth and agreed to accept the Transvaal as their own country'. Most of Jorissen's hearers thought that he spoke with the knowledge of his government.

> The judge's advice to the Uitlanders [continued Greene] to renounce their nationality, and rely on the good faith of the Government of the Republic, could only, I think, be intended as a bait to induce them to abate their confidence in the Imperial Government. At present, in consequence of the recent public utterances of the Secretary of State . . ., the Imperial feeling on the Rand is growing in strength; but when we consider that a considerable proportion of the community entertain a certain misgiving as to the thoroughness of Imperial policy . . . a movement such as that advo-cated by . . . Jorissen might find some . . . support.[3]

At about the same time J. W. Leonard, a leading Johannesburg Uitlander and at one time attorney-general of the Cape Colony, declared in an interview reported to the colonial office: 'It is essential that England should re-establish her lost prestige in South Africa. This is the last chance she will have of retaining the loyalty of English-men and others . . . in the country. . . . Kruger would welcome the sup-port of such men gladly, provided that he was convinced that they had thrown over England. A little time back he sent me a message offer-ing to make me attorney-general of the Transvaal on that condition.'[4]

---

[1] Headlam, i. 267–8; above, p. 159.
[2] Rhodes to British South Africa company, 31 Jan. 1896 (to be handed to Chamber-lain). C.O. 537/130.
[3] Greene to high commissioner, 5 Apr. 1897. African (South), 532, p. 85.
[4] Notes of interview with Leonard by E. A. Altham, deputy assistant adjutant-general. In the original the last sentence of the interview is reported in indirect speech. Ibid., pp. 81–82.

The determination to forestall an independent United States of South Africa lies at the root of British policy after the proving of the deep levels on the Rand. The longer the South African Republic retained her independence the greater seemed the risk that the British colonies would be attracted away from the empire. For some time after the raid there was not much the British authorities could do to checkmate the republic. Their first opportunity to assert themselves came in April 1897.[1] The April demonstration was followed within six months by the assertion of suzerainty. Suzerainty was intended to underpin or legalize paramountcy, and to issue in complete British control over the republic's foreign relations.[2] If this could be achieved the danger of the republic's taking the lead in the formation of an independent federation would be considerably reduced.

The danger might be reduced; it would not be eliminated. It would persist as long as the republican government was a Boer government. It would in fact persist as long as the republic, whether her government were Boer or Uitlander, remained outside the empire. Indeed, it was the prevailing opinion in the colonial office, until Milner appeared on the scene, that it would not be in the interests of Britain to convert the Boer state into an Uitlander republic owing to the risk that the latter would be a more efficient nucleus of an independent federation. Chamberlain himself shared this opinion.[3]

Milner's importance lies in the fact that he converted the colonial office to his solution of the 'duality' problem. He did not fear a republic which admitted the Uitlanders to citizenship. On the contrary he held that she would become a part of the empire,[4] provided that Britain obtained complete political equality for the new citizens without delay and at the same time mastered the republican will to independence.

But if the republican will to independence was not mastered, what would then be the ultimate outcome? Undoubtedly, declared Milner, an independent Republic of South Africa (though the British naval base at Simonstown would be secure for a long time). We have seen that this was also Selborne's view. Milner, however, was the man on the spot and he undertook to enlighten the colonial office on the inwardness of the situation. He came to the conclusion that the independence of the South African Republic was incompatible with

[1] See above, ch. VI.
[2] Headlam, i. 525, 527; *Bulletin* (1954), pp. 187–8.
[3] See above, pp. 87–88, 251.   [4] See Headlam, i. 359.

the interests of Britain because the republic was the prime cause of the growth of Afrikaner nationalism throughout South Africa. Afrikaner nationalism was the real enemy. What was this Afrikaner nationalism of the late 1890's? Its portrait as painted by Milner looks remarkably like the visage it wears today when it has grown to full stature as the result of the Anglo-Boer war and an effort extending over half a century. A nationalist himself, he recognized the symptoms of a malady[1] to which the patient was not to succumb until many years later.[2]

Milner was not interested in the purely cultural aspect of Afrikaner nationalism. It was the political aspect that worried him. 'The Afrikander Nation idea', if it ever came to fruition, meant political independence.[3] 'To afrikanderize' meant to him to become 'a virtual Republican'.[4] This explains how he could lump together all the Cape opponents of his policy—starting from staunch supporters of the imperial connexion like de Villiers and Schreiner and continuing via Hofmeyr, who had no objection in principle to the British flag, to out-and-out republican members of the Afrikaner bond—as the Afrikaner or Dutch party.[5] It appeared to him that even the 'imperialists' among his opponents, in their solicitude for the interests of South Africa and their fear of the disastrous after-effects of war, were willing to take a chance with regard to the imperial connexion. This he was not prepared to do. (In any case he thought that the after-effects of war would be good.[6]) Whether at the cost of war or not it was his firm resolve to secure South Africa's connexion with the empire for ever. That is the explanation of his desire to see the 'Afrikander Nation idea' doomed. That explains also what he meant when he spoke of 'the great game between ourselves and the Transvaal for the mastery in South Africa'.[7] He meant that unless the republic changed its character, its assertion of independence would be copied sooner or later by the rest of South Africa. But the transformation would have to be quick and radical. That was the reason

---

[1] If I may change the metaphor.
[2] Milner to Chamberlain, 23 Aug. 1899 (Chamberlain papers, D); Headlam, i. 262.
[3] Chamberlain, after a long course of instruction from Milner, put the point thus: 'The Dutch [i.e. Afrikaners] in South Africa desire, if it be possible, to get rid altogether of the connection with Great Britain, which to them is not a motherland, and to substitute a United States of South Africa which, they hope, would be mainly under Dutch influence.' Chamberlain's memorandum for the cabinet, 6 Sept. 1899. Chamberlain papers, B.
[4] Milner to Chamberlain, 23 Aug. 1899. Chamberlain papers, D.
[5] Headlam, i. 63.   [6] Ibid. 425.
[7] Ibid. 267. Compare and contrast C.H.B.E. viii. 586–7.

why he insisted that the Uitlanders should be admitted to the republican franchise, not in gradually increasing numbers, but 'wholesale' and on an equal footing with the Boers. If the former course was followed the Uitlanders might 'afrikanderize', i.e. become supporters of republican independence. If they were admitted 'wholesale' by the action of Britain, they would 'burst the existing mould' and the republic would cease to have a will of her own.[1]

IV

The republican government realized too late what it meant to have Chamberlain as a challenger. If it had appreciated its peril, it might sooner have taken appropriate action. As things turned out, the republican record with regard to reform was one of procrastination. The procrastination can be explained. But the fact remains that it was fatal. By the end of 1898 the final crisis had overtaken the republic. Yet as late as the end of April 1899 Smuts still believed that Britain would not go to war unless she had a formally good *casus belli*.[2] As British policy gradually unfolded during the succeeding months, the republican leaders came to the conclusion that Britain was aiming a mortal blow at their independence. Once they had reached that conclusion, they decided to fight. They believed that they stood a chance of winning, especially if they could strike before the British were ready. In spite of a discouraging report from Leyds late in September, they hoped for foreign intervention.[3] Even if they did not win, they may have hoped that Salisbury's government would fall if they held out long enough, and a more sympathetic government take its place. But calculations such as these do not constitute the reason why the republics went to war. After the outbreak of war de Villiers wrote: 'With these people the preservation of their independence is a sacred mission.' Up to the very end he had urged the republicans to give way if they could do so 'without actual dishonour'. Shortly before the Bloemfontein conference his brother Melius[4] wrote to him: 'Men like Mr. Hofmeyr also to some extent forget that the S.A.R. like the Free State has a certain measure of self-respect. . . .' On 16 September the government of the South African Republic sent Hofmeyr its last word: 'We are fully impressed

---

[1] See Headlam, i. 476–9.
[2] Leyds, *Eenige Correspondentie*, 18; see also above, p. 248.
[3] Leyds, *Eenige Correspondentie*, 174; Millin, i. 124–5.
[4] Chief justice of the Orange Free State.

with the very serious position in which we are placed, but with God before our eyes we cannot go further, without endangering, if not totally destroying, our independence. This Government, Parliament and people are unanimous on this point.' The Free Staters' last word had already been spoken by Fischer: 'We have honestly done our best, and can do no more. If we are to lose our independence,[1] since that is what is demanded, leave us at all events the consolation that we did not sacrifice it dishonourably.'[2]

[1] Fischer was identifying his state with the South African Republic.
[2] Walker (a), 338, 355, 369–70; Hofmeyr, 552–3.

NOTES ON SOURCES

I. The Chamberlain papers relating to South Africa have been arranged under a number of headings. These headings are referred to in footnotes by letters of the alphabet, thus:

A Miscellaneous letters to Chamberlain.

B Printed papers, both published and confidential (1896–9).

C Manuscript papers concerning relations between Britain and the South African Republic (1896–9).

D Correspondence between Chamberlain and Milner (1897–9).

E Correspondence between Earl Grey and Chamberlain (1895–8).

F Colonial office minutes and memoranda (1895–6) relating to the Jameson raid. Also a packet of letters relating to the South African Republic (1896).

G Colonial office notes and memoranda, also letters from Bower, Flora Shaw, and others—all relating to the Jameson raid.

H Correspondence between Chamberlain and Hely-Hutchinson.

I Four letters from Rhodes.

J Letters from J. G. Sprigg and John Robinson.

K Correspondence with Loch and Hercules Robinson.

II. Smuts's official and semi-official papers are in the Pretoria archives. His private papers are in the library of the University of Cape Town.

III. The C.O. series comprises the manuscript papers of the colonial office; the African (South) series, papers printed for the use of the colonial office; the C. and Cd. series, papers published by the British government; green books, papers published by the government of the South African Republic.

IV. Published works (including non-official collections of documents and articles in periodicals) referred to in footnotes by brief titles or by the name of the author only:

Agar-Hamilton	Agar-Hamilton, J. A. I. *The Road to the North*. 1937.
Amery	Amery, L. S. (Ed.). *The Times History of the War in South Africa*. 7 vols. 1900–9.
Backeberg	Backeberg, H. E. W. *Die Betrekkinge tussen die Suid-Afrikaanse Republiek en Duitsland tot na die Jameson-inval*. (*Archives Year Book for South African History*, 1949, vol. I.)
Basson	Basson, M. A. *Die Britse Invloed in die Transvaalse Onderwys, 1836–1907*. (*Archives Year Book for South African History*, 1956, vol. II.)
Bell	Bell, E. M. *Flora Shaw*. 1947.
Bixler	Bixler, W. *Anglo-German Imperialism in South Africa, 1880–1900*. 1932.
Botha	Botha, P. R. *Die Staatkundige Ontwikkeling van die Suid-Afrikaanse Republiek onder Kruger en Leyds*. 1926.
Brandenburg	Brandenburg, E. *Von Bismarck zum Weltkriege*. 2nd ed. 1925.
Breytenbach	Breytenbach, J. H. *Die Tweede Vryheidsoorlog*. Vol. I. 1948.

British Documents	Gooch, G. P. and Temperley, H. W. V. (Eds.). *British Documents on the Origins of the War.* Vol. I. 1927.
Bryce	Bryce, J. *Impressions of South Africa.* New ed. 1900.
Buchan	Buchan, J. *Memory Hold-the-Door.* 1940.
Bulletin (1952)	*The Bulletin of the Institute of Historical Research,* vol. XXV, 1952. (Drus, E. *A Report on the Papers of Joseph Chamberlain relating to the Jameson Raid and the Inquiry.*)
Bulletin (1954)	*The Bulletin of the Institute of Historical Research,* vol. XXVII, 1954. (Drus, E. *Select Documents from the Chamberlain Papers concerning Anglo-Transvaal Relations, 1896–1899.*)
Butler	*Sir William Butler. An Autobiography.* 2nd ed. 1913.
C.H.B.E. viii	*The Cambridge History of the British Empire.* Vol. VIII. 1936.
Cecil, Viscount	Viscount Cecil of Chelwood. *All the Way.* 1949.
Coetzee	Coetzee, D. J. *Spoorwegontwikkeling in die Suid-Afrikaanse Republiek.* 1940.
Cook (*a*)	Cook, E. T. *Rights and Wrongs of the Transvaal War.* New ed. 1902.
Cook (*b*)	Cook, E. T. *Edmund Garrett. A Memoir.* 1909.
De Kiewiet (*a*)	de Kiewiet, C. W. *British Colonial Policy and the South African Republics, 1848–72.* 1929.
De Kiewiet (*b*)	de Kiewiet, C. W. *The Imperial Factor in South Africa.* 1937.
De Kiewiet (*c*)	de Kiewiet, C. W. *A History of South Africa, Social and Economic.* 1941.
Du Plessis	du Plessis, J. S. *Die Ontstaan en Ontwikkeling van die Amp van Staatspresident in die Suid-Afrikaanse Republiek.* (*Archives Year Book for South African History,* 1955, vol. I.)
Emden	Emden, P. H. *Randlords.* 1935.
Engelbrecht	Engelbrecht, S. P. *Geskiedenis van die Nederduits Hervormde Kerk van Afrika.* 2nd ed. 1936.
Engelenburg	Engelenburg, F. V. *'n Onbekende Paul Kruger.* 1925.
Ensor	Ensor, R. C. K. *England (1870–1914).* 1936.
Eybers	Eybers, G. W. (Ed.). *Select Constitutional Documents illustrating South African History, 1795–1910.* 1918.
Fitzpatrick	Fitzpatrick, J. P. *The Transvaal from Within.* 1899.
Fitzpatrick (*a*)	Fitzpatrick, J. P. *South African Memories.* 1932.
Fitzpatrick (*b*)	Fitzpatrick, J. P. *Lord Milner and his Work.* 1925.
Foreign and Colonial Speeches	Chamberlain, J. *Foreign and Colonial Speeches.* 1897.
Fuller	Fuller, T. E. *The Right Honourable Cecil John Rhodes.* 1910.
Gardiner	Gardiner, A. G. *The Life of Sir William Harcourt.* 2 vols. 1923.
Garrett	Garrett, E. and Edwards, E. J. *The Story of an African Crisis.* 1897.
Garson	Garson, N. H. *The Swaziland Question and a Road to the Sea, 1887–1895.* (*Archives Year Book for South African History,* 1957, vol. II.)
Garvin	Garvin, J. L. *The Life of Joseph Chamberlain.* 3 vols. 1932–4.
Gedenkschriften	*Gedenkschriften van Paul Kruger gedicteerd aan H. C. Bredell . . . en Piet Grobler. . . .* Geautoriseerde Nederlandsche Uitgave bewerkt door Frederik Rompel. 1902.
German Diplomatic Documents	Dugdale, E. T. S. (Ed.). *German Diplomatic Documents, 1871–1914.* 4 vols. 1928–31.
Grimsehl	Grimsehl, H. W. *Onluste in Modjadjiland, 1890–1894.* (*Archives Year Book for South African History,* 1955, vol. II.)

Große Politik	Lepsius, J., Bartholdy, A. M., and Thimme, F. (Eds.). *Die Große Politik der Europäischen Kabinette, 1871–1914.* 40 vols. 1922–7.
Hammond	*The Autobiography of John Hays Hammond.* 2 vols. 1935.
Hancock	Hancock, W. K. *Survey of British Commonwealth Affairs.* 4 vols. 1937–42.
Headlam	Headlam, C. (Ed.). *The Milner Papers.* 2 vols. 1931–3.
Hertzog-Annale, July, 1953	*Hertzog-Annale van die Suid-Afrikaanse Akademie vir Wetenskap en Kuns.* Julie 1953. (Spies, F. J. du T. [Ed.]. *Briewe uit Transvaal van G. A. A. Middelberg* [1896–1899].)
Hertzog-Annale, Dec. 1955	*Hertzog-Annale van die Suid-Afrikaanse Akademie vir Wetenskap en Kuns.* Desember 1955. (Spies, F. J. du T. [Ed.]. *Reisbriewe van Dr. Hendrik P. N. Muller: 1898.*)
History of 'The Times'	*History of 'The Times'.* 3 vols. 1935–47.
Hobson	Hobson, J. A. *The War in South Africa.* 1900.
Hofmeyr	Hofmeyr, J. H. *The Life of Jan Hendrik Hofmeyr (Onze Jan).* 1913.
Hugo	Hugo, M. *Die Stemregvraagstuk in die Zuid-Afrikaansche Republiek.* (*Archives Year Book for South African History.* 1947.)
Industrial Commission	*The Mining Industry. Evidence and Report of the Industrial Commission of Enquiry, with an Appendix.* . . . Compiled and published by the Witwatersrand Chamber of Mines, Johannesburg, S.A.R. 1897.
Innes	Rose Innes, J. *Autobiography.* 1949.
Jorissen	Jorissen, E. J. P. *Transvaalsche Herinneringen, 1876–1896.* 1897.
Juta	Juta, M. *The Pace of the Ox.* 1937.
Kotze	Kotze, J. G. *Memoirs and Reminiscences.* 2 vols. 1934–41.
Kotze (*a*)	Kotze, J. G. (Ed.). *Documents and Correspondence relating to the Judicial Crisis in the South African Republic.* 1898.
Kruger aan die Woord	du Plessis, J. S. (Ed.). *President Kruger aan die Woord.* 1952.
Kruger's Amptelike Briewe	Engelbrecht, S. P. (Ed.). *Paul Kruger's Amptelike Briewe, 1851–77.* 1925.
Langer	Langer, W. L. *The Diplomacy of Imperialism, 1890–1902.* 2nd ed. 1951.
Laurence	Laurence, P. M. *The Life of John Xavier Merriman.* 1930.
Letters of Queen Victoria	Buckle, G. E. (Ed.). *Letters of Queen Victoria.* 3rd series. 3 vols. 1930–2.
Leyds, *Eerste Jaren*	Leyds, W. J. *Onze Eerste Jaren in Zuid-Afrika.* 1939.
Leyds, *Eenige Correspondentie*	Leyds, W. J. *Eenige Correspondentie uit 1899.* 2nd ed. 1938.
Leyds, *Tweede Verzameling*	Leyds, W. J. *Tweede Verzameling (Correspondentie, 1899–1900).* 2 vols. 1930.
Leyds, *Derde Verzameling*	Leyds, W. J. *Derde Verzameling (Correspondentie, 1900).* 2 vols. 1931.
Leyds, *Vierde Verzameling*	Leyds, W. J. *Vierde Verzameling (Correspondentie, 1900–2).* Part I (2 vols.), Part II (Bijlagen, Index). 1934.
Lovell	Lovell, R. J. *The Struggle for South Africa, 1875–1899.* 1934.
Lugtenburg	Lugtenburg, A. H. *Geskiedenis van die Onderwys in die Suid-Afrikaanse Republiek, 1836–1900.* 1925.
Malherbe	Malherbe, E. G. *Education in South Africa, 1652–1922.* 1925.
Marais	Marais, J. S. *The Cape Coloured People, 1652–1937.* 1939.

Maud	Maud, J. P. R. *City Government. The Johannesburg Experiment.* 1938.
Millin	Millin, S. G. *General Smuts.* 2 vols. 1936.
Milner	Milner, Lord. *The Nation and the Empire.* 1913.
Mouton	Mouton, J. A. *Genl. Piet Joubert in die Transvaalse Geskiedenis.* (*Archives Year Book for South African History,* 1957, vol. I.)
Newton	Newton, Lord. *Lord Lansdowne.* 1929.
Ostrogorski	Ostrogorski, M. *Democracy and the Organization of Political Parties.* 2 vols. 1902.
Phillips	Phillips, L. *Some Reminiscences.* 1924.
Ploeger	Ploeger, J. *Onderwys en Onderwysbeleid in die Suid-Afrikaanse Republiek onder Ds. S. J. du Toit en Dr. N. Mansvelt.* (*Archives Year Book for South African History,* 1952, vol. 1.)
Reitz	Reitz, D. *Commando.* Penguin Books. 1948.
Rose	Rose, E. B. *The Truth about the Transvaal.* 1902.
Saron and Hotz	Saron, G. and Hotz, L. (Eds.). *The Jews in South Africa.* 1955.
Scholtz	Scholtz, G. D. *Die Oorsake van die Tweede Vryheidsoorlog.* 2 vols. 1947.
Seeley	Seeley, J. R. *The Expansion of England.* 2nd ed. 1895.
Selborne Memorandum	*The Selborne Memorandum on the Union of South Africa.* Reprinted 1925.
Smit	Smit, F. P. *Die Staatsopvattinge van Paul Kruger.* 1951.
Taylor, A. J. P.	Taylor, A. J. P. *The Struggle for Mastery in Europe, 1848–1918.* 1954.
Van der Horst	van der Horst, S. T. *Native Labour in South Africa.* 1942.
Van der Merwe	van der Merwe, N. J. *Marthinus Theunis Steyn.* 2 vols. 1921.
Van der Poel (*a*)	van der Poel, J. *Railway and Customs Policies in South Africa, 1885–1910.* 1933.
Van der Poel (*b*)	van der Poel, J. *The Jameson Raid.* 1951.
Van Hoek	van Hoek, K. *Kruger Days: Reminiscences of Dr. Leyds.* 1939.
Van Oordt	van Oordt, J. F. *Paul Kruger en de Opkomst der Zuid-Afrikaansche Republiek.* 1898.
Van Winter	van Winter, P. J. *Onder Krugers Hollanders.* 2 vols. 1937–8.
Vindex	'Vindex'. *Cecil Rhodes. His Political Life and Speeches.* 1900.
Walker (*a*)	Walker, E. A. *Lord de Villiers and his Times.* 1925.
Walker (*b*)	Walker, E. A. *A History of Southern Africa.* 3rd ed. 1957.
Walker (*c*)	Walker, E. A. *W. P. Schreiner, a South African.* 1937.
Walker (*d*)	Walker, E. A. *Lord Milner and South Africa.* 1942.
Webber and Kotze	*The Official Reports of the High Court of the South African Republic.* Translated by Webber, W. S. and revised by Kotze, J. G. Vols. I–III. 1903.
Wilde	Wilde, R. H. *Joseph Chamberlain and the South African Republic, 1895–1899.* (*Archives Year Book for South African History,* 1956, vol. I.)
Williams	Williams, B. *Cecil Rhodes.* 1921.
Wolf	Wolf, L. *Life of the First Marquess of Ripon.* 2 vols. 1921.
Younghusband	Younghusband, F. *South Africa of To-day.* 1898.

V. Unpublished post-graduate theses. They are all in the library of the University of the Witwatersrand, except McGill's, which is in the library of the University of Cape Town:

Bitensky	Bitensky, M. F. *The South African League.*

Etheredge	Etheredge, D. A. *The Early History of the Chamber of Mines, Johannesburg, 1887–1897.*
McGill	McGill, D. C. *History of the Transvaal, 1852–1864.*
Naude, P.	Naude, P. *Boerdery in die Suid-Afrikaanse Republiek.*
Nilant	Nilant, F. G. E. *Jhr. Mr. G. J. Th. Beelaerts van Blokland, Gesant van die Suid-Afrikaanse Republiek.*
Webb	Webb, C. *The Uitlander Movement in the South African Republic before the Jameson Raid.*

VI. Mrs. P. Lewsen allowed me to read the manuscript of her *Life of J. X. Merriman.* I have not referred to the work in footnotes, since it is not yet finished.

INDEX

Afrikaner bond, 16, 51, 96, 165–70, 178, 179, 204 n., 207, 224, 226–7, 296, 330.

Afrikaners, 2, 3, 15–17, 51, 55, 63, 96, 114, 117, 119, 159 and n., 160, 161, 168, 169, 174–6, 178, 179, 183, 196, 205–6, 209, 219–20, 231, 260, 267, 286 n., 297, 318–19, 330–1. *See also* Boers.

Albu, G., 4, 27, 62, 134 n., 162, 228, 325.

Aliens expulsion law, 124–7, 140, 160 n., 223 n.

Altham, E. A., 139, 140.

Amatongaland, *see* Tongaland.

Ameshoff, judge, 141–2.

Anglo-Boer war, 2, 3, 18, 330.

Arbitration in British–S.A. Republic disputes, 165 n., 166, 195–6, 198, 272, 281, 282 and n., 303, 307–8, 309, 313.

Argus company, 131.

Armaments, British, in S. Africa, 91, 106, 115–17, 156–7, 248, 285–6, 288–90, 295, 314, 319–22.

Armaments of S.A. Republic, 27, 28, 32, 96, 115, 116, 157, 161, 193, 205, 210–12, 267–8, 293, 314, 320.

Asiatics, *see* Indians.

Asquith, H. H., 130 n., 267.

Association of mines, 162, 186, 189, 194.

Bailey, A., 4, 328.

Balfour, A. J., 69, 70, 269–70, 303–4.

Barberton, 1, 45, 53, 133.

Barnato, B., 4, 24, 63, 189.

Bechuanaland protectorate, 50, 61, 70, 72, 74, 75, 79–87, 91, 92, 94, 95, 185.

Beelaerts van Blokland, Jhr. G. J., 20 n., 43, 136, 151, 212.

Beit, A., 3, 20, 70, 72, 82, 120, 145, 148 n., 192 n., 229.

Berlin, 100.

Berne award, 154 and n.

Bewaarplaatsen, 20, 249, 254.

Binns, H., 206, 272, 293.

Birmingham, 64, 65, 84, 89, 91, 290 n., 292, 294, 312, 314.

Bloemfontein, 131, 295.

Bloemfontein conference, 273–4, 276–86, 288, 291, 297, 299, 305, 307–9, 317, 331.

Boers, 1–12, 14–19, 46, 55, 68, 71, 93, 94, 96, 101, 104, 107, 108, 115, 116, 125, 139, 140, 146, 157–8, 163, 174, 179, 181, 183, 188–95, 198–201, 205, 211, 220, 235, 242, 247–8, 266, 269–70, 280, 284, 286, 289, 314, 322, 331.

Boksburg, 34.

Botha, Louis, 33.

Bower, Sir G., 72, 74 n., 87, 88, 90, 93 n., 95, 97 n., 104–8, 118, 136, 179.

Britain, 28–30, 37, 38, 46–49, 53 n., 60, 61, 62, 66, 85, 86, 89, 93, 96–100, 103–6, 109, 114, 115, 119, 121–3, 125–6, 128, 129, 148, 152–6, 159, 160, 162–3, 170, 172, 174, 177, 192, 196, 198, 202, 207 n., 208, 211, 213–17, 237, 243, 250, 259, 262, 265, 267–8, 273, 286, 298, 314, 317–18, 328–9, 331.

British empire, 37, 67, 68, 158, 164, 172–4, 210, 265, 296 n., 325, 327, 329–30.

British grievances blue book (C. 9345), 21 n., 234–5, 236 n., 237, 241–2, 261 n., 264, 266, 273, 286–7, 294.

British South Africa company, 70, 72, 74 n., 75, 79, 80, 81 n., 83–87, 91, 94, 95, 99, 111, 112, 121, 224.

British suzerainty over S.A. Republic, *see* suzerainty question.

Brown v. *Leyds* (lawsuit), 140–4.

Bryce, James, 59, 101, 265–6.

Bunu, Swazi chief, 222–3.

Burger, Schalk W., 135 n., 186, 191, 200–2, 204–5, 272, 282, 292.

Burgers, T. F., 5, 6.

Butler, Sir W., 232–3, 236, 239, 241, 242 and n., 286, 289–90.

Buxton, Sydney, 62.

Cape Boys, *see* Cape Coloured.

Cape Colony, 1, 2, 5, 15, 16, 25, 33–40, 51, 53 n., 55, 56, 63, 68, 70, 71, 74 n., 85 n., 86, 91, 94, 96, 108, 114, 117–19,

Cape Colony (*cont.*)
138 n., 144, 146, 159, 160, 161 n., 162, 173–6, 178, 180 n., 185, 205–9, 217, 220, 223–8, 260, 269–70, 273, 276, 278, 287–9, 293, 295–6, 319, 321, 327–8, 330.

Cape Coloured (including Cape Malays) in S.A. Republic, 1, 180–2, 226, 235–7, 249, 258, 261–2, 265.

Cape Times, 102, 118, 120, 161, 165, 166, 179, 239, 287 and n.

Cape Town, 159, 168, 213, 226, 290, 302, 313.

Capitalists (of the Witwatersrand), *see* magnates.

Chamber of commerce (Johannesburg), 56, 253.

Chamber of mines, 4, 20, 27, 29, 30, 56, 58, 59, 141, 162, 186, 189, 190, 192, 194, 201 n., 221, 244–7, 253, 324.

Chamberlain, J., 2, 21 n., 38, 39, 46, Ch. IV *passim*, 96–98, 101 n., 104–28, 130–2, 136–40, 144–51, 153 n., 155–61, 163–6, 171–5, 177–9, 182–5, 191, 194–200, 202, 205–16, 221–4, 226–32, 234–5, 240–6, 249–55, 258–61, 265–79, 281, 284–92, 294–5, 297–8, 302–8, 310–16, 318–24, 327–9, 330 n., 331.

— Mrs. J., 68, 70, 108.

Chartered company, *see* British South Africa company.

Coal and coal mines, 34, 40, 187, 192.

Colonial office, 45, 50, 63, 69, 72–95, 111, 121, 130, 142 n., 145–6, 148, 151, 154, 165, 170, 177, 183–4, 194, 196, 203, 209, 211, 216, 221–2, 228–9, 231, 236 n., 242–3, 249, 254 n., 259, 264, 266, 269, 275, 287, 311 and n., 325, 328–9.

Commandeering crisis, 60, 61.

Commons, house of, 65, 111, 112, 117, 119, 120, 138, 177–8, 254, 304.

Concessions, 20, 23–45, 135 and n., 244. *See also* liquor monopoly; dynamite monopoly; Netherlands and Selati railway companies.

Consolidated Goldfields company, 3, 63, 70, 104, 134 n., 139, 188 n., 228–9, 248, 252, 325.

Cook, E. T., 267.

Corruption (in Cape Colony), 168, 225.
— (in S.A. Republic), 19–22, 27, 31, 32, 34, 42, 44, 119, 235.

Council of education, Witwatersrand, 132–3, 221.

Critic, the, 130–2.

De Kiewiet, C. W., 325–6, 327 n.

Delagoa Bay, 34–40, 41 n., 45, 46–50, 98, 150–6, 214–17, 254 n., 316, 323. *See also* Lourenço Marques.

De la Rey, J. H., 192 n.

Derby, Lord, 197.

De Villiers, Sir H., 9, 58, 140, 144–6, 176–7, 191, 271–2, 282, 299, 301, 305–6, 307–8, 330–1.

— M., 182, 203 n., 307, 331.

De Wet, Sir J., 19, 97, 136, 184.

Disraeli, Benjamin, 65, 66.

'Dopper' Church (*Gereformeerde Kerk*), 7.

Drifts crisis, 38–39, 85–86.

Durban, 35–40, 150, 232, 294, 317, 322.

Dutch Reformed Church (*Nederduitsch Hervormde of Gereformeerde Kerk*), 16, 55, 220, 231.

Du Toit, S. J., 16, 55.

Dynamite monopoly, 27–33, 187–8, 191–2, 194–5, 243–8, 249 n., 250, 253–4, 272, 280, 324.

East London, 38, 167.

Eastern Telegraph company, 74, 75, 152.

Eckstein, H., & co., 148 n., 248.

Edgar, T., 237–9, 241–2, 265.

Education in S.A. Republic, 15, 55–56, 102, 132–4, 220–1.

Eiffe concession, 153–5, 216.

Eloff, F., 42.

Escombe, H., 293–4.

Esselen, E., 16, 21, 57–59.

Evans, J. E., 181, 232, 236, 238–9.

— Samuel, 187, 188 n.

Executive Council (S.A. Republic), 5, 10–13, 17, 21, 22, 26, 31, 42, 43, 102, 103, 108, 124, 129, 133, 134, 139, 141, 190, 191–2, 204, 207, 218, 225, 248, 296, 315.

Expulsion law, *see* aliens expulsion law.

Fairfield, E., 75, 84–86, 89–91, 95, 110 n., 118, 125, 136, 140, 184.

Farrar, G., 4, 100, 134 n., 139.
Fashoda crisis, 217, 250.
Federation of South Africa, *see* South African federation.
Fiddes, G. V., 112 n., 116, 146, 155, 179, 194, 232, 242, 255, 263.
Fischer, A., 217, 276, 282, 290–2, 295–6, 332.
Fitzpatrick, J. P., 1 n., 100, 145, 192–4, 201, 205, 248–9, 252–5, 263 and n., 298 n., 319 n., 325.
Foreign office, 123, 128, 148, 151, 154, 196, 212–13, 216, 254 n.
France and S.A. Republic, 29, 30, 33, 41, 43, 98, 125, 151, 216–17, 250, 316 n.
Franchise in S.A. Republic, 53, 54, 57–60, 62, 102, 107, 112, 132, 134–5, 182, 201, 218, 249, 251 and n., 252, 254–5, 265, 268, 271–2, 280–4, 288–91, 293, 297–303, 306, 308–10, 313–14, 317–18, 321, 328.
Fraser, E., 27, 148 n., 218, 223, 225, 229, 232, 234, 235 n., 236, 238–40, 243–5, 247–8, 256, 258, 261, 265, 286.
Free State, *see* Orange Free State.
Frere, Sir B., 207.

Gaberones, 80, 84, 91.
Garrett, Edmund, 102, 103, 120, 166, 179, 287.
Garvin, J. L., 79, 81–83, 88 n., 90, 99, 269.
Gereformeerde Kerk, *see* 'Dopper' Church.
German South-West Africa, 5, 186.
Germans in S.A. Republic, 1, 3, 4, 15 n., 28, 193, 235.
Germany and S.A. Republic, 29, 30, 33, 39 n., 40, 46–49, 52, 60, 73, 89, 93, 98–100, 106, 110, 125, 150–1, 186, 207 n., 212, 215–17, 250, 254 n., 316.
Gladstone, W. E., 65, 66, 67 n., 131, 171.
Goerz, A., 4, 62, 162, 228, 248, 325.
Gold mines, 3, 4, 19, 20, 27, 30, 31, 35, 36, 52, 69, 71, 104, 136–40, 180, 186–90, 192–3, 218, 228, 249, 253, 256, 264, 324, 327, 329.
Goodenough, general W. H., 157, 159.

Goschen, G. J., 171, 304 n., 305.
Graham, F., 136, 146, 156, 179, 211, 231, 243–5, 251 n., 264, 289, 311–12.
Greene, C., 14, 18, 21, 130, 135 n., 136, 140, 143, 145, 146 n., 148 and n., 149–52, 158, 161, 163–4, 175, 180–3, 189–95, 201–5, 208–10, 217–18, 231–4, 236, 241–3, 245, 249, 252–3, 256–7, 259, 261–4, 267, 274, 279, 286, 288, 292–3, 296 n., 297–8, 302, 306, 308–11, 314, 328.
Gregorowski, R., 203, 288.
Grey, Earl, 74 n., 80–84, 90, 95.
— Sir E., 268 n.
Grobler, Piet, 217, 276 n., 295, 315 n.
Gungunhana (Native chief), 46, 47.

Hammond, J. H., 100.
Harcourt, Sir W., 72–74, 112 n.
Harris, Dr. R., 71–75, 76 n., 79–84, 95, 120.
— Lord, 228–30, 252.
Hatzfeldt, Count, 48, 70, 98.
Hawksley, B. F., 74, 75, 82, 86 n., 90–92, 95 n., 111, 121, 177 n.
Headlam, C., 169 n., 172 n., 178 n., 218 n., 321 n.
Hely-Hutchinson, Sir W., 101 n., 137, 206, 215, 251 n., 260, 268, 271, 272 n., 293–5, 320.
Herff, consul von, 98–100, 122.
Herholdt, A. J., 227, 295–6.
Hess, H., 130, 132.
Hicks Beach, Sir M., 174, 207, 270, 318, 322.
High court (S.A. Republic), 14, 107, 132, 140–5, 147, 182, 184, 191, 201, 203 n., 204, 238.
Hime, A., 206, 293–5.
Hofmeyr, J. H., 51, 97, 112 n., 113, 145, 169, 177, 225, 271, 273, 277–9, 290–2, 295–7, 305, 319, 330–1.
Hollander influence in S.A. Republic, 14–18, 33, 34, 55, 57, 59 n., 113, 125, 133, 140, 158, 190, 217, 219–21.
'Home rule' for the Witwatersrand, 112, 250–2.

Immigration law, 127–9, 140, 149–50, 157, 159, 160 n., 185, 195.
Imperial federation, 68.
Imperialism, 66–69, 171–2.
India, 198–9, 317, 320, 322.

Indians in S.A. Republic, 127 n., 181–2, 249, 258–62, 265.
— elsewhere in S. Africa, 181, 259–60.
Industrial commission, 12, 186, 189–93, 201, 229.
Innes, J. Rose, 165–8, 177, 224, 226–7, 287, 306, 323.

Jameson, Dr. L. S., 8, 70–72, 76–78, 81 n., 86 n., 88, 91–95, 106–8, 112, 118, 184 n.
Jameson raid, 13, 46, 59, 70–73, 79, 96–99, 101–4, 107, 110, 111, 114, 117, 119, 120, 124, 133, 134, 138, 144, 159 n., 160, 162, 167, 174, 178, 179, 210, 217, 220, 245, 250, 251, 281, 303 n., 323–4, 328–9.
Jews, 1, 28, 203 n.
Johannesburg, 1, 5, 24, 25, 34–39, 41, 61, 71, 76, 79, 85–88, 91–95, 97–108, 135, 137, 143, 145, 163–4, 180, 191, 202, 204, 209–10, 232–5, 237, 239–40, 251 and n., 253, 255, 257, 261, 275, 287, 292, 297, 319, 324.
— waterworks company, 24, 25.
Jones, B. S., 238, 242.
Jorissen, E. J. P., 105 n., 328.
Joubert, C., 20.
— P. J. (Piet), 10, 11, 13, 49, 57, 58, 115, 145, 150, 200–2.
Just, H. W., 148 n., 242–3, 266, 284 n., 303, 308.

Katembe concession, see Eiffe concession.
Kimberley, 3, 233.
— Lord, 47, 48, 52, 63.
Klimke, J., 15 n., 31.
Knutsford, Lord, 51 n., 60.
Kosi Bay, 49–52.
Kotze, J. G., 9, 16, 58, 113, 140–5, 146 n., 191–2, 196, 203–5, 209, 218, 238.
Kruger, S. J. P. (Paul), 1 n., 2, 5–23, 26, 28, 31–33, 35–39, 41–43, 46–54, 57–59, 62, 63, 73, 77, 84, 85 n., 92, 96–99, 101, 105–22, 125, 129–31, 138–41, 143–7, 150, 157–60, 162, 165–6, 175, 177, 178, 180, 184, 189, 191–5, 200–7, 216 n., 217–20, 224–5, 228–30, 244–5, 247–8, 249 n., 250–5, 257, 264–5, 271–4, 276–8, 280–4, 286, 288, 291–4, 296 and n., 297–8, 302–6,
308, 312–13, 315 n., 316 n., 319, 322, 325, 328.
Krugersdorp, 34, 45, 71, 264.

Labouchere, H. du P., 73 n., 75, 95 n.
Laing's Nek, 285, 295.
Lambert, H., 130 n.
Lansdowne, Lord, 156, 159, 270.
Law officers of the crown, 121 and n., 123 and n., 125, 127, 128, 130, 147. 154, 196–7, 245 n., 258.
Leonard, C., 56, 57, 100, 101.
— J. W., 56, 170 n., 328.
Leyds, Dr. W. J., 7, 14–18, 21, 28, 29, 31, 32, 42, 43, 46, 51, 59 n., 89, 100, 113 n., 114, 122, 132, 140, 141, 143, 151–3, 179, 189–91, 194 and n., 195 n., 199, 200, 212–14, 217–18, 219–20, 229, 248, 250, 253–4, 256, 276 n., 315–16, 331.
— Mrs. W. J., 15, 17.
Lippert, E. A., 28, 30, 31, 34, 45, 248, 254.
Liquor legislation, 26, 188, 193, 218.
Liquor monopoly, 25.
Lisbon, 151–2, 214, 254 n.
Loch, Sir H., 50–52, 60–63, 196.
Lombaard, field-cornet, 134, 234–8.
London, 44, 61, 62, 212, 253, 290, 304.
London convention, 48, 60, 62, 68, 99, 105, 117 n., 122–9, 144, 145, 148, 149, 158, 165 n., 166, 183, 191, 195–200, 210, 221, 243, 249 n., 259, 262, 269–70, 276, 286, 307, 309, 313, 321, 327.
—— article IV, 48 n., 49, 99, 109, 110, 113, 122–5.
——— XIV, 125–9, 181, 245–6, 258.
Lords, house of, 65, 197.
Lourenço Marques, 25, 47, 151, 153–6, 185, 214, 259. See also Delagoa Bay.
Loveday, R. K., 212, 256.

Macarthur–Forrest cyanide patent, 20, 21, 62, 141.
MacDonell, Sir H., 152.
McMurdo, E., 35, 154 n.
Mafeking, 77–79, 106.
Magnates (of the Witwatersrand), 3, 4, 28, 32, 62, 100, 101 n., 132, 138, 140, 162 and n., 189, 194, 200–1, 221, 228–9, 233–4, 244–5, 247–51, 253–7, 324–5.

Maguire, R., 81 n., 82, 89, 90.
Majuba, battle of, 10, 247, 299.
Mansvelt, N., 55, 132–4, 220–1.
Marais, E., 16.
Marks, S., 4, 25, 30, 45, 63, 108, 109.
Marschall von Bieberstein, Baron A. von, 48, 98–100.
Matabele-Mashonaland, 46, 49, 50. See also Rhodesia.
Meade, Sir R., 61, 74 n., 86 n., 89, 91, 92, 95, 125, 136, 184.
Merriman, J. X., 74 n., 145, 167–8, 170, 176–7, 227, 260, 270, 287.
Meyer, L., 59, 256.
Middelberg, G. A. A., 13, 16 n., 21 n., 22, 38, 59 n., 137 n., 202 n., 219–20.
Milner, Sir A., 2, 26, 27, 46 n., 123, 149, 156, 160 and n., 164, 166, 168–9, 171–83, 185–6, 190–2, 194–6, 199–200, 202, 204–13, 215, 218–19, 221–7, 231–4, 237, 241–5, 247 and n., 248–9, 251–5, 257, 259–99, 301–13, 316, 318–22, 324, 325 n., 328, 329–31.
— Lady, 77, 172 n.
Mines and mining industry, see gold mines.
'Missing telegrams', the, 74 and n., 80–83, 88, 90.
Modderfontein, 31.
Moor, F. R., 293–5.
Morice, judge, 141–2.
Municipal council (Johannesburg), 23 n., 107, 135, 233.

Natal, 1–3, 33, 34–37, 39, 40, 53 n., 117, 118, 160 n., 161, 162, 181–3, 206, 213, 223, 258 n., 259–60, 272 n., 275, 285, 287–9, 293–5, 317, 320, 322, 326–7.
National union, S.A. Republic, 56–63, 100, 163.
Natives (Bantu) in S.A. Republic, 1, 4, 25–27, 52, 54, 60, 130, 180, 183–5, 187–8, 193, 218, 221–3, 235.
Nederduitsch Hervormde of Gereformeerde Kerk, see Dutch Reformed Church.
Nellmapius, A. H., 25, 27.
Netherlands railway company, 13, 22, 32, 33–41, 43–45, 96, 187, 192, 230, 250.
Neumann, S., 4.
Newton, F. J., 72, 78.

Nobel dynamite trust company (Nobels), 28–31.

Oppenheim, E., 42–45.
— R., 43–45.
Orange Free State, 1, 2, 35–38, 96, 117, 147–8, 159, 160, 169 n., 176, 178, 185, 203 n., 206, 209, 217, 247, 267, 293, 304, 307 n., 319–21, 326, 331–2.

Paramountcy, British, in S. Africa, 114, 119, 161, 163, 164, 167, 185–6, 199, 211, 224, 247–8, 252, 268, 274, 297, 304, 306, 310, 312, 314, 320, 326–7, 329.
Paris, 41, 42, 212, 215, 229.
Philipp, M., 31, 246.
— (junior), 31, 246.
Phillips, L., 20, 21, 52, 59, 62, 100, 132, 137–8.
Pietermaritzburg, 294.
Pietersburg railway, 45.
Pitsani, 71, 72, 78 n., 80 n., 84.
Police, S.A. Republic, 27, 189, 218–19, 234–8, 240–2, 274–5.
Port Elizabeth, 180, 259.
Portugal, 25, 35, 37, 46, 47, 98, 122, 150, 152–6, 213–14, 215, 217, 316.
Potchefstroom, 23, 45.
Press law, 129–32, 140.
Pretoria, 14, 15, 17, 20, 24, 31, 36, 42, 55, 87, 97, 144, 145, 161, 184, 202, 210, 220, 232, 251 n., 265, 271, 273, 290–1, 296, 315–16.
Pretoria convention, 68, 145, 176, 197–200, 275–6, 313 and n.
Progressive party (Cape Colony), 167–9, 207–8, 224, 226–8, 271 n.
Progressives (S.A. Republic), 10, 57, 59, 60, 140, 202, 205, 256, 309 n.

Rand, see Witwatersrand.
Rand tram, 34, 40, 45.
Reform committee (Johannesburg, 1896), 102–4, 107, 111, 116, 124, 283.
Reitz, F. W., 21 n., 169 n., 217–19, 223, 237, 239, 246, 248, 250, 253–6, 263 n., 272, 275–6, 302, 306 n., 311–12, 314–15, 322.
Rhodes, C. J., 2, 3, 39, 46–51, 58, 63, 64, 70–99, 104, 106, 111–13, 120–1, 131, 138 n., 139, 144, 146 and n., 166–70, 177–9, 191 n., 207–8, 217,

Rhodes, C. J. (*cont.*)
224–7, 232–3, 287 n., 319 n., 324, 328.
— colonel F., 71, 100.
Rhodesia, 28, 70, 86, 116, 121, 138 n., 185, 259, 261. *See also* Matabele-Mashonaland.
Ripon, Lord, 52, 60–63, 184.
Robinson, Sir H., 49, 50, 63, 68, 70, 72, 75 n., 76–78, 84, 85 n., 87, 88, 90 n., 91–94, 96–98, 101, 103–10, 113, 115–18, 121, 130, 136, 149, 157, 173, 184.
— J. B., 4, 63, 115, 162, 178, 189, 194, 200.
Rosebery, Lord, 63, 64.
Rose Innes, James, *see* Innes, J. Rose.
Rosmead, Lord, *see* Robinson, Sir H.
Rothschilds (London), 36, 155, 212, 229–30.
Rouliot, G., 201 n., 253 n.

Salisbury, Lord, 48, 51 n., 64, 66, 67, 69, 74 n., 85, 88 n., 91, 98, 108, 121 and n., 128–9, 157, 215, 229, 269–70, 288–9, 310, 314, 318, 321–2, 325, 331.
Sanitary board (Johannesburg), 1, 23 n., 24, 54, 56, 135 and n. *See also* municipal council.
Sapte, 139, 188 n.
Sauer, J. W., 145, 167, 170, 176, 225, 227, 273.
Schreiner, W. P., 145, 146 and n., 165, 169, 176–7, 224, 226–7, 233, 260–1, 271–3, 278, 289, 292, 294, 296–8, 305, 319 n., 330.
— ministry, 227–8, 233, 239–40, 266, 271, 279, 290, 294, 296.
Schutte, superintendent of police, S.A. Republic, 275, 316 n.
Selati railway company, 41–45.
Selborne, Lord, 15, 79, 80 and n., 95, 112, 149–50, 155–7, 162 n., 183 n., 194–6, 198, 200, 205, 210, 212, 231, 250–1, 266–7, 268 n., 277, 285–6, 292, 298 and n., 304–5, 327, 329.
Select committee on British South Africa (inquiry into Jameson raid), 46, 71–78, 82, 85, 86, 91 n., 93, 95, 112, 128 n., 138, 144, 146, 165, 166, 169, 177.
Shaw, Flora, 75, 76, 86 n., 92, 97, 146.
Simonstown, 325, 329.

Sivewright, Sir J., 24, 108, 109, 110 n., 225, 271–3, 277, 279.
— agreement, 36–37.
Smit, N., 10, 13.
Smuts, J. C., 217–19, 223, 229 n., 238, 246–8, 250, 253–6, 258, 261, 272, 275, 276 n., 282, 287, 295, 296 n., 298–9, 301–2, 306, 308–11, 314–15, 317–18, 320, 331.
Smythe, C. J., 293–5.
South African association, 170.
South African federation, 46, 50, 60, 63, 68, 144, 147, 159, 163, 176, 215, 222, 224, 233, 296 n., 318, 325–31.
South African league, 160–9, 194, 201, 206, 208.
— — Cape Colony, 124 n., 161, 164–9, 204, 207, 226, 239–40, 287.
— — S.A. Republic, 124, **161**, 162–4, 180, 204, 209, 226, 233–43, 247, 249–50, 253, 257, 263–4, 274–5, 277, 288, 292.
South African party, 224–6, 271 n., 273, 288.
Sprigg, J. G., 118, 167–9, 178, 186, 206, 223–4, 226–7.
Standard and Diggers' News, the, 102 n., 135, 194 n.
Star, the, 59, 103, 131–2, 145, 162, 201–2, 209, 228, 238, 257, 259, 264.
Stellenbosch, 16, 271 n.
Steyn, M. T., 18, 26, 31, 33, 96, 147 and n., 160, 185–6, 271, 273–4, 276, 282, 290, 295, 305, 322.
Supremacy (British) in S. Africa, *see* paramountcy.
Suzerainty question, 99, 119, 125, 126, 129, 142 n., 195–200, 202, 204, 213, 240, 261, 304, 309, 312–13, 329.
Swaziland, 4 n., 49–52, 60, 218, 221–3, 265, 281, 284.
Swaziland convention (first), 51.
— — (third), 52, 54, 210, 221–3.

Taxes on inhabitants of S.A. Republic, 23, 35–36, 39, 102, 192, 228.
Times, The, 75, 101 n., 111, 115, 146, 208, 255, 298.
Tongaland, 49–52, 109.
Transvaal concessions commission, 31, 41.
Treaties of S.A. Republic, 18, 25, 37,

Treaties of S.A. Republic (*cont.*) 96, 122–4, 159. *See also* Pretoria, London, Swaziland conventions.
Tudhope, J., 56 n.

Uitlander council, 264, 288, 292–3, 298.
Uitlanders, 1–6, 8, 19, 23, 24, 35, 52–63, 70, 71, 89–91, 96, 97, 101–8, 110, 112, 114, 117, 119, 124, 132, 134, 138–40, 144, 146 n., 160, 162–4, 166, 174, 182, 189, 192–4, 200–1, 204, 209, 218, 221, 223 n., 229, 233, 235, 242, 247–9, 251–5, 257–8, 263–70, 273–4, 280–4, 286, 292–3, 297, 299–302, 305–6, 308–9, 313 and n., 319, 323, 328–9, 331. *See also* national union; South African league, S.A. Republic.
United States, 68, 88, 89, 125, 126, 142 n., 175.

Van der Poel, Dr. Jean, 177.
Victoria, Queen, 65, 67, 121 n., 176, 288–9, 297.
Viljoensdrift, 35.
Volksraad (first, S.A. Republic), 7–13, 17–24, 26, 29–31, 33, 34, 37, 42, 43, 53–59, 102, 107, 124, 129, 132, 134–5, 141–5, 147, 160 n., 163, 180, 181, 190–4, 201, 203 n., 211–12, 217, 219–20, 222, 223 n., 228–30, 243–7, 250, 255–6, 277, 280–1, 283, 288, 293, 296 and n., 298–9, 301, 306, 308–10, 315 n., 332.
— (second, S.A. Republic), 53, 54, 135, 141, 296.

Volksstem, the, 201 n., 202, 235 n.
Vorster, B. J., 42.
Vorstman, L. G., 28–32, 246.

Walker, E. A., 113, 135 n., 144, 146, 147 n., 150, 192, 195 n., 204 n., 207 and n., 211 n., 227, 235 and n., 244 n., 249 n., 254 n., 264 n., 278 n., 283 n., 285 and n., 292 n., 299 n., 304 n., 305, 311, 312 n., 314–16, 327 n.
War office, 106, 156, 158, 232, 275, 289–90.
Wernher, Beit & Co., 3, 20, 59, 70 n., 137–9, 148 n., 192, 200, 221, 248–50, 298 n., 324–5.
Wernher, J., 3, 250–1.
Wessels, J. W., 308–10.
Westlake, J., 126, 129, 198.
White, Montagu, 85, 92, 118, 121 n., 149.
Wingfield, E., 123, 131, 136, 145, 157, 199 n., 241–2, 245, 277, 303.
Witwatersrand, 1, 19, 25–27, 34–41, 46, 53, 60, 63, 68, 70, 98, 112, 134, 137, 161, 180, 191, 209, 214, 245, 251, 263–5, 281, 296, 299, 314, 327.
Wolmarans, A. D., 282, 292.
— J. M. A., 31.
Wyndham, G., 74 n., 77 n., 170.

Younghusband, F. E., 101 n.

Zarps, *see* police, S.A. Republic.
Zoutpansberg, 42.

PRINTED IN GREAT BRITAIN
AT THE UNIVERSITY PRESS, OXFORD
BY VIVIAN RIDLER
PRINTER TO THE UNIVERSITY